D1707109

THIS ITEM HAS BEEN
DISCARDED BY THE
UNIVERSITY OF PUGET SOUND
COLLINS MEMORIAL LIBRARY

MEDIEVAL ENGLISH STUDIES
PRESENTED TO GEORGE KANE

MEDIEVAL ENGLISH STUDIES PRESENTED TO GEORGE KANE

EDITED BY
EDWARD DONALD KENNEDY, RONALD WALDRON,
AND JOSEPH S. WITTIG

D. S. BREWER

© Contributors 1988

First published 1988 by D. S. Brewer
an imprint of Boydell & Brewer Inc.
Wolfeboro, New Hampshire 03894-2069, USA
and of Boydell & Brewer Ltd
PO Box 9, Woodbridge, Suffolk IP12 3DF

ISBN 0 85991 262 0

Library of Congress Cataloging-in-Publication Data

Medieval English Studies presented to George Kane /
edited by Edward Donald Kennedy, Ronald Waldron,
and Joseph S. Wittig.
  p.   cm.
  ISBN 0-85991-262-0
  1. English literature—Middle English, 1100–1500—
History and criticism.   2. Langland, William, 1330?–
1400? Piers the Plowman.   3. Manuscripts, English
(Middle)   4. Kane, George.   I. Kane, George.   II.
Kennedy, Edward Donald.   III. Waldron, Ronald:
IV. Wittig, Joseph S.
PR251.M35 1988
820'.9'001—dc19   87-27209
                                                          CIP

British Library Cataloguing in Publication Data

Medieval English studies presented to George Kane.
  1. English literature—Middle English,
  1100–1500—History and criticism
  I. Kane, George   II. Kennedy, Edward Donald
  III. Waldron, R.A.   IV. Wittig, Joseph S.
  820.9'001   PR 281

ISBN 0-85991-262-0

Printed in Great Britain by
St Edmundsbury Press Ltd, Bury St Edmunds, Suffolk

TABLE OF CONTENTS

List of Abbreviations   vii

Preface   ix

George Kane   xi

Publications of George Kane   xv

Tabula Gratulatoria   xvii

Guthlac A: Sources and Source Hunting   1
    Jane Roberts

Rhymes in English Medieval Verse: from Old English to Middle
    English   19
    E. G. Stanley

On Some Aspects of the Vocabulary of the West Midlands in the
    Early Middle Ages: the Language of the Katherine Group   55
    Janet Bately

The Use of Coloured Initials and Other Division Markers in Early
    Versions of the *Ancrene Riwle*   79
    Roger Dahood

The Date and Provenance of *King Horn*: Some Interim Reassessments   99
    Rosamund Allen

Patterns in Middle English Dialogues   127
    W. A. Davenport

The Miller's Tale, line 3325: 'Merry Maid and Gallant Groom'?   147
    J. A. Cowen

Chaucer's Host   153
    S. S. Hussey

'Look Out for the Little Words'   163
    C. A. Ladd

Poverty and Poor People in *Piers Plowman*   167
    Derek Pearsall

The Character Hunger in *Piers Plowman*   187
   R. E. Kaske

The Idea of Reason in *Piers Plowman*   199
   John A. Alford

Mede and *Mercede*: the Evolution of the Economics of Grace in the
   Piers Plowman B and C Versions   217
   Robert Adams

The Imperative of Revision in the C Version of *Piers Plowman*   233
   George Russell

Making a Good End: John But as a Reader of *Piers Plowman*   243
   Anne Middleton

Piers Plowman and the Chancery Tradition   267
   John H. Fisher

Some Creative Misreadings in *Le Bone Florence of Rome*: An
   Experiment in Textual Criticism   279
   Nicolas Jacobs

Trevisa's Original Prefaces on Translation: A Critical Edition   285
   Ronald Waldron

Concerning Three Names in *Le Morte Darthur* – 'Roone', 'The
   Welshe King', and 'Chastelayne' – and Malory's Possible
   Revision of His Book   301
   ⋆R. M. Lumiansky

History *and* Literature in the Vernacular in the Middle Ages?   309
   ⋆Morton W. Bloomfield

The Other, the Self: Speculations Concerning an Aspect of Western
   Culture and Medieval Literature   317
   Derek Brewer

⋆deceased

LIST OF ABBREVIATIONS

ABR	*American Benedictine Review*
Archiv	*Archiv für das Studium der neueren Sprachen und Literaturen*
ANYAS	*Annals of the New York Academy of Sciences*
ASE	*Anglo-Saxon England*
BGDSL	*Beiträge zur Geschichte der deutschen Sprache und Literatur*
BuR	*Bucknell Review*
CCL	Corpus Christianorum Series Latina
ChauR	*The Chaucer Review*
DAI	*Dissertation Abstracts International*
EA	*Études Anglaises*
EETS	Early English Text Society (Original Series)
EETS ES	Early English Text Society, Extra Series
EETS SS	Early English Text Society, Supplementary Series
ES	*English Studies*
EStn	*Englische Studien*
E&S	*Essays and Studies*
JEGP	*Journal of English and Germanic Philology*
JHI	*Journal of the History of Ideas*
JWCI	*Journal of the Warburg and Courtauld Institutes*
Kane	*Piers Plowman: the A Version, Will's Visions of Piers Plowman and Do-Well*. Ed. George Kane. London, 1960.
Kane–Donaldson	*Piers Plowman: the B Version, Will's Visions of Piers Plowman, Do-Well, Do-Better and Do-Best*. Ed. George Kane and E. Talbot Donaldson. London, 1975.
LeedsSE	*Leeds Studies in English*
LSE	Lund Studies in English
MÆ	*Medium Ævum*
MED	*Middle English Dictionary*

M&H	*Medievalia et Humanistica*
MLN	*Modern Language Notes*
MLR	*Modern Language Review*
MP	*Modern Philology*
Neophil	*Neophilologus*
NM	*Neuphilologische Mitteilungen*
NMS	*Nottingham Medieval Studies*
N&Q	*Notes and Queries*
OED	*Oxford English Dictionary*
PAPS	*Proceedings of the American Philosophical Society*
PBA	*Proceedings of the British Academy*
PL	J.-P. Migne, ed., *Patrilogiae . . . Cursus Completus*, Series secunda (Latina)
PMLA	*Publications of the Modern Language Association of America*
Pearsall	*Piers Plowman, An Edition of the C-Text*. Ed. Derek Pearsall. London, 1978.
PLPLS-LHS	*Proceedings of the Leeds Philosophical and Literary Society, Literary and Historical Section*
PoT	*Poetics Today*
RATM	*Recherches de théologie ancienne et médiévale*
SAC	*Studies in the Age of Chaucer*
SATF	Société des anciens textes français
SP	*Studies in Philology*
QF	Quellen und Forschungen zur Sprach- und Culturgeschichte der germanischen Völker
TSLL	*Texas Studies in Literature and Language*
ZFSL	*Zeitschrift für französische Sprache und Literatur*

PREFACE

The editors are indebted to those who helped with the publication of this Festschrift honouring George Kane: to Derek Brewer and Richard Barber of Boydell and Brewer, Ltd., for their interest in publishing it; to the English Departments of the University of North Carolina and of King's College, University of London, for support with correspondence and preparation of the manuscript; to Cheryl Baxley and Tobi Schwartzman of Chapel Hill for their secretarial assistance; to George Russell for helping plan the Festschrift during his visit to Chapel Hill in 1983; to the late E. Talbot Donaldson for his interest and encouragement; to the Research Council of the University of North Carolina at Chapel Hill for its generous assistance with the expense of publication; and to the many scholars, libraries and departments listed in the *tabula gratulatoria* who subscribed to the volume and without whose generous participation publication would not have been possible.

GEORGE KANE

George Kane, one of the most distinguished Middle English scholars of his generation, was born on 4 July 1916, in Humbolt, Saskatchewan. In 1936 he graduated with first class honours in English and Latin from the University of British Columbia and received his MA from the University of Toronto in 1937. After spending the academic year 1937–8 as a research fellow at Northwestern University, in 1938 he began reading for the PhD under the direction of R. W. Chambers at University College, London. Like so many others of his generation, he found his education interrupted by the War: in September 1939 he enlisted in the British army; he was commissioned in February 1940 and served until 1946. After being demobilised in 1946, he resumed his studies at London and submitted his doctoral thesis, a critical edition of Passus 18–20 of the B version of *Piers Plowman*, in July of that same year. He taught at University College, London, from 1946 to 1955 and was Professor of English Language and Literature and Head of Department at Royal Holloway College, London, from 1955 to 1965. In 1965 he was appointed Professor of English Language and Medieval Literature at King's College, becoming Head of Department in 1967. In 1976 he accepted appointment as William Rand Kenan, Jr Professor of English at the University of North Carolina at Chapel Hill, where he taught until his retirement in May of 1987. Middle English studies have been permanently enriched by his scholarship and criticism. His work on the text and authorship of *Piers Plowman* and on the general principles of textual criticism and his literary criticism of Langland and Chaucer have all commanded the recognition and respect of his colleagues in these fields. His edition of the A version of *Piers Plowman* was awarded the Sir Israel Gollancz Memorial Prize of the British Academy in 1963. With co-editor E. Talbot Donaldson, he received the Haskins Medal of the Medieval Academy of America in 1978 for their edition of the B version. He was Chambers Memorial Lecturer, University College, London, in 1965 and John Coffin Memorial Lecturer, University of London, in 1979. He was awarded a Leverhulme Trust Research Fellowship in 1962 and again in 1975–6. In 1968 he became a Fellow of the British Academy, a Fellow of University College, London, in 1971, and a Fellow of King's College, London, in 1976. He was elected a Corresponding Fellow of the Medieval Academy of America in 1975 and a Fellow in 1978. In 1977 he was elected to the American Academy of Arts and Sciences.

He conducted summer seminars in paleography and textual criticism at Harvard for the Medieval Academy of America in 1970 and 1982, and at Duke for the Southeastern Institute of Medieval and Renaissance Studies in 1978. He has lectured in many universities in England, on the Continent, and in North America. He represented the British Academy at the Accademia dei Lincei in Rome in 1976 and has delivered featured addresses at many professional meetings, including the Medieval Academy of America, the New Chaucer Society, and the Sewanee Medieval Colloquium.

In addition to his scholarship, teaching, and lecturing, George Kane has always given actively of his time and energy to the university community. He was Public Orator of the University of London (1962–6), Chairman of the Board of Studies in English of the University of London (1970–2), Dean of the Faculty of Arts, King's College (1972–4), and Chairman of the Division of the Humanities at Chapel Hill (1980–3). He served on the Council of the British Academy from 1974 to 1976, as Elector to chairs at Cambridge and Oxford, on committees for the New Chaucer Society and the American Council of Learned Societies, and on the council of the Early English Text Society, the publications committee of the Medieval Academy of America, and on the editorial boards of *Speculum* and *Studies in Philology*.

A list of the offices he has adorned can give, however, only an incomplete impression of George Kane's personal impact on the various institutions he has served. In London he added to the great tradition of Chambers, Gollancz, and others in consolidating the position of Middle English as a major component in the study of English in the University. In the three London colleges at which he taught he attracted a following of promising young graduate students, some of whom have themselves become notable contributors to medieval English scholarship. In the administrative sphere, he is remembered for his rôle in the reshaping of the London English degree syllabus during his period of office as Chairman of the University Board of Studies in English, as well as for his part in the planning of the new Strand Building at King's College in the late sixties.

While a member of the Department of English at Chapel Hill, he became one of the most highly regarded professors in the university. An energetic and rigorous teacher and graduate supervisor, he also became known as a strong advocate for the humanities through his service on many departmental and university committees and his three-year term as chairman of the Division of Humanities of the College of Arts and Sciences.

One of the many visiting lecturers he invited to Chapel Hill commented on both the enthusiasm for medieval studies among the graduate students and the positive relationship between students and faculty. George Kane fostered this enthusiasm both in and out of the classroom. Both as a teacher and as a senior colleague to junior faculty, he balanced frank advice and insistence on hard work with needed encouragement and support. Although busy with teaching, scholarship, and other departmental and university duties, he generously devoted a great deal of time to helping his students and colleagues. Also important were the many social occasions which George and Bridget Kane graciously arranged at their home for the Department's medievalists which helped students and faculty become better acquainted and which added immeasurably to the enjoyment of studying and working in the English Department.

The influence of George Kane's scholarship has gone far beyond the borders of the two countries in which he has taught. His work on Langland and Chaucer and his important contributions to textual criticism have received international recognition. This Festschrift seeks to honour an eminent scholar, a vigorous teacher, and a most valued colleague. The editors hope that it will give some indication of the esteem in which he is held by his students, his colleagues, and his friends.

PUBLICATIONS OF GEORGE KANE

'*Piers Plowman*: Problems and Methods of Editing the B-Text.' *MLR* 43 (1948): 1–25.

'The Middle English Verse in MS Wellcome 1493.' *London Mediaeval Studies* 2.1 (1951): 50–67.

Middle English Literature. London, 1951. Reissued New York and London, 1969, 1970, 1977.

Piers Plowman: the A Version, Will's Visions of Piers Plowman and Do-Well. Volume 1 of the Athlone Press Edition. London, 1960.

The Autobiographical Fallacy in Chaucer and Langland Studies. Chambers Memorial Lecture for 1965. London, 1965.

Piers Plowman: the Evidence for Authorship. London, 1965.

'Conjectural Emendation.' *Medieval Literature and Civilization: Studies in Memory of G. N. Garmonsway*. Ed. D. A. Pearsall and R. A. Waldron. London, 1969. 155–69.

'A Short Essay on the Middle English Secular Lyric.' *NM* 73 (1972): 110–21. (Mustanoja Festschrift.)

Piers Plowman: the B Version, Will's Visions of Piers Plowman, Do-Well, Do-Better and Do-Best. (With E. T. Donaldson.) Volume 2 of the Athlone Press Edition. London, 1975.

'Some Reflections on Critical Method.' *E&S* 29 (1976). 23–38.

'Chaucer and the Idea of a Poet.' *Problemi Attuali di Scienza e di Cultura* 234. Accademia Nazionale dei Lincei. Rome, 1977. 35–49.

'Outstanding Problems of Middle English Scholarship.' *Acta IV, The Four-teenth Century*, ed. Paul Szarmach and Bernard Levy. Binghampton, 1977. 1–17.

The Liberating Truth: the Concept of Integrity in Chaucer's Writings. John Coffin Memorial Lecture for 1979. London, 1980.

'Music Neither Unpleasant nor Monotonous.' *Medieval Studies for J. A. W. Bennett*. Ed. P. L. Heyworth. Oxford, 1981. 42–63.

'Langland and Chaucer: an Obligatory Conjunction.' *New Perspectives in Chaucer Criticism*. Ed. Donald M. Rose. Norman, Oklahoma, 1981, 1982. 5–19.

'Poetry and Lexicography in the Translation of *Piers Plowman.' Medieval and Renaissance Studies*. Proceedings of the Southeastern Institute of Medieval and Renaissance Studies 9. Ed. Frank Tirro. Durham, N.C., 1982. 33–54.

'The Perplexities of William Langland.' *The Wisdom of Poetry: Essays . . . in Honor of Morton W. Bloomfield*. Ed. Larry D. Benson and Siegfried Wenzel. Kalamazoo, Michigan, 1982. 73–89.

'Chaucer, Love Poetry and Romantic Love.' *Acts of Interpretation: the Text in its Contexts, 700–1600: Essays . . . in Honor of E. Talbot Donaldson*. Ed. Mary J. Carruthers and Elizabeth Kirk. Norman, Oklahoma, 1982. 237–55.

'The Text of Chaucer's *Legend of Good Women* in CUL MS Gg.4.27.' *Middle English Studies Presented to Norman Davis*. Ed. Douglas Gray and E. G. Stanley. Oxford, 1983. 39–58.

'John M. Manly (1865–1940) and Edith Rickert (1871–1938).' *Editing Chaucer: the Great Tradition*. Ed. Paul G. Ruggiers. Norman, Oklahoma, 1984. 207–29, 289–91.

Chaucer. Past Masters. Oxford, 1984.

'The Z Version of *Piers Plowman.'* Review Article. *Speculum* 60 (1985). 910–30.

General Editor, Athlone Press Edition of *Piers Plowman*

'An Accident of History: Lord Berners's Translation of Froissart's *Chronicles*.' *ChauR* 21 (1986). 217–25.

'Some Fourteenth-Century "Political" Poems.' *Medieval English Religious and Ethical Literature: Essays in Honour of G. H. Russell*. Ed. Gregory Kratzmann and James Simpson. Cambridge, 1986. 82–91.

'The Text.' *A Piers Plowman Handbook*. Ed. John A. Alford. Berkeley, 1988.

TABULA GRATULATORIA

John A. Alford
Rosamund Allen
Judith Anderson
Shinsuke Ando
Malcolm Andrew
Robert and Ruth apRoberts
William Arfin
Kiyoshi Awaka
Robert Bain
Denise Baker
Richard Beadle
B. S. Benedikz
Robert G. Benson
John F. Benton
Klaus Bitterling
N. F. Blake
Cynthia Bland
Daniel Breen
Elizabeth M. Brennan
Betty Webb Brewer
David Burnley
John A. Burrow
Kenneth Cameron
Mary J. Carruthers
Marie Collins
J. E. Cross
Alfred David
Eirian Davies
Norman Davis
T. P. Dolan
E. Talbot Donaldson
A. I. Doyle
Hoyt N. Duggan
R. D. Eaton
Connie Eble
Charles Edge
A. S. G. Edwards
Robert Edwards
Everett Emerson

Eugene H. Falk
Rosalind Field
John H. Fisher
John V. Fleming
Christine and Joseph Flora
Jaroslav Folda
Robert Worth Frank, Jr
Allen J. Frantzen
Laura Gabiger
Milton McC. Gatch
Helmut Gneuss
Eloise Grathwohl
Douglas Gray
Stanley B. Greenfield
Robert Haig
Anne Hall
Lincoln Hall
Richard Hamer
Howard Harper
James Haar
Trudier Harris
Thomas J. Heffernan
S. K. Heninger, Jr
Dorothy Hill
Joyce Hill
T. F. Hoad
Anne Hudson
Stanley Hussey
Tadahiro Ikegami
Akiyuki Jimura
Henry Ansgar Kelly
Kathleen Ann Kelly
Edward Donald Kennedy
Steven Killion
Kimball King
Thomas A. Kirby
Elizabeth D. Kirk
Michael Kuczynski
Theodore Leinbaugh

xvii

George Lensing
Diane Leonard
Erika Lindemann
Lan Lipscomb
Thomas A. Little
R. M. Lumiansky
Helen Maclean
Jill Mann
John F. A. Mason
David Mills (Liverpool)
Maldwyn Mills
Yoshitaka Mizutori
Charlotte C. Morse
Yuji Nakao
Shunichi Noguchi
Patrick O'Neill
Akio Oizumi
J. Oldaker
Klaus Ostheeren
Charles A. Owen, Jr
Kenneth and Elizabeth Palmer
Derek Pearsall
Richard W. Pfaff
Peter Phialas
Kenneth Phillipps
John C. Pope
Esther C. Quinn
Sir Randolph Quirk
Elizabeth L. Rambo
Mark L. Reed
Alain Renoir
Carter Revard
Felicity Riddy
Marjory M. Rigby
Rossell Hope Robbins
Fred C. Robinson
Pat Rogers
Ann B. Ross
Louis D. Rubin, Jr
George Russell
M. L. Samuels
Fumio Sasaki
R. A. Shoaf
Celia Sisam
T. M. Smallwood
Jeremy J. Smith

Stephen Spector
Diane Speed
Myra Stokes
Albrecht B. Strauss
Eiichi Suzuki
Toshiyuki Takamiya
Sachiho Tanaka
Josephine Koster Tarvers and
    Richard Crawley Tarvers
M. Teresa Tavormina
John J. Thompson
Weldon Thornton
Yoko Wada
Marvin J. Ward
Patricia Ward
Victor Watts
Horst Weinstock
Siegfried Wenzel
James Wimsatt
Joseph Wine
Joseph S. Wittig
Katharine Worth

Englisches Seminar der Universität
    Tübingen
Englisches Seminar der Universität
    zu Köln
Englisches Seminar, Westfälische
    Wilhelms-Universität Münster
King's College (London) Library
Englisches Seminar der Universität
    Bonn
Institut für Englische Philologie der
    Universität München
Institut für Anglistik der Universität
    Regensburg
Institut für Anglistik, Reinisch-
    Westfälische Technische
    Hochschule Aachen
Istituto di Filologia Germanica,
    Universitá degli Studi di Udine
Royal Holloway and Bedford New
    College, English Department
Universitätsbibliothek, Regensburg
University of Salford

Guthlac A: *Sources and Source Hunting*

JANE ROBERTS

Recently, within the context of the *Fontes Anglo-Saxonici*, a proposed Register of 'all written sources which were incorporated, quoted, translated, or adapted in texts composed, in English or Latin, in Anglo-Saxon England',[1] I found myself returning to a brief consideration of the identifiable sources used by the *Guthlac A* poet, when at a *Fontes* meeting in King's College[2] I introduced the preliminary bibliography for the Register being undertaken by Janet Bately and myself. As part of our contribution to the international archiving of the sources used by Anglo-Saxon writers we are at present drawing together a bibliographical guide to published discussions of writings in Old English. As well, we have begun to bring together in King's College source examinations of substance and source texts, thus creating a specialised library collection where such materials can conveniently be consulted. With the hope therefore that George Kane will take a kindly view of a new venture underway in his old department, I should like now to offer to him, in the bibliographical appendix to this paper, a brief foretaste of the Sources Bibliography.[3] And because *Guthlac A* may, it seems to me, have more intrinsic interest for a reader of Langland than much Old English poetry, I hope that discussion of its putative sources will not be thought out of place in this volume.[4]

Within the group of Old English Guthlac materials *Guthlac A* is, so far as sources are concerned, anomalous. Obvious sources can easily be found for the other texts within the group. It is a simple enough task to identify the source of the Old English prose life as ultimately Felix's *Vita sancti Guthlaci*[5]

---

[1] *Old English Newsletter*, 19:2 (1986), 17.
[2] 24 March 1986.
[3] Full bibliographical details for short references in these footnotes will be found in the Bibliographical Appendix.
[4] *Guthlac A* quotations throughout this paper from Roberts, 1979.
[5] Colgrave, 1956, is now generally used as the standard edition. For the prose life Goodwin's text of 1848 is superseded by Gonser, P., *Das ags. Prosaleben des hl. Guthlac*, Anglistische Forschungen, 27 (Heidelberg, 1909).

and indeed to identify that manuscript of the *Vita* nearest to it.[6] The cognate Vercelli homily for the most part goes back to the same original effort of translation.[7] The Old English Martyrology[8] entry is brief, but its few nuggets of information can all be identified within Felix's account of the saint. Although these hardly reflect the most significant events of the life, J. E. Cross has demonstrated that the martyrologist's working methods allow us to assume that he could have taken them directly from the *Vita*.[9] *Guthlac B* has behind it the fiftieth chapter of the *Vita*, Felix's narration of the saint's death, a stylish presentation whose literary forebears have often been explored.[10] In contrast, *Guthlac A* is, in the words of J. C. Pope, a 'thoroughly unrealistic poem, in most respects poles apart from the *Vita*'.[11] Yet, a recent treatment of its sources starts from the proposition that its 'literary source was some form of Felix's *Vita Sancti Guthlaci*', with the *Vita* providing both 'framework and a number of striking images and phrases' elaborated by the poet.[12] Ultimate source it may be, but Kurtz, sixty years ago, did make a good case for the existence of a few non-Felix traditions, for example a scourge for whacking demons and a boiling pot for enclosing the devil, which indicate the possibility at least of other available sources.[13] The proposition that the *Guthlac A* poet must have known Felix's life, however, remains likely, even if he did not work closely from it.

Whereas the main source for *Guthlac B* is plainly Felix, it is unlikely that a recognisable single source will ever be found for *Guthlac A*, a situation shared, it must be remembered, with some of the most admired Old English poems. In any listing of sources it will therefore be necessary to itemise all significant correspondences that have been advanced between *Guthlac A* and the *Vita sancti Guthlaci*, but to do so line by line for *Guthlac B* could well be a pointless exercise within the framework of discovering what was read by Anglo-Saxons. In any case, a reader of *Guthlac B* will want to place his copy of

---

[6] W. F. Bolton, 'The Manuscript Source of the Old English Prose Life of St Guthlac', *Archiv für das Studium der neueren Sprachen*, 197 (1961), 301–3, argues for Corpus Christi College Cambridge MS 307. In his *An Old English Anthology* (1963) Professor Bolton sets text from Corpus Christi College Cambridge MS 389 against an extract from the prose life.

[7] Gonser's text is superseded by Paul E. Szarmach, *Vercelli Homilies IX-XXIII*, Toronto Old English Series 5 (1981).

[8] Herzfeld's text is superseded by G. Kotzor, *Das altenglische Martyrologium*, Bayerische Akademie der Wissenschaften Philosophisch-Historische Klasse, NF 88 (München, 1981).

[9] J. E. Cross, 'On the library of the Old English martyrologist', in *Learning and Literature in Anglo-Saxon England, Studies presented to Peter Clemoes*, edited by Michael Lapidge and Helmut Gneuss (Cambridge, 1985), pp. 227–49.

[10] See especially Kurtz, 1926, Rosier, 1971, and Rugg, 1979.

[11] John C. Pope, review of Roberts, 1979, *Speculum*, 56 (1981), 423.

[12] Cornell, 1976, p. 13.

[13] Kurtz, 1926, 113 and footnote 19; Roberts, 1970.

that poem beside a trustworthy edition of the Latin, if interested in the poet's handling of his main source. Presumably therefore what is needed for *Guthlac B* is indication, division by division, of where Felix is closely followed, together with notes on any additional sources used by the poet. Where sentences, phrases or images derive from Felix, there should be no need to go beyond the *Vita*, unless it seems possible that the poet himself did so. That is a task associated rather with establishing the sources used by Felix. For *Guthlac A* it may be necessary to consider alternative sources even for material paralleled within Felix, given that the poet does not seem to have worked with a copy of the Latin text at his elbow. In this his poem differs markedly from *Guthlac B*, where the use made of Felix is to be compared with Cynewulf's close following of the source for his *Elene*. There even the fitt divisions of the poem sometimes reflect the chapter divisions found in extant texts of the *Inventio Crucis*,[14] and it has been observed that the poem's smooth narrative advance may be the result of closeness to the putative Latin original.[15] By contrast, *Guthlac A* lacks the simple narrative clarity to be found in those parts of the *Vita sancti Guthlaci* with which it has sometimes been compared.

The actual sources that can be itemised for *Guthlac A* are few, if by sources we mean texts in which we can recognise frequent close parallels. If indeed close verbal similarity across a sizeable portion of text be a criterion for identifying a source, it is possible to argue that the sources for *Guthlac A* comprise a passage from the opening of the tenth chapter of Gregory's *Vitae Patrum*.[16] What view then is to be taken of all the evidence that has been put forward both for and against the *Vita* as source? Rather than attempt to rehearse the past interminable disputes, it seems better to look at *Guthlac A* as a text that has revealed only grudgingly its originality and to examine its possible source materials with the hope of casting light upon the organisation of its contents. Understanding of its structure has long been bedevilled by two common approaches. Most obviously, attempts to find a source, willy-nilly in the easiest place, Felix, result in its being compared unfavourably with *Guthlac B*. As well, with line 30 identified as the opening line it has been read either as a single long Guthlac poem that improves once into what we now call *Guthlac B* or as a shorter poem that with the first twenty-nine lines taken away appears ill-organised. The legacy of these approaches has not yet entirely vanished, being apparent most recently in writings on the Guthlac poems by A. H. Olsen[17] and M. E. Bridges.[18]

---

[14] P. O. E. Gradon, *Cynewulf's 'Elene'* (1958), p. 19.
[15] K. Sisam, 'Cynewulf and his Poetry', *PBA*, 18 (1933), reprinted in his *Studies in the History of Old English Literature* (1953), p. 14.
[16] *PL*, lxxi, 1054–5.
[17] Olsen, 1981.
[18] Bridges, 1984.

The Gregory source-passage has long been recognised. Gerould points to it,[19] noting as a possible alternative source a passage from the second book of Lactantius's *De ira dei*[20] earlier proposed by Grau.[21] At first sight it would seem that either passage or similar phraseology in another writer could have triggered off the poet's reflections from line 30:

> Monge sindon   geond middangeard
> hadas under heofonum   þa þe in haligra
> rim arisað . . .   (30–32a)

> Multi variique sunt gradus per quos ad coelorum regna conscenditur . . .   [Gregory]

> Nam cum sint gradus multi per quos ad domicilium veritatis ascenditur . . .   [Lactantius]

Gregory, however, cites from the Psalms a text that is apposite to *Guthlac A*, given Guthlac's rôle in the poem as *bytla* of a *haligne hám* (lines 148–9) which he must defend against the demon inhabitants of the site chosen for his hermitage:

> Nisi Dominus ædificaverit domum, in vanum laborant qui ædificant eam.   [Psalm 126: 1]

And Gregory goes on to describe the different ways in which men may seek God's help:

> Quod adjutorium, non modo martyres, verum etiam et illi quos sacræ vitæ roboravit auctoritas [*Ed.*, celebravit], jugiter inquirentes, ad hoc quod sitis disiderii spiritalis promebat alacres pervenerunt. Nam si ad martyrium mens ascensa est, hujus adjutorii opem poposcit martyr ut vinceret; si jejunii observantiam adhibere studuit, ut ab eo confortaretur afflictus est; si castitati artus reservare voluit impollutos, ut ab illo muniretur oravit; si post ignorantium poenitendi converti desideravit, ut ab eo nihilominus sublevaretur cum lacrymis flagitavit; et si quid operis boni exercere eorum quispiam meditatus est, ut ab hoc adjutorio juvaretur expetiit. Per hos ergo scalæ hujus ascensus tam difficiles, tamque excelsos, tam arduos, cum sint diversi, ad unum tamen Dominum per hujus adjutorii opem conscenditur. Idcirco semper ille poscendus, ille quærendus, ille invocandus erit, ut quod de bono mens concipit, adjutorio suo ipse perficiat, de quo et nobis sine fine oportet dicere: *Adjutorium nostrum in nomine Domini, qui fecit coelum et terram* (Ps. 123: 8). Sicut et ille beatissimis, de quo nunc nobis futurus est sermo, qui inter diversas vel tentationes, vel cruces sæculi, semper hujus adjutorii munimen expetiit.

[19] Gerould, 1917.
[20] S. Brandt and G. Lavbmann, *L. Caeli Firmiani Lactanti opera omnia*, Corpus Scriptorum Ecclesiasticorum, 27 (1983–7), II, 69.
[21] Grau, 1908, 87.

This is in tune with the poet's views of Guthlac as a man who *martyrhád mode gelufade* (line 472) and as a *martyre* who was *from moncynnes synnum asundrad* (lines 514–15). His Guthlac does not endure passively the persecutions that come upon him, but fights to continue in his chosen dwelling-place.[22] In line 31 the translation of *hadas* by 'ranks, grades' can be supported from comparison with *gradus* whether in Gregory or Lactantius. A passage of elegiac reflection follows in the poem, leading naturally to a conclusion that refers back to lines 30–32a:

he fela findeð,   fea beoð gecorene.   (line 59)

[Matthew 20: 16: multi enim sunt vocati, pauci vero electi]

Lines 60–92 describe ways in which men serve God on earth, some in monastic life and some as anchorites. These final thirty-three lines of the opening division, together with lines 30–59, answer the question posed in lines 26–9:

> Hwider sceal þæs monnes   mod astigan
> ær oþþe æfter   þon*ne* he his ænne her
> gæst bigonge   þæt se Gode mote
> womma clæne   in geweald cuman?

The distinction drawn between monastic and anchoritic life is common enough in early medieval writings, but some phrases indicate that the poet may have held the Gregory preface in his mind. He develops carefully the division between *fela* and *fea* of line 59, treating in lines 60–80 the behaviour suited to those who *non modo martyres* serve God among their fellow men, and in lines 81–92 describing briefly the perils that beset those who have minds *ad martyrium . . . ascensa*. The affirmative *witon hyra hyht mid dryhten* (line 90) applicable to the latter group certainly recalls Psalm 123: 8, if not also the Gregory passage in which it appears. There are thus good grounds for assuming that the opening of Gregory's tenth chapter of the *Vitae Patrum* is a convincing source for *Guthlac A*. The closest resemblances are with the poem's first division, and strictly speaking therefore as source the Gregory-passage is local to this division of the poem.

A very different set of issues is raised by the analogy that can be drawn between the opening of *Guthlac A* and the large body of texts that centre on a soul's departure from its body. The suggestion of *einer Visio Pauli* as putative source for the soul-journey material of *Guthlac A* is made first by Grau, who also adduces penitential writings as a proper background not only for this poem but for a good part of *Christ III* as well.[23] L. K. Shook's fuller exploration of *Guthlac A* within this context leads him also to conclude that

---

[22] Compare Kurtz, 1926, 145.
[23] Grau, 1908, 87, 92.

the poet had access to the *Visio Pauli* and possibly such comparable hagiographic texts as the accounts of St Patrick's purgatory and of St Brendan's voyages.[24] Recently A. Healey has given a good account of points of comparison between the *Visio Pauli* and *Guthlac A* lines 1–29 in her edition of the Old English *Visio Pauli*.[25] Within the soul-journey tradition, however, a closer analogue for the framing materials of the poem can be found in the Three Utterances exemplum, a brief narrative episode that assumes varied forms,[26] the more so no doubt as further instances of its use are turned up. Already twelve variants have been identified,[27] and the definitive study being undertaken by Mary Wack and Charles Wright could well throw up a closer analogue than the Dudley text used here.[28] On leaving its body the just soul of a Three Utterances homily exclaims at light, joy, and the pleasant path ahead, whereas the archetypal utterances of a wicked soul focus on *angustia, asperium*, and *tenebrae*. These soul-journey themes are central to the material of the angel's speech at the beginning of *Guthlac A* and to the final section of the poem. Some striking resemblances may be seen between lines 8–9a and the exchange of good soul and angels in for example the Dudley version:

> Wegas þe sindon weþe 7 wuldres leoht
> torht ontyned.

> Suaue est iter. Angeli respondent: Suauius tibi est futurum.

Cornell too recognises line 8a as possibly 'an adaptation' from the exemplum.[29] And we should look forward to lines 767b–768a *sawlum rymeð/ liþe lifwegas* for the return of these themes in the poem's closing division. By contrast, a *frecne fore* (line 566a) is offered Guthlac by his demon persecutors at hell-door. Lines 8b–9a 7 *wuldres leoht/ torht ontyned* can similarly be compared internally with 768b *leohte geræhte*, 814b–815 *wynnum motum/ Godes onsyne georne bihealdan*, and contrasted with 583b–585a *nales dryhtnes leoht/ habban in heofonum*, when set beside another of the exchanges between the exemplum's soul and angels:

---

[24] Shook, 1960, 1961.
[25] Healey, 1978, 44–5.
[26] Roberts, 1973, 1979.
[27] See J. E. Cross, 'Towards the Identification of Old English Literary Ideas—Old Workings and New Seams', in *Sources of Anglo-Saxon Culture*, edited by Paul E. Szarmach, Studies in Medieval Culture, 20 (1986), p. 84. Dr C. D. Wright tells me that he and Dr Wack have now identified 'some twenty-five' further manuscripts in addition to those known to Willard and McNally.
[28] Text cited is L. Dudley, *Egyptian Elements in the Legend of the Body and Soul* (Baltimore, 1911), p. 165. For recent examination of the material see Healey, 1978, and Charles D. Wright, 'Apocryphal Lore and Insular Tradition in St. Gall, Stiftsbibliothek MS 908', in *Irland und die Christenheit*, ed. Próinséas Ní Chatháin und Michael Richter, 1978, 134–7.
[29] Cornell, 1976, 81.

Magnum est lumen! Angeli dicunt: Maius tibi futurum est. Uidebis claritatem domini facie ad faciem . . .

Within this context the opaque but plain noncewords *tidfara* (line 9) and *edergong* (line 11) may be interpreted respectively 'a traveller the time of whose journey is come' and 'seeking of thresholds'. *Edergong* can be given the derived sense 'beggary, penury', but it is worth noting that its limiting element is especially appropriate in being applicable as easily to the margins of heaven as to the eaves of men's houses. Soul-journey motifs so dominate *Guthlac A* structurally that the whole poem becomes, in L. K. Shook's words, 'a long flashback on Guthlac's life'.[30]

Guthlac is introduced only in the poem's second division, so from this point source-hunters have tried to find evidences that the poet used Felix's *Vita*:

> MAgun we nu nemnan þæt us neah gewearð
> þurh haligne hád gecyþed . . . (lines 93–4)

The unlikely interpretation of *þurh haligne hád* 'by men of holy estate'[31] has, for example, been used as evidence that the poet here recalls Felix's references to clerical informants in his Prologue and §xxviii, but Klaeber's 'in a holy (or edifying) manner' is to be preferred to so unusual a collective.[32] Somehow it seems appropriate to have begun examination of the *Vita sancti Guthlaci* as source for *Guthlac A* with a piece of evidence that proves illusory. Doubts as to its likelihood are reinforced by finding that Cornell[33] here puts forward for comparison a sentence from Gregory's *Dialogues*:

> Ea quae mihi sunt virorum venerabilium narratione comperta, incunctanter narro.

Most of the 'proofs' of poet's indebtedness to Felix are similarly vague. Only the three brief verbal parallels identified by Liebermann[34] for lines 150–151b, 699b, and 732b have gained fairly general acceptance, and even they are debated. All three are drawn from what may have been the nucleus of the *Vita*, that part which opens with Felix's second naming of his informants and which reaches its climax with the saint's deliverance *æt heldore* (line 559b) by his patron saint Bartholomew.[35] Coincidentally just these chapters of the *Vita*

---

[30] Shook, 1961, 300.

[31] H. S. MacGillivray, 'The Influence of Christianity on the Vocabulary of Old English', *Studien zur englischen Philologie*, 8 (1902), §123, note 1. See Roberts, 1979, note for line 94, for examples of this reading in some translations of *Guthlac A*.

[32] F. Klaeber, review of A. S. Cook, *The Christ of Cynewulf* (1900), *JEGP*, 4 (1902), 104.

[33] Cornell, 1976, 21.

[34] Liebermann, 1892, 247.

[35] See J. Roberts, 'St Bartholomew's Day: a problem resolved?', *MÆ*, 46 (1977), 16–19.

appealed to the compiler of the Vercelli Book, evidence at least that this part of the *Vita* could be excerpted for use as a Guthlac homily, although the Vercelli homily itself cannot be thought of as anything like an immediate source for Guthlac A. Any fond thoughts in that direction vanish when it is remembered that in the homily the demons play no further part once Bartholomew has arrived, but, it must be assumed, remain *in heolstre*,[36] while Guthlac flies to heaven with Bartholomew. The problems introduced by Dr Olsen's assumption that Guthlac is in the homily taken up to heaven without having died[37] need not be transferred to *Guthlac A*, where the soul-journey background should remove any doubts as to the saint's death. In *Guthlac A* the demons are ordered to return Guthlac safely to the place from which they had snatched him (line 701), and this they do in smooth and gentle flight (lines 731–732a). The poet then focusses briefly on the earthly paradise that Guthlac's hermitage has become:

> Smolt wæs se sigewong 7 sele niwe,
> fæger fugla reord, folde geblowen;
> geacas gear budon; Guþlac moste,
> eadig ond onmod, eardes brucan.
> Stód se grena wong in Godes wære,
> hæfde se heorde se þe of heofonum cwom
> feondas afyrde. (lines 742–748a)

Guthlac has achieved salvation. Accordingly his soul is led lovingly on

> engla fæðmum in uprodor
> fore onsyne eces deman: (lines 782–3)

So too Christ's *cempan gecorene* (line 797a) will journey *to Hierusalem* (line 813b). The striking use of the *locus amoenus* topos in lines 742–748a is not part of the Felix legend. Within *Guthlac A* it fittingly holds together the Guthlac materials, for hints are already present after the *beorg* is won but before the vision-temptations:

> He wið mongum stod
> ealdfeonda elne gebylded,
> sægde him to sorge þæt hy sigelease
> þone grenan wong ofgiefan sceoldan. (lines 474b–477)

As well, Guthlac's return to his earthly paradise, by prefiguring his soul journey in the embrace of angels (lines 781–9), links the main materials of the poem to its frame, as the themes ruminated on in the opening division are picked up in its final lines.

---

[36] Szarmach, *Vercelli Homilies*, 99, line 115.

[37] A. H. Olsen, 'Apotheosis and Doctrinal Purpose in the *Vercelli Guthlac*', *In Geardagum*, 4 (1982), 32–40.

Two of Liebermann's three pieces of evidence for the poet's reliance on Felix occur in one short passage of the *Vita*:

> Tunc deinde sanctus Bartholomaeus catervis satellitum iubet, ut illum in locum suum cum magna quietudine, sine ulla offensionis molestia, reducerent. Nec mora, praeceptis apostolicis obtemperantes dicto citius iussa facessunt. Nam illum revehentes cum nimia suavitate, velut quietissimo alarum remigio, ita ut nec in curru nec in navi modestius duci potuisset, subvolabant.[38]

He suggests that the words *sine ulla . . . molestia* lie behind *ne laþes wiht* (line 699b) and *suavitate . . . quietissimo* behind *smeþe 7 gesefte* (line 732a). Yet, if the poet is recalling these phrases, it is odd surely that he does not follow the structures in which they are set, neither the immediate syntax nor the hyperbolic comparison with being carried along in chariot or ship. The likeness of poem to *Vita* is shown not so much by these phrases as by the actual order of events once Bartholomew arrives, to assume in the poem his rôle of psychopomp of the Vercelli homily, a rôle appropriate also to the framing materials from the soul-journey tradition. For Schaar, *Guthlac A* resembles the *Vita sancti Guthlaci* only in this Bartholomew passage.[39] It is curious, however, that the phrases singled out by Liebermann could as easily be compared with words spoken by the angels in the Three Utterances exemplum:

> Suscitate eam [the soul] leniter de suo corpore, et ut nichil timoris, nichil doloris uideat.

Whether Felix should be identified as its ultimate source is a difficult problem. More interesting than the categorisation of putative source is the evidence the passage affords for the poet's correlation of diverse materials.

Liebermann's third piece of evidence for the *Guthlac A* poet's indebtedness to Felix commands less support:

> Erat itaque in praedicta insula tumulus agrestibus glaebis coacervatus, quem olim avari solitudinis frequentatores lucri ergo illic adquirendi defodientes scindebant . . .[40]

Liebermann would have us compare the poet's statement that Guthlac did not covet transitory well-being in this world:

> nales þy he giemde   þurh gitsunga
> lænes lifwelan   ac þæt lond Gode
> fægre gefreoþode   siþþan feond oferwon
> Cristes cempa.   (lines 150–153a)

---

[38] Colgrave, 1956, §xxxiii.
[39] Schaar, 1949, 40.
[40] Colgrave, 1956, §xxviii.

If this is a 'close' parallel, with *gitsunga/ lænes lifwelan* echoing *avari . . . lucri*, the reference to the Latin is extraordinarily oblique. The Old English lacks explicit lucre, and there is no excavation of a mound. Moreover, the attempts that have been made to establish similarities between the poet's evocation of Guthlac's conversion and Felix's narrative[41] lead me to conclude that for the poet Guthlac is almost an abstraction, not a wanderer or seafarer, but a hermit[42] who lives *ana* (lines 101, 158). He is therefore a *peregrinus* who has made his choice of life *pro amore dei*. If the poet knew Felix's narrative, he wanted none of its validating detail, not even Beccel or Tatwine or a circumstantial journey to Crowland through the fens.

The actual nature of Guthlac's chosen dwelling place is much debated, and discussion of Felix's *tumulus*[43] feeds over into interpretation of the *beorgsepel* (line 102) of *Guthlac A*. Colgrave visualises the *tumulus* as 'like a chambered long barrow'[44] and writes of Guthlac's 'dwelling on a barrow',[45] both notions that have trickled into discussion of *Guthlac A*. To my mind, Reichardt has the right of it, the *beorg* is 'as much a symbol of interior spiritual achievement as a geographical location in the fens of Crowland',[46] although spirited attempts have been made, most notably by Wentersdorf,[47] to arrive at a narrower identification. L. K. Shook's explanation of the *beorg* as 'grave, burial mound' is buttressed by two unconvincing textual points:[48] that the shelter of the *beorg* is such that it bows or makes stooped the man who lives daily in its discomfort; and secondly that it is in the marsh (line 274, but *mos* 'food' is generally read here). Neither reading proposed is likely to gain acceptance. And although the word *beorg* is used in Old English both in verse and prose for 'grave, burial mound', there is generally contextual reinforcement for such interpretation. Wentersdorf knits to Shook's ancient burial mound or barrow a new element, 'the presence of powerful heathen forces, whose continued existence there was a constant threat to Christianity'. For him therefore:

> The battle for the tumulus represents not merely the faithful Christian's spiritual war against his personal demons but also the unremitting campaign by the Church to suppress the lingering remnants of heathendom in England.

The saint's action in taking over the *tumulus* becomes 'a courageous public

---

[41] See especially Gerould, 1917, and Cornell, 1976.
[42] Forstmann (1902) gives *Guthlac A* the title *Guthlac der Einsiedler*.
[43] Colgrave, 1956, §xxviii. See quotation in preceding paragraph.
[44] Colgrave, 1956, 182.
[45] Colgrave, 1956, 20.
[46] Reichardt, 1974, 335.
[47] Wentersdorf, 1978, 136.
[48] Shook, 1960.

challenge' in the *mearclond* (line 174) or rather 'disputed borderland where the followers of God and Satan clashed'. That the *beorg* is twice described as *on bearwe* 'in a grove' (lines 148, 429) leads on to Wentersdorf's designation of the *bearu* as 'no ordinary grove' but 'a technical term for a sacroneme, the combination of *beorg* and *bearu*'. To *beorg* as burial chamber an imaginative stroke has added a new religious sense for *bearu*, and Crowland is therefore 'a latter day Calvary'. The identification of a saint's trials with the suffering of Christ may very properly lead to the symbolic alignment of the place of Guthlac's temptation with Calvary, but Wentersdorf's sacroneme is too heady. There is nothing in the poem to suggest that the *beorg* was an old, hallowed and haunted spot or that it was ever used for political assemblies and hundred business transactions or that it had once been closely associated with pagan religious beliefs. There is not even any sufficiently explicit detail to allow firm identification of the *beorg* as 'gravemound', for the poet does not draw upon the large conventional vocabulary in which mounds with burial associations are elsewhere presented.[49] It is therefore unlikely that the poet thought of the *beorg* as having any connection with burials. The whole passage, following on from his account of anchorites *on westennum* (lines 81–92), is reminiscent rather of the lives of the desert fathers, where hills and desert places are usual, than of Felix's *tumulus* set in the fens. A lot can be made depend on the single word *beorg*, either with or without relating it to Felix's *tumulus*.

Overall the landscape of *Guthlac A* lacks sharp definition. It would not seem out of place in a life of Anthony or Paul or Fursey. Guthlac's secret spot (*dygle stowe*, line 159) is set in a desolate countryside, and is hidden from men (*bimiþen fore monnum*, line 147) until revealed by God. To this place comes Guthlac, a builder (*bytla*, line 147), to raise up his *haligne hám* (line 149). It is apposite to recall again Gregory's citation of Psalm 126: 1: *Nisi Dominus ædificaverit domum, in vanum laborant qui ædificant eam*. Certainly the delights of Guthlac's *eorðlic eþel* (line 261), despite its position, become dear to him. In the presentation of the *beorgseþel* we see something akin to the paradoxical choice made by the seafarer for whom *Dryhtnes dreamas* were *hatran* than *þis deade lif*.[50] Guthlac deprived himself of delights and worldly pleasures, life's luxuries, having too great a fear of God in his heart to wish to devote himself to pleasure in a life of worldly glory (lines 163–9). The choice presented in the first division of *Guthlac A*, between *eorðwela* and *þæt ece lif* (line 62), lies more clearly behind Guthlac's disdain of *lænes lifwelan* (line 151a) than do the words *avari . . . lucri* advanced by Liebermann from Felix. The poet later reflects again on Guthlac's rejection of *longeþas lænra dreama* (line 330) and

---

[49] See Roberts, 1979, note for line 140 *on beorhge*.
[50] *The Seafarer*, lines 64–5.

has Guthlac himself twice affirm his lack of interest in earthly weal (lines 319, 386b–389). Where the seafarer's choice is between *lifes wyn in burgum* and *iscealdne sæ* on *wræccan lastum*,[51] Guthlac's is between his *beorg* in a secret place *from moncynnes synnum asundrad* (lines 514b–515) and life to be enjoyed *þurh lust . . . idlum æhtum 7 oferwlencum* (lines 417–18). The devils accuse him of having made his choice *for wlence* (line 208), which could prompt the reflection that Guthlac's abstinence from all intoxicating liquids *excepto communicationis tempore*,[51a] was not entirely popular at Repton according to Felix. Their many threats and taunts do not move Guthlac from his determination to hold the desolate place in which he has raised Christ's cross (line 180) as his standard.

Four divisions of the poem centre on Guthlac's wresting from demons possession of his *eorðlic eþel*, the perspective changing in the sixth division of the poem. The demons, allowed to lay hands on Guthlac, test his constancy first by raising him into the heavens to look upon a vision of monastic luxury and afterwards by taking him to the gates of hell. The second of these visions is familiar enough. Containing, as we have seen, those phrases sometimes held to have close verbal parallels in Felix's *Vita*, it is certainly central to the saint's legend. No source has, however, been found for the vision of abused monastic luxury. Instead of being tempted to scourge his flesh with *abstinentiae flagellis*,[52] Guthlac:

> . . . fore eagum eall sceawode
> under haligra   hyrda gewealdum
> in mynsterum   monna gebæru
> þara þe hyra lifes þurh lust brucan
> idlum æhtum   7 oferwlencum,
> gierelum gielplicum: swa bið geoguðe þeaw
> þær þæs ealdres   egsa ne styreð.   (lines 414–20)

The vision sets the scene for an episode unparalleled in Old English verse, and the *Guthlac A* poet is unusual for his time in regarding the theme as one suitable for English poetry. Long before the days of the friars so berated by Langland here is an English poet choosing to comment on the misdemeanours of men in religion. Not even a close analogue has been found for this episode of *Guthlac A*, and unfortunately Gerould does not identify the 'single detail from Felix' which he found within it and there is nothing in Felix that might obviously have prompted it.[53] A chapter from the *Vita Martini* has been compared by Wolpers,[54] but only in default of anything more convincingly alike. Guthlac's constant trust in *þam myrcelse* (line 458), the symbol of his

---

[51] *The Seafarer*, lines 27–9, 14–15.

[51a] Colgrave, 1956, §xx.

[52] Colgrave, 1956, §xxx.

[53] Gerould, 1917, 82, notes the lifting of Guthlac into the sky as possibly adopted from Felix's hell vision.

[54] Wolpers, 1964, 114–15; Cornell, 1976, 58–60.

chosen way of life, is not shaken by the vision of monastic laxity, though the poet has a few sharp words to deliver on the shortcomings of others bound by such forms:

(In þam mægwlite   monge lifgað
gyltum forgiefene, nales Gode þigað,
ac hy lichoman   fore lufan cwemað
wista wynnum: swa ge weorðmyndu
in dolum dreame   dryhtne gieldað.
Fela ge fore monnum miþað   þæs þe ge in mode gehycgað,
ne beoð eowre dæde dyrne   þeah þe ge hy in dygle gefremme.)
                                                    (lines 460–6)

His forthright criticism, already softened by lines 419b–420, is tempered in Guthlac's reply to a devil's tauntings:

God scop geoguðe   7 gumena dream;
ne magun þa æfteryld   in þam ærestan
blæde geberan   ac hy blissiað
worulde wynnum   oððæt wintra rim
gegæð in þa geoguðe   þæt se gæst lufað
onsyn 7 ætwist   yldran hades . . .   (lines 495–500)

Despite this gentler interpretation of misconduct, the criticism stands, revealing to us a poet prepared to comment on social issues, albeit his canvas is small. *Guthlac A*, after all, can hardly have been much above 900 lines when complete.

A vision of monastic luxury abused provides a strange but effective prompting to despair, analogous to the soft lives enjoyed by men *on foldan* in *The Seafarer*.[55] And although overt reference to monastic life is unusual in the major codices of Old English poetry, such material does not come altogether as a surprise in *Guthlac A*, given the alternative modes of religious life, monastic and solitary, introduced in the first division. There already the shortcomings of monks are mooted:

Sume him þæs hades   hlisan willað
wegan on wordum   7 þa weorc ne doð:
bið him eorðwela   ofer þæt ece lif
hyhta hyhst   se gehwylcum sceal
foldbuendra   fremde geweorþan.
Forþon hy nú hyrwað   haligra mod
ða þe him to heofonum   hyge staþeliað;   (lines 60–6)

and a whiff of monastic corruption is suggested by Guthlac's decision to eschew the delights of *seftra setla 7 symbeldaga* (line 165). The vision itself, if new to the legend, is well prepared for within *Guthlac A*. Who are we to

---

[55] *The Seafarer*, line 13.

object that Felix does not have it, when it plays so satisfying a part within the structure of *Guthlac A*?

As a final example of the kinds of sources that have been found for *Guthlac A* it is worth examining the passage which deals with the saint's renunciation of *seftra setla 7 symbeldaga*:

> Oft þurh reorde abead
> þam þe þrowera þeawas lufedon
> Godes ærendu þa him gæst onwrah
> lifes snyttru, þæt he his lichoman
> wynna forwyrnde 7 woruldblissa,
> seftra setla 7 symbeldaga,
> swylce eac idelra eagena wynna,
> gierelan gielplices: him wæs Godes egsa
> mara in gemyndum þonne he menniscum
> þrymme æfter þonce þegan wolde. (lines 160b–169)

Something similar can be found in Felix, whether in §xix[56] or §xxvii,[57] if fleeting resemblances are diligently sought. More relevant to an understanding of the passage, however, is its relationship to the 'three temptations' of 1 John 2: 16:

> quoniam omne quod est in mundo/ concupiscentia carnis et concupiscentia oculorum est et superbia vitae/ quae non est ex Patre sed ex mundo est.

The poet's use of this commonplace is fully explored by Charles Wright,[58] who argues that juxtaposed with it is the biblical motif of the seven gifts of the Holy Spirit:

> et requiescet super eum spiritus Domini/ spiritus sapientiae et intellectus/ spiritus consilii et fortitudinis/ spiritus scientiae et pietatis/ et replebit eum spiritus timoris Domini . . . [Isaiah 11: 2]

Wright identifies the first and last gifts revealed by Guthlac's *gæst* (line 162) with *lifes snyttru* (line 163) and *Godes egsa* (line 167), comparing other biblical verses in which the fear of the Lord is seen as the beginning of wisdom. Whether or not the poet had in mind some phrase from the *Vita*, perhaps *abrenuntiatis saecularibus pompis*,[59] the 'three temptations' commonplace is more convincing as source for lines 160b–169. Both the commonplace and the *Vita* parallels should be entered in the *Fontes Anglo-Saxonici* Register, together with some indication of respective importance.

[56] Gerould, 1917, 80.
[57] Cornell, 1976, 197.
[58] Wright (1982) points out and develops Abbetmeyer's identification of this commonplace in *Guthlac A*.
[59] Colgrave, 1956, §xix; Gerould, 1917, 80, compares the preceding sentence.

Hunting the sources of the *Guthlac A* poet is an enticing game, with sides too often taken for and against Felix. The many examinations that have been published make it hard to be unsympathetic with Gerould, who began by approving Forstmann's demonstration of the poem's independence from the *Vita sancti Guthlaci*[60] but came to believe that 'in phrase it frequently recalls the Latin'.[61] In his turn Kurtz refuted Gerould's evidence, arguing against literary indebtedness:

> . . . no proof has been adduced to show that *A* could not have been derived in part, at least, from Felix, or that any part of it must have been derived from him.[62]

The recent re-examination of the problem by C. E. Cornell, starting from the hypothesis that the poem had a literary source which was 'some form of Felix's *Vita Sancti Guthlaci*',[63] accepts Gerould's demonstration of the poem's dependence upon *Vita* 'as elaboration, generalization, epitome, or direct translation of its materials'.[64] Proof either way, as Calder and Allen indicate,[65] is hard to sustain. Dr Cornell provides among the appendices to her thesis a clear conspectus of possible parallels, information which will be extremely useful to the *Fontes Anglo-Saxonici*. She does not however seek to provide proof that the *Vita* itself was the poem's actual source and describes only §xxxii (Bartholomew's arrival) as having a close parallel in lines 685–720 of *Guthlac A*. In the face of the reiterated and unsuccessful attempts by many to prove or disprove literary indebtedness, it might be safer to categorise Felix's *Vita sancti Guthlaci* as an analogue rather than source for *Guthlac A*. If a source categorisation is advanced, it cannot be anything other than ultimate. That one of the two balanced *visio* episodes of *Guthlac A* is without close parallel, yet integral to the poem's development, is not to be gainsaid, and for this episode at least no source is known. For the whole poem there is no obvious single source. Unfortunately evidence of originality is not something that will be sought out for the *Fontes Anglo-Saxonici* Register, although the possibility it will afford of confirming a lack of source will contribute to the recognition of a writer's originality.

Itemisation of sources for the *Fontes Anglo-Saxonici* Register can properly begin once there is final agreement as to the conventions to be used. Some of us involved in the project have already contributed sample entries for use in

[60] Gerould, 1904, 96.
[61] Gerould, 1916, 80.
[62] Kurtz, 1926, 143.
[63] Cornell, 1976, 13.
[64] Cornell, 1976, 25.
[65] D. G. Allen and M. J. B. Calder, *Sources and Analogues of Old English Poetry* (1976), p. 108.

testing the sigla at present under discussion. Meanwhile the compilation of a Sources Bibliography at King's College is one of the necessary preliminaries for the Register, and the establishing of a complementary specialised library collection should allow easier recording and assessment of identified sources once the sigla are agreed. As work progresses, it could be useful to have such a back-up library collection, especially where multiple sources are proposed. The sigla, no matter how firmly elaborated, will in use be subject to differing interpretation from one contributor to another. This may seem an unduly pessimistic note to strike at the outset of so huge and exciting a project as the *Fontes Anglo-Saxonici*, but an analogy might perhaps be drawn with the subject and style markers of the *Oxford English Dictionary*. These are found in some but not all volumes of the dictionary. Where they are used, they are invaluable indications of register, but their usefulness is diminished both because they are sometimes used inconsistently and because they are not applied throughout. However, the drawing of such an analogy indicates the wealth of information that is to be hoped for from the *Fontes* Register. A perfect terminology is hard to envisage, when, as we have seen, source hunting can be such a slippery business, but what looks like a perfectly workable set of sigla has been devised and is being tested. The King's College Sources Bibliography is underway, and as it progresses any works of substance listed in it and not already available at King's will be brought into the college, consolidating what is already an excellent working library for Anglo-Saxonists. The long tradition of teaching English at King's, where among George Kane's predecessors in Old and Middle English are to be found such names as Wrenn, Garmonsway and Gollancz, has left the college well equipped for the establishing of a specialised collection of this sort, for many of the necessary monographs and papers are among the current library holdings. In a way, therefore, the grounds on which we can put forward both the Sources Bibliography and the Sources Archive is in part our legacy from George Kane, and I hope he will approve of this King's project.

King's College, London

BIBLIOGRAPHICAL APPENDIX

Standard editions of Felix's *Vita sancti Guthlaci*

Birch, W. de G. *Memorials of Saint Guthlac of Crowland*. Wisbech, 1881.
Colgrave, Bertram. *Felix's Life of Saint Guthlac*. Cambridge, 1956.

Materials containing discussion of sources for *Guthlac A* and *Guthlac B*. (Some of these range more widely than the Guthlac poems)

Bjork, Robert E. *The Old English Verse Saints' Lives*. Toronto, Buffalo, London, 1985.

Bridges, M. E. *Generic Contrast in Old English Hagiographical Poetry*, Anglistica, 22 (1984).

Cornell, Cynthia E. 'Sources of the Old English Guthlac Poems.' Diss. University of Missouri. Columbia, 1976.

Forstmann, Hans. *Das altenglische Gedicht 'Guthlac der Einsiedler' und die Guthlac-Vita des Felix*. Halle, 1901.

——. 'Untersuchungen zur Guthlac-Legende.' *Bonner Beiträge zur Anglistik*, 12 (1902).

Gerould, G. H. Review of Forstmann 1902. *EStn*, 34 (1904), 95–103.

——. *Saints' Legends*. Boston and New York, 1916.

——. 'The Old English Poems on St Guthlac and their Latin Source.' *MLN*, 32 (1917), 77–89.

Grau, Gustav, 'Quellen und Verwandtschaften der älteren germanischen Darstellungen des jüngsten Gerichtes.' *Studien zur englischen Philologie*, 31 (1908).

Lefèvre, P. 'Das altenglische Gedicht vom hl. Guthlac.' *Anglia*, 6 (1883), 181–240.

Kurtz, B. J. 'From St Anthony to St Guthlac.' *University of California Publications in Modern Philology*, 12, no. 2 (1926), 103–46.

Olsen, Alexandra Hennessey. '*De Historiis Sanctorum*: A Generic Study of Hagiography.' *Genre*, 13 (1980), 407–29.

——. *Guthlac of Croyland*. Washington, 1981.

17

Roberts, Jane. 'An Inventory of Early Guthlac Materials.' *Mediaeval Studies*, 32 (1970), 193–233.

——. *The Guthlac Poems of the Exeter Book*. Oxford, 1979.

Schaar, C. *Critical Studies in the Cynewulf Group*. LSE, 17, 1949.

Thundyil, Z. P. *Anglo-Saxon Thought*. Madras, 1972.

Wolpers, Theodor. *Die englische Heiligenlegende des Mittelalters*. Tübingen, 1964.

Materials containing discussion of sources for *Guthlac A*

Healey, A. diP. *The Old English Vision of St. Paul*. Speculum Anniversary Monographs 2. Cambridge, Massachusetts, 1978.

Hill, Thomas D. 'The Middle Way: *idel-wuldor* and *egesa* in the Old English *Guthlac A*.' *RES*, n.s. 30 (1979), 182–7.

Liebermann, F. 'Über ostenglische Geschichtsquellen des 12, 13, 14. Jahrhunderts, besonders den falschen Ingulf.' *Neues Archiv der Gesellschaft für ältere deutsche Geschichtskunde*, 18 (1892), 225–67.

Lipp, F. R. '*Guthlac A*: an Interpretation.' *Mediaeval Studies*, 33 (1971), 46–62.

Olsen, Alexandra Hennessey. 'Guthlac on the Beach.' *Neophil*, 64 (1980), 290–6.

Shook, L. K. 'The Burial Mound in *Guthlac A*.' *MP*, 58 (1960), 1–10.

——. 'The Prologue of the Old-English *Guthlac A*.' *Mediaeval Studies*, 23 (1961), 294–304.

Reichardt, Paul F. '*Guthlac A* and the landscape of Spiritual Perfection.' *Neophil*, 56 (1974), 331–8.

Roberts, Jane. '*Guðlac A, B*, and *C*?.' *MÆ*, 42 (1973), 43–6.

——. 'The Old English Prose Translation of Felix's *Vita sancti Guthlaci*.' In *Studies in Earlier Old English Prose*. Ed. Paul E. Szarmach, 1986, pp. 363–79.

Wentersdorf, Karl P. '*Guthlac A*: The Battle for the *Beorg*.' *Neophil*, 62 (1978), 135–42.

Wright, Charles D. 'The Three Temptations and the Seven Gifts of the Holy Spirit in *Guthlac A*, 160b–169.' *Traditio*, 38 (1982), 341–3.

Materials containing discussion of sources for *Guthlac B*

Palumbo, Edward M. *The Literary Use of Formulas in 'Guthlac II' and Their Relation to Felix's 'Vita Sancti Guthlaci.'* The Hague and Paris, 1977.

Rosier, James. L. 'Death and Transfiguration: *Guthlac B*.' In *Philological Essays, Studies in Old and Middle English Language and Literature in Honour of Herbert Dean Meritt*. The Hague, 1971, pp. 82–92.

Rugg, Phillis. 'A Critical Edition of *Guthlac B*.' Diss. Oregon, 1979.

Rhymes in English Medieval Verse:
from Old English to Middle English

E. G. STANLEY

1. Rhyming in Old English

The history of rhyming in English verse has often been traced back to its beginnings, best perhaps in F. Kluge's article, now more than a hundred years old, in which Anglo-Saxon rhyming is seen in the context of Germanic.[1] Kluge interested himself in all kinds of internal rhyming such as is manifested in Old English compounds like *wordhord* 'store of words' or *searofearo* perhaps 'vessel of deceit', or less exact manifestations like *waroðfaruða* 'shore-waves' and *sundorwundra* (gen. pl.) 'special marvels'. In this paper I shall content myself with rhyme at the end of the line (or halfline), and shall disregard internal rhyming.

Kluge endeavoured to account for the phenomenon in the language and was not unwilling to speculate on what rhyming there might have been in popular speech and popular proverbialism. Of course, some of the rhyming utterances sound proverbial; and they were made to look so from an early period of Anglo-Saxon scholarship by printing those in the Anglo-Saxon Chronicle as verse;[2] for example, from the annal for 1075 on the bridal of Norwich:

> Þær wes þ brydeala
> mannum to beala.[3]

['Then turned that bridal into a woe to people.']

[1] 'Zur Geschichte des Reimes im Altgermanischen', *BGDSL*, 9 (1884): 422–50.
[2] First printed as verse by J. Ingram, *The Saxon Chronicle* (London, 1823), 280, and in subsequent editions, for which see S. B. Greenfield and F. C. Robinson, *A Bibliography of Publications on Old English Literature to the end of 1972* (Toronto and Buffalo; 1980), 346.
[3] The version in Cotton MS Tiberius B.iv is less neat in rhythm:

> Þær wæs þ brydealo
> þwæs manegra manna bealo.

['There was that marriage-feast which was the destruction of many men.']

In both versions the rhyme is exact. The Tiberius reading is given in J. Earle and C. Plummer, *Two of the Saxon Chronicles Parallel*, I (Oxford, 1892), 210. The Chronicle is edited from this manuscript by E. Classen and F. E. Harmer, *An Anglo-Saxon Chronicle from British Museum, Cotton MS. Tiberius B.IV* (Manchester, 1926); see p. 93 for the rhyming couplet, in that Chronicle wrongly s.a. 1076.

Two central concerns of the student of Middle English rhyming are to be considered also in connection with rhyming in Old English:

(a) Except for the very small number of poems extant in holograph, none of them pre-Conquest, the texts have come down to us transmitted by scribes most of whom show little respect for the integrity of their exemplars, little respect even for their author's wording and usually none at all for his orthography. Old and Middle English had no standard spelling. In Old English, the inconsistently pursued, dialectal standardisation of the manuscripts was often at variance either with the superficial Anglian colouring of poetic texts, or, worse still, when rhymes are analysed for their purity, with the genuinely Anglian origins of some of the poems. In Middle English dialectal variety was, till near the end of the period, such that scribal translation of texts from their author's dialect into the scribes' own often obscures the forms of rhyme words, if anything even more than in Old English.

(b) With a few exceptions, Old English poets used rhymes as an occasional ornament only, not as a prosodic device recurring regularly (for example, in couplet after couplet, or alternating in various rhyming patterns within a stanza) as they did in Middle English, and, of course, as they did and often still do in Modern English. Can we assume that poets strove to achieve true rhymes for such occasional ornaments? If, as I think, they did not, hearers (or readers) would not expect true rhymes. Having been accustomed to rhymes less than true for occasional ornament Old English poets might not have striven to provide consistently true rhymes when rhyme recurs regularly, and hearers (or readers) would not have expected true rhyming only. To the extent to which early Middle English rhyming is based on Old English practice, early Middle English poets too need not have striven to provide true rhymes only, and modern philologists may have little reason to look for purity in rhyming, unless there is cumulative evidence that a poet rhymes accurately and does not follow those of his predecessors whose practice was looser.

2. Rhyming verse in the Anglo-Saxon Chronicle; occasional rhymes from the earliest verse onward

The history of rhyming in English begins earlier than 1075 in dated verse, and probably considerably earlier in undated and undatable verse. Discussion of it is best undertaken by considering first the dated verse. The first poem in the Chronicle is *The Battle of Brunanburh*; it has no rhyming, as its editor, A. Campbell, says:[4]

---

[4] A. Campbell, *The Battle of Brunanburh* (London, 1938), 33.

As a final instance of the conservative nature of the versification of the *Battle of Brunanburh*, the absence of rhyme must be mentioned. This is a feature which is shared by all the *Chronicle* poems in regular metre [*The Capture of the Five Boroughs* (942), *The Coronation of Edgar* (973), *The Death of Edgar* (975) and *The Death of Edward* (1065), but not *The Death of Alfred* (1036) in which there is rhyming],[5] and, as a sporadic use of rhyme is found in most of the earlier poems [Campbell is not here referring to the earlier of the Chronicle poems, but to the poems in the great poetic codices], it seems likely that the tenth- and eleventh-century poets, who preserved the old style, deliberately avoided rhyme to differentiate their work clearly from that of the popular writers of the time, with whom rhyme was becoming more and more a favourite device, as may be seen from *Maldon* and the *Chronicle* poems in irregular metre.

A footnote adds, 'The absence of rhyme in these poems seems to be complete', and he disputes Sedgefield's statement that these poems contain 'one perfect rhyme'.[6] It is difficult to be sure if absence of rhyme is the result of deliberate avoidance. As we shall see, in the poems of MSS Corpus Christi College Cambridge 201 and Junius 121, which were probably also written in the late tenth or the eleventh century, rhyming is relatively common in *The Judgment Day II* but not otherwise, and rhyming (other than of suffixes) is avoided in the metrical psalms of the Paris Psalter – perhaps the versifier found it hard enough to get the psalms into alliterative metre without adding rhymes.

Campbell's account contains a factual description of rhyming in these poems, but underlying it there is a theory of popular verse of the end of the Anglo-Saxon period in which versifiers resort to rhyming with greater frequency than did the poets of an earlier period, with whom rhyme was an occasional ornament. In some late verse in which rhyme is used, rhyme is sometimes so inexact that it is difficult to tell if rhyme or assonance describes it properly. I exclude from consideration such rhythmical but virtually non-alliterative and non-rhyming passages as those on the martyrdom of King Edward (979) and Archbishop Alphege (1011), and the arrival of the atheling Edward (1057) in MS Tiberius B.iv only. I do wish to consider further the

---

[5] Throughout this paper I use the titles (and the line-numbering) of poems as given in *The Anglo-Saxon Poetic Records*, ed. G. Krapp and E. V. K. Dobbie (New York and London, 1931–54). The Chronicle poems are in vol. VI; see especially pp. xxxii–xxxiii.

[6] W. J. Sedgefield, *The Battle of Maldon and Short Poems from the Saxon Chronicle* (Boston, etc., 1904), ix. Sedgefield seems to be referring specifically to *The Battle of Brunanburh*, not, as Campbell makes it seem, to all the 'regular' verse in the Chronicle. Either way, Campbell appears to be right: there is no rhyme.

Wulfstanian alliterative (prose) lines on Edgar (959)[7] in MS Tiberius B.iv as well as in the Peterborough Chronicle and (much abridged) in Cotton MS Domitian A.viii, the rhythmical note on the death of Edgar (at the beginning of the annal for 975) in MS Tiberius B.iv and the Peterborough Chronicle, the Wulfstanian alliterative (prose) lines on the death of Edgar (later in the annal for 975) in MS Tiberius B.iv only, *The Death of Alfred* (1036) in the same manuscript and also in Cotton MS Tiberius B.i, a few rhythmical phrases with a rhyme on Malcolm and Margaret (1067) in MS Tiberius B.iv only, and the atrocities at the bridal of Norwich (1075) from MSS Tiberius B.iv and B.i (of which the first couplet has been quoted above), the lines on King William in the Peterborough Chronicle s.a. 1086 (for 1087),[8] and a couplet in the Peterborough Chronicle s.a. 1104. Perhaps the short pieces in the annals for 1075 and 1104 will be generally regarded as snatches of popular verse, though I doubt it; but, as C. Clark's note makes clear, that the lines on King William are popular is a matter for debate:[9] she inclines to the view that they are 'popular and oral in origin'; B. J. Whiting gave them to the chronicler. I think there is enough doubt at least for an impartial reader of Old English verse not to regard as beyond question the popular and oral origin of late Old English metrically 'irregular' and, specifically, rhyming verse. Popular origins for loosely alliterative and rhyming entries in the Chronicle seem to me to be particularly unlikely when it is remembered that the only author scholars have associated with them, identifying him by his characteristic 'prose' style, is Wulfstan, who, very far from being an author of the common people, stood, in church and state, at the centre of affairs. And the earliest of these entries are in his style, though, of course, they are not likely to have been written contemporaneously, that is, they probably replaced, at some later time, the prose entries extant in the other versions. Wulfstan died in 1023; his style is to be seen in the first two items in the list of alliterative but metrically 'irregular'

---

[7] Preserved best in MS Tiberius B.iv (see n. 3, above), and also in the Peterborough Chronicle, ed. Plummer, see n. 3, also). The ascription to Wulfstan of alliterative passages of the annals for 959 and 975 in two of the versions of the Chronicle, Cotton MS Tiberius B.iv and Bodleian MS Laud Misc. 636 (the Peterborough Chronicle) was first proposed by K. Jost, 'Wulfstan und die angelsächsische Chronik', *Anglia*, 47 (1923), 105–23. Cf. D. Whitelock, *Sermo Lupi ad Anglos*, 3rd edn. (London, 1963), 27–8.

[8] See B. J. Whiting, 'The Rime of King William', *Philologica: the Malone Anniversary Studies* (Baltimore, 1949), 89–96, as well as the editions of the Chronicle, including especially C. Clark, *The Peterborough Chronicle 1070–1154*, 2nd edn. (Oxford, 1970), 13–14, 76.

[9] The term 'popular' was firmly attached to these poems in an early account, still of use for its collection of material under various heads: D. Abegg, *Zur Entwicklung der historischen Dichtung bei den Angelsachsen*, QF, 73 (1894), who gives the heading 'Gedichte volkstümlicher Art' (p. 57) to his section on the rhythmical, but metrically imprecise, parts of the annals, or of some of the versions of them, for 959, 975, 1011, 1036, 1067, 1076 (1075).

entries. The two Wulfstanian pieces are, of course, to be regarded as rhythmical prose rather than as verse.

Outside the Chronicle rhyming verse is also to be found. I do not wish to consider in detail the sporadic use of rhyme which occurs from the earliest extant verse onward, as in line 7 of *Cædmon's Hymn* (Leningrad MS):[10]

tha middingard   moncynnæs uard

['then the earth, Guardian of Mankind'].

---

[10] The rhyme in the Moore MS is less exact, at least in orthography:

tha middungeard   moncynnæs uard.

Our knowledge of seventh-century Northumbrian is insufficient for us to know if breaking of *æ* after labials never occurred, and if it was invariable after palatalised *g*; but the Leningrad form *middingard* is not easily paralleled – *middangardes* is recorded from Corpus Christi College Cambridge MS 41 (fo. 414ᵛ, 5–6) in R. L. Venezky and A. diP. Healey, *A Microfiche Concordance to Old English* (Toronto, 1980). For the texts of *Cædmon's Hymn* see E. V. K. Dobbie, *The Manuscripts of Cædmon's Hymn and Bede's Death Song*, Columbia Studies in English and Comparative Literature, 128 (1937), especially pp. 13 and 17. For breaking in early Northumbrian see K. Luick, *Historische Grammatik der englischen Sprache* I/1 (Leipzig, 1914–21; reprinted Oxford and Stuttgart, 1964), §§147 and Anm. 1 and 2, 157; A. Campbell, *Old English Grammar* (Oxford, 1959; reprinted 1983), §144 and footnote.

The difference between Leningrad MS *middingard* and Moore MS *middun geard* is described by C. J. E. Ball (in M. B. Parkes, *The Scriptorium of Wearmouth-Jarrow*, Jarrow Lecture, 1982, 26, n. 27) as one of the fourteen distinctions between the texts of the poem in these two manuscripts, and is included, with Leningrad *and* and *to* against Moore *end* and *til*, among the distinctions which 'simply contrast different words, or forms of words'. For my present purpose it is to be regretted that there is no discussion of the rhyme. The Leningrad scribe of the poem is the last of the four who wrote this important and very early witness to the text of Bede's *Historia*. He is 'probably a house author', if Parkes's view, pp. 5–6, is right; and he is conceivably Bede himself, if full significance is to be attached to a daring speculation of Paul Meyvaert's that 'Scribe D may have been Bede himself', though Meyvaert and Parkes, aware of the insufficiency of the evidence for so weighty a conclusion, tell us that 'at this stage, we would both prefer to leave the question open' (p. 27, n. 45). Is the Leningrad form *middingard* the result of a scribal attempt to get the rhyme with Northumbrian *uard* more nearly true? Does this form go back to what Cædmon dictated? Was the initial consonant of *-gard* a stop in Cædmon's pronunciation, or in Bede's, or in the Leningrad scribe's? We must recall that the late Northumbrian form is *middangeard* in the Lindisfarne Gospels (also with the variant *e* for *ea*), and similarly in the Durham Ritual (see A. S. C. Ross and E. G. Stanley, 'The Anglo-Saxon Gloss', in T. D. Kendrick et al., *Evangeliorum quattuor Codex Lindisfarnensis*, 2 (Olten and Lausanne, 1960), book ii, s.v. (*middan-*) *geard*, and in T. J. Brown et al., *The Durham Ritual*, Early English Manuscripts in Facsimile, 16 (Copenhagen, 1969); Rushworth Northumbrian has *middengeard* and *middengeord*, see U. Lindelöf, *Glossar zur altnorthumbrischen Evangeliarübersetzung in der Rushworth-Handschrift*, Acta Societatis Scientiarum Fennicæ, 22.5 (1897), s.v. *middengeord*. It looks as if the Leningrad scribe botched the form in an attempt to make the (imperfect?) rhyme look better.

There are many examples in 'regular' verse, such as *Beowulf*, line 1014:

fylle gefæægon;[11]   fægere geþægon

['rejoiced in the feast; partook of it with relish']

or a more complex set of rhymes, as at the climax of *Andreas*, lines 1585b–1589, with internal rhymes *hlyst ȳst* and *brimrād gebād*, the latter strengthened by end-rhyme with *tohlād*:

Geofon swaðrode
þurh haliges hæs,   hlyst yst forgeaf,
brimrad gebad.   Þa se beorg tohlad,
eorðscræf egeslic,   ond þær in forlet
flod fæðmian,   fealewe wægas.

['The ocean subsided at the saint's behest: the storm gave up listening,[12] the sea-path stood still. Then the hill split apart, a terrible earth-cave, and there let in the flood, the dusky waves, to overwhelm it.']

Like *Andreas*, line 1586, *Vainglory*, line 33, combines internal rhyme with end-rhyme (in describing the devil):

Wrenceþ he ond blenceþ,   worn geþenceþ
hinderhoca.

['He deceives and cheats, devises a multitude of tricks.']

In late verse, as all commentators have noted, the use of exact and inexact rhyme including assonance is not uncommon, though it is not certain that there are significantly more such devices. Thus in *The Battle of Maldon*, clearly in line 42 (and, very similarly, line 309):

Byrhtnoð maþelode,   bord hafenode

['Byrhtnoth spoke, raised his shield']

---

[11] The semicolon is editorial, and represents an accepted, modern analysis of the difficult passage, for which see the editions.

[12] Line 1586b is difficult: 'the storm gave up listening', which has been interpreted as 'the storm passed out of earshot' by K. R. Brooks, *Andreas and the Fates of the Apostles* (Oxford, 1961), 150 s.v. *hlyst*, but in his notes (p. 116) he remains closer to the wording of the text, and translates 'the storm gave up hearing', i.e. 'became inaudible', the latter following C. W. M. Grein, *Dichtungen der Angelsachsen*, 2 (Göttingen, 1859), 43, 'verhallt war der Sturm', and similarly in Grein's *Spachschatz der angelsächsischen Dichter*, 2 (Göttingen, 1864), retained in J. J. Köhler's revision (Heidelberg, 1912–14), s.v. *hlyst* 'auditum procella reliquit i.e. non amplius audita est'. Whatever the precise meaning, this internal rhyme is not exact: the *y* of *hlyst* is short, that of *ȳst* is long.

And line 47:

> ættryne ord   and ealde swurd

['poisonous point and ancient sword']

And line 271 (a foretaste of Laȝamon's rhythm and rhyme) lacking alliteration to link the two halflines, unless *st* were allowed to rhyme with *s*:

> æfre embe stunde   he sealde sume wunde

['time and again he gave some wound']

and (also rather like Laȝamon) line 282:

> Sibyrhtes broðor   and swiðe mænig oþer.

['Sibyrht's brother and very many others'].

In this poem true assonance is, in fact, not found. Perhaps lines 19–20 provide an example of a different pattern of linking four halflines, especially if the manuscript reading *randan* (for *randas*) is left unemended – as if a forerunner of Laȝamon's nunnations:

> hu hi sceoldon standan   and þone stede healdan,
> and bæd þæt hyra randan   rihte heoldon.

['how they must stand and hold the field, and commanded that they should bear their shields properly.']

Late religious verse too has some rhymes, as I have said above. *The Judgment Day II* has exact rhymes in lines 3, 6, 82, 147, 266; inexact rhymes in lines 28, 126 (with an internal echo in the first halfline); true assonance does not occur, but perhaps the less exact *ræplingas | onbindan* of line 48 should be regarded as a near-rhyme, and perhaps even *ælmihtig | atihtum* of line 69; and a different form of linking, *gesælig . . . ofersælig . . . gesæligost* occurs in lines 247–8 (where line 247 could, if one so wished, be regarded as a rich rhyme). No clear examples of rhyming are to be found in the other poems in Corpus Christi College Cambridge MS 201, nor in the poems in MS Junius 121.

Rhymes at the end of each of the two halflines forming a long line are used frequently in *Judith*,[13] and persistently in *The Riming Poem*; and there is a

---

[13] Kluge (see n. 1, above) commented on the frequency of rhyme in *Judith*, pp. 444–5. The poet's practice is discussed fully by A. S. Cook, *Judith*, 2nd edn. (Boston, 1904), lxix–lxx. Of the various kinds of rhymes listed by him, only the following lines are linked exactly enough to be considered as truly rhyming: 2, 20 (suffixal, according to Cook), 29, 63, 115, 116, 123, 231, 272 (suffixal), 304, 348–9; and as truly assonating 163–4 (internal); and more imperfectly (either in vocalic quality or length) 36, and 60 (though probably lengthening would have made the rhyme perfect).

long run of rhymes at the beginning of Cynewulf's epilogue to *Elene*, lines 1236–50. These persistent uses have been much discussed, usually in connection with the original dialect of *The Riming Poem*[14] and of Cynewulf.[15]

Line 1247 of Cynewulf's epilogue to *Elene* well illustrates the difficulties that stand in the way of comfortable solutions:

mægencyning ámæt   7 on gemynd begeat

['the powerful king granted and seized into the mind'].

Though the most recent editor, Dr Pamela Gradon, has purity of rhymes in Cynewulf's practice as an underlying assumption, she makes it clear that not only Kentish but also late Northumbrian share in the merging of short *æ* and *e*; and that the rhyme *amæt* / *begeat* (usually taken to depend on an original *amæt* / *begæt* or *amet* / *beget*) with the second rhyme-word with short *æ*, from *begi(e)tan*, 'to get', would make better sense if taken to have long *ēa* as the preterite of *begēotan*, as Grein had it in *Dichtungen der Angelsachsen*, 2, 137, 'und ins Gemüt mir eingoß', accepted by Bosworth's *Anglo-Saxon Dictionary* s.v. *be-gēotan*, 'he poured knowledge into my mind', not retracted by Toller in the *Supplement*;[16] but Köhler, in his revision of Grein's *Sprachschatz*, wondered if the reading should not be *begæt*.

Two aspects of the problem raised by this rhyme are of central importance, both for Old English and, in continuation, for Middle English rhyming verse. First, assuming exactness of rhyme, the poet's original dialect will be sought

---

[14] See, for example, O. D. Macrae-Gibson, *The Old English Riming Poem* (Cambridge, 1983), 1–4. The poem is often the starting-point for considering the history of rhyming in early English poetry, both in general historical accounts, beginning with J. J. Conybeare, 'Observations on the Metre of the Anglo-Saxon Poetry', *Archaeologia*, 17 (1814), 265–6 (cf. Macrae-Gibson, p. 11 and n. 1), and E. Guest, *A History of English Rhythms* (London, 1838), 2.102 (after quoting and translating nearly sixty lines of the poem); more recently, both R. P. M. Lehmann, 'The Old English *Riming Poem*: Interpretation, Text, and Translation', *JEGP*, 69 (1970), 437–49 (especially 437–9), and Macrae-Gibson's excellent section on 'Rhyme in Old English', pp. 21–5.

[15] K. Sisam, 'Cynewulf and his Poetry', *Studies in the History of Old English Literature* (Oxford, 1953), 1–28, especially p. 2. It was first published in *PBA*, 18 (1932), 303–31 (and separately). For the rhymes of the poem as evidence for its original dialect, see P. O. E. Gradon, *Cynewulf's Elene* (London, 1956), 13–14 and 72 (note on line 1247). The suggestion that the rhyme might require *begæt* goes back to R. Simons, *Cynewulfs Wortschatz*, Bonner Beiträge zur Anglistik 3 (1899), 12, 'begēotan *eingiessen*, begēat on E 1247 (oder wegen des reimes mit āmæt = begæt zu begitan?)', and the next headword, *begitan*, gives *begeat* at *Elene* 1151.

[16] I am not convinced by A. S. Cook, *The Old English Elene. Phoenix, and Physiologus* (New Haven and London, 1919), 97, that Cynewulf's halfline echoes Tobias 3:22, 'et post lacrimationem et fletum exultationem infundis', though Latin *infundere* 'to instil (ideas, feelings, or sim.)', in the definition of *Oxford Latin Dictionary*, may help to explain the unique, metaphorical (but strangely intransitive) use in Old English.

by philological reasoning most conveniently in an area where the smallest number of differences in the configuration of the rhyming part of the rhyme-words manifests itself, either, genuinely, because of a simplification in the phonemic system compared with other dialects, or, apparently, because of a reduction in, or superficially undisciplined handling of, graphemes leading to what in the versification of Modern English would be regarded as eye-rhymes. The Kentish and (more relevantly for *Elene*) West Mercian merging of several vowels in *e* is probably (and is usually accepted as) an example of genuine simplification; Aldred's divers spelling practice in the Lindisfarne Gospels and the Durham Ritual is an example of apparent confusion, which, if he had been a rhymester rather than a glossator, would have allowed him to make his rhymes look more exact than they need have been in sound. Secondly, philologists, eagerly searching for dialectal evidence, tend to value sound above sense in the rhyme-words they analyse.

In discussions of the persistent use of rhymes in Old English verse purity of rhyme is usually assumed, often leading to emendation, though increasingly some licences have been accepted by scholars. Even Holthausen, who is one of the most energetic emenders among editors of and commentators on Old English verse,[17] left unemended some assonances in the fifteen lines of Cynewulf's rhyming verse: *f* with *s wæf* / *læs* 1237, *nd* with *ng gebunden* / *beþrungen* 1244, guttural fricative *g* with *d onlag* / *had* 1245, *nd* with *md ontynde* / *gerymde* 1248. There are other assonances and impure rhymes in late Old English rhyming verse. Kluge drew attention to the rhyme *selle* / *willes* in the third (that is, the final) line of the Sutton brooch inscription, the second line of which rhymes exactly:[18]

> Drihten hine awerie   ðe me hire ætferie,
> buton hyo me selle   hire agenes willes.

['May the Lord curse him who removes me [the brooch speaking] from her, unless she gives me of her own accord.']

---

[17] F. Holthausen, *Cynewulfs Elene*, Alt- und mittelenglische Texte, 4, 2nd edn. (Heidelberg, 1910), 46, has no fewer than ten alterations in the rhyme-words of the fifteen lines of rhyming verse. He edited *The Riming Poem* three times, in 1913, 1931, and 1953; his many emendations are recorded in Macrae-Gibson's apparatus.

[18] See note 1, above: 'Der reim *selle : willes* verdient hier besonderer beachtung' (p. 447); but there is no further comment. See my study, 'The Late Saxon Disc-Brooch from Sutton (Isle of Ely): Its Verse Inscription', in my *A Collection of Papers with Emphasis on Old English Literature* (Toronto, 1987), 406. I had the privilege of first reading it in the presence of George Kane and some of his colleagues and students in the course of a wholly delightful visit to Chapel Hill in March 1985. For the text, see E. Okasha, *Hand-List of Anglo-Saxon Non-Runic Inscriptions* (Cambridge, 1971), 117.

3. Impure rhymes in the Chronicle verse

The assonances and impure rhymes in the metrically 'irregular' Chronicle poems may be analysed as follows:

(Wulfstanian alliterative prose 959: no rhyme of any kind.)

Rhythmical opening of 975 on the death of Edgar: *rang | strang*; assonances *wide | swiðe, cyninge | gecynde*; possibly a rhyme *wide | beoda*.

Wulfstanian lines on Edgar 975: probably none, but note *wiþærsacan | brǣcon*; and perhaps even *myrdon | tostǣncton | todrǣfdon | fesedon*.

The persistently rhyming and rhythmical as well as alliterative piece on the earl Godwine and the atheling Alfred in 1036 is worth quoting in full (from MS Tiberius B.i and parallel with it from MS Tiberius B.iv), printed 'hudibrastically' to indicate better how the halflines form couplets, and provided with editorial punctuation:[19]

Ac Godwine hine þa gelētte,		
7 hine on hæft sette;		Đā lēt hē hine on hæft settan;
7 his gefēran he todrāf,		and his gefēran he fordrāf,
7 sume mislīce ofslōh;	4	and sume mislīce ofslōh;
sume hī man wið fēo sealde,		sume hī man wið fēo sealde,
sume hrēowlīce ācwealde,		sume hrēowlīce ācwealde,
sume hī man bende,		sume hī man bende,
sume hī man blende,	8	and ēac sume blende,
sume hamelode,		
sume hættode.		and hēanlice hættode.
Ne wearð drēorlicre dǣd		Ne wearð drēorilicre dǣd
gedōn on þison earde	12	gedōn on þisan earde
syþþan Dene cōmon		siððan Dene cōman
7 hēr frið nāmon.		and her fryð nāman.
Nū is tō gelȳfenne		Nū is tō gelȳfanne
tō ðān lēofan Gode	16	tō þām lēofan Gode
þæt hī blission		þæt hī blission
blīðe mid Criste,		blīðe mid Criste,
þē wǣron būtan scylde		þē wǣron būtan scylde
swā earmlīce ācwealde.	20	earmlīce ācwealde.
Se æþeling lyfode þā gȳt,		Se æþeling leofode þā gȳt,
ælc yfel man him gehēt,		ælc yfel man him behēt,
oðþæt man gerǣdde		oðþæt man gerǣdde
þæt man hine lǣdde	24	þæt man hine lǣdde
tō Ēligbyrig,		tō Ēlibyrig,
swā gebundenne.		ealswā gebundenne.

[19] The editions by Plummer and Classen and Harmer (see n. 3, above) underlie the parallel versions given by me; but their punctuation, word-division and expansion of abbreviations have not been followed, and length-marks have been added.

Sōna swā hē lende		Sōna swā hē lende
on scype man hine blende,	28	on scype man hine blende,
7 hine swā blindne		and hine swā blindne
brōhte tō ðām munecon;		brōhte tō þām munecum;
7 hē þār wunode		and hē þær wunode
ðā hwīle þē hē lyfode.	32	þā hwīle þē hē leofode.
Syððan hine man byrigde,		Syððan hine man byrigde,
swā him wēl gebyrede		swā him wēl gebyrede:
ful wurðlīce,		þæt wæs full weorðlīce,
swā hē wyrðe wæs,	36	swā hē wyrðe wæs,
æt þām west ende,		æt þām west ende,
þām styple ful gehende,		þām stypele ful gehende,
on þām sūð portice:		on þām sūð portice:
sēo sāul is mid Criste.	40	sēo sāwul is mid Criste.

['But then Godwine stopped him and put him in captivity (had him put in captivity); and he dispersed his companions, and in various ways killed some; (5) some of them were sold for money, some cruelly killed, some of them were bound in fetters, some of them were (also) blinded, some were mutilated, (10) some were (shamefully) scalped. No more horrible deed was committed in this country since the Danes came and made peace here. (15) Now we must put our trust in dear God that they rejoice happily with Christ who without guilt were (20) killed so wretchedly. The atheling was still alive, threatened with every cruelty, till it was decided to take him (25) to Ely thus bound. As soon as he arrived he was blinded on board ship, and thus blind (30) he was brought to the monks; and there he dwelt as long as he lived. Then he was buried, as was very fitting for him (35) very honourably (that was very honourably), as he deserved, at the west end very close to the steeple, in the south porch. (40) His soul is with Christ.']

In addition to the exact rhymes at lines 1–2, 5–6, 7–8, 9–10, 23–4, 27–8, 31–2, and 37–8, there are less exact rhymes at lines 13–14, 19–20, and 21–2, and perhaps even 3–4; and with a different kind of linking at lines 33–4.

The rhythmical phrases on Malcolm and Margaret (1067): *heortan | sceortan*, and perhaps repetition of *wolde* at the end of what could be regarded as two irregularly alliterative long lines.

The snatches on the bridal of Norwich (1075): *eala | beala* quoted above, (*geblende |*) *lande | scande*.

The lines on King William (1086): rhymes *stearc | marc*, *wihte | unrihte*, *landleode | neode*, probably *befeallan | ealle*, *deorfrið | þærwið*, *haran | faran*, *stið | nið*, probably *eahta | sehta*, *mildheortnesse | forgifenisse*; assonance *wyrcean | swencean*; perhaps loosely rhyming *hinde | blendian*, *libban | habban*, *ahebban | tellan*.

The couplet summing up 1104: rhyme or assonance *gremienne | tregienne*.

In these lists, and throughout my discussion, I have left out of account rhyming unstressed syllables, suffixal rhyme. If one were to look for the antecedents in Old English of some kind of Middle English alliterative verse with rhymes, such as that of Laȝamon, suffixal rhyme would be of great interest. It is not uncommon in Old English, and Kluge (p. 437) maintains that there are some 150 cases in *Beowulf* alone, but then he counts not merely rhyming halflines constituting a long line which can be regarded as a couplet, but succeeding long lines ending in the same suffix, as well as second halflines ending in the same suffix as the following first halfline. Thus he finds two pairs (italicised by me) in lines 1605–7:

> selfne gesaw*on*. – Þa þæt sweord ong*an*
> æfter heaþoswate hildegicel*um*,
> wigbil wanian; þæt wæs wundra s*um*.

['they saw it. – Then the sword began to diminish, the battle-glaive to war-icicles, because of the battle-blood. That was a marvel indeed.']

Suffixal rhymes occur in verse in which rhyme of stressed syllables is avoided, as in the versified psalms of the Paris Psalter, 73: 2 (in both lines):

> Gemun þin mannweorod, þæt þu, mihtig God,
> æt fruman ærest fægere geworhtest.

['Remember thy congregation, which thou, mighty God, in the beginning at first didst make beautiful.']

Since such rhymes seem, therefore, to have had different usage in Old English and since they play little part in the development of English rhyming poetry other than in alliterative rhyming verse especially of the Transitional period, which would require, and would merit, separate study, I shall say no more about them in this paper.[20]

4. Peculiarities of Old English rhymes and their relationship to early Middle English rhyming verse

Let me sum up what I regard as the significant peculiarities of Old English rhymes before I move on to Middle English rhyming in verse either non-

---

[20] In logic, the fact that suffixal rhyme occurs in poems in which other rhymes are avoided seems to conflict with the occasional practice in verse with rhymes, variously strict and inexact, of disregarding the suffix of the rhyme-word, as in the Sutton brooch inscription, *selle* / *willes* (the rhyme presumably presupposes development to *sylle*, *sille*, for which see Campbell, *Old English Grammar*, §325). In the former the prosodic linking depends on the suffixes, in the latter the linking disregards them. It is inconsistent when considered as a whole, but we are dealing with two or more kinds of verse by several versifiers, and overall consistency is not to be expected.

alliterative or using alliteration only as an ornament, so that the debt to Old English may be assessed.

First of all, the basic structure of some Middle English verse lines is to be identified in a non-alliterative, rhyming line (271) in *The Battle of Maldon*:

$$\angle \ \times \angle \ \times \ \angle \ \times \ \times \ \angle \ \times \ \angle \ \times \ \angle \ \times$$

æfre embe stunde   he sealde sume wunde.[21]

That, however, is a rare case in Old English. With hindsight we see it as a precursor of rhyming, non-alliterative lines of Transitional verse, as, for example, in the twelfth-century Worcester Fragments (B 15):

Ac nu heo beoþ fuse   to bringen þe ut of huse.[22]

['But now they are ready to bring you out of your house.']

Perhaps in that line *beoþ* alliterates; though finite parts of the verb 'to be' do not alliterate in Old English, they seem to have been capable of bearing alliteration in alliterative verse of the later Middle English period, as in *Piers Plowman* B.10.351:

That is baptiȝed beþ saaf,   be he riche or pouere

at least *be* of the second halfline, and perhaps *beþ* too.[23] There is no alliteration in the following rhyming line (E 38) of the Worcester Fragments:

Is þiin muþ forscutted,   for deaþ hine haueþ fordutted.[24]

['Your mouth is quite shut, for Death has stopped it.']

---

[21] According to the standard rules of alliteration *st* in the first halfline cannot, of course, alliterate with *s* in the second halfline. That Ælfric alliterates *s* groups indiscriminately with one another and with simple *s* is probably not relevant; cf. J. C. Pope, *Homilies of Ælfric*, 1, EETS, 259 (1967), 128–9: 'Ælfric may be reflecting, or exaggerating, a tendency in late Old English poetry.' The following unit of Ælfrician alliterative prose provides an example:

stala and leasunga   and forsworennyssa

(W. W. Skeat, *Aelfric's Lives of Saints*, I, 2, EETS, 82 [1885], 356, No. xvi, line 283). More important, in Ælfric's practice, where end-rhyme is used there is not always alliterative linking as well (see Pope, pp. 131–4; Pope refers to rhyme either of stems or merely suffixal, but he says that the former is very rare).

[22] R. Buchholz, *Die Fragmente der Reden der Seele an den Leichnam*, Erlanger Beiträge zur englischen Philologie, 6 (1890), 3; and cf. pp. lxxii and lxxvi.

[23] Kane–Donaldson, 428; cf. Professor George Kane's important discussion of such alliteration, Kane–Donaldson, 134–6. An earlier, not quite conclusive example of alliteration on finite *beo* (subjunctive) is Worcester Fragments B 39 (Buchholz, 3):

Ær þu beo ibrouht   þær þu beon scalt.

[24] Buchholz, 7. (Buchholz adds *Nu* at the beginning of the line, perhaps because there is a manuscript lacuna at this point. The emendation is irrelevant to my purpose, and,

The lines in *The Battle of Maldon* which seems to anticipate Laȝamon's *Brut* are *Maldon* 271:

> æfre embe stunde   he sealde sume wunde

with which one may compare rhyming lines in the *Brut* like 15633:

> Cadwalan somnede uerde.   mucle in þissen ærde.[25]

['Cadwala summoned the army mightily in this land'.]

And *The Battle of Maldon* 282:

> Sibyrhtes broðor   and swiðe mænig oþer

which may be compared with *Brut* 12710:

> he wes Walwainnes broðer.   næs þer non oðer.[26]

---

unless it fills a lacuna, it is unnecessary.) For an alliterative problem similar to that of E 38, see G 17 (Buchholz, 9) on the prefix *bi-* but without rhyme other than perhaps suffixal rhyme:

> Heo was faken biforen   7 atterne bihinden.

['It [your tongue] was false in front and poisonous behind.']

The prefixes *a-*, *bi-*, *for-*, *i-*, *on-*, and *to-* cannot be shown to alliterate in the Worcester Fragments, though at B 16 (Buchholz, 3) *bedæled* could perhaps have cross-alliteration on *b* [and cf. G 9 (Buchholz, 9) with alliteration on *t* and conceivably cross-alliteration on the prefix *a-* in *atrukied* and *ascorted*, also perhaps with suffixal rhyme]; and conceivably the prefix of *bedæled* could provide treble alliteration in the halfline *þine bon beoþ bedæled* at E 9 (Buchholz, 6). Similar to B 16, prefixal cross-alliteration on the initial vowel of *afursed* might be regarded a possibility at E 37 (Buchholz, 7), and at F 34 (Buchholz, 9) the two occurrences of the prefix *i-* could possibly be regarded as providing transverse alliteration as could conceivably the same prefix at F 36. There are, of course, several more lines in which a vocalic prefix might be thought to supply some kind of alliteration, but since I do not believe in that kind of alliteration I do not list them all. (The position of the unstressed conjunction *ond* in the alliterative system seems similar to me: once alliteration on *ond* is regarded as possible, many doubtful examples can be found.) The most plausible case of prefixal alliteration is perhaps F 17 (Buchholz, 8):

> Mid clutes þu ert forbunden,   7 loþ alle freonden

['you are bound up in shrouds, and hateful to all friends)]

a line which is regarded by Buchholz, lxxiv, as having neither alliteration nor end-rhyme, a view which seems right to me. On the other hand, I do regard some kind of linking of two halflines by means of prefixes possible at E 38 and G 17, without considering it in terms of alliteration.

[25] G. L. Brook and R. F. Leslie, eds., *Laȝamon: Brut*, vol. 2, EETS, 277 (1978), 818.
[26] Brook and Leslie, 664.

5. Rhyme (and full stress?) on the penultimate (originally half-stressed) syllable in words of three or more syllables

Of greater interest, however, is perhaps the rhyme on the half-stressed -*ode* at
The Battle of Maldon 42 (and 309):

> Byrhtnoð maþelode, bord hafenode

and similarly Chronicle AD 1036, lines 9–10:

> sume hamelode,
> sume hættode.

We have not yet reached the stage where the half-stressed medial syllable is elevated by rhyme above the stem-syllable,[27] for the stems *hamel-* and *haett-* alliterate, and must, therefore, carry full stress. The stress on the medial syllable is as in the couplet of *Poema Morale* 119–20 (MS Trinity College Cambridge 335, that is B.14.52):

> Ac drihte ne demeð no man after his biginninge
> Ac al his lif sal ben teald after his endinge.[28]

['But the Lord judges no one according to his birth, but one's entire life shall be brought to account according to one's end.']

In Orm, that is, probably as early as the 1170s,[29] the stage had been reached where the half-stressed medial syllable is elevated in scansion above the fully

---

[27] The transfer of metrical stress to the originally half-stressed medial syllable in trisyllabic words is mentioned from time to time by Leo Pilch, *Umwandlung des altenglischen Alliterations-verses in den mittelenglischen Reimvers*, diss., U. Königsberg, 1904, but he deals with too many texts, and his treatment is cursory.

[28] J. Hall, *Selections from Early Middle English 1130–1250* (Oxford, 1920), 1.37; cf. H. Lewin, *Das mittelenglische Poema Morale* (Halle, 1881), 58; J. Zupitza, 'Zum Poema Morale', *Anglia*, 1 (1878), 14, who prints the lines:

> Drihte ne demeð nenne man
> bi his biginninge:
> al his lif sel ben iteald
> bi his endinge.

Cf. also A. C. Paues, 'A Newly Discovered Manuscript of the Poema Morale', *Anglia*, 30 (1907), 230, lines 113–14.

[29] The only complete edition is that by R. M. Holt, *The Ormulum with the notes and glossary of Dr R. M. White* (Oxford, 1878). I have altered the quotations in line with the current understanding of Orm's orthography, but have not checked the readings against the manuscript. For the date of the *Ormulum* see M. B. Parkes, 'On the Presumed Date and Possible Origin of the Manuscript of the "Orrmulum": Oxford, Bodleian Library, MS Junius 1', in E. G. Stanley and Douglas Gray, *Five Hundred Years of Words and Sounds . . . for Eric Dobson* (Cambridge, 1983), especially p. 125.

stressed stem-syllable. (The *Ormulum* has, of course, no rhyme.) Thus we may contrast *Ennglísshe* in lines 129–30 of Orm's Dedication:

> 7 tærfore hafe icc turrnedd itt:
> inntill Ennglisshe spæche

with *Énnglissh* in lines 147–8:

> Hemm hafe itt inntill Ennglissh wennd:
> forr þeȝȝre sawle nede

or with the verbal ending of the present participle 8165–6:[30]

> Abutenn þatt stinnckennde lic:
> þær itt wass brohht till eorþe.

Orm's scansion is more flexible than he has been usually credited with, and we must always remember that those who impose slavish regularity on Orm have only themselves as model readers when they tell us that he follows the septenarius without deviation, as, for example, J. Hall:[31]

> Orm's verse is monotonously regular; every line has its fifteen syllables exactly counted out and ends in x́ x; the caesura comes after the eighth syllable; the rhythm is iambic without substitution. For the sake of uniformity he does violence to the natural accent in Niþþrédd 35, Bisscópess 51, Enngléss 69, sahhtnésse 140, drihhtíness 171.

The metre of these lines bears closer inspection. In trisyllabic words accentuation of the middle syllable is, as we have seen, regular for early Middle English verse. Thus in the lines referred to, 51, 140, and 171 need detain us no longer; it may be that their metre does violence to natural accentuation in the words singled out by Hall, but that is in line with Middle English practice and with some late Old English practice. On the other hand, lines 35 and 69 bear the accent on the second syllable of *Niþþredd* and *Enngless* only if the modern reader departs from what must be the normal stress on the first syllable: it is he who forces the accentuation away from what is normal in the belief that he is doing what Orm means him to do. There is no evidence for that belief, and it seems better to me to read the former line with accent on the stem syllables of *Niþþredd* and *wánnsedd* and the latter with the accent on the stem of *Énngless*:

> Niþþredd 7 wannsedd wunnderrliȝ;
> 7 laȝhedd inn himm sellfenn.

['Humbled and diminished marvellously, and brought low in themselves.']

[30] Similarly lines 1067 and 17447; see B. Thüns, *Das Verbum bei Orm*, diss., U. Leipzig, 1909, 17.
[31] See n. 28, above. Hall, p. 486. The corresponding line numbering in the edition by Holt and White is: line 35 = 3730–1, 51 = 3762–3, 69 = 3798–9, 140 = 3940–1, 171 = 4002–3.

And

> To frofrenn swillke senndeþþ godd;
> Énngless 7 hall3he sawless.

['To help such, God sends angels and holy souls.']

In both cases the 'natural' accentuation, that is, with the accent on the stem-syllable, seems good: it brings some grace to the use of the two participles in the former; and in the latter it throws the emphasis on *Enngless* as the sense requires. This kind of more flexible reading of the *Ormulum* brings out more fully the meaning of many lines, where harshly enforced 'unnatural' metrical regularity offends against both linguistic and literary good sense. Orm's accentuation of the penultimate, originally half-stressed syllable in words of three or more syllables, however, is in line with the treatment of these syllables in late Old English verse, as is shown by such lines, considered above, as *The Battle of Maldon* 42 and 309 *mapelode | hafenode*, and in the Sutton brooch inscription the pure rhyme on the stem and endings of *awerie | ætferie*, probably with the -*i*- of the ending syllabic.[32]

6. The rhyme looks less good in the transmitted text than it may have been in the poet's original

Sometimes what looks like an imperfect rhyme may have been more nearly perfect in the poet's original; and when changes brought about by textual transmission are considered by editors they may improve the appearance of the rhymes as transmitted by emendation. Thus the rhymes in *Elene* 1240–1

> be ðære [rode] riht   ær me rumran geþeaht
> þurh ða mæran miht   on modes ⌐þ⌐eaht

['By the truth of the Cross before to me more extensive knowledge through that greater might in thought of mind.']

The rhymes in these lines are improved phonologically in Holthausen's edition:[33]

> be ðære [rode] reht,   ær me rumran geþæht
> þurh ða mæran mæht   on modes æht.

---

[32] See E. Sievers, *Altgermanische Metrik* (Halle, 1893), 126, §79, 1.

[33] See n. 17, above. In the last word of 1241, *þ* has been added before *eaht*, later according to the apparatus of J. Zupitza, *Cynewulfs Elene*, 3rd edn. (Berlin, 1888), confirmed by Gradon in the apparatus to her edition (see n. 15, above). The other editors do not comment on when the letter was added; and Cook (see n. 16, above) in his note on the line (p. 97) seems to ascribe the repetition neither to the confused main scribe nor to a subsequent scribal attempt at correction, but to the author himself: 'þeaht. It seems rather inartistic to repeat this syllable from the preceding line.'

In Holthausen's reading the last word, *æht* for West Saxon *eaht*, must have some such meaning as 'consideration'; Holthausen's glossary gives the senses 'Acht' (the cognate in Modern German, with the sense 'attention, care') and 'Beratung' (but that seems to go with the occurrence of the word at line 473).

Sometimes, in spite of the frequency of imperfect rhyming in Old English, editors abandon the good sense of the transmitted text when it rhymes imperfectly, and, as we have seen,[34] give preference to their emendation designed to 'restore' a perfect rhyme though the sense is less good, as in *Elene* 1247 *ámæt | begeat* where the second rhyme word is emended to *begæt*.

7. The tradition of rhyming: truly or more loosely

There is a tradition in early English of rhyming at many levels of purity. We have the term assonance for one kind of impure rhyming, namely when the vowels are identical and the consonants close in sound. H. Löhe, discussing some of the inexact rhymes in *The Judgment Day II*, speaks of *Anklang*, and that German term for which English has no equivalent may cover a wider set of loose rhymes;[35] he is referring specifically to line 4 *gehæge | secge* and line 28 *hleorum | tearum*. He does not discuss the internal assonance in the first halfline used in conjunction with an inexact end-rhyme in line 126:

> amasod and amarod,   mihtleas, afæred.

['amazed and stupefied, the powerless, terrified.']

It would be useful to have a term like *Anklang* for all kinds of inexact rhyme-like linkings, but we lack it. We have not even in regular use a term to correspond to *skothendingar*,[36] the half-rhymes of Scaldic verse.

It may be that rhyming in English is, as has often been suggested, due to, and subject to the influence of, rhyming in Church Latin, also variously impure. Specifically, it may be that absence of alliteration in rhyming lines within what is otherwise alliterative verse is due to Latin influence, as Guest thought in his important discussion of English writers of Latin verse and the interrelation of Latin and vernacular, rhythmical and rhyming practice.[37] It is, however, likely that influence in the reverse direction may also have taken

---

[34] See p. 26 above.

[35] Cf. H. Löhe, *Be Domes Dæge*, Bonner Beiträge zur Anglistik, 23 (1907), 65.

[36] The use of rhymes and especially half-rhymes, *skothendingar*, in Scaldic verse has affinities, at least by analogy, with the rhymes, true or in various ways inexact, of early English verse. For details, see R. Frank, *Old Norse Court Poetry: The* Dróttkvætt *Stanza*, Islandica, 42 (Ithaca and London, 1978), 36–7, and elsewhere (see the excellent index).

[37] E. Guest, *A History of English Rhythms* (London, 1838), 2.419:

> Writers of Latin 'rhythmi' have influenced, in a very marked manner, both the sentiments and the versification of English poetry. Many of the rhythmical models, which our critics have perversely sought for, in some one or other of

place, that is, that some of the practices of English poets writing in the vernacular, in both Old and Middle English, may have been imitated by English poets writing in Latin, though that is not relevant to the present discussion; what is probable is that the influence on English of Medieval Latin and, later, of Old French rhyming verse had the result that English versifiers could not escape rhymes and increasingly made use of rhymes instead of alliteration.[38] Whether at the beginning of this process, that is, in the Old

> the Romance dialects, were familiar to our Latinists, long before any of these languages possessed a literature.

And p. 420:

> Their accentual rhythms have a peculiarity which deserves notice, as being directly opposed to the great law of Anglo-Saxon versification. Whenever they alliterate the rhythmus, the alliteration is always subordinate to the rhime, and often rests on unaccented syllables.

A good, brief modern account of such problems within Medieval Latin, but not, of course, in relation to English vernacular verse, is to be found in the chapter 'Assonance, rime et allitération', in D. Norberg, *Introduction à l'étude de la versification latine médiévale*, Studia Latina Stockholmiensia, 5 (1958), 38–49. I am indebted to David and Ian McDougall (*Dictionary of Old English*, Toronto) for drawing my attention to three important earlier accounts, which have a direct or indirect bearing on Medieval Latin rhyming practice: E. Wölfflin, 'Der Reim im Lateinischen', *Archiv für lateinische Lexikographie und Grammatik*, 1 (1884), 350–89; Wölfflin, 'Zur Alliteration und zum Reime', in the same journal, 3 (1886), 443–57; V. Lundström, 'Zur Geschichte des Reims in klassischer Zeit', *Eranos*, 2 (1897), 81–6, 104–16.

[38] Cf. W. Meyer, 'Ein Merowinger Rhythmus über Fortunatus und Altdeutsche Rhythmik in lateinischen Versen', *Gesammelte Abhandlungen zur mittellateinischen Rhythmik*, 3 (1936; Hildesheim and New York, 1970), 95–6. [= *Nachrichten der Königlichen Gesellschaft der Wissenschaften zu Göttingen*, Philologisch-historische Klasse, 1908, 79–80], especially p. 96 [= 80], after discussing Old High German rhyming verse and the extinction of alliterative verse in Old High German:

> Anders die Engländer; sie hielten die Alliteration fest und kümmerten sich zunächst wenig um den Reim. Da aber in der altfranzösischen Dichtung der Endreim ebenso feste und nie fehlende Eigenschaft der Verse geworden war wie in der deutschen, und da im Laufe des 11. Jahrhunderts der Endreim ein nothwendiges Stück auch der mittellateinischen Rythmik geworden war, so konnte auch die mittelenglische Rythmik sich dem Reim nicht entziehen; der Reim wurde also ein wichtiges Stück auch der mittelenglischen Rythmik.

> ['It was otherwise with the English. They clung to alliteration, and at first they cared little about rhyme. But because end-rhyme had become a firm and never absent peculiarity in Old French verse, as much as in German verse, and because end-rhyme had in the course of the eleventh century become an essential element also of Medieval Latin verse, therefore Middle English verse could not escape rhyme: and so rhyme became an important element also of Middle English verse.']

English period, Irish played a part, as has sometimes been thought,[39] especially with reference to *The Riming Poem*,[40] seems more questionable to me. The treatment of half-stress in Latin rhyming verse seems to run parallel to that in vernacular rhyming verse (whatever the causal relationship, if any).[41] And there are parallels between some recurring licences in Latin rhyming and licences in Old and especially Middle English.[42]

From what has been said so far of earlier English rhyming it will be apparent that purity in Middle English rhyming is not to be regarded as inevitable. Far from it; if we could imagine a reader who, by some kind of academic ontogenesis, comes to Middle English verse, not, as we all have done, from Modern English poetry and by way of Chaucer (the Middle English poet whom we read first), but from Old English and Medieval Latin verse including some of the earliest period written by Anglo-Saxon and Irish poets, such a reader would find the expectation of purity surprising; it would seem a deliberate exclusion of many less exact forms of prosodic linking, all of them in frequent early use. Yet to a modern reader who has come to early Middle English by way of Chaucer, it is clear also that, unless Chaucer were unique in purity of rhyming, at some stage some poet must have begun to favour purity in rhymes: but who, and when, and how far?

8. *The Proverbs of Alfred*

In considering early Middle English rhyming practice, one might do worse than begin with *The Proverbs of Alfred*. Of course, the connection with the

---

[39] Cf. H. Brinkmann, 'Der Reim im frühen Mittelalter', in W. Iser and H. Schabram, eds., *Britannica: Festschrift für Hermann M. Flasdieck* (Heidelberg, 1960), 62–81 [reprinted in H. Brinkmann, *Studien zur Geschichte der deutschen Sprache und Literatur*, Literatur (Düsseldorf, 1966), 2.58–78], especially 70–2 [= 67–9] with an expression of belief in magic and mantic implications of rhyme in which I have no faith. Meyer's important discussion of these difficult connections is less speculative, and therefore more persuasive to me: 'Reim und Assonanz bei den lateinischen Dichtern der Iren', in 'Die Verskunst der Iren in rythmischen lateinischen Gedichten', *Nachrichten der Königlichen Gesellschaft der Wissenschaften zu Göttingen*, Philologisch-historische Klasse, 1916, 616–23 [= *Gesammelte Abhandlungen*, 3.315–23], and on Aethilwald in the same paper, pp. 635–7 [= 336–8].

[40] Cf. Brinkmann, p. 75 [= 72]; and G. Baesecke, *Das lateinisch-althochdeutsche Reimgebet Carmen ad Deum und das Rätsel vom Vogel federlos* (Berlin, 1948), 25–31.

[41] Cf. W. Meyer, 'Ein Merowinger Rhythmus', *Nachrichten*, 1908, 63–4 [= *Gesammelte Abhandlungen*, 3.50–1].

[42] Meyer analyses impure rhymes in Latin in 'Der Rythmus über den h. Placidas-Eustasius', *Nachrichten*, 1915, 253–69 [= *Gesammelte Abhandlungen* 3.284–302]. He has a skilful comparative discussion of the prosodic practice, both Latin and English, in the Towneley Plays, in 'Lateinisch-mittelenglische Gedichte in Hexametern und Vagantenzeilen', *Gesammelte Abhandlungen*, 3.349–52 (not previously published).

great Anglo-Saxon king is merely twelfth-century antiquarian piety. But in many ways this is a text that conveniently typifies the literary and especially the textual problems of early Middle English verse. As the manuscript witnesses are considered it soon emerges that Jesus College Oxford MS 29 (J) introduces a neater system of rhymes than that of the other manuscripts, namely Trinity College Cambridge 323 (T), Maidstone A. 13 (M), and Cotton Galba A.xix (C). In other words, the Jesus reviser is not a faithful transmitter of the text but a man who thrusts regularity upon its rhymes, often by means of empty rhyming tags.[43] As Arngart says,

> The transcriber of J, or the transcribers of one or more of the series of copies through which it is descended from the archetype, was not content with copying his original as faithfully as he could, like the T scribe, but he revised the text of the original to a fairly great extent. Especially in certain sections . . . he gave free rein to his imagination, and the result is that these sections . . . offer readings which differ from those of the other MSS. and where the text can be shown to be unauthentic.

Arngart goes on to characterise the Jesus redactor (or the redactors leading to Jesus). In an important footnote he draws attention to the violence which Jesus has done to texts transmitted in that manuscript:

> On the possibility that the reviser is identical with the scribe of the Jesus MS., cf. Hall (p. 293),[44] who points out that the copy of the Poema Morale in the same MS. has undergone a drastic revision, which sets it apart among the versions of that poem, and the J version of the Owl and the Nightingale has suffered, though not to the same extent.

That *The Owl and the Nightingale* seems to have 'suffered' less alteration in the Jesus MS is undemonstrable in absolute terms: Arngart's statement may mean no more than that the only extant other witness, the scribe of Cotton MS Caligula A.ix, is the faithful copyist of 'one or more of the series of copies through which it [J] is descended from the archetype'. Arngart goes on immediately in his characterisation of the Jesus redactor of *The Proverbs of Alfred*:

> He is fond of rhyme or assonance. The Proverbs of Alfred are composed in a kind of alliterative verse which forms a continuation of the Old English alliterative line, but differs from it in many respects. Though the old rules were still to a great extent observed, the Proverbs of Alfred show alliterative verse in an advanced state of decay as

---

[43] See O. S. A. Arngart, *The Proverbs of Alfred*, 1. A Study of the Texts, Skrifter utgivna av Kungl. Humanistiska Vetenskapssamfundet i Lund, 32.1 (1942), chapter ii, 'Inferior Matter in J', 74–98. The quotation is from p. 74.
[44] See n. 28, above.

compared with classical Old English patterns. All the OE types of alliterating lines may be found in the Proverbs, but the number of irregular lines is great. The staves are sometimes correctly placed, but often they are not. Finally, the half-lines are not rarely connected by rhyme or assonance. On the whole, the characteristics of the verse of the Proverbs of Alfred are the same as those of some late OE alliterative pieces, though in the Proverbs the decay of the alliterative line has advanced farther than in these. Judging by a comparison of the texts, however, the alliterative line of the archetype was considerably more regular than the line found in J. The redactor of the version represented by J in many cases spoils the old verse pattern by the introduction of rhyme or assonance . . .[45]

Arngart's 'Study of the Texts' gives examples of departure in the Jesus MS from what must be regarded as more nearly the original, better preserved in the other manuscripts of the text, and he points to some extensive cases, of which sections 8 and 9 show a great profusion of improved rhymes of varying degrees of looseness. I give them here from Arngart's edition:[46]

TRINITY	MAIDSTONE	JESUS	
Þus quad Alfreð:		Þus seyþ Alured:	
Sorȝe it his to rowen	Sorwe hit is to rowen	Strong hit is to reowe	
aȝen þe se-flod,	aȝen þe se-flode,	ayeyn þe see þat floweþ,	
so it his to swinkin	so it is to swinken	so hit is to swynke	
again honiselþe.	aȝenes vniselþe.	ayeyn vnylimpe.	5
Ach wel is him a ȝueþe	ac wel is him on ȝuþe	þe mon þe on his youhþe	
þe suinch was ȝauen	þe swinch was iȝiuene	swo swinkeþ	
her on werlde	her on werlde	and worldes weole	
welþe to winnen;	wele to winnen;	her iwinþ,	
7 he muȝe on helde	and he muȝe in elde	þat he may on elde	10
hednisse holdin,	ednesse helden,	idelnesse holde,	
7 he mist in his welþe	and he mis welþe	and ek myd his worldes weole	
werchin Godis wille.	wirche Godes wulle.	God iqueme er he quele.	
Þenne his his ȝueþe	Þanne is his ȝuȝeþe	Youþe and al þat he haueþ idrowe	
swiþe wel bitoȝen.	swiþe wel bitoȝen.	is þenne wel bitowe.	15

[45] pp. 74–5.
[46] O. S. A. Arngart, *The Proverbs of Alfred*, 2. The Texts Edited with Introduction, Notes and Glossary, Skrifter utgivna av Kungl. Humanistiska Vetenskapssamfundet i Lund, 32.2 (1955), 84–9. Accents, brackets, italics have been ignored, and the punctuation has been modernised here.

Þus quad Alfred:		Þus queþ Alured:
ȝif þu hauest welþe awold	Ȝif þu hauest welþe	Yf þu seoluer and gold
i þis werlde	in þisse werlde	yefst and weldest in þis world
ne ȝin þu neure forþi	ne gin þu nefre forþi	neuer vpen eorþe
alto wlonc wurþen.	alto wlonc wurþen;	to wlonk þu nywrþe. 20
Aycte nis non eldere stren,	for ahte nis non eldere stren,	Ayhte nys non ildre istreon,
ac it is Godis lone.	ac is Godes lone.	ac hit is Godes lone.

['Thus spoke (J says) Alfred: it is a sad thing (J hard) to row against the ocean-current (J the sea that flows), as it is to toil (5) against misfortune. But it is good for him to whom in his youth (J The man who in his youth) the toilsome task was given (J so toils) here in the world (J and worldly prosperity) to gain prosperity (J gains here,); (10) and (J that) he may in old age possess bliss (J idleness [!]), and he could in his prosperity (M and he with his [?] prosperity; J and also with his worldly wealth) do God's will (J please God before he dies). Then his youth will have been (J youth and all that he has experienced) (15) very well spent (J will then have been well spent).

'Thus spoke Alfred: if you have wealth at your disposal (M if you have wealth; J if silver and gold you) in this world (J give and control in this world) do not ever begin for that reason (20) to become too proud. Possessions (M For possessions) are no hereditary gain, but they are God's gift.']

The Jesus MS adds a rhyme at lines 2–3, loose because *rowe* (spelt *reowe*) rhymes with the stem but not, of course, the ending of *floweþ*, but T and M have no rhyme at all. J seems to add some kind of very inexact rhyme (*swynke / vnylimpe*) at lines 4–5 where T and M seem to have no rhyme at all. At line 13 J adds a tag to introduce the rhyme word *quele* which goes with *weole* (12), and similarly J introduces the rhyme word *idrowe* to go with the last word of the next line, *bitowe*. In the next section J has a great deal of rewriting, but not, it seems, to produce rhymes. It would be possible to think of reasons for such changes, for example, that *forþi* (19) is a feeble word for the end of a line; but I want to use this rewriting for no other purpose than to indicate how unreliable a textual witness the Jesus MS is. And if the manuscript is so unreliable, how can we use its rhymes as evidence of dialectal provenance? Another reason for looking at this text transmitted by three manuscripts, two of them in some agreement against the third, Jesus, is to let the evidence of these versions undermine any certainty a modern reader may feel when trying to assess the nature of the prosody: is this verse basically alliterative, each line as given here providing an alliterative halfline, or is it basically rhyming verse, though very inexact? Alliterative lines include, for example, the following with alliteration on *w* and on vowels (I use M, because T has inorganic *h* before the alliterating vowels):

> her on werlde   wele to winnen,
> and he muȝe in elde   ednesse helden.

When we consider the rhymes even in manuscripts less freely improved than Jesus, we are at once in the familiar world of Middle English rhyming tags. Thus for lines 17–24:[47]

TRINITY	JAMES TRANSCRIPT[48]	JESUS
Alfred he was in Enkelonde a king,	Alfred he was on Engelond	Alured he wes in Englene lond,
wel swiþe strong 7 lufsum þing.	a king wel swiðe strong.	an king wel swiþe strong.
He was king 7 cleric; ful wel he louede Godis werc.	He was king 7 clerc: wel he luvede Godes werc.	He wes king and he wes clerek: wel he luuede Godes werk.
He was wis on his word	He was wise on his worde	He wes wis on his word
7 war on his werke.	and ware on his speche.	and war on his werke.
He was þe wisiste mon þad was in Engelonde on.	He was þe wiseste man þat was on Engelond.	He wes þe wysuste mon þat wes englelonde on.

In origin *The Proverbs of Alfred* appears close to the descendants in Transitional English of Old English alliterative verse, close perhaps even to Laȝamon's alliterative verse with frequent rhymes at various levels of looseness. In transmission, especially in the Jesus MS, it is brought into greater proximity to rhyming verse with alliterative ornament. That in the Jesus MS it is written out like prose, and not in lines like verse, is irrelevant, for even some of the stanzaic lyrics in MS Harley 2253 are written continuously like prose; for example, 'Wiþ longyng y am lad' on fo. 63ᵛ and 'The Man in the Moon' on fos. 114ᵛ and 115ʳ.[49] Yet I cannot help feeling that, in view of the insecurity of the textual basis for this poem and in view especially of the mingling of alliterative and rhyming verse in the text as we have it, most

---

[47] Arngart, 2. 72–3.

[48] This copy of Cotton MS Galba A.xix (mutilated in 1731 in the Cottonian fire when this part of the text was lost) was made about 1620–34. See Arngart, 2.17; and F. Madan, H. H. E. Craster, and N. Denholm-Young, *A Summary Catalogue of Western Manuscripts in the Bodleian Library at Oxford*, 2.2 (Oxford, 1937), 752–3, No. 3843.

[49] See N. R. Ker, *Facsimile of British Museum MS. Harley 2253*, EETS, 255 (1965), xi–xiii, xvii–xviii.

strikingly in the Jesus MS, Arngart's statement about the metre is too absolute:

> The metre is a modification of the advanced type of O.E. alliterative line showing greater freedom of construction and alliteration, extended use of rhyme within the alliterative long line and, in lines which rhyme only but do not alliterate or which use alliteration merely for ornament, a transition to the rhymed couplet. Metrically the closest parallel is Layamon's *Brut*.[50]

9. Early Middle English shorter poems, and *Meidan Maregrete*

The Proverbs of Alfred is not uniquely insecure in textual transmission among early Middle English texts. These and related manuscripts underlie some early Middle English short poems, well discussed by Karl Reichl.[51] His concern is, in the first place, with the Trinity MS, one of the manuscripts in which *The Proverbs of Alfred* is also preserved. Other manuscripts containing short Middle English poems related to those in Trinity are also used by him; they are: Jesus 29, Egerton 613, Arundel 248, Digby 2, Digby 86, Corpus Christi College Oxford 59, Royal 2 F.viii, Royal 12 E.i, Cotton Caligula A.ix, Cotton Nero A.xiv, Tanner 169, St John's Cambridge 111, Corpus Christi College Cambridge 8, Guildhall, British Library Add. 27909, Maidstone A.13, Laud Misc. 471, Rawlinson G.18, Gonville & Caius 512; also Arundel 292, Bodley 57, Trinity College Dublin 432, McClean 123, Harley 2253, Digby 4, Lambeth 487, and many others. What emerges with clarity is the great number of substantive variants, amounting to rewriting in some cases. I do not wish to enter into the problem of aural as opposed to scribal transmission, for I know how unreliable conclusions are when based on impressions of bookishness, or, for that matter, of singability.

Some of the poems edited by Reichl from several manuscripts manifest not merely great differences in wording, but also a wide range of inaccurate rhymes. Did the scribes find these rhymes acceptable when they wrote out the poems? By way of reference I use the numbers of *The Index of Middle English Verse* and its *Supplement*[52] together with page and line numbers in

---

[50] Arngart, 2. 225.

[51] *Religiöse Dichtung im englischen Hochmittelalter – Untersuchung und Edition der Handschrift B. 14. 39 des Trinity College in Cambridge*, Münchener Universitäts-Schriften: Texte und Untersuchungen zur Englischen Philologie, 1 (1973). See especially pp. 60–82, 107–11.

[52] Carleton Brown and Rossell H. Robbins, *The Index of Middle English Verse* (New York, 1943); R. H. Robbins and John L. Cutler, *Supplement to the Index . . .* (Lexington, Kentucky, 1965).

Reichl's edition to bring together some of the more interesting or glaring examples:

4211: 154.6–7 misnomen (p.p.) / bouen ('above').

2672 and 203: 174/33–6 telle / helle / quelle / selle; Cambridge Add. 4122 (15th c.) selle / helle / qwelle / twelve.

do.: 178/45–8 Maregrete / strete / bihete / furlete; Bodley 779 (1st half 15th c.) to mete ('to meet') / chepe ('sheep') / bede ('offer') / forlete.

do.: 179 st. 13 (the following is the full text in the manuscripts):

TRINITY
Þe sergaunz deden ar ernde, feire ant fele siþe.
'Meidan Maregrete, nulle we nout mitte fike:
Olibrius is loverd of Auntioge þe riche,
He wil het þe to wiue, wel it may þe like.'

AUCHINLECK
Þe seriaunce of her erand wald hir nouȝt biswike.
'Damisel, we say it þe, ful wele may þe like:
Olibrious is louerd of Antiage rike,
He ȝerneþ þe to wyue, he nil þe nouȝt biswike.'

BODLEY 779
Þe knyȝtus toldin here erande, nolde hy noþing swike.
'Damesele, we seggeþ, we nolleþ þe bystrike:[53]
Olibrius oure lord of Antioche is ryche,
He desireþ þe to wyue, ful wel may hit þe like.'

RAWLINSON
The knyghtes dedene here eraunde welle fayre and curteslye.
'Maidene, we behote welle the, we wylle the noughte besweke:
Olybrius, the lorde of Antyoche and of alle Assyȝe eke,
He desyrethe to haue the to wyffe and that may welle the lyke.'

CAMB. ADD.
The Saryssones her erande to done forthe þei gunne stryke.
'Damysel,' þei sayden, 'we wolle þe not smyte:
Olibryus, oure lord of Antioche so ryche,
He desyres þe to wynne, fulle welle it maye þe lyke.'

---

[53] *MED* has no suitable entry for *bistriken* 'strike at'; the sense is confirmed by the reading of Camb. Add., *we wolle þe not smyte*. This variant well exemplifies the unreliability of the doctrine of *lectio difficilior* for editors of medieval English vernacular texts.

BLACKBURN　　The sergeauntys whan þei her herde,　they wolde
　　　　　　　　　no lenger on her seke.
　　　　　　　　'Dameselle,' they sayden,　'we wyl nouȝt the
　　　　　　　　　beswyke:
　　　　　　　　Olebrius, that is lorde　of alle Antioche the ryche,
　　　　　　　　He desyreth the to be his wyfe,　fful welle hit
　　　　　　　　　may the lyke.'

do.: 191–2 st. 25: Trinity bot / god (adj.) / fot / mod; Auchinleck: bote / gode / fot / mode; Bodley: bote / sote ('sweet') / fote / mode; Blackburn (beginning of 15th c.) boot / good / feet / meet.

do.: 194 Rawlinson 117–20: thinge / kinge / wonynge / manassynge.

do.: 196 Trinity 117–20: striue / riue / swiþe / liue; Cambridge 119–22: dryve / stryve / schyve⁵⁴ / lyve; Blackburn 118–22: blyue / swythe / clyffe / lyfe.

do.: 201 Trinity 137–40: sore / here / care / nammore; other manuscripts do better.

do.: 205 Rawlinson 173–6: thene / mane / fontstone / Jordone; other manuscripts do better.

do.: 209 Cambridge 171–4: it (pron.) / bryȝte / wyȝte / nyȝte.

do.: 210 Cambridge 175–8: sente / wente / warde / wende; other manuscripts do better.

The faults of transmission in this poem, *Index* 2672 and 203, have been amply exemplified. Rhyming impurities from other poems edited by Reichl are given by me more briefly now:

2992: 298/31–2: liue / bliþe.

885: 302/33–5: sine ('sin') / cunne / dimme.

3078: 315–16: Trinity: brom / don; hosebonde / wolde; British Library Add. 11579: brom / don.

912: 333/34–5: wombe / fonden.

1129 and 2694: 334–6: Reichl divides the transmission into two branches, using the rhymes *suere / bere* (of two manuscripts including Trinity) as against *stele / bere* (of four manuscripts) and the attempted correction in Harley 2391 *stelle / delle* ('steal / deal') as important evidence.

1461: 358: Trinity 91–2 londe / þange (for ȝange); Digby 86 and Harley 2253 londe / ȝonge.

---

⁵⁴ The halfline seems best in Auchinleck (and similarly Rawlinson and Blackburn): *as water doþ fram cliue.* Cambridge Add. *as watyr dos of schyve* may again exemplify the unreliability of *lectio difficilior* – but cf. *OED* s.v. *Shive,* sb.² which can mean 'the refuse of hemp or flax', though only in the plural. Water running off such a greasy mess may give sense, less hackneyed sense than water running off the cliff. Reichl (p. 274) suggests that the underlying *clyve* may have been miscopied *chyve* by an intermediate scribe.

do.: 362: Trinity 117–20: fles ('flesh') / reunes ('rueness, repentence') / les ('false') / roties ('rots'); Harley: fleysh / reunes / les / endeles.

1649: 376/29–30: þat / spec.

4170: 389/23–4: slepen (MS damaged) / furleten; 393/57–60: eten / biyeten / mete / weope.

3967: 412/29–32: Trinity: honde / stonden / sconde / londe; Caligula A.ix and Jesus 29, and similarly Digby 86: honde / stondeþ / schonde / londe.

4119: 443/18–19: bouen / comen.

4141, 3966, 3968, 3965, 3961, 3964, 4107: 488–92. The seven versions of the short poem based on St Bernard's 'Respice in faciem Christi tui' are, as Reichl says (p. 492), all corrupt or altered in transmission. He has tentatively advanced a short lyric which is something like a nucleus of the transmitted versions, perhaps not too far from the presumed original. It includes the assonance *wepen / leten* found in four of the seven extant versions. He accepts into his *Kerngedicht* the impure rhyme *rode / stonde* from MSS Royal 12 E.i and Harley 7322, somewhat later witnesses than the earliest, of the thirteenth century, though, of course, early need not mean better, and earliest certainly need not mean best. This is not an exercise, therefore, of getting the divergent and often impure rhymes back into the better shape of a hypothetical original, but of finding the nucleus of the transmitted, divergent versions, and assuming for it impure rhyming practice such as is not uncommon in the verse contained in the Trinity MS and similar collections. Of course it would be possible to produce a hypothetical *Kerngedicht* with pure rhymes, perhaps taking from MS Bodley 57 the lines

> Weil aut i sinne lete
> An neb wit teres wete

which in that manuscript take the place of the couplet in the Trinity MS

> Sore he may wepin
> Ant bittre teris letin

or in MS Royal 12 E.i

> Wel ou hic to wepen
> And sinnes for te leten.

10. The Harley Lyrics, and *King Horn*

We may now move forward to rhymes in major Middle English poetry, the Harley Lyrics, *The Owl and the Nightingale*, and some in Chaucer's, with which I mean to end this brief account of rhyming in English medieval verse. The Harley Lyrics preserved in MS Harley 2253 and *The Owl and the*

Nightingale preserved in Cotton MS Caligula A.ix and Jesus College Oxford MS 29 are in transmission close to the Trinity lyrics edited with variants by Reichl. MS Caligula A.ix also contains (and is very likely to have contained from the first) Laȝamon's *Brut*. N. R. Ker's account of the manuscript and of the hands in it is important.[55] Neither of the two (or perhaps more) hands of the *Brut* is the same hand as that of *The Owl and the Nightingale*, but is close to it. MS Harley 2253 contains, of course, many poems other than the lyrics, among them political poems by means of one of which, in French and Latin 'Dieu roy de mageste', the date is established as after 1338,[56] and *King Horn*.

The Harley Lyrics do not contain pure rhymes only; for example, using the numbers in G. L. Brook's edition[57] (with the *Index* numbers in brackets):

6 (3874): 25–31 wot ('know') / lot ('behaviour' cf. OIcel. lát) / mot (= mod 'sorry') / blod. From the evidence of the stanza form elsewhere in the poem these four words should rhyme. *MED* brands *mot* for *mod* as 'error'; but the spelling may be designed to direct the reader to consider the words as rhymes, perhaps even in pronunciation by unvoicing final *d*.[58] The similar rhymes of Harley Lyric 21 (discussed below) confirms the rhyming of voiced with unvoiced in Lyric 6.

8 (1449): 1–7 fremede / glemede / kenede / gremede.

9 (105): 48–50 syke ('sighing') / whyte.

14 (1395): 14–16 longe / fonde / monge.

20 (3211, also in MSS Digby 86, St John's College Cambridge 111, and Royal 12 E.i):[59] 7–8 wepinge / monkynde (Royal wepinge / mannes thinge).

21 (1705): 5–9 (god / blod /) fot / blod; 12–14 ouerwerpes / werkes.

24 (2236): 13–16 man / am / sham / lemman.

26 (1407, also MS Egerton 613):[60] 9–12 wan / man / am / can; Egerton won / forþan / kan / man.

27 (359): 26–7 wymman / cam ('came') / man; 49–53 wymman / cam / nam / wymman.

---

[55] *The Owl and the Nightingale* (facsimile), EETS, 251 (1963), especially pp. ix, xvi.

[56] See N. R. Ker, *Facsimile of British Museum MS Harley 2253*, EETS, 255 (1965), xxi.

[57] *The Harley Lyrics. The Middle English Lyrics of MS Harley 2253*, 4th edn. (Manchester, 1968).

[58] Unvoicing of final *d* preceded by a vowel in a stressed syllable would be exceptional. Cf. R. Jordan, *Handbook of Middle English Grammar: Phonology*, trans. E. J. Crook, Janua Linguarum Series Practica, 218, The Hague and Paris, 1974, §200. The first pair of rhyme-words, of course, has long open *o*, the last pair has long close *o*; lines 1, 3, 5, and 7 rhyme in the other stanzas of the poem, and elsewhere in poems of this stanza form.

[59] Digby and Royal are edited by Carleton Brown, *English Lyrics of the XIIIth Century* (Oxford, 1932), No. 49, with St John's in the notes, pp. 203–4.

[60] Egerton is edited by C. Brown (see n. 59, above), No. 55.

32 (parody of 31, which has better rhyming; both 1921): 2–6 stonde /
fonde / longe / wronge (31 ybounde / wounde / sounde / grounde); 7–8
þohte / ofte (31 þohte / bohte).

King Horn[61] rhymes in couplets. The following rhymes are inexact:

23–4 sones / gomes; 29–30 beste / werste; 45–6 yherde / onsuerede, also
207–8; 55–6 gripe / smyte; 151–2 gode (adj.) / moder; 159–60 fleoten /
weopen; 215–16 stille / hulles (Laud snille ('quickly') / hulle; Gg schulle
('clearly, resoundingly') / hulle); 239–40 listes / wistest; 245–6 vnderstond /
song (Laud vnderfonge, Gg vndervonge / songe); 255–6 dohter / þohte;
361–2 blyþe / olyue ('alive'; Laud swiþe, Gg siþe 'time'); 369–70 wille /
telle; 391–2 soþte ('softly') / dohter; 409–10 reste / lyste ('pleases'); 543–4
proue / wowe ('woo'); 699–700 dohter / ofte; 759–60 passe / westnesse
(Laud wisse / westnisse); 777–8 ryde / bridel; 793–4 man / cam; 799–800
wowen ('woo') / glouen ('gloves'); 819–20 fyhte /knyhtes; 835–6 borde /
wordes (Laud worde); 873–4 Murry / sturdy, on second syllable only, cf.
1345–6 Mury / hardy; 885–6 furste / huerte ('heart'); 935–6 sherte
('short') / derste ('durst'); 1005–6 haue / felawe; 1067–8 cloþes / loþe;
1155–6 wyne / pelryne (Laud wyn / pylegrim, Gg wyn / pilegrym); 1173–4
damoisele / palmere; 1207–8 sette / kepte (Laud lette); 1263–4 belle /
fulfulle (Laud fullen, Gg felle; 1271–2 chayere ('chair') / yhere; 1279–80
lond / strong; 1467–8 sone ('son') / welcome; 1479–80 listes (Laud and Gg
liste) / wiste; 1481–2 shewe ('show') / felawe (Laud drawe / felawe, Gg
schewe / fewe); 1485–6 sherte / suerde (Laud gyrte / schirte); 1493–4
harperis / fyþelers (Gg harpurs / gigours).

The rhymes of *King Horn* in the Harley MS are, in some respects, less
accurate than those of most of the other Middle English rhyming poems we
have considered, especially in ignoring the presence or absence of final
consonants of unstressed endings. Words of more than two syllables, especially
those with dissyllabic endings, are allowed to rhyme inexactly. In some cases
the variant readings provide stricter rhymes, but in some of these stricter
rhymes one gets the impression, subjectively, that we are dealing with scribal
improvements.

11. *The Owl and the Nightingale*, Dan Michel, William Herebert, and *Sir Ferumbras*

As we turn to *The Owl and the Nightingale* from earlier English verse, rather
than from a reading of later, more accurately rhyming verse, not only will use

---

[61] Edited by J. Hall, *King Horn. A Middle-English Romance* (Oxford, 1901), who
prints the three extant texts in parallel, MS Harley 2253, Bodleian MS Laud Misc. 108
and Cambridge University Library MS Gg.iv.27.2. I confine my discussion in the first
place to the Harley text. The rhymes in Laud have a bearing on the rhyming practice of
Havelok the Dane in that manuscript.

of assonance be regarded as part of the tradition of thirteenth-century English rhyming, but also some further inexactness, exceeding recognised licences, will not be found surprising. Often it might be possible to improve the rhymes, if one were inclined to emend; but there are many cases in Middle English rhyming verse, including *The Owl and the Nightingale*, where an editorially improved rhyme does not give sense as good as the inexact text of the manuscripts. The late professor E. J. Dobson has discussed the rhymes of the poem,[62] and with more faith in their accuracy than I showed in my edition,[63] and with more faith in it than I have now. He says:

> The assumption of imperfect rhymes and 'assonances', in order to give preference to readings or interpretations that offend against true rhyming, seems to me the arbitrary rejection of one of the most valuable tools of ME. textual criticism.[64]

There are only two or three writers of Middle English rhyming verse whose work survives in holograph, all of them later than *The Owl and the Nightingale*, Dan Michel, William Herebert, and the author of *Sir Ferumbras*: none of them rhymes exactly. Dan Michel and William Herebert are both of the earlier fourteenth century, that is a century or so later than *The Owl and the Nightingale*. Dan Michel rhymes are discussed by J. K. Wallenberg;[65] he refers to *yzed* 'said' / *bread* / *red* 'advice' / *dyad* 'dead':

> Here words with O[ld]K[entish] *ēa* and OK. *ē* undoubtedly rhyme with each other. In my opinion too great importance has been attached to these rhymes. The rhyme-words in the Ayenb. are altogether too few (in all 53) to show how far Michel was a careful rhymer. Such rhymes as *sseld* : *uend*, 1, 5 and *domb* : *rond*, 1, 16 justify doubt on this point. Furthermore, in order to get a rhyme-word Michel often had recourse to a form which is not his usual one in the prose text.

William Herebert's inaccurate rhymes include *on* 'one' / *mon* 'man', *kynedom* / *þorn*, *kunde* 'kind' / *bunde* 'bound' / *munde* 'mind'.[66]

---

[62] 'A New Edition of *The Owl and the Nightingale*', *N&Q*, 206 (1961), 373–8; continued pp. 405–11, 444–8.
[63] E. G. Stanley, ed. *The Owl and the Nightingale* (London and Edinburgh, 1960; corrected edn. Manchester, 1972).
[64] p. 378.
[65] *The Vocabulary of Dan Michel's Ayenbite of Inwyt* (Upsala, 1923), 306. Wallenberg gives examples of dialectal forms not found in Dan Michel's prose, but to which he is driven by the need to rhyme. The page and line references are to R. Morris's edition, EETS, 23 (1866; 2nd edn. rvsd. P. O. E. Gradon, 1965). The first group discussed is at p. 262.
[66] See Carleton Brown, *Religious Lyrics of the XIVth Century*, 2nd edn. rvsd. G. V. Smithers (Oxford, 1952), No. 14 lines 5–6, No. 15 lines 31–2, and No. 19 lines 2–9 (with *u* from both OE *y* and *u*).

The holograph of *Sir Ferumbras* is extant in Bodleian MS Ashmole 33 of *c*. 1380. Its editor, S. J. Herrtage, says of its rhymes:[67]

> The rymes are full and true, to effect which, however, the author frequently has had recourse to some very curious spelling (see for instance 11. 260–1 [*keem* 'came' / *Eem* 'uncle']). Occasionally we have instances of half-rhymes, as in 11. 76–7 [*frenschemen* / *hem* 'them'], 86–7 (first-half [*bane* 'ruin' / *name*]), 370–1 [*Balaan* / *cristendam*],[68] 1545–6 [wrong reference, perhaps 1548–9 *cure* / *þere*], &c.

The following rhymes in *The Owl and the Nightingale* are discussed by Dobson just before he speaks of rhyming as 'one of the most valuable tools of ME. textual criticism':

63–4: Caligula MS vuele ('evilly') / fuȝele, Jesus MS vuele / vowele. Accepting an emendation, Dobson follows C. T. Onions:[69]

> Onions is relying on the principle that in dealing with a ME. rhyming text one is entitled to assume that a form or a development which makes a rhyme perfect was that of the original author unless (i) it can be shown to be inherently improbable or (ii) an equally valid alternative explanation is available.

277–8: C foȝle / þuuele ('thicket'), J vowele / þuuele.

283–4: betere / chatere.

415–16: ȝomere ('miserably') / sumere. Dobson: 'but even this need not be accepted as imperfect', and he explains it as shortening of long *o* > *u* in the trisyllabic form as used here.

> 807–8: Do þine craftes alle togadere
> Ȝet is min on [on] horte betere.

['Put all your tricks together, yet my single one is fundamentally better.']

The couplet assonates on dissyllabic ending, especially if the original had *togedere*.

> 809–10: Oft þan hundes foxes driueþ
> Þe kat ful wel him sulue liueþ.

liueþ to rhyme exactly should have a long *i*; either some unparalleled form of *bileven* 'remain' or (different word) 'trust' without prefix. Possibly an inexact rhyme of long *driueþ* with short *liueþ* 'lives'.[70] But the sense is not easy;

---

[67] EETS ES, 34 (1879), xviii.

[68] The author's extant draft for this rhyme is better: *Balahen* / *cristen men*.

[69] 'An Experiment in Textual Reconstruction', *E&S*, 22 (for 1936), 86–102.

[70] Such rhymes can, of course, occur at all times in the language; thus *Tom Tyler and His Wife*, ed. G. C. Moore Smith and W. W. Greg, Malone Society, 1910, line 741, internal rhyme:

> If Destinie drive poor Tom for to live.

perhaps 'Often when hounds pursue foxes the cat itself lives very contentedly'.

1555–6: lokeþ / spekeþ. Dobson suggests an original *lekþ* 'plays' / *spekþ*, for the phonology of the rhyme is unparalleled in the poem. Probably the final consonant of the stem together with suffixal rhyme is enough.

Other inexact rhymes in the poem include the following:

475–6: J ywune / frume ('beginning'); cf. 1319–20 C kume / iwune.

501–2: itrede / iqueþe ('speak' inf.).

505–6: heisugge ('hedge-sparrow') / stubbe ('stubble').

631–2: cradele / aþele.

763–4: C liste / sholde miste. Mätzner, who edited part of the poem for his *Sprachproben*,[71] was probably right to explain the rhyme as having led the poet to alter the normal infinitive *misse* to an exceptional *miste*. If so, it is an important example of the poem changing a grammatical form owing to the exigencies of rhyme; and that is the opposite of the principle so commonly invoked, that rhyme confirms a form.

791–2: luuieþ / shunieþ; rhymes on the middle syllable -*i*- as well as assonating. 291–2 *gidie* 'the giddy one(s)' / ʒonie 'yawn' (subjunct. sg.) has no assonating stem-syllable.

987–8: wepen / forleten.

1071–2: tunge / songe. Impure rhymes on *ong* / *ung* are widespread in Middle English, and were exact in some areas, especially of the Midlands, which is not likely to have been the area where the poem originated.

1397–8: luste ('lusts' dat. pl) / custe ('qualities' dat. pl.); the rhyme appears to be /u/ with /y/ (< OE *cyst*).[72]

1467–8: wite (subjunct. sg.) / utschute ('gadding about'); if the original was south-eastern the rhyme would be of short *i* with short *e*; if south-west Midlands (as is believed by some),[73] the rhyme would be /i/ with /y/. Similarly 1505–6: ofligge ('may lie on' subjunct. sg.) / bugge ('buy' inf.); and probably 1767–8: stude ('place') / heom . . . mide ('with them'), *mide* is a possible adverbial form.

1523–4: gulte ('sin(s)' v.) / pulte ('copulate'). It appears that to provide a rhyme the poet uses the subjunctive *gulte* where the indicative *gult* would be normal syntax.

1531–2: wiue ('wife' dat.) / ischire ('utter').

1587–8: C oflonged ('seized with longing') / ongred ('grieved').

---

[71] E. Mätzner, *Altenglische Sprachproben*, 1.1, Poesie (Berlin, 1867), 42: 'miste, fail st[att] *misse*. Das nur assonirende Wort scheint wegen *liste* in *miste* verwandelt.' For other suggestions see the note in my edition.

[72] In some early Middle English texts *custe* alternates with *costes*. See Arngart, *The Proverbs of Alfred*, 1 (see n. 43, above), 32 note on line 269, and 113 note 4.

[73] See Sherman M. Kuhn, review of B. Sundby's *The Dialect and Provenance of . . . The Owl and the Nightingale*, *Language*, 27 (1951), 423.

The rhymes of the *The Owl and the Nightingale* are of interest because, by the standards of early Middle English, the poet is generally regarded as very good; and it is an assumption sometimes made, though hardly ever expressed explicitly, that if the poet is good his rhymes should be good too. The transmission of the poem rests on two closely related manuscripts which, in those lyrics included in them as well as in other manuscripts – for example, in Digby 86, the Trinity MS which Karl Reichl takes as his starting point, Royal 2 F.viii, and the Maidstone MS – can be seen to go back to a lost, common, scribally 'edited' exemplar. Shared errors in the two texts of *The Owl and the Nightingale* confirm that. The rhymes of *The Owl and the Nightingale* include assonances usual in early Middle English, impure rhymes on dissyllabic endings, and rhymes on forms to which the poet seems to be driven by the need to rhyme, of which *miste* for *misse* (764) is a striking example.

12. Chaucer

At the end of this study I wish to glance briefly at Chaucer's rhyming practice. It has, of course, received much attention, notably from Ellis,[74] ten Brink,[75] Wild,[76] and Masui,[77] as well as from the editors of Chaucer. The exactness of Chaucer's rhymes is accepted as a rule; but even the relatively mechanical ten Brink lists exceptions in the paragraphs devoted to rhymes. Among them the following:

Long with short vowel: *cas* / *was* (*Book of the Duchess* 725–6); later evidence suggests that *was* underwent lengthening,[78] so that perhaps as early as Chaucer the rhyme may have been true.

[74] A. J. Ellis, *On Early English Pronunciation, with especial reference to Shakspere and Chaucer*, Chaucer Society, 2nd series, 1 (1869), ch. IV. Pp. 249–53 bear the running title 'No real faulty rhymes in Chaucer'; that doctrine is established under the first principle of investigation: 'When few people can read, rhymes to be intelligible must be perfect' (p. 245), for which no demonstration is advanced by Ellis.
[75] B. ten Brink, *Chaucers Sprache und Verskunst*, 3rd edn., rvsd. E. Eckhardt (Leipzig, 1920), especially pp. 189–95. Most general books on Chaucer's language or on his style have sections devoted to his rhyming practice.
[76] F. Wild, *Die sprachlichen Eigentümlichkeiten der wichtigeren Chaucer-Handschriften und die Sprache Chaucers*, Wiener Beiträge zur englischen Philologie, 44 (1915).
[77] M. Masui, *The Structure of Chaucer's Rime Words. An Exploration into the Poetic Language of Chaucer* (Tokyo, 1941); and cf. M. Masui, 'Further Consideration of Chaucer's Rimes', *Hiroshima University Studies: Literature Department*, 29 (1970), 92–124.
[78] Lengthening could perhaps have taken place as early as Middle English. For the evidence (all of it much later than Chaucer) for lengthening in *was*, see E. J. Dobson, *English Pronunciation 1500–1700*, 2nd edn. (Oxford, 1968), 1.301 and 443, 2, §§4, 53(3) and n. 4.

Long *i* with long close *e*: *riden | abiden | yeden* (*Troilus* II, 933–6).

Open and close long *e*: *dremes | lemes* 'flames' (*Nun's Priest's Tale* *4119–20); *lief* 'dear' | *leef* 'leaf' (*Knight's Tale* 1837–8).

Open and close long *o*, according to ten Brink (§32) in early poems only: *Book of the Duchess* 513–14 (519–20, 1189–90) *wroth | soth*; *Second Nun's Tale* 167–8 *sothe | bothe*: when *to* is involved the rhyme may be true, because the pronunciation of *to* developed divergently in unstressed positions, and that pronunciation could have led to long open *o* when stressed;[79] thus *Monk's Tale* *3510–15 *mo | therto | wo | go*.

That Chaucer occasionally resorts to dialectal forms in rhymes at variance with his normal rhyming practice is often mentioned. Thus *Reeve's Tale* 4275–6 *fest* 'fist' (< OE *fȳst*) | *brest* (but with development of OE /y:/ > /i:/ as usual in Chaucer, *Troilus* IV, 506–9 *hire* 'hire' (< OE *hȳr*) | *desire* |*afyre* 'afire'). Endings in early Chaucer include *Book of the Duchess* 73–4 *it telles | elles*.

In spite of these occasional impure rhymes and rhymes involving exceptional forms to which Chaucer was driven by the need to rhyme, the general impression is that Chaucer avoided impure rhymes, but not so studiously as to reduce the possibilities open to him for the deployment of his art of expression. He did, however, avoid in later verse some of the impurities to which he had recourse in early rhymes.

13. Conclusions

At the end of this study it may seem, as so often when rhyming practice is discussed, that the philologists have been at a great feast of language and stol'n the scraps. And so we have, but my excuse for presenting the scraps is that, though impressions are valuable in assessing rhyming techniques, the impressions of a modern reader of Old and Middle English verse should be weighed against an unprepossessed analysis of the rhyming practice of the early English poets. My impression is that *The Owl and the Nightingale* is far less exact than Chaucer's poetry in rhyming. The early history of English rhyming poetry should make one cautious about emending to introduce purer rhymes into an early Middle English and, even more, an Old English poem. Certain licences were very common, especially assonances and impure rhymes in words with dissyllabic endings. But impurities of all kinds occur from time to time. It is usually easy to emend them away; so easy that many a scribe did so. This is a temptation to be resisted.

But let the baby not be thrown out with the bath-water. With much inaccurate rhyming practice in early English no generalisation about the

[79] See Dobson, *English Pronunciation*, 2, §4, pp. 460–1.

accuracy of a poem is valid when the poem is short. For a long poem, however, say, a poem of several hundred lines at least, we can generalise on the basis of cumulative evidence. We should keep an open mind, and while recognising that Chaucer, a great poet, is an accurate rhymer, unusually so among Middle English poets, it is not necessary for a poet to rhyme accurately to be a good poet. If by consistent translating seemingly imperfect rhymes into one other dialect than the one in which the poem has come down to us, we can with some regularity achieve greater accuracy in the rhymes than appears from the extant versions, we may even be able to form a juster idea of the poet's original rhyming practice. For all of Old English and for most of Middle English, however, all the evidence we have points to a looser rhyming practice than many philologists would think ideal.

Pembroke College, Oxford

On Some Aspects of the Vocabulary of the West Midlands in the Early Middle Ages: The Language of the Katherine Group

JANET BATELY

The five works that compose the Katherine Group – *Seinte Iuliene* (SJ), *Seinte Marherete* (SM), *Seinte Katerine* (SK), *Sawles Warde* (SW) and *Hali Meiðhad* (HM)[1] – are preserved together in Oxford, Bodleian Library, MS Bodley 34. A second manuscript, London, British Library MS Royal 17 A xxvii, contains the three saints' lives and *Sawles Warde*. MS B seems to have been written about 1220–5,[2] MS R slightly later, that is, about 1220–30.[3] A third manuscript, British Library, Cotton Titus D. xviii (MS T), dating from the second quarter of the thirteenth century ('towards 1250'),[4] contains *Seinte Katerine*, *Sawles Warde* and *Hali Meiðhad*. The archetype of all five texts in the Katherine Group appears to have been written in what has come to be known as 'language AB'. This language, which is also the language of *Ancrene Wisse* and the so-called *Wohunge* Group,[5] shows not only a consistent phonology

---

[1] Editions cited are *Þe Liflade ant te Passiun of Seinte Iuliene*, ed. S.T.R.O. d'Ardenne (Liège and Paris, 1936); repr. as EETS 248 (London, 1961); *Seinte Marherete: þe Meiden ant Martyr*, ed. Frances M. Mack, EETS 193 (London, 1934); *Seinte Katerine*, ed. S.R.T.O. d'Ardenne [*sic*] and E. J. Dobson, EETS SS 7 (London, 1981); *Sawles Warde*, ed. R. M. Wilson, Leeds School of English Language Texts and Monographs, 3 (Leeds, 1938) (see also *Early Middle English Verse and Prose*, ed. J. A. W. Bennett and G. V. Smithers, 2nd ed. [1968; repr. with corrections, Oxford, 1974], 246–61); *Hali Meiðhad*, ed. Bella Millett, EETS 284 (London, 1982). See further *Middle English Prose: a Critical Guide to Major Authors and Genres*, ed. A. S. G. Edwards (New Brunswick, N.J., 1984), 1–33.
[2] Facsimile, ed. N. R. Ker, EETS 247 (London, 1960), diplomatic edition by S.T.R.O. d'Ardenne, *The Katherine Group, edited from MS Bodley 34* (Paris, 1977). For a description of the manuscript see *Seinte Katerine*, pp. xliii–xlvii.
[3] For a description of the manuscript see *Seinte Katerine*, pp. xlvii–xlix.
[4] *Seinte Katerine*, pp. xlix–liii.
[5] See *Þe Wohunge of ure Lauerd*, *On Ureisun of ure Louerde*, *On Lofsong of Ure Louerde* and *On Lofsong of Ure Lefdi*, in *Þe Wohunge of Ure Lauerd*, ed. W. Meredith Thompson, EETS 241 (London, 1958). For editions of *Ancrene Wisse* see *Middle English Prose*, ed. Edwards, pp. 20–2.

and grammar, but also a distinctive and regular spelling-system.[6] Tolkien described it as 'either a faithful transcript of some actual dialect of nearly unmixed descent, or a "standard" language based on one'.[7] There are a number of verbal parallels, which 'could indicate either a single author or a closely-knit group of authors well acquainted with each other's work'.[8] The use of words not only of Scandinavian but also of Welsh origin, coupled with language AB's affinities with the Worcestershire dialect of Laȝamon and with the language of the Westerly lyric, appears to indicate that the Katherine Group originates from an area in the West Midlands, near the Welsh border. Wigmore Abbey in Herefordshire has been proposed as a possible centre.[9]

On the basis of internal evidence, it has been suggested that *Sawles Warde* was certainly written later than 1196 and in all probability later than 1200, and *Hali Meiðhad* between roughly 1190 and 1220.[10] Tolkien argues that none of the works can well be dated before 1190, on the assumption that any greater interval between the date of composition and the date of the Bodleian MS would have produced more signs than there are of two linguistic strata, the author's forms and the scribe's.[11] D'Ardenne and Dobson suggest the order of composition (i) *Seinte Marherete* and *Seinte Iuliene*; (ii) *Seinte Katerine* and *Sawles Warde*; (iii) *Hali Meiðhad*.[12] The basis of this dating is not only the differing textual histories of the works, but also 'the varying proportions of French-derived vocabulary used in the several works'.[13]

I propose in this paper to explore two different, but not unconnected, aspects of the vocabulary of the Katherine Group: its relationship to the vocabulary of roughly the same area in the Old English period (Mercia) and the possible significance of the distribution of French loan-words in the five texts.

---

[6] J. R. R. Tolkien, '*Ancrene Wisse* and *Hali Meiðhad*', *E&S*, 14 (1929), 104–26. For a detailed analysis of this language see *Seinte Iuliene*, ed. cit. in n. 1, pp. 177–250.

[7] Tolkien, 106.

[8] See *Seinte Iuliene*, pp. xl–xlvii; *Hali Meiðhad*, p. xxi. For the theory of single authorship of the contents of Bodley 34 and Royal 17 A xxvii and the *Ancrene Wisse*, see, e.g., J. Hall, *Selections from Early Middle English* (Oxford, 1920), 2.505. For a single author for SM and SJ only, see, e.g., E. Einenkel, 'Ueber den Verfasser der neuangelsaechsischen Legende von Katharina', *Anglia*, 5 (1882), 91–123. For syntactical evidence see R. M. Wilson, 'On the Continuity of English Prose', *Mélanges de Linguistique et de Philologie, Fernand Mossé in Memoriam* (Paris, 1959), 486–94.

[9] See especially D. Brewer, 'Two Notes on the Augustinian and possibly West Midland Origin of the Ancren Riwle', *N&Q*, 201 (1956), 232–5, and E. J. Dobson, *The Origins of Ancrene Wisse* (Oxford, 1976), 114–73.

[10] Dobson, *Origins*, 165 ('in all probability later than 1210'); Millett, *Hali Meiðhad*, xvi–xvii.

[11] Tolkien, esp. pp. 114 and 122.

[12] *Ancrene Wisse* is taken to be last in the series. See, e.g., Dobson, *Origins*, 155.

[13] Dobson, *Origins*, 156–63; *Seinte Katerine*, p. xxxix; Cecily Clark, '*Ancrene Wisse* and the *Katherine Group*: A Lexical Divergence', *Neophil*, 50 (1961), 117–23.

The 'Mercian' vocabulary of the Katherine Group

In phonological and morphological studies, language AB is most usually compared with the language of the Old English Vespasian Psalter gloss.[14] This gloss is in a hand which appears to date from the mid- to late-ninth century and was possibly written at Canterbury, but its dialect is similar to that of texts from the Midlands.[15] However, for their definition of the 'Mercian' dialect, Old English lexical studies have generally concentrated on the language of texts such as the *OE Bede*, Werferth's translation of *Gregory's Dialogues*, and the *Life of St Chad*, all traditionally assigned to the late ninth century, with a wider 'Anglian' perspective including tenth-century glosses from both Mercia and Northumbria.[16]

Some of the most recent of these lexical studies not only isolate words which are exclusively Anglian, they also assemble lists of items which appear to have been common Old English in the late ninth century but either do not appear or are of restricted occurrence in West Saxon texts of the late tenth century.[17] It is possible that this restriction may be associated with the creation of the so-called Winchester School and the general adoption of a literary standard based on late West Saxon usage.[18]

It is also possible that the true linguistic situation in Anglo-Saxon England has been obscured not only by the general adoption of this West Saxon-based standard by the scribes of surviving late Old English manuscripts but also by the virtual absence of texts from the more northerly parts of the country. The

---

[14] Cf. Dobson, *Origins*, 115: 'This was certainly a West Midland dialect . . .; more particularly it was almost directly descended from the Mercian dialect of the Old English gloss to the Vespasian Psalter (which itself has not been precisely located) and there are resemblances to the language of the Worcester version of the Old English Chronicle.'

[15] N. R. Ker, *Catalogue of Manuscripts containing Anglo-Saxon* (Oxford, 1957), says that the gloss in British Library MS Cotton Vespasian A.1 is 'probably of s.ix med.'. For the Vespasian Psalter as a witness of Mercian learning at Canterbury in the ninth century see K. Sisam, *Studies in the History of Old English Literature* (Oxford, 1953), 4, n. 2. For the presence of the manuscript at St Augustine's Canterbury in the eleventh century see Ker, *Catalogue*, no. 203.

[16] Richard Jordan, *Eigentümlichkeiten des anglischen Wortschatzes* (Heidelberg, 1906); Jackson J. Campbell, 'The Dialect Vocabulary of the OE Bede', *JEGP*, 50 (1951), 349–72; *The Life of St Chad*, ed. R. Vleeskruyer (Amsterdam, 1953); Gregory George Waite, *The Vocabulary of the Old English Version of Bede's Historia Ecclesiastica*, diss. U. Toronto, 1984; Franz Wenisch, *Spezifisch anglisches Wortgut in den nordhumbrischen Interlinearglossierung des Lukasevangeliums* (Heidelberg, 1979). I am indebted to Dr Waite for making a copy of his thesis available to me at King's.

[17] See especially the studies by Vleeskruyer and Waite.

[18] See Helmut Gneuss, 'The Origin of Standard Old English and Æthelwold's School at Winchester', *ASE*, 1 (1972), 63–83.

only surviving major dialect texts from the Midlands and North that can be confidently assigned to a period later than the first half of the tenth century are the glosses in the Lindisfarne and Rushworth Gospels and the Durham Ritual, and the textual history even of these is not altogether clear.[19] Other Anglian texts, along with most early West Saxon works, have survived only in copies made in the late tenth, eleventh, and even twelfth centuries[20] with a late West Saxon veneer.[21]

Before examining the vocabulary of the Katherine Group in detail, therefore, I propose to survey briefly the usage of a range of early Middle English texts from the Midlands, with the aim of discovering how much of the Anglian, or more specifically Mercian, vocabulary of Old English can be shown to have survived in this area after the Conquest.

On the very limited evidence available to us, many Old English words considered by Anglo-Saxon scholars to be diagnostic of 'Anglian' appear to have been totally lost by the late twelfth century. Thus, for instance, there are no entries at all in Middle English dictionaries for the verbs *leoran* and *sceþþan*, the nouns *brord, cennes, feoung, firstmearc, forhogednes, geornnes, herenes, hleoþor, meord, oferhygd, sigor, swinsung*, the adjectives *fram, til, wilsum*, and the adverbs *gen, recene, semninga*.[22]

---

[19] For instance, some of the so-called Rushworth glosses in Oxford, Bodleian Library MS Auct.D.2.19, also known as the Macregol Gospels, may be copied from the Lindisfarne Gospels (British Library, MS Cotton Nero D.iv), while 'eye-error' appears to suggest that the Lindisfarne gloss itself has been copied from another manuscript.

[20] See, e.g., MS Corpus Christi Cambridge 322 (Werferth's translation of Gregory's *Dialogues*, s.xi[2]); Oxford, Bodleian Library, MS Bodley 180 (Alfred's *Boethius*, s.xii[1]) and London, British Library MS Cotton Vitellius A. xv (Alfred's *Soliloquies*, s.xii med.). See further the list in Ker, *Catalogue*, pp. xv–xviii.

[21] For revisions and alterations in late copies of early West Saxon or Anglian texts see, e.g., David Yerkes, *The Two Versions of Wærferth's Translation of Gregory's 'Dialogues'; an Old English Thesaurus* (Toronto, 1979); Dorothy M. Horgan, 'The Old English *Pastoral Care*: The Scribal Contribution', *Studies in Earlier Old English Prose*, ed. Paul E. Szarmach (New York, 1986), 109–27; Jackson J. Campbell, 'The Differences in Vocabulary in the Manuscripts of the Old English Version of Bede's Ecclesiastical History', diss. Yale, 1949.

[22] Spellings of OE words are normally those of the works of reference from which they are cited. See Wenisch, pp. 143–4 (*feoung*), 161–5 (*gen*), 165–8 (*geornness*), 175–8 (*leoran*), 183–4 (*meord*), 208–11 (*recene*), 211–15 (*sceþþan*), 221 (*hleoþor*), 303–4 (*swinsung*); Waite, pp. 270 (*brord*), 271 (*cennes*), 272 (*firstmearc, forhogednes*), 280 (*til*), 282 (*wilsum*); Jordan, pp. 102 (*herenes*), 107 (*sigor*), 61–3 (*semninga*); H. Schabram, *Superbia: Studien zum altenglischen Wortschatz* 1 (Munich, 1965), passim (*oferhygd*); Campbell, pp. 24–5 (*fram*). References in Waite, pp. 268–82, are to 'Anglian words and rare words with Anglian associations'; references on pp. 283–90 are to 'words which appear in early West Saxon and Anglian texts'. From the Old English Bede Waite lists 267 words in the first category and 146 in the second and adds a list of

Other words labelled as Anglian in Old English lexical studies are recorded in Middle English dictionaries[23] but are confined to a group of texts in manuscripts copied very early in the post-Conquest period and containing material that is either derived from pre-Conquest sources or recorded in a linguistic form which may be defined as 'Old English': thus, OE *carcern* and *medmicel* occur in *The Holy Rood Tree*, *elcor* in a late copy of the Old English *Medicina de Quadrupedibus* and in the Lambeth Homilies, and *afedan* in a couple of homilies in British Library MSS Cotton Vespasian A xxii and Cotton Vespasian D xiv. Recorded only from the twelfth-century Trinity Homilies is the noun *hidercyme*.[24]

A somewhat greater number of 'Anglian' words, however, occur in a range of *bona fide* early Middle English texts from both East and West Midlands. The *Ormulum* (apparently composed in the East Midlands in the late twelfth century)[25] has the nouns *praȝhe*, *uhhtenntid* and *weorelldlif*, the verbs *blinnenn*, *ȝellpenn*, *lipenn* ('to proceed') and *winnenn* (in the sense 'to labour'), the adjectives *atell* and *naniȝ* and the adverbs *dafftelike* and *lefliȝ*.[26] It also has the

words found in the OE Bede only; from the glosses to St Luke in the Lindisfarne and Rushworth Gospels Wenisch lists 138 *'gemeinanglisch'* words, 80 Northumbrian words and 139 other words that are exclusive to the two glosses. The two lists have fewer than fifty words in common. However, the great rarity of some of these words, combined with the fact that certain distribution patterns may well be the result of authorial choice, make it quite conceivable that not all of them were in fact exclusively Anglian or even typical of that region throughout the Old English period. See J. M. Bately, 'Some Words for Time in Old English Literature', *Problems of Old English Lexico-graphy*, ed. Alfred Bammesberger (Regensburg, 1985), 47–64.

[23] See F. H. Stratmann, *A Middle English Dictionary*, rev. H. Bradley (Oxford, 1891, repr. 1967), and *MED*. At the time of going to press the *MED* had reached part R5.

[24] For the identification of these words as 'Anglian', see Wenisch, pp. 113–20 (*carcern*), 124–8 (*elcor*); Waite, pp. 269 (*afedan*), 274 (*hidercyme*); Vleeskruyer, p. 31 (*medmicel*). The Latin loan *carcer* is found in Bod. Hom. Dom. Quadr.; see also *Brut quarcerne*, discussed below, p. 61, n. 40. The question of 'when Middle English begins' is a difficult one. For Kemp Malone ('When Did Middle English Begin?', *Curme Volume of Linguistic Studies*, ed. J. T. Hatfield *et al* (Baltimore, 1930), 110–17) the distinctive features of Middle English first appear in early tenth-century manuscripts: see also D. Amborst, 'Evidence for Phonetic Weakening in Inflectional Syllables in Beowulf', *Leeds SE*, NS 9 (1977), 1–18. For R. M. Wilson (*Sawles Warde*, v–xxx), Old English extends up to 1150.

[25] *The Ormulum with the Notes and Glossary of Dr R. M. White*, ed. Robert Holt (Oxford, 1878).

[26] For the identification of these words as 'Anglian' see Jordan, 90 (*prag*); Waite, 269 (*atol*), 275 (*leoflice*), 281 (*uht(a)tid*), 282 (*woruldlif*), 284 (*gedæftlice*), 286 (*gylpan*), 287 (*lipan*); Wenisch, 112–14 (*blinnan*), 189–205 (*nænig*), and 251–4 (*winnan* 'labour'). Orm also has the noun *daffteleȝȝc*.

forms *fraʒʒnenn*,[27] and *wifmannkinn*.[28] A slightly later text from the East Midlands, the poem *Genesis and Exodus* (apparently composed in Norfolk, c. 1250),[29] has the nouns *geming, swaðe, wifkin,* the adverbs *leflike, tidlike,* and *unghere,* and the verbs *blinnen, freinen, frigten,* and *miðen.*[30] It also uses the noun *werk* with the meaning 'pain'.[31] We may compare *The Owl and the Nightingale* (apparently composed in the south-east after 1189 and before 1216),[32] which yields far fewer such words. In this text I have noted only the noun *proʒe* and the verbs *anhon* and *biwerien.*[33]

A more substantial body of words that in an Old English context are considered diagnostic of 'Anglian' appears in Laʒamon's *Brut* (Worcestershire, late twelfth century).[34] Interestingly the *Brut* shares with the *Ormulum* and *Genesis and Exodus* only three words that are considered to be 'Anglian' in Old English and three that are 'early West Saxon and Anglian'. In the first category we have the noun *weorldlifen,* the verb *fræinien,* and the adverb *leofliche,* and in the second category the noun *prowe* and the verbs *ʒælpen* and *liðen.* The adjective *soðfest* (in the sense 'just') occurs alongside *rihtwis* and its related noun *rihtwisnesse* 'justice',[35] and there is a single instance of

---

[27] The Anglian word *frignan* (Wenisch, 156–60), is not recorded in ME dictionaries; however, descendants of the cognate forms *(ge)frægnian, fregnan* have survived, and the distribution of these forms in OE texts leads me to label them also as Anglian. See Antonette diPaolo Healey and R. L. Venezky, *A Microfiche Concordance to Old English* (Toronto, 1980).

[28] The form *wifmanncyn* is not recorded in Old English. However, I include Orm's form here as a variant of 'Anglian' *wifcynn* (Waite, 282). Orm similarly has *weppmannkinn,* not a form of 'Anglian' *wæpnedcynn* (Waite, 281). Another word, *ammbohht,* may be of Mercian origin (cf. Wenisch, 129–31, for the masculine *embeht, ambeht*). However, MED suggests an Old Norse origin for this word, at least in the form in which it has survived.

[29] *The Middle English Genesis and Exodus,* re-ed. Olof Arngart (Lund, 1968), 45–7.

[30] For 'Anglian' *gyming* see Jordan, 12; Campbell, 26; see also Waite, 281 (*ungeara*), 287 (*miðan*), 289 (*swaðo, tidlice*); Wenisch, 289 (*fyrhtan*). We may compare *Havelok* with *prawe* and *blinne.* In view of the frequency of occurrence of *tidlice* ('quickly, early, in good time') in Old English prose from the Alfredian period on, I do not accept the derivation (by d'Ardenne and Dobson and *MED*) of ME *tidlike, tidliche* from ON *títt.*

[31] See OE (Anglian) *wærc* (Wenisch, 125).

[32] *The Owl and the Nightingale,* ed. Eric Gerald Stanley (1960; repr. Manchester, 1972).

[33] For OE *onhon* see Waite, p. 288; for *bewerian* see Wenisch, pp. 106–8.

[34] *Laʒamon: Brut,* edited from British Museum MS Cotton Caligula A.ix and British Museum MS Cotton Otho C.xiii, ed. G. L. Brook and R. F. Leslie, vols. 1 and 2, EETS, 250 and 277 (1963 and 1978).

[35] Jordan (p. 43), Wenisch (pp. 221–8) and Waite (p. 278) take *soþfæst* 'iustus' and *soþfæstnes* 'iustitia' to be specifically Anglian, and by implication these same words with the meaning 'faithful, true' to be common Old English. However, in the Vespasian Psalter gloss *soþfæstnes* translates 'veritas' and *rihtwisnes* 'iustitia', etc. See Bately, 'Lexical Evidence for the Authorship of the Prose Psalms of the Paris Psalter', *ASE,* 10 (1982), 69–95, esp. p. 76. In Stratmann's *Middle English Dictionary* only the sense 'truthful' is recorded.

wapmoncun. Like the surviving manuscripts of *The Owl and the Nightingale* Laȝamon's poem also has the verb *anhon*. However, the *Brut* in addition contains a considerable number of 'Anglian' words not present in these texts. Thus, we find the nouns *broc* 'stream', *burinæsse, comp, los* ('loss'),[36] *morþre, seine, stral, strund, wonderwork*, the adjective *latemiste*, the adverbs *forwhan* and *ȝære*, and the verbs *aqueðen, awundred, beoteden, fellen, sturmden, toluken*, and *tunden*.[37] In addition the *Brut* has a single instance of *þræt* in the sense of 'multitude' and several instances of *ifæied, iued*, etc., 'hated'.[38] Some of the words from both these groups occur in the Caligula MS only, the Otho MS either using instead words that had no specifically Anglian connections in Old English or employing a different expression. These are the nouns *comp, stral, strund, þræt* ('multitude'), *þrowe*, and the verbs *beoteden, fræinien, sturmden*.[39] Unique to the Otho MS are *morþre, seine, wonderwork*, and *latemiste*.[40] It is in this context that we must assess the 'Anglian' vocabulary of the Katherine Group.

(a) *The Saints' Lives*

'Anglian' forms in the three saints' lives are the noun *strunde* (SJ), the verbs *awundrin* (SJ and SK), *edwiten* (SK), *freinin* (SJ, SK), *ȝelpen* (SK), *spitten* (SJ), *toluken* (SM, SJ, SK), *wreoðien* (SK), past participle *itunet* (SM), the adjective *wlech* (SJ), and the adverbs *ȝare* (SJ), *leofliche* (SM, SJ, SK), and *tidliche* (SK). *Preat* also occurs (in SJ and SK, though it there has the meaning

---

[36] *los* occurs 4x. However, the preferred word in *Brut* is *lure*.

[37] For the identification of these words as 'Anglian', see Campbell, 19 (*broc*) and 62 (*beotian*); Waite, 270 (*byrgnes* and *camp*), 278 (*segn* and *stræl*), 282 (*wundorgeweorc*), 284 (*cypeman*), 286 (*fyllan*), 289 (*styrman*), 290 (*tolucan*); Jordan, 15 (*los*); Wenisch, 100–2 (*acweþan*), 150–6 (*forhwon*), 184–9 (*morþor*), 228–9 (*strynd*), 239–40 (*tynan*), 274 (*awundrian*), 297–8 (*lætemest*); Vleeskruyer, 28 (*geara*). Cf. GenEx *birigels, biriele*.

[38] For the distribution of the word *þreat* in OE see Wenisch, 242–6. It also appears – but only in the 'common OE' sense of 'threat' – in O and N and GenEx. *Ifæied* appears to be related to Anglian *feogan*, for which see Wenisch, 134–7.

[39] Instances of words for which MS O has variant readings are *comp* (O *fiht*: see 4632, 12489, and 13787, beside 2169 *comp 7 ifiht* C, *werre and eke fiht* O); *strales* (O *stremes*: see 2840 *stockes 7 stanes 7 strales hate* C; *stockes and stones and swiþe hote stremes* O; and 4340 'mid stocken 7 mid stanen 7 mid stelene orden'); *strund* (O *streone* 1368); *fræinen* (O *axien* 12757 and passim); *sturmden* (O *sweinde* 9145); *isturmede* (O *iwraþþed* 837); *Liþen* is sometimes replaced in O, sometimes retained (see, e.g., O 6195 *flowe* O, 6577 *wende*, 2270 *laþ*). See also *anhongen* 514 C, *hangie* O; *anho* 3354 C, *fordo* O, but *anhon* 11291 both MSS. Words in C without equivalent in O are *þræt* 4882 C; *þrowe* 322 C; *beoteden* 10239 C (see also *beot* 10238, C only).

[40] For MS O *morþre* see 13024, 10460, 14329 (*morð* C); for *seine* see 4630 ('nam he his seine and his sceald briþte' O; 'nom he his burne 7 his gold-ileired bord' C); for *wonder(work)* see 8676 O, *sellic werc* C; for *latemiste* see 5527 O, ute[m]esten C. It is possible that *carcern* has also survived at least partially in *quarcerne* 365 (both MSS) and 510 C (*prisune* O), beside *quarterne* 9627 (C), *tour* (O) and 1882 (C only).

'threat' and is therefore not indisputably an inherited 'Anglian' feature), while *blinnen* occurs once (in SK, MS T) as a manuscript variant.[41]

(b) *Sawles Warde* and *Hali Meiðhad*

These texts have the noun *alesnesse*[42] and the verbs *edwiten* and *freinin*. *Sawles Warde* also has the verbs *ʒelpen* and *tunen* and the adverb *leofliche*, and *Hali Meiðhad* has the verbs *awundrin* and *spitten* and the adjective *wlecche*.

Of these words four are found also in the *Ormulum* (three if we exclude the manuscript variant *blinnen*), three (or two, excluding *blinnen*) in *Genesis and Exodus*, and five in *Brut*.

We may compare the *Ancrene Wisse*,[43] which uses ten of the fourteen 'Anglian' words found in the Katherine Group, that is, the verbs *awundrin*, *edwiten*, *freinin*, *spitten*,[44] *toluken*,[45] *tunen*, and *wreoðien*, the adjectives *leatemeste* and *wlech* and the adverb *ʒare*. In addition we have four words not found in the Katherine Group but used in the *Brut*, that is, the nouns *brok* and *morþre* and the verb form *ibleachet* and the adjective *soþfest*, ('true'); we have one word, *warch* ('pain, grief'), found also (as *werk*) in *Genesis and Exodus*, and we have two words, the noun *dahunge*[46] and the weak verb *duuen*, not otherwise recorded from texts of this period.[47]

The Katherine Group, then, has only one diagnostically 'Anglian' word that is not found also in the other texts from the Midlands – *alesnesse* – and it has significantly fewer such words than Laʒamon's *Brut*, the work which in terms of dialect is closest to it and to the *Ancrene Wisse*. Moreover, as the details in brackets show, not all of these 'Anglian' items are found in all five members of the Katherine Group. Indeed on occasion one text has the 'Anglian' form and another a form which was of general occurrence in Old English. Thus, corresponding to *alesnesse* in *Sawles Warde* and *Hali Meiðhad* (MS T) we find *alesunge* in *Seinte Katerine* and *alesendnesse* in *Hali Meiðhad* (MS B). Corresponding to *Sawles Warde tuneð* we find *bitunen* in the three saints' lives and *Ancrene Wisse*, while *Sawles Warde* and *Ancrene Wisse* also

---

[41] For *edwitan* and *spittan* see Wenisch, pp. 122–4 and 228, for *wreþian* and *wlæc* see Waite, p. 290. For *carcer* see below, p. 63, n. 53.

[42] See OE *alysnes* (Waite, p. 269).

[43] For details of manuscript variations see Arne Zettersten, *Studies in the Dialect and Vocabulary of the Ancrene Riwle*, LSE, 34 (Lund, 1965). In my references to the vocabulary of AW I am heavily indebted to Zettersten's study.

[44] MS N, however, has forms of *speten*, from OE *spætan*, the usual form in West Saxon; cf. O and N *speten*.

[45] MS N substitutes *tetereð*.

[46] For Anglian *dagung* see Waite, 271. Cf GenEx *daigening*, *daning*, etc.

[47] So MS N; A *deueð*, G *dewed*. For Anglian *dyfan* see Waite, p. 285. In place of Katherine Group *þreat*, AW has *þreatung*.

have *biloke*.⁴⁸ Both *freinin* and *easkin* occur in *Seinte Iuliene*, *Seinte Katerine*, *Hali Meiðhad*, and *Sawles Warde*, but *easkin* alone is found (2x) in *Seinte Marherete*.⁴⁹ Some of these variants may be due to scribal intervention, as the presence of alternative readings in surviving manuscripts demonstrates. Thus, as we have seen, the verb *blinnen* occurs only once, in MS T of *Seinte Katerine*, the other manuscripts having forms with initial *l*, which alliteration suggests must have been in the original text.⁵⁰ Since this verb is absent also from the *Brut* and *Ancrene Wisse*,⁵¹ and the great majority of instances of it cited in the *Middle English Dictionary* are from the East Midlands and the North, it may perhaps not have been characteristic of West Midlands usage in the early Middle English period.⁵²

Other non-Anglian forms found in these texts include *cwarterne* (SM, SK), not *carcern*,⁵³ *ʒeme* (SM, SJ, SK, SW, HM, also AW), not *geming* as in *Genesis and Exodus*;⁵⁴ *culure* (SM, SK, and AW) and not *turtur* or indeed the typically West Saxon *turtul*, as in Orm and *Genesis and Exodus*;⁵⁵ *fla* (SJ and HM) and *(e)arewe* (SJ, HM), not *stral*, as in the *Brut*;⁵⁶ *schadewe* (SM, SW), not *skue* as in *Sir Gawain*;⁵⁷ *smoke* (SM, SW), not *rek-* as in *Cursor Mundi*,⁵⁸ and the adjective *(e)atelich(e)*, *eateluker* (SM, SJ, HM, and AW), not *atel* as in Orm (*atell*).⁵⁹

---

⁴⁸ See also SK *bicluset*. In SJ, MS R, *bitunet* corresponds to MS B *ethalden*; see also AW, and Brut MS O *bituned* (9301, etc., MS C *biclused*). Orm and GenEx have the form *biluken*.

⁴⁹ SM 30/32 *cuð me þet ich easki*, 38/16–17 *cuð me ⁊ ken þet ich easki efter*. MS R of SJ has only *freinin* (2x); MS B has *freinin* (1x) and *easki* (3x). *Aske, axien*, is also frequent in GenEx and Brut.

⁵⁰ SK 622: MS R *linneð*, MS B *limieð*, MS T *blimneð*.

⁵¹ The related noun, which always occurs in collocation with *bute, butan*, also seems to have caused difficulty to scribes. See SK 614 *linunge* MS R, *blinnunge* MS T, *lungunge* MS B); 791 *linunge* MS R, *longunge* MS B, *ende* MS T. SM 26/28 also has *linunge* MS R, *linninge* MS B, and SW has *linunge* MS R, *linnunge* MSS BT.

⁵² Cf. the East Midlands Harley lyric 'My deþ Y loue' (Bennett and Smithers, p. 125), with *blynne*, 1. 17.

⁵³ For the possibility that the form *carcern* lies behind SJ *dorchus*, see *Seinte Iuliene*, ed. d'Ardenne, p. 148.

⁵⁴ *ʒeme* occurs also in GenEx (*gem*) and Brut (MS O; *ʒemen* C, in a line ending with *icweme*). Old English *giemnes* and *giemeleasnes* (Wenisch, 168, and Waite, 274) are never found. Cf. Orm *ʒemelæste*, AW *ʒemeleaste*. For 'care' Orm has the forms *gom* and *ʒemsle*.

⁵⁵ Laʒamon and Orm *culure*, etc., Orm *turrtle* and GenEx *turtul*; GenEx *duue*. See Wenisch, 305.

⁵⁶ For Brut *stral* see above, p. 61 and n. 39. This text also has *arwe*.

⁵⁷ For Anglian *scua*, see Wenisch, 215–16.

⁵⁸ For Anglian *rec* see Campbell, 362. GenEx has the verb *rekeð*, 'smokes', as well as the compound *rekefille*. However, the noun form in this text is *roke* (1x, beside *smoke* 2x). Cf. Orm *recless smec*, AW *rechles* 'incense', and the nouns *smorþre* (AW), *smeche* and *smeke* (SW, MS B), *smoke* (SW, MSS RT). Brut has the verb *smokien*.

⁵⁹ Brut *atteliche*.

It may also be noted that unlike the *Ormulum* (with *snoterr*), the Katherine Group and *Ancrene Wisse* do not use any derivative of Old English *snotter*, *snyttro*, or *snoternesse*, selecting instead *wise* and *wisdom*.[60] They also have the forms *for hwi* (SK, HM, AW), not *forhwon*,[61] *hongin*, *ahongin*, *ahon* (SM, SJ, SK, AW), not *onhon*,[62] *lure* (SK, HM, AW), not *los*,[63] *offruht* (SM, SJ, SK, AW), not forms of Old English *fyrhtan*,[64] and *coss* (SJ, HM, AW), *smirles* (SK, HM, AW), *sy* (SM, SJ, HM), *hearmin* (SM, SJ, SK, HM, SW, AW), and *eisfule* (SK, SM AW), not versions of Old English *cossetung*, *smireness*, *sigor*, *sceþþan* and *egesfullic*.[65]

The 'Anglian' element in the Katherine Group, therefore, is not a pronounced one, and the question that arises is whether this could be the result of late Old English standardisation and the development of a literary *koine* by the 'Winchester School'. The Old English words that have been identified as typical of writers of this 'school' are as follows: *cypere* (not *þrowere* or *martyr*), *weofod* (not *alter*, *altare*), *cnapa* (not *cniht*), *gylt* (not *scyld*), *modig*, *modignes*, and *pryte* (not forms of *ofermod*-), *ælþeodig* and *ælfremed* (not *fremde*), *wuldorbeag*, *gedyrstlæcan*, *gerihtlæcan*, *geefenlæcan*, *hæfen*, and *onhrop*. *Sunu* is preferred to *bearn*, *miht* 'virtue' to *mægen*, *leahtor* to *unþeaw*, *þæþ* to *stig* or *siþfæt*, *werod* to *swete* or *myrig*, *(ge)blissian* to *(ge)fægnian*, *utanydan* to *adræfan* or *adrifan*, *forswælan* to *forbærnan*, and possibly *afeormian* to *(ge)clænsian*.[66]

Reference to the Middle English dictionaries reveals that of the twenty-four 'Winchester' words no fewer than half have failed to survive into early Middle English – at least as far as can be determined from the small corpus of texts dating from that period.[67] Of the remainder, five belong to the category of

[60] For OE *snytru* see Wenisch, 218–21. The only instances of *snoternesse* in Stratmann are from Hom. I. 95, 97; *snoter* is cited only from Orm and Hom. I. 117. *Wis* and *wisdom* are also found in Brut, Orm, GenEx, and AW.

[61] Cf. *forr whi* Orm, *forquat* GenEx, *forwhon* Brut. See above, p. 61.

[62] See SM 8/9 *ahon*, 8/16 *hongeden* (MS R *ahongen*), 12/16, 14/32, 16/3, 42/12 *hongin*, etc.; SJ 469 *ahon* (MS R *hongin*), 238 *hongede* (not MS R). See also SJ (MS R) 200 *hon up ant hongin*; SK 119 *ahongeden* (MS R *ahongen*, MS T *hongeden*); AW *hongin*, *ahongen*. Cf. Orm *henngde*, *heng*; GenEx *heng*, *hangen*, Brut *anhon*, and see above, p. 60.

[63] For Brut *los* and *lure* see above, p. 61, n. 36. GenEx has *lire*.

[64] Brut *offurht*, GenEx *ofrigt*.

[65] See Wenisch, 313 and 216–17; Jordan, 107; Wenisch, 211–15; and Waite, 271. Brut has the forms *cossen* (pl.), *æiȝesful* (8968 C, *witfol* O), *hærme*, *siȝe* (MS C only); Orm *smere* ('ointment'), *siȝe*, *siȝȝefasst*; GenEx *smerles*. cf. *eiful* SK (MST) and *aȝhefull* Orm. Instead of a derivative of OE *sceþþan* Orm has *skaþenn* (from Old Norse) and adjective *skaþelæss*; cf. the noun *scaðe* in Brut and GenEx.

[66] See Gneuss, op. cit.

[67] See *leahtor*, *afeormian* and *gerihtlæcan*, recorded by *MED* and Stratmann only in late copies of OE originals; also *cypere*, *ælfremed*, *wuldorbeag*, *gedyrstlæcan*, *geefenlæcan*, *onhrop*, *utanydan*, and *werod*. The need for caution in describing words as 'lost' is illustrated by the existence of a single instance of the root *werod* in the compound *wordness*, AW, MS N. It is worthy of note that the noun *wuldor* itself is recorded by Stratmann only from Orm and a fragment copied from OE.

'preferred' alternatives, and in each of these cases the 'unpreferred' word has also survived into early Middle English, along with four words not used by the Winchester school, *alter*, *cniht*, *martyr*, and *fremde*. We also find the adjective *scyldig*.[68] The distribution of these words in the early Middle English texts from the Midlands is of some interest. Thus, descendants of the Winchester preferences *gylt*, *miht* ('virtue'), *blissian*, *sunu*, and *pryt*, are found in both East and West Midland texts.[69] However, *cnape* (*knape*), 'boy', is confined to the *Ormulum* and *Genesis and Exodus*, along with the compound *knapechild*,[70] while *modiʒnesse*, like the hybrid compound *modiʒleʒʒc*, is recorded only in the *Ormulum* – though the adjective *modi* is of greater currency, being used in *Genesis and Exodus*, *Ormulum*, *Brut*, *Seinte Iuliene*, *Seinte Katerine*, and *Hali Meiðhad*.[71] The use of descendants of Old English *pæp*, *weofod*, *forswelan*, and *elpeode*, on the other hand, is a feature of the West Midlands texts, with *papes*, *weofed*, and *forswælde* in *Brut*, *weoued* in *Seinte Katerine* and *elpeodie* and *weoued* in *Ancrene Wisse*.[72] At the same time it is of significance that these texts also use a number of the words that were apparently deliberately rejected by the writers of the Winchester School[73] or rarely used by them. Thus, *unpeaw* occurs in *Ormulum*, *Brut*, *Sawles Warde*, *Hali Meiðhad*, and *Ancrene Wisse*. The descendants of *stig* occur in *Sawles Warde*,[74] *Ormulum* and *Genesis and Exodus*, and (alongside *pap*) the *Brut*. *Fægnian* is preserved in *Genesis and Exodus*, the *Brut*, and *Ancrene Wisse*, *fremde* in the *Ormulum* and *Ancrene Wisse*, *myrig* (in a range of meanings) in *Genesis and Exodus*, *Brut*, *Ancrene Wisse*, and all the Katherine Group except *Seinte Iuliene*, *forbærnan* in *Brut*,

---

[68] The selection of *martyr* and *altar* may of course have been influenced by the presence of similar forms in Old French. For a distributional distinction between *gylt* and *scyld* in early Old English see Bately, 'Lexical Evidence for the Authorship of the Prose Psalms in the Paris Psalter', *ASE*, 10 (1982), 69–95; see also G. Büchner, *Vier altenglische Bezeichnungen für Vergehen und Verbrechen (Fyren, Gylt, Man, Scyld)*, diss. Berlin, 1968.

[69] For OE *gylt* see Orm, GenEx, Brut, HM, AW (cf. SK *gultelese*, SM *gulteð*, SJ, HM *forgulten*, HM *unforgult*, and SW *gulteð*, *agulteð*); for *meaht*, *miht* see Orm, GenEx, Brut, SM, SK, SJ, HM, AW; for *blissian* see Orm, Brut, SM, SK, HM, SW, AW; and for *pryd*, *pryt* see GenEx, SM, SJ (MS R), SW, AW, and Brut. OE *sunu* is found in all the texts under examination.

[70] Cf. GenEx and AW *cn(e)aue*, Brut *cnaue* and *cnaue child* (MS O 7748, MS C *cnihtbærn*).

[71] *Modiʒnesse* and *modi* are also found outside the East and West Midlands, in *The Owl and the Nightingale*. For *ofermodi* and *ofermod* see Hom.I.5, 9 and 19. See also *orʒel*, *orhel* SM, AW, *orgelprid* GenEx, *orʒhellmod* Orm; *ouergart* SM (cf. 26/6–7 'his ouergart 7 his egede orhel').

[72] With *weofed* (Brut, AW and SK) cf. *allterr* Orm; with *elpeodie* (AW) cf. Brut *albeodene*, *alpeodisc* (MS O *aluis*). For OE *hæfen* see *The Bestiary* and *Cursor Mundi*.

[73] As can be seen from the revisions to older texts. See above, p. 58, n. 21.

[74] MSS B and R; MS T *wei*. For the distribution of the words *stig* and *pæp* in OE charters, see the forthcoming paper by Peter Kitson.

Seinte Marherete, *Seinte Iuliene*, *Sawles Warde*, and *Ancrene Wisse* (in contrast with *Genesis and Exodus*, which has the variants *forbrende* and *forsweðen*), while *alter* occurs in the *Ormulum* and *Genesis and Exodus*, and *martyr* (*martir*), *martirdom* in the *Ormulum*, *Genesis and Exodus*, *Brut*, *Seinte Marherete*, *Seinte Iuliene*, *Seinte Katerine*, *Sawles Warde*, and *Ancrene Wisse*. *Mægen*, alone or in compounds, not only survives alongside *miht* in *Brut*, *Seinte Iuliene* (MS R), *Seinte Marherete*, and *Seinte Katerine*, it is sometimes collocated with it. However, as in the Winchester Group it is *miht* which occurs with the sense 'virtue'. In *Genesis and Exodus*, *Ormulum*, *Hali Meiðhad*, and *Ancrene Wisse* the reduction has been carried still further, with no instances of *mægen* recorded in any of its senses.[75] Also surviving into the Middle English period are the words *(ge)clænsian* (Orm, GenEx, Brut, AW), *adrifan* (SJ, MS R), *bearn* (SM, HM, Brut, Orm), and *cnihtbearn*, 'boy' (Brut).[76] The adjective *schuldi* is a feature of *Seinte Katerine*, *Hali Meiðhad*, and *Ancrene Wisse*.

We may compare *The Owl and the Nightingale*, with *modines*, *gult*, *blissen*, but with *unþew* and with *miʒte* and *maine* only in the sense 'strength'.[77]

It would therefore appear that the literary standard of the late West Saxon Winchester School was not handed down to the authors of the Midlands in the early Middle English period, and certainly not to the authors of the Katherine Group, who are so often claimed to be the direct heirs of the alliterative prose tradition of which Ælfric was the prime expositor.[78]

To appreciate the true significance of lists of words such as these, however, it is necessary to examine all the contexts in which the different words occur, to discover what other alternatives exist and what their status is, and to attempt to determine the effects of borrowings from Old Norse and Old French on the English literary registers.[79] For instance, sometimes neither the 'Winchester' word nor a native equivalent is recorded, simply because their place has been taken by a loan-word. So both *beag* and *wuldorbeag* have vanished, along with the Latin loan *coronan*, the current term being the

---

[75] SJ (MS R) *mihte 7 mein* 417; MS B *mihte* only. Cf. *meinful* SJ, SK, SM, and SW (MS R, *weolefule* MSS BT). See, e.g., SM 28/3–4 'merren wið his muchele mein þe mihte of þi meiðhad'.

[76] SJ 762, MS B 'draf him adrenchet', MS R 'warp ham adriuen'. For Brut *cnihtbærn* see above, p. 65, n. 70. The normal meaning of *cniht* in ME is 'servant, knight'.

[77] See also Pet. Chron. *adrifan*, *forhwan*.

[78] d'Ardenne, *Seinte Iuliene*, xxviii, refers to 'direct continuity' with Ælfric's *Lives of the Saints*. See also Dorothy Bethurum, 'The Continuity of the Katherine Group with Old English Prose', *JEGP*, 34 (1935), 559.

[79] For d'Ardenne (*Seinte Iuliene*, 178), language AB is 'a literary idiom', containing 'much that was ancient (for us here last recorded) and indeed, it may be suspected, purely literary and traditional. . . . It preserves elements of archaic diction'. Zettersten, 24, regards language AB as 'a purely literary dialect'. It is, of course, necessary to take into account the possibility of scribal change and updating. As d'Ardenne shows (xxxv–xl), there are not inconsiderable differences between MSS B and R of SJ.

French loan-word *crune*. Such an examination, if carried out fully, would of course be a major undertaking, well beyond the scope of my present study. However, I will endeavour to demonstrate its importance in the second part of this paper, where I shall scrutinise those concepts for which words of French origin are found in the Katherine Group.

The French vocabulary of the Katherine Group

The number of words of French origin in the three saints' lives is relatively small, with an estimated 2.5% in *Seinte Marherete*, 2.9% in *Seinte Iuliene*, and 3.9% in *Seinte Katerine*. Of the other major texts in 'language AB' the closest to the three saints' lives is *Sawles Warde* with 4.2% words of French origin. In contrast the figures for *Hali Meiðhad* are 6.3% and those for *Ancrene Wisse*, parts VI and VII, 10.7%.[80]

Recent editors have taken the different percentages in the texts as an indication of the 'progressive infiltration of French words into English',[81] and propose an order of composition based on these figures.[82] However, a detailed survey of the whole of the vocabulary of the Katherine Group (including words of Latin origin which may have come in to Middle English either direct or via French), shows that variety in subject-matter, differences in approach, and the heavy use of alliteration in some of these texts[83] all have a significant rôle to play and that as a result these percentages have to be interpreted with care.

A. *The Saints' Lives*

1. The noun
The number of nouns of French or Latin origin in the three saints' lives which can confidently be said to have been borrowed in the Middle English period ranges from twenty-six in *Seinte Marherete* to thirty-one in *Seinte Iuliene* and to

[80] Dobson's revised figures, based on Clark: see *Origins*, 157 and 166. Some scholars consider that this small number of words is the result of 'deliberate minimisation' of the French element for 'literary reasons' and suggest that it is due (at least in part) to the fact that 'the alliterative style tends to encourage native vocabulary'. See, e.g., *Seinte Iuliene*, 177.

[81] What Mary S. Serjeantson (*History of Foreign Words in English* (London, 1935), 104) sees as 'the gradual creeping in of one word after another' may have taken place at different times in different areas and even perhaps in different strata of society. French influence, Miss Serjeantson suggests, 'travelled more quickly across country to the West Midlands than up-country to the North-East Midlands' (120).

[82] Clark attempts no such classification. Of HM and AW, Dobson, *Origins*, 166, writes that 'if the two are by different men, . . . the much greater proportion of French words in *Ancrene Wisse* might be an individual feature of its author's vocabulary and not a sign of later date'.

[83] For a discussion of style see Bethurum, 553–64.

thirty-six in *Seinte Katerine*.[84] However, between them the texts have a total of no fewer than sixty-eight different nouns (seventy, if we include words in *Seinte Iuliene* and *Seinte Marherete*, MS R, which apparently did not occur in the original text). Only nine words are common to all three texts: *beast, crune, eoli (eoile), grace, lei,*[85] *maumez, parais, passiun,* and the proper noun *Gius, Giwes* (OE *Iuþan, Iudan*). For two of these (*crune* and *maumet*) equivalents are found in the *Brut*.[86] Two others, *beast* and *grace*, occur only in the Otho MS of *Brut*, where they replace the *deor* and *milce* of the Caligula MS.[87] Yet another, 'paradise', is used in the *Brut* in the older form *paradis*.[88]

Six other words occur in two of the three saints' lives: *merci, patriarche,* and *prisun* are found in *Seinte Marherete* and *Seinte Iuliene*, *prince* and *turn* (*toturn, ȝeinturn*)[89] in *Seinte Marherete* and *Seinte Katerine*, and *weorre* in *Seinte Iuliene* and *Seinte Katerine*. In MS R the *incipits* of *Seinte Marherete* and *Seinte Iuliene* both have the word *uie*. Once again a couple of these words are found in the *Brut*, with *weorre* in both manuscripts and with *prisune* as a variant of *quarcerne* in MS O.[90]

<hr />

[84] Twenty-seven and thirty-two in *Seinte Marherete* and *Seinte Iuliene* respectively if the *uie* of the *incipits* is included. Cf. Clark's figures of SM, SJ each 34; SK 55, SW 29, HM 80. These figures are for all parts of speech of Romance origin. From my lists here and subsequently I have omitted long-established words of Latin origin (e.g., *acofrian, fals, iacinct, Iulium, kalende, lilie, pel, pin, psalm-, rose, seil, iseilet*), words whose possible French origin has been challenged (as *gabb, igabbet* and *cang, acangin*), words which could be derived from Latin via either OE or Old French or which could be OE loans remodelled under the influence of Old French – perhaps even by a scribe – (as *apostel, castel, Latina, liun, martyr, meister, purpre, temple, tur,* and *offrin*). For some of these words in early Old English see the *Old English Orosius* and Alfred's translation of the *Pastoral Care*. For 'martyr' and 'pride' see above, p. 65. I have also excluded from my lists some words of French origin, as *sot*, which are already recorded in late Old English texts.

[85] In SJ the single instance of *lay* occurs only in MS R, the corresponding passage in MS B having been accidentally lost; cf. *lahe* (SJ, SK, SM, HM, SW, AW) from Old English *lagu*, Old Norse *lagr*.

[86] See also Brut *kinehelm, mahum* 'idol' and *onlicnesse*; cf. SJ *weon*.

[87] Brut 663 and 3298. I do not wish to pursue here Miss Serjeantson's comment (p. 117) that 'many of the English words in [MS C] which are replaced by French words in [MS O] are words which do not occur at all in late ME, and had presumably become archaic and obsolete when the second version [i.e. MS O] was made'.

[88] Scribal intervention in a word of this kind cannot, of course, be ruled out. See also Orm *crune, paradis*; GenEx *beste, crune, Iewes, lay, olie, parais,* and *paradis*; AW *beast, grace, parais, passiun, Giwes*. Cf. Orm *ele* (from OE *ele*), *Judei, Judeow, Juþewess* (cf. OE *Iudei, Iuþei*); Brut *ieled* (O *iheled*), GenEx *ideles*. Pet. Chron. *coronan*; *eoli, Iudeus*.

[89] *Ȝeinturn* and *toturn* may be derived from OE; cf. OE *tyrnan*, etc., and *turnung*.

[90] MS O 510. Cf. Orm *patriarrke, flumm,* beside *deor, hehenngell,* and *cwarrterrne*. See also Orm *millce, mildherrtleȝȝc* and *mildheorrtnesse*; GenEx *merci* (beside *milce*), *prince, prisun* (beside *chartre*), *turn, were*; AW *merci, meister, patriarche, prisune, weorre*; O and N *merci*. Brut, however, has only *milce*, with O once using the variant *grace* (3298). See also Pet. Chron. *prisune, uuerre*.

The remaining words occur only in one of the three saints' lives. These are distributed as follows:

(a) in *Seinte Marherete* only: *bascins, chapele, chere, coste, grandame, lake, lampe, mantles, samblant, sauur, warant,* and the hybrid compound *eil-þurl*.

(b) in *Seinte Iuliene* only: *arcanglene, baptiste, cendals, ciclatuns, cure* ('triumphal chariot'), *ernesse* (MS B only), *ewangeliste, Feouerreres, flum, furneise, hurtes, Mearch, peis, postles* ('posts'), *rente, seruise* (MS B only), *sire*. Confined to MS R of *Seinte Iuliene* and apparently the result of scribal error is *gencling*.[91]

(c) in *Seinte Katerine* only: *aromaz, atine, barren, clearc, clergesse, clergies, curt, dame, desputunge, dute, eritage, gin, marbrestan, meistrie, miracle, pilegrimes, place, prophete, puisun, reisun, schurgen, strif, uirgnes,* and *ymage*.

The *Brut* has sixteen of these words, using *chere, clerc, flum,*[92] *ginne, hurte,*[93] *lak, mantel, pilegrim, postles,*[94] *seruise,*[95] *sire,* and (in MS O) *chapel* as a variant of *chireche, marbre-ston* as a variant of *marme-stan, peis* as a variant of several words including *friþ* and *sæhtnesse, strif* as a variant of *flit,* and *ymages* as a variant of *imaken*.[96]

Seinte Katerine, then, is the saint's life with the largest number of nouns of Latin or French origin, *Seinte Marherete* having the fewest. However, of the twenty-five French nouns found in *Seinte Katerine* but not in *Seinte Marherete* more than half represent concepts for which there is no equivalent either in *Seinte Marherete* itself or in the other purportedly 'early' saint's life, *Seinte Iuliene;* that is to say, we cannot know whether the author would have selected the French word or its native equivalent had he needed to refer to the concept which they both represent. These are the words *aromaz, barre, clearc, clergesse,*

---

[91] See *Seinte Iuliene*, p. 95. Also in MS R only and probably non-original, are *dute, ofseruinge* (MS B *wurðes*), *prude* (MS B *selhðe*).

[92] *Flum* Brut 273 (*water* O) and 652, also GenEx, beside *æ* (Brut, Orm) and *stræm* (Brut).

[93] 920 C, *harmes* O; 4078 C only. See also the regular use of the noun *harm* in O, where C has *burst*.

[94] Brut 660, MS O *postes*. Brook and Leslie emend the reading of MS C to *postes*.

[95] Brut 4025. See also 4038 *seruuinge*, MS O *seruise*, and 4046 (C only) *sereuunge*.

[96] See, e.g., Brut 13046; 571; 242, 4353, 4994; 12459; 9085. See also *paisinge* 5819 (C *hustinge*); *paisi, paise* 4408, 4380, C *sæhtnien*, etc.; *costninge* 11251; *striuinge* 7765 (O *to struiende*). The equivalent forms in Orm are *bapptisste, prophete* (beside *wite*); cf. also *wunnderr*. GenEx has the forms *mentel, clerc, miracle, pais, place, prophete, strif* (beside *striuing*), *seruise;* cf. also *costful*. AW has the forms *aromaz, clergesse, clerc, curt, dame, dute, hurt, mantles, meistrie, miracle, peis, pilegrim, place, prophete, reisun, sauur,* and *sire*. *Owl and Nightingale* has the forms *disputinge, gin, rente*. See also Pet. Chron. *clerc, curt, miracle, pais,* and *rente;* also (interpolated under annal 656 *lac*). MS A of the Chronicle has *serfise*, s.a. 1070.

clergies, eritage, gin, marbrestan, pilegrimes, reisun, schurgen, strif, ymage. One other noun without either native or foreign equivalent in *Seinte Marherete* – the word *weorre* – is in fact used in *Seinte Iuliene.*[97]

Two of the concepts for which these French words are used in *Seinte Katerine* are also expressed through their native equivalents in that text. Beside *strif* we have *flit* and *feht*; beside *ymage* we have *ilicnesse.*[98] So it is not surprising to find that of the eleven French words for which *Seinte Marherete* and *Seinte Iuliene* do have native equivalents a number are similarly found alongside those equivalents in *Seinte Katerine.* And in assessing the possible significance of the way in which any given pair of native and foreign words is distributed among the texts, it is essential also to consider the contexts in which they occur within them. So, for instance, in *Seinte Katerine* the loan-word *strif* is the 'normal' word for 'strife, contest', occurring six times in both alliterative and non-alliterative or neutral contexts. *Feht* in contrast is found only once in this sense, alliterating with *fearlac* in a passage with an extended metaphor of battle in which the verb *fehten* is also used, while the two instances of *flit* also alliterate, with the 'leading' word in 1.317 being the proper noun *Filistiones.*[99]

In the case of other pairs, the French word cannot be said to be the 'normal' word, yet it is the native equivalents whose selection appears to have been determined by contextual considerations. So, for instance, the learned French word *prophete* occurs once in *Seinte Katerine* and the native *witege* twice. Both the instances of *witege* appear to have been selected to meet the needs of alliteration: thus 175–6 'ant toc me him to lauerd ant makede him mi leofmon þe þeos word seide þurh an of his witegen', and 179–80 'Ich herde eft þeos word of an oðer witege, *Deus* . . .'. In each case the previous use of the form *word* makes selection of *witege* rather than *prophete* desirable. *Prophete,* on the other hand, appears in a neutral context where neither it nor *witege* would contribute to the alliterative patterns: 665–6 'as he dude Daniel þurh Abacuc þe prophete i þe liunes leohe þer he in lutede'. *Seinte Marherete* and *Seinte Iuliene,* in contrast, have single instances of *witege* in alliterative contexts: thus, SJ 360 'þen muchele witti witege Ysaie', and SM 44/18–19 "þet Dauið þe witege wrahte . . . Criste to wurdmunt'.[100]

---

[97] SM, like SJ and SK, has the related verb *weorrin.*

[98] *Ymage* is here used of a statue (OE *onlicnes, gelicnes*) and *ilicnesse* for 'likeness', (God's) 'image'. Brut also has *onlicnes, anlicnes* (beside *imaken* 9085 C, *ymages* O), Orm *onnlicnesse.* See SK 664 'i culurene iliche' (R *liche*) and SM 44/6 'o culures iliche' (MS R *lich*), SM 28/3 'drake liche'; and SJ 196 'lilies ilicnesse' (MS R *iliche*), SK 365 'ne makede he mon of lam to his ilicnesse?', SJ 736 'ne lef þu neauer to þi va þin ilicnesse . . .'

[99] Cf., for instance, SK 260–1 'Ant tu schalt sone etsterten al þe strengðe of þis strif þurh a stealewurðe deað', 256–7 'þe flit of þine fan swifteliche auellen'.

[100] *Witege* is SJ MS B only; MS R 'þen wittie ysaye'. For lists of concepts see Einenkel.

However, more frequently it is the French word the use of which appears to have been determined by the context. For instance, both *leafdi* and *dame* are used as terms of address in *Seinte Katerine*. The native word *leafdi* is the norm, occurring in both alliterative and non-alliterative contexts, with, for instance, the vocative phrase 'ȝe leafdis and ȝe meidnes' (855) beside 'te riche leafdis letten teares trondlin' (853). The single instance of *dame* occurs in an alliterative pattern, in the seemingly colloquial 'Hu nu, dame, d[o]test tu?' (760), the 'leading' word *dote* being coincidentally also of French origin.[101]

Seinte Katerine's choice of the word *uirgnes* in 1.846 rather than its usual *meidenes* is again determined by context, with 'þe feire ferredene of uirgnes in heouene' as a variation of 261–3 'i þe feire uerredene ant i þe murie mot of meidnes . . . in heouene',[102] while the French word *curt* (Latin text *palatium*) is used in an alliterative collocation that may at the same time have had a legal flavour: 145 'to curt cume . . . ant kinemede ikepen'. We may compare the author's use of the native *halle* in the expressions 'hehest in his halle' 152 and 'in halle ant i bure' 534. *Seinte Iuliene* has *halle* in 584 'þe ȝungeste hap i Pharaones halle'.[103]

The use of technical terms may similarly account for the appearance of the word *reisun* in SK 810 'ȝelde reisun',[104] while the use of the word *place* in 479 'ȝef he come i place, nere he neauer se prud' is possibly used as much for reasons of register as of alliteration.[105] The native word *stude* occurs no fewer than three times in *Seinte Katerine*: 'i keiseres stude' (1); 'i stude ant i stalle' (254); 'I þet ilke stude' (899). We may compare *Seint Iuliene*, with *stude* twice, both in an alliterative pattern.

The desire to make use of alliterative patterns must surely also have contributed to the choice of *meistrie* in *Seinte Katerine* 48 'þe meistrie ant te menske', as of the native part-equivalent *sy* in SM 54/3 'i sy ant i selhðe', SJ 97 'þy sy 7 ti selhðe', etc. We may compare the choice of words for 'miracle' and 'folly' in *Seinte Katerine* – concepts for which there is no equivalent in *Seinte Marherete*. In *Seinte Katerine* the native word *wundres* (6x in this sense) is preferred to the borrowed *miracle* (2x). And in each case of 'miracle' there is a special reason for its use. Thus, in 518 'þet wes miracle muchel' the choice of *miracle* serves to set up an alliterative pattern with the adjective *muchel*; in 393–5 'Ant ȝef þu nult nanesweis witen þet he wrahte þulliche *wundres*, lef

---

[101] See the related form *grandame* in SM, and cf. SM 28/8–9 'Ah lef me 7 let me gan, leafdi, ich þe bidde'; SJ 206 'Mi lif 7 mi leofmon 7 leafdi, ȝef þu wel wult . . .'; SJ 495–6, 'Mi leoue leafdi Iuliene, ne make þu me. . . .'

[102] Cf. SM 4/13 'þet seli meidnes song singen, wið þis meiden 7 wið þet heouenliche hird, echeliche in heouene' and SW 290–1 'þet schene ant þet brihte ferreden of þe eadi meidnes ilikest towart engles'.

[103] *curt* is found already in Pet. Chron., annal 1154.

[104] *reisun*. See MED *resoun* 6.

[105] *place*. See MED *place* 8.

lanhure þet tu isist – *miracles* þet bi his men beoð imaket ȝette'; the choice is obviously made for the sake of variation. The normal collocation is *wunder* + *wurchen* (e.g. 341 'Swa þet we wite wel, þurh wundres þet he wrahte þet na mon ne mahte . . .') as in *Seinte Marherete*. We may also compare the distribution of the terms *atine, desputunge* and *mot* in *Seinte Katerine*, where *mot* with the meaning 'disputation' is used three times in conjunction with the verb *meistrin* and once with *meidenes*, and *atine* (alliterating with *tunge* and *teuelin*) and *desputunge* are each used only once.[106] *Seinte Marherete* has a single instance of *mot*, while the context is totally absent from *Seinte Iuliene*.

However, although it is *Seinte Katerine* which has the largest percentage of French words, a significant number of terms of French origin are used in *Seinte Marherete* and *Seinte Iuliene* which are not found in that text, and once again context appears to loom large among the possible reasons for this. For instance, the concepts 'river' (*flum* SJ), 'injury' (*hurtes* SJ, beside *hearm*), and 'patriarch' (*patriarche* SM, SJ) do not occur there, nor do 'basin', 'chapel', 'grandmother', 'lake', or 'lamp'. There is only one instance of 'archangel', and in the context the choice of *heh-engel* seems inevitable, with SK 263–5 'Ich hit am Michael, Godes heh-engel, ant of heouene isent forte seggen þe þus' recalling SJ 321–3 'Ich hit am, quoð þe unwiht, godes heh-engel, forte segge þe þis isent te from heouene', beside SJ 455–6 'englene feolahe, ant arch-anglene freond'. The concept 'peace' is also only found once, and then only through emendation, in SK 360: 'Heo ne sohte nawiht [sahte][107] ah seide aȝein ananriht . . .' We may compare *Seinte Iuliene* with *peis* in 731–2 'custe ham coss of peis', and *Seinte Marherete* with *grið* in 48/24–5 'gleadien i godes grið 7 i gasteliche luue'. OE *frið* is never found in the Katherine Group, though the related verb continues to be used.[108] In other instances, it is the context in *Seinte Iuliene* or *Seinte Marherete* that appears to have prompted the use of a French rather than of a native (or Scandinavian) word. Thus, for instance, we may compare SJ 268 'to prisunes pine',[109] and SM 52/26 'i pine of prisun' and 10/3 'in cwarterne 7 i cwalhus' with SK *cwarterne* 4x, twice with alliteration and once in the phrase 'i cwarterne ant i cwalmhuse'. We may compare *Brut* 'quarterne in ane quale-huse'.

Similarly the use of *sire* rather than *lauerd* in SJ 526–7 'ti sire Sathanas' is surely prompted by its association with the 'leading' word *Sathanas*, and

---

[106] For SK *mot* see, e.g., 203 'ha wið hire anes mot meistreð us alle', 466 'te mihte ant te mot of a se meoke meiden schal meistren ow alle'; *atine* (457 'nefde hare nan tunge to teuelin atin[e] wið') is described by d'Ardenne and Dobson as 'one of the trickiest problems in the text . . . presumably adopted . . . *ad hoc*'. SM *mot* also alliterates.

[107] No reading MSS.

[108] Cf. *friþien* SK (MS R 1093; MS BT *firstede*, for *fristede*); SJ *friðien*. Although *friþ* is found in MS C of Brut, the corresponding passages of O have *blisse, griþe*, etc., while *unfriþ* 9682 is replaced by *no griþ*.

[109] See also *dorchus* SJ, and above, p. 63, n. 53.

seruise and *chere* may well also have been selected for reasons of style.[110] Finally, the greater frequency with which the concept 'mercy' appears in *Seinte Marherete* and *Seinte Iuliene* may explain why in these texts it is represented by both *milce* and *merci* (sometimes in collocation), while *Seinte Katerine* has only *milce* (2x).[111]

2. Other parts of speech

A similar picture emerges if we examine the very much smaller body of adjectives, adverbs, and verbs[112] which were apparently borrowed from French or Latin in the early Middle English period and which are found in these texts. Only three words in this category (*crunin*, *ofseruin* / *unoseruet* and *weorrin*) are found in all three texts. One other (*crauant*) is found in *Seinte Katerine* and *Seinte Marherete* but not *Seinte Iuliene*, three (*seruin*, *kecchen*, and *riche* in the sense 'rich') in *Seinte Iuliene* and *Seinte Katerine* but not *Seinte Marherete*, and two, *forschaldin* and *unhurt*, in *Seinte Iuliene* only.[113] Yet another, *seinte*, is found in the *incipits* of *Seinte Iuliene* (MSS R and B) and *Seinte Marherete*, but not in the *incipit* of *Seinte Katerine*, which has the form *sancte*,[114] while the masculine form *sein* is found (alongside masculine *seinte*) in *Seinte Iuliene* only.

The majority of the remaining thirteen words occur in *Seinte Katerine* only,

---

[110] SJ 180 '7 softe me bið euch sar in his seruise'; MS R 'ant softe me bið euch derf hwen ich him serui . . .' For *chere* see below, p. 74, and cf. *bleo, leor, nebscheft, wlite*.

[111] Compare SK 106–7 'þurh his milce ant godlec of his grace' and 504 'þurh his milde milce', with SJ 459 'for moncun milce haue 7 merci' and 461–2 'merci nan nis wið þe; for þi ne ahest tu nan milce to ifinden'. Cf. 502–3 'merciable 7 milzfule. . . . Haue merci of me'. The converse, infrequency of occurrence, makes the drawing of firm conclusions dangerous. Cf., e.g., *puisun* (SK) and *atter* (SM) each lx, with *atter* used in an alliterative pattern (20/6–7 'ful of atter his ontfule heorte') but not *puisun* (847 'fordrenct wið þes deoules puisun'). In these circumstances it is not significant to the matters under discussion in this paper that SK has *puisun* and SM has *atter*.

[112] For a recent study of the distribution of verbs of French origin in the Katherine Group and Ancrene Wisse see Juliette de Caluwe-Dor, 'Divergence lexicale entre le *Katherine Group* et l'*Ancrene Riwle*: Valeur statistique des premières attestations de mots d'origine française en anglais', *EA*, 30 (1977), 463–72.

[113] *Kecchen* and *seruin* are not found in SJ, MS B, which has the verb *ilecche* and a construction with the noun *seruise* (see above, n. 110). For *ofseruin* as a half translation of OF *deservir*, see d'Ardenne, *Seinte Iuliene*, 117. SK, MS T, has *ofearnin* 1467 and 1526, and d'Ardenne and Dobson, *Seinte Katerine*, emend MSS BR *ofseruin, ofseruet* to 781 *ofearnin*, 814 *deseruet*. Cf. SM *iþeinet*.

[114] The *incipits* of the three saints' lives are of special interest. In MS B SJ and SM open similarly with 'Her biginneð þe liflade ant te passiun of Seinte Iuliene/Margarete', while SK has '[Her biginne]ð þe martyrdom of Sancte K[aterine]'. In MS R, however, we find 'Her cumseð þe uie of seinte iuliane ant telleð of liflade'; and 'Her seinte Marherete uie þe meiden 7 martir'. The differences may indicate that the original texts had no *incipit*, and at the same time point to separate textual histories for the three saints' lives. The corresponding noun in *halhen* (SJ, SW).

and it is these which give the text its percentage lead. They are *hardi* (with the compound *hardiliche*), *mate*, *poure*, *sauure*, *icuplet*, *meistrin*, *iginet*, *sauuin*, *sputi*.[115] *Seinte Marherete* has the verbs *changede* (collocated with another French loan, *chere*) and *ibreuet*; *Seinte Iuliene* has *merciable* and *cumseð* (MS R *incipit*). We may compare the *Brut*, with *cruneden*, *werren*, *riche*, *cacchen*, *pouere*, *changen*, *seint*, and MS O *serue*.[116]

Once again there is no good reason to suppose that the occurrence of a larger number of such words in *Seinte Katerine* than in *Seinte Marherete* and *Seinte Iuliene* has any special significance in terms of date or authorship. Thus, for instance, the concept 'tasty' is found only in *Seinte Katerine*, where it is represented not only by the French *sauure* but also by the native *beatewil*, the word chosen in each case contributing to the alliterative patterning, with 560 'al me þuncheð sauure ant softe þet he sent me', beside 617–18 'For nis þear nawt bittres, ah is al beatewil'. Choice between *hardiliche* and *baldeliche* likewise appears to have been influenced by a desire for alliteration, while the use of only one word for the concept 'to dispute' in *Seinte Marherete* and *Seinte Iuliene*, where *Seinte Katerine* has two has no significance at all, given that only *Seinte Katerine* uses that concept more than once.[117]

Many of the words of French or Latin origin that have been discussed above occur also in *Sawles Warde* and *Hali Meiðhad*. Thus, of the nouns previously mentioned five are found in both texts, two in *Sawles Warde* but not in *Hali Meiðhad* and twelve in *Hali Meiðhad* but not in *Sawles Warde*.[118] In *Sawles Warde* we find the nouns *archangles*, *chere*, *grace*, *patriarches*, *prophetes*, *semblant*, and *turn*, all with their equivalents in one or more of the three saints' lives; in *Hali Meiðhad* we have *beast* (and *beasteliche*), *chere*, *crune*, *dute*, *earnesse*, *eolie*, *eritage*, *grace*, *lampe*, *meistrie*, *merci*, *pes*, *poisun*, *prophete*, *semblant*, *seruise*, *turn* (alongside *turnunge*, from OE *tyrnung*), and *weorre*. As for the other parts of speech, *Sawles Warde* uses the verb forms *cruneð*, *enbreuet*, *meistreð*, *seruið*, *weorreð*, and the adjectives *ouerhardi*, *poure*, *riche*, and *seinte*. *Hali Meiðhad* contributes the verbs *changin*, *cruni*, *serui*, *weorrin*, and the adjectives *poure*, *riche*, *seint*, and (the comparative) *sauurure*. 'New' words in *Sawles Warde* – that is, words not found in the saints' lives – are *chatel* (MS R),[119] *cunestable*, *cunfessurs*, *leattres*, *mealles*, *meoster*, *meosure*, *ordres* (MS R), *tresor*, *tresorers*, and *trone*, the verb forms *aturnet*, *chasti*, *meallið*, *iordret*, *preouin*, *irobbet*, *spealie*, and the adjective *fol*. 'New' words in

---

[115] See also *cointe* SK (MS T) and *ofdutet* SK (MS R).

[116] MS C 12287 *þæinen*, O *saruy*. Cf. GenEx *hardi*, *poure*, *riche*, *seruen*, *kagte*; Pet. Chron. *uuerrien*.

[117] In SJ, SK, and SM the instances of *motin* 'dispute' alliterate (usually with *meiden*). See also *fliten* (SK), *teuelin* (SM, SK) and, for the noun, above, p. 72.

[118] Once again a significant number of words in the saints' lives are not found in SW or HM.

[119] MSS BT *castel*.

Hali Meiðhad are the nouns *adamantines, angoise, aturn, aureola, basme* (cf. OE *balsam), blame, (weater-)bulge, cangun, charbucle, confort, cuntasses, degre, delit, dignete, eise, estat, flurs, frut, gerlondesche, huler, leccherie, mesure, nurrice, priuileges, reng, richesce* (beside *richedom), sabaz, sawter, simplete, spuse, stat, treitres, tresor, trubuil, vanite, uertu;* the verbs *asaili, chastien, cunqueari, desiri, greueð, hantið, hurten, ipaiet, passeð, preouin, robbin, itricchet,* and *wastið,* the adjectives *chaste, cwite, feble,* and *gentile,* and the hybrid adverbs *folliche* and *largeliche.*[120] It will be noted that a number of the French words whose derivatives are represented in this list (as the adjectives *fol* and *large*) are sufficiently well-established in the language for functional conversion to have been applied to them and for compounds with English components to have been formed from them.

Once again these 'new' words sometimes represent concepts for which there is no equivalent in the saints' lives, for instance, *aureola, blame, cunestable, cuntasse, iacinct, mesure, tresurer.* Indeed the majority of 'new' words in *Sawles Warde* belong here, while, as Cecily Clark has pointed out, a number of the 'new' words in *Hali Meiðhad* owe their presence in that text to the use of theoretical argument by its author.[121] Sometimes, however, the concepts are ones also used in the other texts and once again stylistic considerations, in particular the desire for alliteration, appear to have determined choice of one or other form. Thus, for instance, *Sawles Warde* and *Hali Meiðhad* both have the form *tresor,* but its absence from *Seinte Katerine* and *Seinte Marherete* may be related to context. *Seinte Katerine* uses *gersum* in the phrase 'wið gold ant gersum igrette' (295–6), and 'wið gersum 7 wið golde' is found also in *Seinte Marherete* (6/15).[122] Again, *Hali Meiðhad* collocates *feble* and *flesch* twice, using *wac* with *wil* also twice. *Seinte Katerine* collocates *wac* and *flesch* as part of a larger pattern: 780–1 'þet tet wake ules ne wursi neauer mi mod'.

However, in *Hali Meiðhad,* more general stylistic considerations frequently apply. Thus, for instance, desire for variety of diction and rhythm seems to have prompted the use of *richese* alongside its native equivalent *weole* in HM 15/10–11: 'þet ter walde wakenin of wif ant weres somnunge richese ant worldes weole', beside 13/16–17 'of wif and weres gederunge worldes weole awakeneð'. *Weole* is the usual word for 'wealth', 'riches' in the texts of the Katherine Group, though *Seinte Iuliene* and *Seinte Katerine* also have *ahte,* and *Seinte Katerine* in one place uses this in conjunction with the Scandinavian loan *orcost:* 624 'ȝef þear is orcost oðer ei ahte'. Similarly *Hali Meiðhad* uses

---

[120] Cf. Brut *hurten, riches, tresur, ipaid, passi, wasten,* MS O *fol, lettre, atyr, caðel;* GenEx *lettre, mester, flur, fruit, lecheri, greueð, chasthed, feble;* Pet. Chron. *cuntesse, tresor.*

[121] Clark, 120–1.

[122] Cf. Brut *gærsume, æhte, wele* and the adjective *weoleȝen.*

both French *vertu* and native *þeaw*,[123] and French *desiri* and native *wilnin*: 5/10–11 ' "Ant þenne wule", seið Dauið, "þe king wilni þi wlite", þe king of alle kinges desiri þe to leofmon'.[124]

Angoise, too, is only one of a range of terms (in which the Katherine Group is particularly rich) for the concept 'suffering, pain'. *Hali Meiðhad* also uses *bale, þralunge, þrahen, teone, wa*, and *weane*, as well as *sar* and *sorhe*,[125] for this and related concepts, only the last two of these seemingly inappropriate in the immediate context: 18/7 'þet sore sorhfule angoise, þet stronge ant stinkinde stiche'.

The concept 'honour' is represented in *Hali Meiðhad* by *dignite* as well as *wurðschipe* and *menske*, and again stylistic considerations appear largely to determine choice, with *menske* usually used in collocation with *meiðhad*[126] and with *dignete* on one occasion used in the same passage as *wurðschipe*: thus, 2/20 'of se swiðe heh stal, of se muche dignete, ant swuch wurðschipe'.[127]

Again 'comfort' may be represented by *confort* only in *Hali Meiðhad*, but the native equivalent *froure* occurs no more than three times in the other texts in the Group, on all three occasions in an alliterative pattern.

Sometimes, however, there appears to be no special contextual reason for the adoption of one or other term. So, for instance, the French loan *trone* is used twice in *Sawles Warde* in the collocation *sitten in a trone*; *Seinte Iuliene* and *Seinte Katerine* also refer to 'sitting on a throne', using the verb *sitten*, but *Seinte Katerine* selects the word *kineseotle* and *Seinte Iuliene heh(e)seotel*.[128] That difference of date need not be responsible for this is illustrated by the distribution of another loan, which I have not included in my list since it would seem to have been well established already in Old English, the word *fals*. *Fals* and *falschipe* are found four times and twice respectively in *Hali Meiðhad*, in both alliterating and non-alliterating contexts. The corresponding nouns in *Seinte Iuliene* and *Seinte Katerine* are *leas* (SJ and SK each 1x) and *leasunges* (SK 2x).

At the same time it must not be forgotten that although the percentages of

---

[123] 20/18–20 'þet beoð þe uertuz þet he streoneð in þe . . . as rihtwisnesse ant warschipe aʒeines unþeawes'. Cf. *custe* Brut; and *duʒuþ*. Cf. SW 4/32–3 'vnseheliche gasttes wið alle unwreaste þeawes 7 aʒein euch god þeaw'.

[124] *Wilnin* occurs 7x in HM and *desiri* only once; in the saints' lives only *wilni* is found, with SK 3x, SJ 4x, SM 2x. The figures therefore are not statistically significant.

[125] All of these words are found in one or more of the saints' lives.

[126] SM 4/12 'meiðhades menske'; 4/26 'þe meske of hire meiðhad'; 34/9–10 'meiðhad, meidenes menske'. Cf. SK 48 'þe meistrie ant te menske'; SJ 175 'to meiðhades menske'; 484 'o meiðhades mihte, hire to muche menske'.

[127] *wurðmunt* SM, SK; *wurðschipe* HM, SK; *are* SM (cf. 10/27 'he ne alið neuer, ah liueð a in are, 7 his muchele mihte lesteð a mare'). None of these words are found in SW. See also the pairs *confort / froure, fol / sotte, flur / blostme, treitres / sweoke*.

[128] SJ (MS R) 140 'to his hehseotel as he set in dome'; 378 (R) 'þ hauest iset in hehseotel'.

French words in *Hali Meiðhad* and *Sawles Warde* are far higher than those in the saints' lives, no fewer than fifty-four of the loan-words recorded in the three saints' lives are absent from *Hali Meiðhad* and from *Sawles Warde* also, a fact which again serves as a salutary reminder of the great problems involved in using statistics to determine authorship or date. And a number of the native words for which *Hali Meiðhad* and *Sawles Warde* provide French alternatives are still to be found in texts of the late Middle English period – some of them in the work that has of recent years formed one of the major preoccupations of the recipient of this Festschrift and which is perhaps the greatest of compositions to originate in the West Midlands, *Piers Plowman*.[129]

King's College, London

---

[129] Forms discussed in this paper and recorded by Skeat as found in the several versions of *Piers Plowman* include *brok, dyuen, edwiten, fellen, fliting, fraynen, lesyng, spitten, stude, þewes, wilnen, worschipe*.

The Use of Coloured Initials and Other Division Markers in Early Versions of Ancrene Riwle

ROGER DAHOOD

The *Ancrene Riwle* comes down to us in a number of versions, which may be classified as early and late. The late versions, excluded from the present study, have been drastically condensed, rearranged, or otherwise heavily rewritten.[1] The early versions, which survive in six manuscripts and have generally similar texts, preserve the treatise apparently much as the author conceived it. The earliest version, preserved in the Nero MS (*c.* 1225–50), was composed for three consanguineous sisters.[2] Authorially revised versions, aimed at a wider audience of female recluses, survive in English in MSS Cleopatra (*c.* 1225–30), Corpus (*c.* 1230), and Vernon (late fourteenth century), and in a French translation in the Vitellius MS (early fourteenth century).[3] The text of Vernon, though imperfect through loss of leaves at the

---

[1] The list of editions in this and the following notes is necessarily selective. I have published a more inclusive list in *Middle English Prose: A Guide to Major Authors and Genres*, ed. A. S. G. Edwards (New Brunswick, New Jersey, 1984), pp. 20–1. The late versions of *Ancrene Riwle*, available in the following editions, are the Latin, preserved in four manuscripts, ed. Charlotte D'Evelyn, EETS, 216 (1944); the second French version, also called the 'Compilation', preserved in three manuscripts, ed. W. H. Trethewey, EETS, 240 (1958); and the English versions in Cambridge, Gonville and Caius College MS 234/120, ed. R. M. Wilson, EETS, 229 (1954); London, British Library MS Royal 8. c. i., ed. A. C. Baugh, EETS, 232 (1956); and Cambridge, Magdalene College MS Pepys 2498, ed. Arne Zettersten, EETS, 274 (1976).

[2] London, British Library MS Cotton Nero A. xiv. The manuscript has been edited twice, first by James Morton, Camden Society, 57 (1853), and more recently by Mabel Day, EETS, 225 (1952). The information that the treatise is addressed to three sisters appears on fo. 50.

[3] The Introduction, Part One, and some of Part Two (corresponding to Nero fos. 1ʳ1–15ʳ14) of the text in Oxford, Bodleian Library MS Eng. Poet. a. 1, better known as the Vernon MS, have been edited by Kikuo Miyabe in *Poetica: An International Journal of Linguistic–Literary Studies*, 11 (Tokyo, 1979), 80–107, and 13 (1982), 1–14. Texts from the other manuscripts are available in the following volumes: London, British Library MS Cotton Cleopatra C. vi, ed. E. J. Dobson, EETS, 267 (1972); Cambridge, Corpus Christi College MS 402, ed. J. R. R. Tolkien, with an introduction by N. R. Ker, EETS, 249 (1962); and London, British Library MS Cotton Vitellius F. vii, ed. J. A. Herbert, EETS, 219 (1944).

end,[4] is closely related to that of Nero, but also shares readings with Corpus; the French of Vitellius was translated from a text closely resembling but not identical to that in Cleopatra.[5] At some time fairly early in its history the treatise was superficially and carelessly revised, probably not by the author, for the use of men, as can be seen from the imperfect Titus MS (*c.* 1230–40), containing a version fundamentally similar to that in Nero.[6] One folio of a seventh early version survives in the Lanhydrock fragment (first half of the fourteenth century), related to Nero and Vernon.[7]

Editions of *Ancrene Riwle* are not always reliable in their treatment of manuscript divisions. The EETS editions, for example, which regularly print coloured initials as large bold-face letters displacing one or more lines of text, and thus give an appearance of reproducing the situation of the letters in the manuscripts, sometimes alter crucial features of size and placement.[8] What follows is a comparison of the ways different manuscripts of the early versions mark divisions, along with some hypotheses about what the similarities and differences in scribal practice may signify.

The six manuscripts included in the present study (Nero, Cleopatra, Corpus, Vernon, Vitellius, and Titus) exhibit a variety of formats, page layouts, and decoration. Text is written in single and double columns. Decoration ranges from the plain to the ornate. Different manuscripts employ different colour schemes. The variety suggests that to some extent matters of format and layout were decided independently by the persons responsible for producing each manuscript.

Beneath the variety, however, are some common features. Although the

---

[4] E. J. Dobson describes the condition of the Vernon text in detail in 'The Affiliations of the Manuscripts of *Ancrene Wisse*', *English and Medieval Studies Presented to J. R. R. Tolkien on the Occasion of His Seventieth Birthday*, ed. Norman Davis and C. L. Wrenn (London, 1962), pp. 153–4.

[5] E. J. Dobson, 'Affiliations', 133, 154–7.

[6] London, British Library MS Cotton Titus D. xviii, ed. Frances M. Mack, EETS, 252 (1963). Mack provides a brief account of the revisions in her introduction, pp. xiv–xvii. Leaves containing the Introduction and most of Part One are now missing from the manuscript. Also missing is a leaf from Part Three and one from Part Four (Mack, ed., p. ix).

[7] Oxford, Bodleian Library MS Eng. th. c. 70, the Lanhydrock fragment, ed. Arne Zettersten, EETS, 252 (1963). In the text of the fragment three division markers appear: space intended for a two-line initial never executed (fo. 1r9–10), an indentation (1r15), and a double slash (1r28). The divisions marked by the initial and the double slash correspond to divisions marked albeit by different means in Corpus and Vitellius. None of the other early manuscripts marks a division corresponding to that marked in Lanhydrock by the indentation.

[8] See, e.g., below, notes 17 and 26.

later among the six manuscripts mark more divisions than the earlier, there is a core of agreement across the stemma, indicating that some divisions were already marked in the ancestors of the extant manuscripts.[9] How far back in the manuscript tradition division markers originated is impossible to say with precision, but in view of the short time that could have elapsed between the probable date of composition and the earliest extant copies, either the author himself or a copyist very early in the tradition must have been responsible.[10]

The proliferation of initials is but one indication of an ongoing effort in the thirteenth and fourteenth centuries to make the text of *Ancrene Riwle* more accessible by carefully ordering it into visually manageable units on the page.[11] Even in the earliest surviving manuscripts of *Ancrene Riwle* efforts were made to mark divisions in helpful ways, and, as the Cleopatra MS testifies, division markings in early manuscripts could be supplemented by later users.[12]

The manuscripts provide evidence of two radically different approaches to layout, one most clearly exemplified by Corpus (and to a lesser degree by Cleopatra and Titus), the other by Nero. The essential feature of the Corpus design is that placement, size, and ornamentation of initials indicate degrees of subordination among textual divisions. Blue and red initials of various size, the colours usually alternating, appear at the heads of lines of text, and

[9] Dobson has produced a stemma ('Affiliations', 137), but because it is based on only a partial collation of the manuscripts, it must be used with care. E. G. Stanley has published a critique in *Archiv*, 201 (1964), 130–2. Out of fifty-two divisions marked by coloured initials in the Introduction and Part One of Corpus, thirty-one are marked either by initials or some other means in the other manuscripts. (Titus, lacking the Introduction and most of Part One, is excluded from the count.) Another ten are marked in three of the other manuscripts. Eleven are marked in only one or two other manuscripts, but of these eleven, five are of uncertain significance because one or more manuscripts lack the relevant passage.

[10] *Ancrene Riwle* is thought to have been composed in the early thirteenth century. Estimates range from 'about the year 1200, and on the whole probably after, rather than before 1200' (Geoffrey Shepherd, ed., *Ancrene Wisse: Parts Six and Seven* [London, 1959], xxiv) to about 1215–22 (E. J. Dobson, 'The Date and Composition of *Ancrene Wisse*', *PBA*, 52 [1966], 206).

[11] The desire, widespread in the thirteenth and fourteenth centuries, to facilitate reference and methodical study by attention to layout is attributed to the rise of scholasticism; see M. B. Parkes, 'The Influence of the Concepts of *Ordinatio* and *Compilatio* on the Development of the Book', *Medieval Learning and Literature: Essays Presented to Richard William Hunt*, ed. J. J. G. Alexander and M. T. Gibson (Oxford, 1976), pp. 115–41.

[12] Cleopatra Scribe D, working in the late thirteenth century, added subheadings and at the tops of folios running heads for each Part (Dobson, ed., pp. cxli–cxlii).

one-line initials[13] appear either at the heads of lines or within lines. Initials at primary divisons (i.e., the beginnings of the Introduction and eight parts) are larger and more profusely decorated than initials marking subdivisions, and initials at primary and secondary divisions (i.e., the main internal divisions within the Introduction and parts) are sometimes accompanied by rubricated headings.[14] Some attempt was made, furthermore, to indicate levels of subordination within primary divisions. This is most clearly evident in the Introduction and Parts Two and Eight.

At the beginning of the Corpus MS degrees of subordination are marked with great consistency. The Introduction consists of two secondary divisions, one treating of matters pertaining to the anchoritic life, the other, functioning somewhat as a table of contents, briefly describing the eight parts of the treatise. The beginning of the first subdivision coincides with the opening of the treatise, marked by a rubric and an ornate blue and red *R* more than five lines high and extending into the top margin. The beginning of the second is marked by a rubric and a red, two-line *N* at the head of a line (fo. 4^a17–20). Each of the secondary divisions is further subdivided. The first consists of four sections, each dealing with a different matter pertaining to anchoritic life: the two kinds of rule, inner and outer (fos. 1^a1–1^b12); the extent to which the anchoresses must observe each kind of rule (fos. 1^b12–2^a20); a caution against making vows that are too hard to keep (fos. 2^a20–2^b27); and the propriety of the anchoresses' claim to membership in a religious order (fos. 2^b28–4^b17). The scribe begins each section with a new line distinguished by a coloured one-line initial at the head of the line. The beginning of the English text, a partial translation and expansion of the opening Latin passage, is marked by a one-line initial within the line. The initial's small size and

---

[13] The terms 'one-line', 'two-line', and so forth refer to the height of initials. One-line initials occurring within lines of text occupy approximately the same vertical space as an ordinary capital and do not intrude on the lines above or below. Initials occurring at the heads of lines are described as one-line, two-line, etc., depending on how many lines of ordinary text they displace to the right. The nomenclature is not entirely precise, for initials such as *I*, *F*, *H*, and *L* are often written with their ascenders or descenders in the margins and may in fact be much larger than the nomenclature implies. Initial *I* so written displaces no lines of text to the right, yet may be comparable in size and visual impact to a two-line or larger initial. Editors have not always dealt with such letters satisfactorily (e.g., Tolkien, ed., prints the *I* at fo. 8^a19 as a two-line initial, although the letter is written entirely in the margin of the manuscript, but the *I* at 7^b10, of comparable size, he prints as one-line, perhaps because it is the extension of the stem of *F* at 7^b4). Additional cases are mentioned in note 17, below.

[14] Although space was left for rubrics at the beginning of each of the eight parts, no rubrics appear after the beginning of Part Two (fo. 12^a). In his description of the manuscript Ker does not mention the initial and space for a rubric on fo. 81^a at the beginning of Part Five (introduction to Tolkien, ed., xv-xvi, cited in note 3, above).

mid-line position give it reduced prominence, appropriate to the degree of subordination of the passage it marks, yet distinguishing the passage as the beginning of the English text of the treatise.

In outline form the structure of the Introduction appears as follows:

I. Matters pertaining to the anchoritic life
    A. Distinction between the inner and outer rules
        1. Latin passage beginning *Recti*
        2. Partial translation and expansion of the Latin passage
    B. Extent to which the anchoresses must observe each rule
    C. Caution against making vows that are too hard to keep
    D. Propriety of the anchoresses' claim to membership in a religious order
II. Summary description of Parts One to Eight

The Corpus scheme indicates degrees of subordination almost as precisely as the above outline. It fails only in that where the beginnings of two or more categories coincide, a single initial marks all, its size and placement determined by the largest category. That is, the Corpus scheme cannot distinguish, for example, between the categories given on the outline as I., I. A., and I. A. 1., since all begin at *Recti*. Otherwise, the system is unambiguous. The passages indicated in the outline as I. B., I. C., and I. D. each begin in Corpus with a one-line initial at the head of a line, whereas the account of the eight parts, indicated in the outline as II., begins with a two-line *N* at the head of the line in Corpus. Had the pattern been continued throughout Corpus, it would have been a useful aid to comprehension, for a reader would have been able to discover at once the structural level of any passage in the treatise.

After the first few folios, however, the pattern begins to break down. Because the descriptions of the eight parts are logically co-ordinate, strict observance of the pattern of the early folios would require that they all be marked in the same way, with one-line initials at the heads of lines. Instead, the scribe wrote some initials at the heads of lines, others within lines, placement being of no significance. Size, however, remains a reliable indicator of structural relationships throughout the Introduction, for the initials marking the tertiary divisions are smaller than the *N* marking the secondary division.

Correlation between size of initial and degree of subordination is maintained throughout the treatise in the case of primary divisions, for, as I have already noted, the initials at the beginnings of the Introduction and the eight parts are larger than any at the beginnings of lesser divisions. In the case of subordinate divisions, however, the correspondence is not consistently maintained. In Part One, whose highly stratified composition would particularly lend itself to representation through a system of graduated initials, size and placing of initials correspond only intermittently to degree of subordination. For example, some of the eight obviously co-ordinate passages detailing the way of saying *Pater nosters* begin with one-line initials at the heads of lines, some with one-line initials within lines, and some with two-line initials at the heads of lines (fos. 6^{b}26–8^{a}6).[15] In every case but one (the one-line initial *F* at fo. 7^{a}23) where an initial appears at the head of a new line, it is clear from the spacing or other evidence that the positioning of the initial at the head of a new line was deliberate. Passages not structurally co-ordinate, on the other hand, sometimes get equivalent treatment. Thus, the section on devotions after dressing and some of its constituent prayers are alike marked by one-line initials within lines (fos. 4^b–5^a).

Frequent inconsistencies notwithstanding, however, there is reason to suppose that whoever devised the system intended in at least some places outside of the Introduction to indicate structural relationships below the level of primary divisions, for intermittently there are stretches where initials receive consistent treatment; for example, the sixteen co-ordinate sections on shrift all begin with two-line initials (fos. 82^{b}11–92^{b}14). Somewhat more impressive is the evidence of Parts Two and Eight. Part Two consists of six main subdivisions, one for each of the five senses (except that speech replaces taste as the main 'sense' of the mouth) and a sixth, at about the midpoint of the part, treating sight, speech, and hearing together. In Corpus the six subdivisions are marked with coloured initials. The first, dealing with sight, is treated as a continuation of the prefatory discussion with which Part Two opens. The ornamental initial at the beginning of the part (larger than four lines high and extending well into the top margin) thus simultaneously marks the beginning of the discussion of sight. Each of the other five subdivisions begins with a two-line initial at the head of a line (see illustration on p. 86).[16] The remaining initials in Part Two mark tertiary and lesser subdivisions, and with few exceptions are one-line. The exceptions, five two-line initials marking tertiary subdivisions, somewhat obscure the neat pattern of graduation; on the whole, however, in Part Two of Corpus size of initial corresponds to degree of subordination down to the level of secondary divisions.[17] Yet

---

[15] Similar inconsistencies occur elsewhere in the manuscript, e.g., among the initials marking the eight reasons for fleeing the world (fos. 44^a–45^b), the seven deadly sins (fos. 52^a–55^a), and the nine aids against temptation (fos. 61^b–64^a).

[16] The initial *Z*, marking the passage on sight, speech, and hearing together, is indented but probably only because the scribe wished to avoid writing across a tear in the membrane (fo. 23^b). The indentation is probably not significant as a structural indicator.

[17] The exceptions occur at fos. 14^{a}16–17, 14^{b}4–5, 21^{a}21–22, 21^{b}5–6, and 26^{a}13–14. Tolkien prints a number of other initials as two-line which in the manuscript are one-line. Also, the initial *I* at fo. 28^{a}7–8 is entirely in the margin in the manuscript and though comparable in size to a two-line initial, displaces no text to the right. It is worth noting that the five exceptions seem to result from local considerations taking precedence over the general scheme. The first two mark examples from the Bible, illustrating the dangers of unguarded sight. They are part of a group of three, the first of which begins with a one-line *L* at the head of a line (fo. 13^{b}9, printed as a two-line

there seems to be no attempt made to distinguish between tertiary and lesser divisions. Part Eight, the account of the non-devotional aspects of the outer rule, consists of a prefatory opening, the body of the account, and a conclusion. The body of the account touches upon many topics, but as the author explains in the Introduction and mentions again at the beginning of Part Eight, they are grouped in seven subsections, which he calls *stucchen* (fos. 4^b8–15; 111^a21–22): (1) food, drink, and related subjects; (2) things that the anchoresses may receive, keep, or have; (3) clothing and related matters; (4) works; (5) haircutting and bloodletting; (6) governance of maid-servants; and (7) instruction of maidservants.

In Part Eight a four-line initial at the head of the line marks the beginning of the part (fo. 111^a). Two-line initials at the heads of lines mark the beginnings of the first, second, and seventh *stucchen* and the conclusion (fos. 111^a, 112^b, 116^b, and 117^a), but one-line initials within lines mark the other *stucchen* (fos. 113^a22, 114^a16, 114^b26, and 115^a21). All other coloured initials in Part Eight are one-line, either at heads of or within lines. It is apparent that the size and placing of initials in Corpus does not accurately reflect the structure of Part Eight, for logically co-ordinate elements, i.e., the *stucchen*, are marked differently, some in the manner of lesser divisions. What is significant is that two-line initials mark only secondary divisions, never tertiary (although one-line initials mark some secondary divisions). Tertiary divisions, on the other hand, are invariably marked by one-line initials. Such a pattern seems unlikely to result from chance. It can be better explained as either the vestige of a scheme in which secondary and tertiary divisions were regularly and systematically distinguished, or as evidence of an only partly successful attempt at some point in the transmission to impose such a scheme.

That the scheme probably did not originate with the Corpus MS is suggested by the presence of a similar pattern in the Cleopatra MS, which, if Dobson is correct, is slightly older.[18] The Cleopatra design differs from the Corpus design in a number of ways. Whereas Corpus relies mainly on coloured initials (occasionally in conjunction with rubrics) to mark divisions

---

letter in Tolkien). Because its ascender rises several lines high in the margin, the *L* compares in size to two-line initials. In marking the last two examples with two-line initials, the scribe may have been concerned to make them appear parallel with the first. A similar situation obtains in the case of the fifth exceptional two-line letter, marking the second of a pair of biblical examples. The first of the pair begins with a large one-line *L* (fo. 25^b16, printed as two-line in Tolkien). Again the size of the second initial of the pair may have been determined by the apparent size of the first. The remaining two exceptions introduce the discussions of the two worst kinds of poisonous speech, backbiting and flattery. In all five cases the scribe may have used the larger initials intentionally and regardless of relative subordination in order to give passages of especial interest or importance greater prominence.

[18] Dobson, ed., ix–x.

Cambridge. Corpus Christi College
MS 402, fo. 30ᵃ

London. British Library MS Cotton
Nero A. xiv, fo. 27ʳ

London. British Library MS Cotton
Titus D. xviii, fo. 31ᵛ

London. British Library MS Cotton
Vitellius F. vii, fo. 21ʳ

The photographs show how four manuscripts mark the beginning of a main subdivision of Part Two. In Corpus the subdivision, which treats feeling, the fifth bodily sense, opens with a coloured two-line 'P' at the head of the line. Because of its size, placement, and decoration, the 'P' stands out from coloured initials nearby marking lesser subdivisions. In Nero the corresponding 'P' is treated like nearby coloured initials marking lesser divisions; all are two-line red capitals at the heads of lines. The 'P' in Titus is a heavily inked black letter (col. i, l. 5). Only its width and the thickness of its penstrokes distinguish it from surrounding text, and it is treated like neighbouring initials marking lesser subdivisions. Vitellius prominently marks the subdivision with an ornamented, red, two-line 'L' and a rubricated heading. (The photograph of the Corpus MS is here reproduced by permission of the Master and Fellows of Corpus Christi College, Cambridge, the photographs of the Cotton MSS by permission of the British Library, London.)

of the text, Cleopatra uses a mix of coloured and uncoloured initials, rubrics, and paragraph symbols. Often a paragraph symbol alone marks a division in Cleopatra that in Corpus is marked by a coloured initial.[19]

Still, among the Cleopatra initials a pattern of graduation similar to that in Corpus, albeit less perfect, can be detected.[20] Usually initials marking primary divisions are larger than those within divisions. Cleopatra opens with a large, four-line initial, and most of the parts begin with three-line initials at the heads of lines. Part Six, however, begins with a two-line initial (fo. 178[v]) and Part Four with a one-line initial within the line (fo. 74[r]18). Also, a three-line initial occurs within Part Two, further confusing the pattern (fo. 36[r]).

Below the level of primary divisions in Cleopatra the familiar pattern can be detected within Parts Two and Eight.[21] Within Part Two the six secondary divisions are distinguished by coloured initials. As in Corpus the section on sight is treated as a continuation of the opening of the part and so has no initial of its own. The beginnings of the sections on speech, smell, and feeling are marked with two-line initials (fo. 26[v], 42[r], and 44[v]). Graduation is not perfectly carried out, however, for the section on hearing begins with a one-line initial within the line (fo. 33[r]5), and the section treating sight, speech, and hearing together begins with a three-line initial (fo. 36[r], as noted above). Lesser divisions are marked with one-line coloured initials, either at the heads of lines or within lines, or with paragraph symbols. In the case of these lesser divisions there seems no consistent relationship between type of marker and degree of subordination.

---

[19] In Corpus paragraph symbols are used almost exclusively to separate runovers from following text, and therefore almost always appear in conjunction with coloured initials. The few exceptions occur in special circumstances: a paragraph symbol precedes the rubricated heading on fo. 12[a], and another precedes the *Explicit* on fo. 117[b]. Also paragraph symbols are twice used erroneously in place of coloured initials (fos. 6[b] and 7[b]). Otherwise in Corpus paragraph symbols are used only to mark runovers and so appear at the ends of lines that begin with coloured initials.

[20] The intelligent Scribe B, whom some identify with the author, did not revise the pattern of graduation, which remains as the main scribe, designated A, copied it. The most complete statement of the case for Scribe B's authorship may be found in Dobson, ed., xcvi–xcvii.

[21] The pattern is absent from the Cleopatra Introduction, which makes no distinction between secondary and tertiary divisions. The description of the parts, marked by a two-line initial in Corpus, begins with a one-line initial in Cleopatra, and the tertiary divisions in the first portion of the Introduction, marked by one-line initials at the heads of lines in Corpus, are marked in Cleopatra by one-line initials placed indifferently at the heads of lines or within lines. Also, in Cleopatra initials without counterparts in Corpus appear unsystematically at other breaks in sense. Thus, the passage on the rule of the body, the less important of the two rules, is marked with a coloured, one-line initial (but the passage on the more important rule of the heart is unmarked, fos. 4[r]15, 20), and a prominent black capital marks the name 'Pauwel' in the section on religious order (fo. 7[r]22).

The leaf in Cleopatra containing the beginning of Part Eight and the beginning of the first of the seven *stucchen* has been lost. In what remains of Part Eight, two-line initials mark only secondary, never tertiary, divisions, just as in Corpus. Four of the surviving six beginnings of divisions, further-more, have two-line initials (the second, fo. 192^v; the fourth, 194^r; the sixth, 195^r; and the seventh, 197^v), and five are provided with coloured headings in red and blue (the second, fo. 192^v; the third, 193^v; the fifth and sixth, 195^{r}9, 16; and the seventh, 197^v).[22]

Cleopatra is a problematic manuscript, copied by a scribe whose under-standing of the text was not always sound.[23] He is most unlikely to be responsible for creating the system of graduated initials, which would seem rather to be the work of someone more keenly interested in the structure of the treatise. Was the system in perfect or near-perfect shape in the exemplar, and first corrupted in Cleopatra? The inconsistent use of one-line initials is most frequent early in the manuscript. If the inconsistencies had originated with the Cleopatra scribe, their high concentration at the beginning could in ordinary circumstances be plausibly explained by supposing that at first the scribe was especially confused by the system but came to understand it better after settling into his task. Since, however, the first three quires were not copied first, a more likely explanation is either that he was following his exemplar, as Dobson suggests,[24] or, possibly, if we suppose that the exemplar was consistently imperfect throughout, that as he copied and perceived no apparent system in the exemplar, he began to size and place initials according to his own perception of the text.[25]

The implication in either case is not only that the pattern of graduated initials probably existed before Cleopatra, but that if it ever did exist in a perfectly or nearly perfectly realised form, it must have done so very early in the manuscript tradition and must have deteriorated very rapidly in the course of transmission. There is of course no certainty that the pattern ever did exist in a perfectly realised form or that a single system of graduation was ever used throughout the treatise. Some parts and not others could have been singled out for graduated initials. The author himself could have used initials inconsistently and unsystematically in his holograph. It could be that in the Corpus MS the pattern appears in as perfect a realisation as it ever attained.

---

[22] The rubric at 195^{r}9 is placed a few lines after the beginning of the sixth division and does not mention haircutting, the subject with which the division opens. Cf. the corresponding heading, which appears at the beginning of the division in Vitellius: *Quant vous devez estre tondu. ou seignee* (Herbert, ed., 310). Probably the Cleopatra rubric is innovative and misplaced.

[23] Dobson, ed., lvi.

[24] Dobson, ed., xxix–xxxvi, lxiv–lxv.

[25] I am grateful to T. F. Hoad for suggesting this alternate possibility.

Whether or not it was ever perfectly realised, however, it was a system likely to go awry in the course of transmission, first, because of the many grades of letter size involved and, second, because the significance of the graduation, never made explicit, had to be inferred from a closer knowledge of the text than the copyists seem to have possessed. Most vulnerable to loss or confusion would have been markings of more subordinate divisions and divisions occurring where explicit lexical cues to the structure of the text are absent.

The Titus MS is probably an example of how radically the Corpus style could be altered for the worse. With its double-column format and red–green colour scheme, Titus is at first glance strikingly different from Corpus and Cleopatra. Titus, furthermore, has relatively few coloured initials, relying instead on black initials, some touched with colour, and coloured or uncoloured paragraph symbols to mark most divisions.[26] Despite the differences, however, the Titus, Cleopatra, and Corpus layouts must be related, for those coloured initials that appear in Titus exhibit the familiar pattern of graduation. Primary divisions, the beginnings of the surviving parts, are marked with three-line initials, larger than any initials within parts. Within Part Two Titus distinguishes secondary divisions about as consistently as Cleopatra does. Like Corpus and Cleopatra, Titus treats the beginning of the first of the six secondary divisions as coincident with the beginning of the part. The second, third, and fifth of the secondary divisions in Titus begin with two-line initials (fos. 19^r, 23^r, and 30^r). The fourth has an ordinary capital and the sixth a prominent black, one-line capital within the line (fos. 25^{vb}19 and 31^{va}5; see illustration, p. 86).[27] In Part Eight the pattern of two-line initials in Titus is exactly as in Corpus: only the first, second and last of the seven *stucchen* and the conclusion have two-line initials. In the case of the other *stucchen* Titus follows no consistent pattern. The third has a red, one-line initial within the line, preceded by a red paragraph symbol; the sixth also has a red, one-line initial within the line but is preceded by a black paragraph symbol, whose position to the left of the line in the margin suggests

---

[26] Titus includes only fifty-one coloured initials (not counting the two hundred or so black initials touched with colour), as compared to hundreds in Corpus and Cleopatra. Even if the few initials that probably appeared on the folios now lost from the beginning of Titus are taken into account, the disparity is substantial. Three-line initials, of which Titus has seven, and two-line initials, of which Titus has thirty-nine, are always coloured. Two-line initials appear more frequently in the second half of the manuscript. The highest concentration occurs in Part Five, on confession, where there are fifteen, with space left for a sixteenth that was never executed (quires *h* and *i*, fos. 70^r–91^v; the empty space is on fo. 75rb). Titus has five coloured, one-line initials. Mack, ed., does not print one-line initials, coloured or uncoloured, in distinctive type, but they occur as follows (references are by page and line to Mack): *Hwa*, 88:18 (printed as two-line); *Ondes*, 97:7; *Mine*, 123:13; *For*, 155:32; and *Anker*, 157:11.

[27] Mack, ed., 19:35 and 28:10.

that it was added after the line was written (fos. 102^{vb}9 and 103^{va}10).[28] The fourth begins with a slightly prominent black capital preceded by a green paragraph symbol and the fifth with an ordinary capital preceded by a green paragraph symbol (fos. 103^{ra}18 and 103^{rb}17).[29]

The tables opposite allow convenient comparison of the size of initials marking secondary divisions within Parts Two and Eight in the three manuscripts. In the marking of secondary divisions in Part Two, Corpus is consistent in employing two-line initials after the opening of the part, Cleopatra and Titus less so. In Part Eight Corpus and Titus display a strikingly similar pattern of two- and one-line initials at secondary divisions.

Although it is conceivable that Titus preserves an earlier stage in the development of the graduated scheme than either Cleopatra or Corpus, it seems more likely that the differences between the layouts of Titus and the earlier manuscripts originated in Titus. Titus is the work of a careless and sometimes innovative scribe.[30] Such a person might well have substituted a new colour scheme and reduced the number of coloured initials.[31] The Titus layout is a retrograde step in the history of *Ancrene Riwle* page design. The replacement of coloured initials with less conspicuous division markers makes for a volume not well suited to reference and study.

The deficiencies in manuscript layouts of the Corpus type seem to have been evident at least to some medieval readers of *Ancrene Riwle*, for even in Corpus itself there are indications of a competing system. In Part One, after the first three initials marking the serial *Pater nosters*, the scribe, perhaps following his exemplar, all but abandons one-line initials in favour of two-line initials at the heads of lines. The two-line system predominates until the end of Part One (fos. 6^b–12^a). A similar change occurs in Part Three partway through a series of eight reasons for fleeing the world (fos. 44^a–45^b). In Parts Four and Five two-line initials predominate. It is as if the scribe is moving uncertainly and with some hesitation towards the exclusive use of two-line initials.

In the Nero MS the two-line system prevails, although in the Nero Introduction and Part One traces of a Corpus-like graduation remain. In the Introduction the capital *R* at the beginning of the treatise is three-line, the

---

[28] Mack, ed., 155:32 (the *e* immediately following the red initial *F* is touched with red) and 157:11 (the *N* immediately following the red initial *A* is an elaborate, small black capital).

[29] Mack, ed., 156:19, 34. The reliance on paragraph symbols instead of coloured initials to mark subdivisions in Part Eight first appears in Titus.

[30] Mack, ed., xiii–xvii.

[31] Mack reasonably suggests that concern for economy may have prompted the reduction in the number of coloured initials (xi).

[32] By 'ordinary' I mean a majuscule letter form not distinguished from other letters by prominent inking, decoration, or colour.

INITIALS MARKING SECONDARY DIVISIONS

PART TWO

	Corpus	Cleopatra	Titus
Opening/Sight	4-line	3-line	3-line
Speech	2-line	2-line	2-line
Hearing	2-line	1-line within line	2-line
Preceding three together	2-line	3-line	ordinary[32] capital within line
Smell	2-line	2-line	2-line
Feeling	2-line	2-line	prominent black capital within line

PART EIGHT

	Corpus	Cleopatra	Titus
Food, drink, and related subjects	2-line	wanting	2-line
Things anchoresses may have, keep, or receive	2-line	2-line	2-line
Clothes and related subjects	1-line within line	1-line within line	¶, red 1-line within line
Works	1-line within line	2-line	¶, heavy, 1-line, black capital within line
Haircutting and blood-letting	1-line within line	1-line within line	¶, ordinary[30] capital within line
Governance of maids	1-line within line	2-line	black ¶ in left margin, red 1-line initial within line
Instruction of maids	2-line	2-line	2-line
Conclusion	2-line	1-line within line	2-line

largest size used in Nero, and as in Corpus, a one-line initial within the line marks the beginning of the English text. With few exceptions all other initials in the Nero Introduction are red, two-line letters at the heads of lines.[33] In Part One in Nero as in Corpus red, one-line initials within lines mark the beginnings of Latin prayers, Nero marking many more than Corpus. After Part One, however, almost all marked divisions in Nero, whatever their degree of subordination, begin with red, two-line initials at the heads of lines (see illustration, p. 86).[34]

Which of the two designs, the system of graduated initials or the system of uniform initials, is the older? Corpus, Cleopatra, and Nero are of approximately the same age. Corpus, usually considered to preserve the most authoritative text, and Nero, preserving the earliest version of the treatise, contain evidence of both systems. Cleopatra, on the other hand, which may be slightly earlier than Corpus, makes some use of the graduated system but no use of the uniform system. In Nero there is evidence, albeit inconclusive, that may point to an answer. At the beginnings of Parts Five and Seven Nero has text not corresponding to any in Corpus but found with slight dialectal variation in Cleopatra headings.[35] Presumably, then, the Nero pedigree includes a manuscript that, like Cleopatra and Corpus, used headings at the beginnings of parts. If the headings, like many in Cleopatra, were unrubricated, a copyist might easily have mistaken them for ordinary text and copied them as such. At what point in the transmission they were incorporated into

---

[33] The exceptions occur in the passage at the end of the Introduction, describing the parts of the treatise. One, the technically one-line initial marking the description of Part Five at the beginning of the last line of the folio, is only apparently exceptional. Because of its position on the folio it displaces only one line of text, but it extends the equivalent of another full line below the last line and is comparable in size to two-line initials. The second is the one-line initial marking the description of Part Seven, at the top of the next folio. It is noticeably smaller than the preceding two-line initials but somewhat larger than other one-line initials. Day prints both as two-line (6:21–24). The descriptions of Parts Six and Eight are marked with one-line initials within the line. The mid-line initials here may result from the scribe's desire to avoid short lines and hence white space in a passage that he recognised as a unit. Or they may be the result of carelessness. Carelessness seems the most likely explanation for his failure to mark the description of Part Two in the same passage even by so much as an ordinary capital letter.

[34] Exceptionally there is a three-line initial within Part Two at fo. 11v3–5 (Day, ed., 21:24–26). Also there is a blue initial in Part Three at fo. 45v1–2 (Day, ed., 77:30–31). The exceptions seem to be capricious.

[35] The Cleopatra headings are as follows (letters in brackets are Dobson's reconstructions of missing text): [He]r biginneð þe fifðe dale [of] schrift (fo. 135v) and her biginneð þe seoueðe dale of luue (fo. 178v). The corresponding text in Nero reads as follows: her biginneð ðe uifte dole of schrifte (fo. 80v) and her biginneð ðe seoueðe dole of luue (fo. 105v). Also, cf. Vitellius: Ici comence la quinte distinction qest de Confession (fo. 47r) and Ici comence la septime partie qest damour (fo. 62r).

the main text is impossible to say, but if as seems possible the Nero ancestor, like Corpus and Cleopatra, had graduated initials as well as headings, then it would follow that the graduated system existed prior to the uniform. It is interesting to note that the last of the mid-line initials in Nero appears on fo. 10v, the last folio of the gathering. This may indicate that in its use of initials the Nero exemplar indeed resembled Corpus, that the Nero copyist followed the layout of the exemplar until he completed his first gathering, and that thereafter he regularly replaced one-line initials with two-line initials at the heads of lines. Whatever the particular history of Nero, however, the uniform system has every appearance of an attempt to streamline the presentation of the text by eliminating the complexity of the graduated system. The uniform system is easy to understand and copy accurately. Its very simplicity, furthermore, facilitates reference. The uniform size and placement of initials enables quick scanning of the folios, for the eye need move only down the left-hand side of the page to locate new divisions. The answer to the question of which system, the graduated or the uniform, came first is not certain, but the hypothesis is attractive that the graduated system was first, and that when its complexity proved too great for copyists to master, the uniform system was introduced as a replacement.

The designs of the two fourteenth-century manuscripts, Vitellius and Vernon, are in different ways developments of the earlier designs. Basic similarities can be readily seen in Vitellius, which like Corpus and Cleopatra has an alternating red–blue colour scheme and coloured headings, and like Titus is written in double columns. Also, the initials in Vitellius exhibit some graduation. In most cases initials marking primary divisions are larger and more ornate than others.[36] The graduation, however, does not extend beyond distinguishing primary from lesser divisions. Initials within parts are almost always two-line, as in Nero, and without exception appear at the heads of lines (see illustration, p. 86).[37] Frequently, and especially in Parts One and Eight, they are accompanied by rubricated headings. Latin passages in Vitellius are underlined in red. Lesser divisions are sometimes marked by red or blue

---

[36] Herbert, ed., does not reproduce the size differences, printing all coloured initials as two-line, with the exception of the *R* of *Recti* at the beginning of the treatise. In the manuscript the treatise begins with an *R* that before fire damage must have been ten or more lines high (fo. 2[r]). A five-line initial begins Part Two (fo. 9[r]), four-line initials Parts Three, Five, Seven, and Eight (fos. 22[v], 47[r], 62[r], and 67[r]), a three-line initial Part Six (fo. 55[v]), and a two-line initial Part One (fo. 4[r]). The beginning of Part Four was omitted from Vitellius, apparently accidentally (Herbert, ed., xiii-xiv). As in the case of Corpus, there seems to be no obvious reason for the differences in size. What seems to matter is that on the whole the initials at the beginnings of parts are larger than those within parts.

[37] In Part Two the discussion of speech begins with a coloured heading and four-line initial (fo. 13[r]), and the discussion of sight, speech, and hearing together begins with a three-line initial (fo. 18[r]), both printed as two-line in Herbert.

paragraph symbols, usually in alternation.[38] The scribe wrote double slashes, many of them still visible, to guide the rubricator's insertion of paragraph symbols, a practice found also in thirteenth-century Latin manuscripts.[39] Paragraph symbols are also used as in Corpus to mark runovers.

The text of *Ancrene Riwle* is more accessible in Vitellius than in any of the earlier manuscripts, solely because of improvements in layout. First of all, the Vitellius scribe exercised restraint in marking lesser divisions. Because paragraph symbols in Vitellius are always coloured and used sparingly, the folios have a clean, uncrowded appearance that those of Titus do not, while at the same time the text is visually broken into manageable sections. Also contributing to the success of the Vitellius design is the increased reliance on rubrics, especially helpful in allowing for speedy access to any of the numerous provisions of the outer rule. Another improvement is that in Vitellius different kinds of markers serve different functions. Because initials and rubrics mark only the more important divisions and red underlining only Latin text, opportunities for readers to be misled about the significance of a given division marker are diminished. Also, in so far as the damaged state of the manuscript allows us to say, it appears that in the Introduction and Parts One and Eight the scribe uses paragraph symbols only to mark new subdivisions, whereas elsewhere in the manuscript, with the exception of a few instances in Part Two, he uses them only to mark runovers. In other words, although in this manuscript paragraph symbols serve two functions, the scribe seems fairly consistently to separate the functions, again lessening the chance of confusion. In addition, Vitellius combines two of the most helpful features of the Corpus and Nero schemes. Like Corpus, it uses graduated initials, albeit only to distinguish primary from lesser divisions. The graduation is not perfectly executed, but for the most part larger initials indicate primary divisions. In theory, at least, a reader looking for the beginning of a part need look only for three-line or larger initials, and a reader looking for an important subdivision within a part need look only for two-line initials. Furthermore, because as in Nero all initials are at the heads of lines, a reader looking for any important division need only scan the left-hand side of the page.

Vitellius evidently was laid out with readers' convenience in mind, but the same cannot be said of MS Vernon, produced towards the end of the

---

[38] Herbert did not print all paragraph symbols, especially those occurring in badly damaged early folios. The following, in blue ink badly faded in the Ashburnham House fire and not easily visible except under ultraviolet light, are absent from his edition (numbers refer to page and line of the Herbert text): 1:13 (before *Recti*); 1:24 (before *li une*); 2:9 (before *Ceste*); 11:1 (before *La primere*); 11:12 (before *La tier-*); 11:23 (before *La* [*siste*]); 11:29 (before *La vtisme*); 13:1 (before *Quant*); 13:26 (before *Apres*); and 14:28 (before *A*). In addition Herbert omits a red paragraph at 11:25 (before *La*).

[39] Parkes, 'Influence', 121.

fourteenth century. Originally consisting of more than 420 leaves measuring about 23 × 15.5 inches, Vernon remains a huge book, even in its present state, with seventy-one leaves missing.[40] *Ancrene Riwle*, almost complete and written in double columns usually of eighty lines each, occupies not quite eighteen of its folios, verso and recto. The sheer size and bulk of the volume put certain limitations on its use. It has been observed more than once that Vernon is not an easily portable book.[41] In addition, its size and lavishly decorated borders make reading in it awkward. The folios are so large that in scanning a single page a reader must repeatedly change position and refocus his eye. Folios must be turned carefully with both hands to avoid damaging the ornamentation. Beyond these difficulties there are shortcomings in the details of layout.

The format, in some ways standardised throughout the manuscript, was not designed particularly for *Ancrene Riwle*. Some of the shortcomings are associated with the standardised features. For example, the text is laid out with little or no white space between divisions, which are marked mainly by ornate initials (usually at the heads of lines) and paragraph symbols (at heads of lines or within lines). The initials, however, do not always stand out very well, for in many cases they are incorporated into the pattern of vines bordering each page. Thus submerged in the page frame, they tend to be perceived more as part of the background design than as part of the text, and their effectiveness as division markers is correspondingly reduced. The paragraph symbols are too numerous to be effective. The result is a page offering few places for the eye to rest. Instead of visually manageable units, the pages appear as continuous blocks of text running the length of each column, within which individual items are difficult to find.

Certain features of layout suggest that the exemplar of the Vernon *Ancrene Riwle* may have had a Corpus-style format. Although as in Nero most coloured initials appear at the heads of lines, the Vernon initials are of various

---

[40] Mary S. Serjeantson, 'The Index of the Vernon Manuscript', *MLR*, 32 (1937), 222–61, concluded that before losses Vernon contained 377 individual items, but the numbers vary depending on what is counted as an individual item. A. I. Doyle, 'The Shaping of the Vernon and Simeon Manuscripts', *Chaucer and Middle English Studies in Honour of Rossell Hope Robbins*, ed. Beryl Rowland (London, 1974), 329, observes that of Serjeantson's 377 items, 'the last comprises 27 distinct poems, making a total of 404 [*sic* for 403]; but 113 constitute the Southern Legendary, 42 the miracles of Our Lady, and 114 the *Northern Homilies*'.

[41] Doyle, 'Shaping', 331. In the same place Doyle also notes that it 'weighed more than fifty pounds when complete'; Robert E. Lewis quotes Doyle in 'The Relationship of the Vernon and Simeon Texts of the *Pricke of Conscience*', *So Meny People Longages and Tonges: Philological Essays in Scots and Mediaeval English Presented to Angus McIntosh*, ed. Michael Benskin and M. L. Samuels (Edinburgh, 1981), 251–2.

sizes, and there is limited use of graduation.[42] For the most part primary divisions are marked with initials larger than any marking lesser divisions. A six-line *R* marks the beginning of the treatise (fo. 371[vb]), four-line initials within the parts mark the beginnings of Parts One and Six (fos. 372[rb] and 388[rb]), and five-line initials the beginnings of Parts Two to Five (fos. 373[vb], 377[rb], 380[ra], and 386[ra]).[43] Within the primary divisions a few four-line initials occur, but one-, two-, or three-line are more usual, with two-line and three-line initials predominating. The size of internal initials for the most part bears no relationship to degree of subordination. In the Introduction and Part Two two-line and three-line initials are used indifferently to mark the beginnings of secondary and tertiary divisions (no coloured initials appear in the surviving few lines of Part Eight). In Vernon consistent use of graduation occurs only in Part Five, on confession, where secondary divisions in most cases begin with three-line initials; tertiary divisions, if given initials, begin with two-line initials. Thus, the sixteen sections on the requirements of confession begin with three-line initials and their subsections with two-line initials (e.g., fos. 386[v]–387[r]).

Graduation in Part Five, absent from Corpus and Cleopatra, may have originated with Vernon, for the Vernon scribe seems to have been especially concerned to make Part Five accessible for reference. The only heading in the Vernon *Ancrene Riwle* appears at the beginning of Part Five. It is in the main hand. Also in the main hand, in the left margin of folio 386[v], are the roman numerals i–iiii, indicating four subtopics within a passage on the bitterness of confession.[44] Such features seem most likely intended to facilitate reference and study.

---

[42] The Vernon *Ancrene Riwle* includes a few initials within the line, chiefly in Part One at the beginnings of pre-matinal Latin prayers (fo. 372[v]). Outside of Part One I have found only two instances of initials within the line: the initial of *Idel*, Part Two, fo. 375[rb], eight lines from the bottom (= Corpus, fo. 20[b]26), and the initial of *Now*, Part Five, fo. 388[ra]20 (= Corpus, fo. 92[b]21). The manuscript, now in the process of being photographed for a facsimile edition, has been unavailable for consultation, but, so far as I can judge from comparative shading in the microfilm, the *N* is not coloured. There are also isolated cases of indentation marking divisions (e.g., fo. 371[vb]7), but the spaces may have been intended for paragraph symbols that were not executed.

[43] The design seems to have called for a five-line initial at the beginning of Part Six, but the scribe skipped a line between the last two lines of Part Five, writing the last words of Part Five in a space that appears to have been meant for the top of the initial beginning Part Six, thereby forcing the illuminator to keep the initial to four lines. Missing from Vernon are most of Part Six (the text breaks off at the place corresponding to Corpus fo. 97[b]18), all of Part Seven, and all but an abridged segment of Part Eight (corresponding to Corpus fos. 113[b]22–114[b]20).

[44] The heading reads *Her biginneþ þe fyfþe Book* (fo. 386[r]4). Working from photographs, Dr A. I. Doyle has kindly confirmed in private correspondence that the heading and the roman numerals are in the hand of the main scribe. In particular, he notes the main scribe's characteristic form of the ·j· (i.e., the roman numeral ·i·) and

Taken as a group the six manuscripts testify that manuscript layouts were not fixed in the early versions of *Ancrene Riwle*. Copyists evidently felt free to adapt format to specific needs and preferences, usually but not invariably in the direction of greater ease of reference. Perhaps the most ambitious scheme is found in the two earliest manuscripts, the system of graduated initials in Cleopatra and Corpus. Expertly executed the scheme would have provided readers with reliable visual indicators of the structure of the text. In practice, however, it appears to have been too complex for the scribes to master. The simpler, cleaner pages of the Nero and Vitellius styles turn out to be far more convenient to use.

It is worth noting that in the earliest extant manuscripts, and as we have seen probably earlier still, *Ancrene Riwle* was in some measure set out as a study text. Whoever first imposed the system of graduated initials was concerned that readers grasp the relationships between divisions and not just focus on discrete passages. This concern is compatible with the author's express concern, evident from the lexical cues in the text, to make the structure clear. I am not aware of manuscripts of other works, Latin or vernacular, with quite this style of graduation. Oxford, Bodleian Library MS Bodley 34, closely linked to Corpus linguistically, is more like Nero than Corpus in its use of initials. Bodley uses red initials only, and in the lives of St Margaret and St Juliana these were intended to be exclusively two-line.[45] It might enhance our knowledge of the origins or at least the early history of *Ancrene Riwle* if in contemporary manuscripts specific models for the Corpus style of graduation could be identified.[46]

The University of Arizona

emphasises that the hand of the heading is not that of the preliminary quire, contents list, and any rubrics supplied where spaces were left by the main scribe. From the evidence of the microfilm the heading appears to be in black ink. The Vernon heading is differently worded from and less specific than the corresponding headings in Cleopatra and Vitellius, the only other manuscripts having headings at the beginning of Part Five, and the heading-like text of Nero (all given in note 35, above). The different wording suggests independent invention and, because of his great interest in Part Five, probably by the Vernon scribe himself.

[45] Not all initials were executed, but at each new division the scribe left a space for a two-line initial. *Facsimile of MS Bodley 34: St Katherine, St Margaret, St Juliana, Hali Meiðhad, Sawles Warde*, EETS, 247 (1960), fos. 18–52, and N. R. Ker's comments in the introduction, xi-xii.

[46] I am grateful to Carl Berkhout, T. F. Hoad, and R. A. Waldron for reading and commenting on earlier drafts of this essay.

The Date and Provenance of King Horn: Some Interim Reassessments*

ROSAMUND ALLEN

In each of the three extant manuscripts of *King Horn* (*KH*) the scribes have 'translated' the language of the original poem into their own dialectal forms. Each of the three manuscripts, Cambridge University Library MS Gg.4.27 (2) [C], Oxford Bodleian Library MS Laud Misc. 108 [O], and British Library MS Harley 2253 [L], reflects the dialectal colouring imposed by the last scribe to work on it. In varying degrees, underlying the 'translations' are relict forms from previous stages of copying. The prevailing dialect of C has been identified as Hampshire, O is West Norfolk, and L from North-West Herefordshire.[1]

Nevertheless, there were restraints upon these scribes' translation of their exemplars, which may have been written copies or memorised performances

*For their generous help with material advice and information I am most grateful to Dr J. J. Smith, Prof. M. L. Samuels, and Mr T. F. Hoad; to Mr David Mills and Dr David Carpenter of Queen Mary College; and to Drs Derek Keene and Paul Brand. I am also indebted to Prof. Kane for having suggested that I make a textual study of *King Horn*. All responsibility for the interpretation of data in this article, and for any errors, is naturally my own.
[1] See A. McIntosh, 'A New Approach to Middle English Dialectology', *ES*, 44 (1963), 1–11, esp. 8f.; also M. Benskin and M. Laing, 'Translations and *Mischsprachen* in Middle English Manuscripts', *So Meny Peple Longages and Tonges: Philological Essays Presented to Angus McIntosh*, ed. M. Benskin and M. L. Samuels (Edinburgh, 1981), 55–106. The dialect of C has been identified by M. L. Samuels (in a private communication), who has also recently located L to the district around Leominster: 'The Dialect of the Scribe of the Harley Lyrics', *Poetica* [Tokyo], 19 (1984), 39–47. C. Revard has found a series of Ludlow deeds in the hand of the scribe of Harley 2253; see 'Richard Hurd and MS Harley 2253', *N&Q*, 224 (1979), 199–202. In Samuels's opinion this may indicate that the scribe migrated nine miles north to Ludlow to his place of work. The dialect of Scribe O was identified by A. McIntosh, 'The Language of the Extant Versions of *Havelok the Dane*', *MÆ*, 45 (1976), 36–49. A. McIntosh, M. L. Samuels, and M. Benskin, ed., *A Linguistic Atlas of Late Medieval English* (Aberdeen), covering the period 1350–1450 in particular, was not yet available when this paper was prepared.

they had heard: where translation would spoil a rhyme or mismetre a line, they tended to preserve the original form.

Besides such deliberate retention of the dialect forms of the original in the process of transmission, scribes might also restore rhymes to what they assumed to be their original form: the scribe of L apparently corrects rhymes to forms not current in his own dialect.[2] Perhaps L had heard the poem sung in its original dialect at some stage and retained a memory of the performance. However, L also sophisticates, that is, rewrites copy or fills lacunae on his own initiative, and not all readings where L stands alone will be found to be restorations of original forms; yet where L has a reading which is both demonstrably superior to the other two manuscripts, and is also almost certainly the source of the inferior readings of C and O, it does seem that L has, by some untraceable means, recovered the original form. Establishment of the original dialect of *KH* cannot be separated from the complex editorial situation imposed by the tradition.

Because each extant manuscript of *KH* presents a mixture of forms, estimates of the original dialect have differed widely. Most critics and editors seem to have considered the poet's dialect to be South-Western or South Midland, the Midlands being the locale selected by Lumby (1866).[3] As recently as 1981 W. A. Quinn and A. S. Hall designated the dialect 'South-Western or South Midland',[4] while in 1983 Brewer opted for 'Dorset or Somerset'.[5] Gibbs described the dialect of *KH* as 'Southern, with South-Eastern and Midland forms',[6] thus accepting Wissmann's identification of South-Eastern features in *KH*: Wissmann himself thought that the particular

---

[2] Rhymes corrected by L include 89 L *feyrhade*:*made*, 109 L *adrenche*:*penche*, 131 L *horn þe ȝyng*:*tidinge* (and other occurrences of *ȝing*), 661 L *ferste*:*berste*. Other instances of 'correction' are 523 L *geste* 'deed' (CO *gestes* 'guests'):*feste*, 885 L *flyten*:*smiten*, 951 L *in lutel spelle* (O *feyr of felle*, C *if beo þi wille*):*telle*, and 431 L *vnbowe* (O *nam boþe*, C *buȝe*):*yswowe*. In the last case, L's *vnbowe* makes sense, explains the O reading as thorn/wynn confusion, and has original *w* in place of C's *ȝ*. The rhyme is proved correct by *wowe*:*bowe* of *Seven Sages* (another Type II London Text): see M. L. Samuels, 'Chaucer's Spelling', *Middle English Studies Presented to Norman Davis*, ed. Douglas Gray and E. G. Stanley (Oxford, 1983), 18, and G. V. Smithers, *Kyng Alisaunder*, EETS, 237 (London, 1957), 40ff., where *o* between [u] and [u] becomes *u*; cf. R. Jordan, *Handbuch der Mittelenglischen Grammatik*, rev. H. Ch. Matthes (Heidelberg, 1934), §115, Anm. 2.

[3] *King Horn, Floriz and Blauncheflur, The Assumption of Our Lady*, EETS, 14 (London, 1866), rev. G. H. McKnight (1901).

[4] W. A. Quinn and A. S. Hall, *Jongleur, A Modified Theory of Oral Improvisation and its Effects on the Performance and Transmission of Middle English Romance* (Washington, 1982), 25.

[5] *English Gothic Literature* (London, 1983), 73f.

[6] A. C. Gibbs, ed., *Middle English Romances* (London and Evanston, Ill., 1966), 42.

area of the South-East in question was Essex;[7] Joseph Hall tentatively proposed Surrey, as 'possibly satisfying the conditions' of being near the Midlands (to account for a 'considerable admixture of Midland characteristics') but also near the middle South to account for influence from there.[8] The presence of both Midland and Southern characteristics in *KH* is not simply evidence that it originated in a border area, as Hall asserts, but may additionally indicate that *KH* was written in an area where the indigenous dialect was undergoing influence from elsewhere. London was such an area, where there was immigration in the late thirteenth and early fourteenth centuries from first the East Midlands, and later the Central Midlands. During this period, as Ekwall describes, and Samuels confirms, the originally Essex-based dialect of the City was modified by the adoption of Midland characteristics.[9] The Westminster dialect was not distinct from that of the City in being Middlesex-based, as used to be claimed, and, moreover, the Middlesex dialect had originally much in common with those of Essex and Kent. Heuser, in seeking to identify texts composed in the dialect of early London, concluded that there was too little evidence to locate *KH* in London;[10] since then, however, others have made more confident identification of London texts which provide data for comparison with the dialect of *KH*, and much place-name material has been published.

There is, however, another possible explanation for the Midland forms in *KH*: probably because it was popular, the poem was disseminated across Southern England as far North at least as Norfolk, and West to the Welsh

---

[7] *King Horn: Untersuchungen zur mittelenglischen Sprach- und Literaturgeschichte, QuF*, 16 (1876); supported but with a query and a suggestion of Essex by H. C. Wyld, *A Short History of English*, 3rd ed. (London, 1927), 103. W. Breier, 'Zur Lokalisierung des *King Horn*', *EStn*, 42 (1910), 307–9 is certain that the dialect is SE.

[8] *King Horn*, ed. Joseph Hall (Oxford, 1901), xliv.

[9] B. O. Eilert Ekwall, *Two Early London Subsidy Rolls* (Lund, 1951), 67–8, observes that immigration was largely from the Home Counties in the period prior to 1300, but considers that large numbers of immigrants from Norfolk and Suffolk in the first quarter of the fourteenth century, who were of the merchant class, may have affected the 'upper-class' London dialect. In *Studies on the Population of Medieval London* (Stockholm, 1956), Ekwall is more cautious on the immigration theory, but believes it was a chief factor in the dialectal change of early London (xiif., lxi–lxiii). Cf. M. L. Samuels, *Linguistic Evolution, with Special Reference to English* (Cambridge, 1972), 165–70 (esp. 169), and id., 'Chaucer's Spelling', 30, n. 27. Midland influence through trade was suggested by E. Dölle, *Zur Sprache Londons vor Chaucer* (1913; Tübingen, 1973), 88–90. H. C. Wyld, 'South-Eastern and South-East Midland Dialects in Middle English', *E&S*, 6 (1920), 113, 145, considered that the London dialect extended over Middlesex, part of Herts., and part of Essex, but did not derive features from S of the Thames; he thought that 'Kentish' features were probably from Essex, but he failed to identify $\bar{a} < \bar{æ}^1$, $\bar{æ}^2$ in both Essex and London dialects (see 116f., 132).

[10] W. Heuser, *Altlondon, mit besonderer Berücksichtigung des Dialekts* (Osnabrück, 1914), 58, 62.

Border, and the surviving manuscripts contain both original forms as relicts, and later accretions from scribes' or oral redactors' personal usage of Midland dialects. There are indeed many shared errors in the extant manuscripts which must derive from their exclusive common ancestor (e.c.a.), and in theory this could have been in Midland dialect. However, there seem to be no cases of shared error where a rhyme has been spoiled because the e.c.a. had been translated from the original dialect (unless of course these have been repaired by scribal correction like L's but on an extensive scale). This would seem to suggest that the e.c.a. was in the original dialect, and that the poem circulated first in the area of its composition. The possibility that this may have been London now has to be explored, together with the possible date of composition, because the London dialect changed in the late thirteenth century through extra-linguistic factors such as immigration, and *KH*, as has been suggested above, may contain an admixture of forms consistent with the later thirteenth-century London dialect.

Estimates of the date of composition of *KH* have varied widely. The Bibliography of the *Middle English Dictionary* and Severs's *Manual* give the long-accepted conventional dating of *c.* 1225.[11] This is far in advance of the period from *c.* 1280–1300 when other romances were translated into English, including *Havelok* (*Hav*), *Guy of Warwick*, *Beves*, *Arthour and Merlin* (*AM*), and *King Alisaunder* (*KA*); *Floris and Blauncheflour* is usually dated somewhat earlier at 1250, but it is also found in MS C, as the item preceding *KH*, and the date formerly assigned to C (see below) may be a reason for this dating. *Horn et Rigmel* (*HR*), the Anglo-Norman story of Horn and his beloved, was composed by 'Thomas' about the year 1175. During the period 1150–1250 most literature of entertainment was in Anglo-Norman.[12] There is no record that English was used for chivalric romance before 1250 – apart from *KH* itself, and then only if we assign to *KH* the date 1225. Although the aristocracy seem to have spoken English as their mother tongue from probably the early twelfth century, one would expect any version of the Horn story additional to *HR* before 1250 to be also in Anglo-Norman, unless *KH* were written for a very different audience or different purpose. Although some have recently assigned the rather later date of 1250 to *KH*,[13] no one seems to

[11] *MED*, 1, 12, '?1225', under the heading 'Southwestern Texts'. E. Severs, ed., *A Manual of the Writings in Middle English 1050–1500* (New Haven, 1967), 1. 13.
[12] *The Romance of King Horn*, vol. 1, ed. M. K. Pope, Anglo-Norman Text Society, 9–10 (Oxford, 1955); vol. 2, rev. and completed T. B. W. Reid, Anglo-Norman Text Society, 12–13 (Oxford, 1964). Reid dates *HR* 'not much later than 1170' (2, 124). M. D. Legge, *Anglo-Norman Literature and its Backgrounds* (Oxford, 1963) considers *HR* 'perhaps written in connexion with the Christmas festivities of 1171' celebrated by Henry II outside the walls of Dublin (99).
[13] E.g., D. Pearsall, *Old English and Middle English Poetry* (London, 1977), 113; Pearsall dates MS C to *c.* 1260 (295).

have made a case for dating the work after the de Montfort rebellion and the crisis of 1260–5, for example. *KH*, with its tale of a threatened royal family and a usurper, might form a stern *exemplum* at that time, especially for those who supported de Montfort even after his defeat.

There seem to be two reasons why *KH* has been dated 1225: one is the apparently early stage of development of phonology, syntax, and metrical form in the poem; the other, presumably, is a tacit acceptance of the date previously assigned to MS C, namely 1250/1260. Current opinions on the date of C, however, reckon this MS up to ninety years more recent than 1250; a consensus of opinion now gives a date of 'around 1300'.[14] This postdates the generally accepted date for O of *c*. 1290, and makes C only thirty to forty years older than L. The ages of the MSS do not, therefore, preclude our dating *KH* to the last quarter of the thirteenth century.[15] I shall, therefore, attempt to ascertain on linguistic grounds a more precise location and a later date for *KH* than those hitherto ascribed.

More precise information than is currently available on the written forms of dialects in thirteenth-century England will be to hand in a decade or so with the publication of an atlas of the dialects of Early Middle English, now being undertaken by members of the team which has just produced the *Linguistic Atlas of Later Middle English*. If that survey isolates a set of scribal forms which can be identified as typical London spellings, it may then be possible to find some of these preserved as relics in the extant manuscripts of *KH*; this might support a case for considering *KH* as a London poem, but would not prove more than that the e.c.a. was recorded in London dialect: it could have been taken down by a London scribe from actual performance, for example, after circulating orally; the authorial dialect was not necessarily that of the e.c.a.

The authorial dialect is traditionally identified by examining rhymes and attempting to locate the sounds which seem to be represented in them to an area in which, from other evidence available, they were probably indigenous. Because, even in copies far removed from the original, rhymes are very likely

---

[14] C. Hardwick, ed., *Catalogue of the Manuscripts Preserved in the Library of the University of Cambridge* (Cambridge, 1858), 3, 172–4, Art. 1526: 'xivth century'. *MED* dates MS C to 1300; G. Guddat-Figge, *A Catalogue of Manuscripts Containing Middle English Romances* (Munich, 1976), 99f., Item 13, dates it *c*. 1300, as does Severs, *Manual*, 1, 145 (under *Floris*). Malcolm Parkes suggests the first quarter of the fourteenth century (M. B. Parkes and R. Beadle, *Facsimile of Cambridge University Library MS Gg.4.27* [Cambridge, 1982]), while the extreme upper limit is suggested by P. Robinson, 's. xiv med.' ('A study of Some Aspects of the Transmission of English Verse Texts in Late Medieval Manuscripts', diss., Oxford, 1972, 111).

[15] Smithers has recently suggested that *Havelok* may date from the last decade of the thirteenth century, or even later: see 'Four Notes on *Havelok*', *So Meny Peple Longages and Tonges*, 191–209.

to be preserved in the authorial rhyme-spelling, and because accident may preserve the original spellings even in the body of the line as relicts, it seemed allowable to make preliminary analysis of the dialect of *KH* under the following headings: (a) evidence from rhymes; (b) identification in the three manuscripts of relict forms which seem to coincide with the dialect area suggested by the evidence in (a), but which do not correspond to the respective dialects of the three individual scribes.[16] Since *KH* is certainly from somewhere in the SE, I have compared the forms in (a) and (b) with those forms assigned to this general area in dialect studies and maps published by members of the dialect survey, and with those texts which they designate London dialect, Type II, Early Fourteenth Century. I have tried to use as evidence the place-names in the dialects of Essex, Kent, Middlesex, Surrey, and the City.[17] I have also compared other texts already associated with the SE: the rhymes in *The Owl and the Nightingale [O&N]*, and the forms of four localised texts from the South-East: the Essex *Vices and Virtues [VV]* (MSS Stowe 24 and Stowe 240, dated *c.* 1200); the Proclamation of Henry III issued in 1258 *[Proc1258]* (Public Record Office MS); the *Kentish Sermons [KS]* (MS Bodley Laud Misc. 471, *c.* 1275); and Dan Michel's *Ayenbite of Inwit [AI]* (1340). My aim was to assess what *KH* had in common with these, and what any similarity might indicate about its provenance.

In the following quotations from *KH*, the line references correspond to those of the edition of Joseph Hall; the reference corresponds to Hall's numbering of MS C in that edition, unless the sigil O or L is cited immediately following the line reference, when it refers to the independent numbering of O (Laud MS) or of L (Harley MS) in Hall's edition.

[16] The term 'relict' is defined in Benskin and Laing, 'Translations and *Mischsprachen*', 58.

[17] In addition to charts and maps published in the works cited in note 1 above, I have also used: M. L. Samuels, 'Some Applications of Middle English Dialectology', *ES*, 44 (1964), 81–94; M. L. Samuels, *Linguistic Evolution*, esp. 167; A. McIntosh, 'Word Geography in the Lexicography of Medieval English', *ANYAS*, 211 (1973), 55–66; M. L. Samuels and J. J. Smith, 'The Language of Gower', *NM*, 92 (1981), 295–304; J. J. Smith, 'Linguistic Features of Some Fifteenth-Century Middle English Manuscripts', *Manuscripts and Readers in Fifteenth-Century England*, ed. Derek Pearsall (Cambridge, 1983), 103, 107, 109; M. L. Samuels, 'Chaucer's Spelling', 17–37, esp. 22f.; M. L. Samuels, 'Langland's Dialect', *MÆ*, 54 (1985), 232–47. The place-name volumes used, and the abbreviations by which they are referred to in the text, are the following: J. E. B. Gover, A. Mawer, F. M. Stenton, *The Place-Names of Surrey [PNSur]*, English Place-Name Society, 11 (Cambridge, 1934); P. H. Reaney, *The Place-Names of Essex [PNEsx]*, English Place-Name Society, 12 (Cambridge, 1935); J. E. B. Gover, A. Mawer, F. M. Stenton, *The Place-Names of Middlesex, Apart from the City of London [PNMsx]*, English Place-Name Society, 18 (Cambridge, 1942); Eilert Ekwall, *Street-Names of the City of London [StNLdn]* (Oxford, 1954); and Eilert Ekwall, *Early London Personal Names [PersN]* (Lund, 1947).

(a) Evidence of Rhymes

Although this evidence is obviously difficult to identify and interpret, because of the textual complications, it is by no means an impenetrable tangle of non-authorial strands. Even where scribes did translate rhymes into their own dialect, this is frequently obvious. The underlying original reading is often recoverable, either because variants in other manuscripts preserve the original dialect form, or because the translation into scribal dialects produces such poor or non-existent rhymes that it is not difficult to deduce the original from which each clearly descends by independent variation. For instance, it appears that the poet himself used the form *ȝing* 'young' throughout. This form is normally described as Northern (Anglian *ȝing*, OED s.v. *young*),[18] but could perhaps be derived from OKt *ȝeng*; it is similar to the sb. *ȝingþe* in *KA* 269 (Auchinleck MS Hand 1) and to *ȝyngþe* in the Earliest Prose Psalter [*EPPs*], Ps. 87:6 (but contrast Ps. 24:7 *ȝengþe*), both early London Type II in Samuels's schema. The Norfolk scribe of O simply converted *ȝing* to *ȝong* in each of the ten occurrences, and so destroyed the rhymes on *king* and *ring*. It emerges that the heroine's full title in the original was *Rimenhild þe ȝing*, and the Hampshire scribe, C, availed himself of the assonance *-hild/ring* (*king/wedding*) at lines 614, 874, 1034, 1287, and 1484, and simply omitted the epithet *ȝing* altogether in these instances; in 443 he substituted *þat swete þing* for *ȝyng* (L; *ȝenge* O) to secure a rhyme on the verbal noun *swoȝning*; at 127, 279, 566, and 1188 he used the form *ȝonge*, despite the bad rhymes. Only the West Midland scribe L retained *ȝing*, or possibly restored it by conjecture.

Frequently when rhymes contained an unfamiliar dialect form or an unusual word or syntactical construction, the scribes simply dropped the entire couplet rather than produce a non-rhyme, for preservation of rhyme, even more than sense, governed their actions as scribal editors. The scribe of O was especially inclined to drop couplets which contained some difficult rhymes, and so, at times, was C. Consequently, when scribes do preserve a form which is not native to their dialect, in many cases this is likely to be original; e.g., *kesse*, which C preserves at 583 in rhyme and may have supplied in 431, where L has *cusse* both times (:*blesse*, *wisse*), while O omits the first

---

[18] Dickins and Wilson, *Early Middle English Texts* (London, 1951), 174, were unconvinced that the form was restricted to the North in OE; and A. Campbell, *Old English Grammar* (Oxford, 1959), §176, shows that, while *ȝing* was more common in Northumbrian than *giung* and *gigoð* is found exclusively there, nevertheless *ging* occurs in Vespasian Psalter (beside *gung*) and in other texts with a Mercian element, where it has arisen through development of a glide after the palatal, followed by shifted stress, loss of the second element of the diphthong, and loss of rounding through influence of the initial palatal. Breier thought *ȝing* could have arisen earlier than the fourteenth century in South (by a similar process): see 'Zur Lokalisierung des *King Horn*', 308.

couplet and has *kusse*:*blisse* at 583; at line 1208, however, both C and O read *cusse*/*kusse* while L has *kesse*. In these instances, the form either comprised part of the passive repertoire of C and L (whose own dialects would have had the form *cusse*) or has been restored by a process of 'guess-editing'. That O may have used a SW Midland exemplar seems to be indicated by nine instances of *kusse*/*kuste* beside the *kisse*/*kiste* forms of his own dialect. When seeking out the original dialect forms, therefore, we must bear in mind the caution that O frequently omits couplets when the going gets tough, so depriving us of one out of only three witnesses; that L, rising to the challenge, but perhaps over-emending, *may* have given us a non-authorial form; and that C, who is content with half-rhyme and assonance, may not in every instance have formed his inexact rhymes on one half of an original couplet at all, but have rewritten entirely (a tendency L is even more prone to when his editorial skills desert him).

With these provisos, the following meagre facts can be deduced about the original dialect of *KH*.

1. OE *ǣ¹* (Gmc *ǣ*) rhymes frequently with OE *ē̜*:

> 218 *forlete*:*swete*; 657 *aslepe*:*wepe*; 1257 *ete*:*suete*.

This rules out the West Saxon area as the place of composition, although scribe C (Hampshire) in fact lived within its boundaries.

2. Palatal diphthongisation does not seem to have occurred in the dialect which gave rise to the poet's forms, as the following examples show:

> 482 *ȝelde*:*welde*; 513, 558, 1301 *scheld*:*feld*; 915, 1085, 1403 *ȝerne* (but perhaps from *ȝeornian*):*werne* 'forbid' (cf. O 1413 *ȝerne*:*sterne* (:*hurne* L); 1217 *geste(s)*:*feste* 'feast'.

This contrasts with Essex *VV*, where *ȝiven*, *ȝiernan*, *ȝieldan* (etc.) are regular, but coincides with *KA* 6950 *ȝare* (:*care*) where *æ¹* has not undergone PD (Smithers, *KA*, p. 48); *KH* 75 *ȝare* 'year' (:*mare*) (om. OL) may present the same form, but if the rhyme is correct, then *ā* has not rounded (contrast 19 below).

3. In the dialect of OE from which the language of *KH* descends *i*- mutation of *ēa* was to *ē* rather than to *īe* as in W Saxon:

> 469 *nede*:*mede*; 677, 1261, *ihere* 'hear': *dere*, *chaere*; 397 *here* 'hear': *were*.

4. However, fracture of **æl* > *eal* (rather than retraction to *al*) is reflected in some rhymes, and not in others:

> (fracture): 845 *bihelde* (infin.):*felde*.

Such instances as 601 *bihelde*:*belde* 'bold' and 901 *welde*:*helde* are ambiguous (OL read *holde*:*bolde* in the former instance, although the W Norfolk O has the e- rhymes with fracture in 901f. and also 1391 *(h)elde* CO *(olde* L): *helde* CO *(holde* L), whereas the unfractured retracted type would be usual; cf. 375 *bolde*: *holde* COL.

But fracture has not taken place in the rhyme 87 *bald*: *admira[l]d*. Even the Central Southern MS C has *wolde*: *holde* at line 305, where it may be a relict form, either from the original or from a more northerly or easterly dialect in the course of transmission of the poem from its area of composition. In London, fractured and unfractured forms are found: *Proc1258* has both *healdan* and *halden*, but in *KA* the fractured type is more common (Smithers, *KA*, p. 48). *Old Ford (olim* Stepney) is *Eldeford(melne)* (cf. also 5, below) in the period 1230–1313, but *Oldeforde* is recorded in the same period (*PNMsx*, 136); *e* is more common in Middlesex, cf. *Harrow Weald*, with only occasional *a* forms from 1294 (*PNMsx*, 53). The situation is apparently similar in Essex, where OE *eald* occurs as *eld* or *ald* (later *old*) and *weald* is spelled with *e* occasionally, but almost invariably *a* (*PNEsx*, xxxv); cf. the simplex forms *North Weald*, 1086 *Walda*, *a* forms in majority in 13c, but *South Weald*, 1062 *Welde*, *a*/*e* about equal in 13c (*PNEsx*, 86, 135). *VV* has both *wealden* and *walte*; *KA* 3123 *belde*: *elde*, beside 6706 *to wolde*: *golde*, 7191 *bolde*: *Thorolde*. P. H. Reaney states that London originally had the fractured type, replaced, as in Essex, by *-ald* > *-old*.[19]

5. The case is simpler with OE *ẏ*, for which the reflex is regularly *e* in *KH* (Jordan §40), as in:

> 402 *fulle*: *pelle* (OE *pæll* or OF *paile*); 473 *leste* 'listen': *beste* (also 1263 C *luste*: *beste*, om OL); 861 *leste* 'wish': *reste*; 583 *kesse*: *blesse* (OL *kusse*); 609 *dunte*: *wente*; 633 *kyn*: *Men* (OL *kenne*: *menne*); 865, 985, etc., *kunne*: *Suddenne*; 1057 *legge* 'lay': *rigge* (OE *hrycg*), cf. *AI ope þe regge*; 1155 *fulle* 'fill' *(felle* L): *telle*; 1189 *custe* 'kissed': *reste* (cf. *keste*: *reste* OL); probably 661, 1191 *furste* 'first': *berste* (unless *berste* is *bürst* < *⋆brustiz-* 'injure'); 1207 *cusse*: *Westernesse* (*kesse* L); 1254 *felle* *(fulfulle* L): *belle*; cf. *KS uuluelden, folvellet* (imper. pl.), *AI uoluelle*; 1271 *reme* < OE *ryman*: *fleme*, < Angl. *fleman*; 1386 *merie*: *werie* (OL).

The textual complexity of the *KH* tradition, and the dialectal layering which results from this, are shown in 1209, where C avoids the original rhyme *keste*: *leste* by rewriting, which produces *ywisse*: *blisse*, while the E Midland MS O presents Western forms *kuste*: *luste*, and W Midland L the Central and Midland *kyste*: *lyste*. In 1377 O retains *kende* 'kind, species': *fende* 'fiend' of the original, while L omits the couplet and C varies to *cunde*: *þende* 'the end'. In 1254 the original form was probably *[fulfelle]* 'fulfil': *belle(n)* 'bells', but C reads *felle*, O *fullen* and L *fulfulle*. This SE *e* is regular in *KA* and frequent in

---

19 'On Certain Phonological Features of the Dialect of London', *EStn*, 59 (1925), 341, 345; and 'The Dialect of London in the Thirteenth Century', *EStn*, 61 (1927), 18.

AM.[20] *Cornhill* in London is *Cornhelle* 1193–1211 and *Cornhell* 1259–60, but *Cornhilla* 1115/6, *Cornhill*, *Cornhull(e)* in 1055, 1274–5, 1283/93, 1324, etc. (*StNLdn*, 186ff.); *Lambeth Hill* is recorded with *e* and *u* in 13c but *u* and *i* in 14c (*StNLdn*, 178). Tandridge, on the Surrey–Kent border, which has OE *hrycg* as its second element, is often *Tenregge* from 1086–1316, but *u/i* forms predominate; within Tandridge Hundred, OE *pynd* is *Pendell Ct, La Pende* 1259, cf. *KH* 1138 L *pende* 'enclosure, pond': *hende*. On the N Surrey bank of the Thames, Rotherhithe (OE *hryðer* + *hyð*) is *Rederheia* in 1100, *Retherhethe* 1224–1408, *u/o* forms appearing for the first element in 12c, and *i* for the second in the same period. However, *Geldeford* is the form used for Guildford (prob. OE *gylden*) in W Surrey in 13c, giving way to *i/u* spellings later in the century (*PNSur*, 9ff.). Stepney (*Stybbanhype*) has *e* in the second element 12 times, *i/u* 9 times in 13c, and *e* in the first element 9 times, *i/u* 18 times in 13c; for 1274 there is an entry *Stibbeneie al. Stebenuthe* (*PNMsx*, 149). Ek locates the incidence of OE $\breve{y} > e$ in an area centred on Kent, Essex, and Suffolk, with E Sussex, E Surrey, Middlesex and London City, Herts. and Cambs. as border areas.[21]

6. OE *ēa* + *h/g* has been smoothed to *e* in 1036 *iʒe* 'eye': *adriʒe*, infin. (< OE *adrēogan, dreʒe: eʒe* L), cf. *VV astrehte*, and also *AI heʒ, eʒe, leʒe*.[22] The sp. *i* in C reflects the 13c S and Midland change *e* + *g* > *i*: (Jordan §97.1b dates this to early 13c).

7. The evidence so far examined would not exclude the Middlesex/Kent/E Surrey area in the thirteenth century. This area is not ruled out by rhymes of *ǣ¹ : ǣ²* (Gmc *ai*) in:

> 1407 *mete* 'dream': *swete* 'sweat'; possibly 183 *rede* 'advise': *lede* 'lead', if *rede* < Gmc *rǣðan* (but there may be influence from wk vb *rǣdan*, = Goth *raiðjan, ǣ²*[23]); Reaney, 'Phonological Features', 339, suggests that tense *ẹ̄* for *ǣ¹* in London may have been introduced from Kent or Surrey. But *ǣ¹ : ǣ²* is not necessarily Kentish,[24] and see ref. in 11, below.

8. Rhymes of OE *ǣ² :* OE *ē* are not confined to Kent (where *ǣ²* appears as *ẹ̄*),

[20] O. D. Macrae-Gibson, ed., *Of Arthur and of Merlin*, vol. 2, EETS, 279 (London, 1979), 61.

[21] Karl-Gustav Ek, *The development of OE ȳ and ēo in S.E. Middle English* (Lund, 1972), 122f.

[22] Pamela Gradon, *The Ayenbite of Inwyt*, vol. 2, EETS, 278 (London, 1979), 25, points out that *ēa:* before [ ] and [ ] joins tense [e:].

[23] S. R. T. O. d'Ardenne, ed., *Þe Liflade ant te Passiun of Seinte Iuliene*, EETS, 248 (London, 1961), §127.

[24] E. J. Dobson, 'A New Edition of "The Owl and the Nightingale"', *N&Q*, 206 (1961), 374 (rev. of the ed. by E. G. Stanley [London, 1960]).

and such rhymes apparently occur in 217 *swete*:*forlete*; 715 *sprede* 'spread': *stede* 'steed'; 797 *fairhede*:*spede*; 907 *lede*:*bede* (*beodan*). However, rhymes between slack and tense *e* are fairly common in Middle English; see 11, below. In 1393 *lede*:*spede* C appears as *lade* 'lead':*made* 'made' L and *lede*:*made* 'made' O, probably indicating original [*lade*] (infin.):*made* (pret.), i.e. $\bar{æ}^2$:ā; this is a rhyme influenced by the Essex ā < $\bar{æ}^{1,2}$ (assuming that *lade* = 'lead').[25]

9. The form *slon*:*vpon* COL in 43 is matched in 85 *slon*:*flon* OL (*slen*:*flen* C) 'flay', OE *flēan* (cf. *sle*:*fle* 1369 C); *slon* is a Kt form and occurs in *KS he hit wolde slon*: Bennett and Smithers compare OKt Glosses 829 *ofslanne*,[26] and cf. *KA slo* (Smithers, *KA*, p. 46).

10. The rhyme *bure*:*foure* 1161f., which Dickens and Wilson reject as not a good rhyme (173), shows raising of tense *ō* to *ū* by preceding [i] in the diphthong [īo] developed by shifted stress from *ēo* (Kt *īo*) + *w*, as in *KS furti*, *yu*, *ywe* (Bennett and Smithers, 391), and *Proc1258 ʒew* 'you', *AI uour*, *uourti*, *you*, *your* (Gradon, 33, derives this from OKt [e:o] + w, under influence of preceding labial in the case of *uourti*); contrast *Proc1258 fowertiʒ(þe)*.

11. On the other hand, one might not expect OE *ēa* to rhyme with OE $\bar{æ}^1$ or OE $\bar{æ}^2$ in Kent,[27] where $\bar{æ}^1$, $\bar{æ}^2 > \bar{ę}$, whereas it is obvious that $\bar{æ}^1$ and $\bar{æ}^2$ would rhyme with *ēa* in a dialect of WS antecedent type, while $\bar{æ}^2$ would rhyme with *ēa* in an Anglian-based dialect, and $\bar{æ}^1$ with *ēa* in Essex, Herts., Beds., and Hunts., where *ēa* > $\bar{ę}$ (Jordan, §50, Anm. 1). An example of the last occurs in 309f., but is obscured by the Hants/Oxon spelling of C: *ire* 'ear':*were*. There seems to be an instance of $\bar{æ}^2$:*ēa* at 463 *eue* 'evening':*leue* 'leave' (sb.). But Dobson postulates a theory in which all ME $\bar{ę}$ words had a variant in $\bar{ę}$, and more specifically notes an apparently common raising of ME $\bar{ę}$ to $\bar{ę}$ in the 'Eastern' dialects (Essex, Suffolk, and Norfolk), especially Essex;[28] Dobson dates this raising of $\bar{ę}$ to the late 13c or early 14c, according to dialect, and refers to Fischer, *EStn*, 64 (1929), 1–19, who shows that in SE texts of the Alisaunder Group, ME $\bar{ę}$ of all origins, not only OE *ēa*, rhymes with ME $\bar{ę}$. Reaney, 'London in Thirteenth Century', 12, shows that 'both $\bar{æ}^1$ and $\bar{æ}^2$ were slack in London but both sometimes appear as tense vowels in

[25] So E. Mätzner, *Altenglische Sprachproben* (Berlin, 1867), 1. 229; cf. *The Earliest Complete English Prose Psalter*, ed. K. D. Bülbring, EETS, 97 (London, 1891), 158, Psalm 124:5 *laden*. Hall, *King Horn*, 213, took *lade* as possibly meaning 'load', as did W. H. French, *Essays on King Horn* (Ithaca, N.Y., 1940), 92n., 1393–4.

[26] J. A. W. Bennett and G. V. Smithers, *Early Middle English Verse and Prose*, 2nd ed. (Oxford, 1968), 393.

[27] Gradon, on the other hand, comments that OKt diphthong *ēa* produces a phoneme [ɛ:] in the first instance, which may have become tense by the time of lengthening in open accented syllables (37).

[28] E. J. Dobson, *English Pronunciation 1500–1700*, 2 vols. (Oxford, 1957), 2. 611.

the thirteenth century', although he insists that slack [ɛ:] is characteristic of the London dialect.

The above instances show the area of composition within a circle whose centre is N rather than S of the Thames, but not further N than SW Essex, nor further W than E Herts. Essex features are found in the following.

12. Rhymes based on the Essex reflex $\bar{a}$ for both OE $\bar{æ}^1$ and OE $\bar{æ}^2$ rule out Kent itself as the provenance; Ek locates this $\bar{a}$ < OE $\bar{æ}$ in a belt from Essex, Middlesex, London, Herts., S and E Beds., Hunts. and S and W Cambs., but centred on Essex, E Middlesex and London; the ousting of *a* by *e* started earlier in London and Middlesex; this feature has a very narrow border area, and is not found in Surrey, unlike 13:[29]

> 616 *laste* (OE *lǣsta*, 'least'): *haste* (OF hasté) in C (but L sophisticates with *beste*: *leste*, and O has the half-rhyme *haste*: *leste*); 659 *ilaste* 'last, endure' (infin.), O reads *ileste*: *i* (1 sg. pron.) *caste* (ON *kasta*) may be an instance of shortening (OE $\bar{æ}^2$ > æ̆ > ă); 892 ʒare (OE *gearo*): *bare* 'bier' (NWS *bēr*, WS *bǣr*); 799 *Cristesmasse*: *lasse* (with shortening? contrast 6 L *ileste* 'lasted', *laste* C, *lasten* O: *weste*); 1473 *late* 'let' (infin.): *gate*, where the noun is either a sg. formed on analogy with the OE pl. *gatu*, or OE *gæt*, without PD; OE *geat* is *gate* in *Stonygate*, Middlesex (1316), and *gate* is regular in the City street names (*StNLdn*, 190ff.); 1417 *slape* 'sleep' (sb): *rape* (prob. ON, cf. *hrapa* vb. or AN *raap* 'rape, sudden fear'). Cf. *Baremanlane* 1285 in the City < OE *bǣrman*/*bǣrmann* 'porter(s)' (*StNLdn*, 111). When shortened, OE $\bar{æ}$ is *a*: 20, 1046 *ladde*: *hadde*. *Proc1258* has *æ*, *ea* and *e* for $\bar{æ}^{1,2}$: *ilærde*, *ileawede*, and *lestinde*; there are ten rhymes of OE $\bar{æ}^2$ on $\bar{a}$ in *KA*, against five on $\bar{e}$.

13. However, the reflex of OE ă + *n* + *i*/*i* as *a* does not seem to occur in *KH* unless possibly in 67f. *of all wymmanne*: *þanne* CL (*wimmenne*: *onne* O), where it is most unlikely that *wimmanne* can be derived from the OE dat. pl. *wifmannum* (contrast 1366 *menne*: *Suddenne*). The *a* is usual in Essex (*Bulphan* < OE *burh* + *fænn* Bolegefanne 1269, with *fenne*/*fanne* forms in equal numbers in 13c and early 14c, and cf. *Four Wantz* < *wente*, and *Myland Lodge*, < *mīl* + *ænde*, where *a* sp. is preserved); *a* is also found in parts of Middlesex, cf. *Anedehea* < OE *ened* 'duck' (lost, formerly between Charing Cross and Westminster, *PNMsx*, 168). Zachrisson cites modern Essex dialect *wants* 'a meeting of three or four roads'.[30] The *a* occurs regularly in London documents of the 13c and 14c. No extant MS of *KH* has the *a* form at 733

---

[29] Karl-Gustave Ek, *The Development of OE æ̆ (i-mutated ă) before Nasals and OE ǣ in South-Eastern Middle English* (Lund, 1975), 56–8.

[30] R. E. Zachrisson, 'Notes on the Essex Dialect and the Origin of Vulgar London Speech', *EStn*, 59 (1925), 349.

ende : sende, 371f., 1117f. *hende : wende*, 911f., 121f. *(y)wende : ende*, 679, 1401 (O 718) *wende : schende*. Cf. *Proc1258 ænde*; in *AM a* is regular as a derivative of Gmc *ă* + nasal + *i/i* (ed. Macrae-Gibson, p. 61), but less so in *KA*: Macrae-Gibson would argue for an earlier date for *AM* because of this. Ek (*OE æ*, 26) locates this feature in Essex, E Middlesex, and London, centred on SW Essex, whence it spread in ME, with a residual area in E Surrey and E Sussex, and spreading into Kent in early 13c. *VV* has *wænd* for 'wend'. Zachrisson notes *Danecourt, Shottendane* in Kent (349).

14. The Essex–London form *sigge* is attested in the rhyme 1276 *segge : ligge* O, where O, alone of the three MSS, has the original rhyme; cf. *KA siggeþ* (pl.), and with 1240 *nekke : þikke* cf. *nykken AI*, page 56.

15. In 538 *sedes* (pret. 2sg.) 'said' : *dedes* (sb) OE *ĕ* + *g* has contracted to *-ēde* with lengthening of the vowel. This is also a S feature, cf. Bennett and Smithers, 277, and *VV sade, sæde, sede* 'said' (Jordan, §191 Anm.).

There seems to be no evidence in *KH* of the *ēo* > *ie* change which Ek locates in Essex, Cambs., Herts., Mx., Kent, and London (*OE ȳ and ēo*, 122, 124). The dialect of *KH* is not, therefore, pure Essex, but seems to belong near the border with London or Middlesex, and after the spread of other speakers into the London area had modified the original Essex-based dialect there. It cannot be pure Kentish either, for the reasons given, and because OKt *e* does not appear as a reflex of OE (WS) *æ*, nor *ie* for OKt *īo/ēo* (this would be concealed in any case by self-rhymes, e.g., 377, 673 *trewe : rewe*). Some further hints of dating are furnished by the following.

16. As in 14c London English, the pret. of *shall* is *scholde* (395) : *wolde(st)*, cf. *Orfeo* 467 *schold : hold*, *AI ssolden*, *KS solde*, *VV scolde*.

17. OE *æ* + *g* is usually kept separate from OE *e* + *g*, cf. 186 *pleie : galeie*; 1007 *weie : galeie*; *deie : abeie* (109), : *tweie* (888, 1346); 763 *preie : seie*; *deide : preide* 1185 (? error). The contrary may be true of 271 *seide : maide* (here O has the wrong reading *mede* 'bribe, reward', which may point to a misunderstood form *mede* < OKt *megden* in his exemplar). Jordan dates the change *ei* > *ai* to the second half of 13c (§95 Anm.).

18. Open accented syllable lengthening (OAS) may have taken place in the poet's dialect, but because he tends to rhyme open accented syllable words together, this cannot be proved. Two possible instances are: 75 *gode* 'God' : *forbode* (cf. *MED* s.v.*God*: inflected forms of the word *God* with a long vowel are attested in ME rhymes); 1266 *name : blame* (C only), but *blamen* in *AI* does not fall in with OE Class II weak verbs with long vowel, and may have been borrowed with short *a* (*blasmer*) (Gradon, 100f.). Jordan dates OAS to the first half of 13c in South (§25 and Anm. 4).

19. OE *ā* appears as *o* in, e.g., 335f. *oȝe:þroȝe* (OE *þrāȝ, þrāh*), but this may reflect scribal speech habits only; 4467 *ȝare* (nWS *garu*):*ifare* is equally ambiguous. 597 *stonde:honde* 'dogs' (C only) is probably an error (cf. *grounde: hounde* L). *Proc1258* has *moare*, implying rounding. In London, Broad St is *Bradestrete* (street, and Ward) from 1293 until 16c (apart from one instance of *Brodestrate* in *c.* 1215–30, the *a* is universal); in E Surrey, *Oxted* (< OE *āc*) is *Axstede* in 1219, but *Ocsted* from 1225 on, indicating about 1220 for *ā* > *ǭ* in that area, about 20 miles S of the City (*PNSur*, 332). Jordan, however, dates the rounding of *a* to late 12c in Kent (§44).

20. In the poet's dialect, [ɣ] > [w]: 669, 1205 *þinowe:knowe*, 984 *oȝe:iknowe*, 1010 *þroȝe* (OE *þrāg*):*blowe*, 1079 *loȝe:rowe*. This rules out Kent itself as the provenance, since there [ɣ] was retained in late Middle Kentish;[31] Jordan dates the vocalisation of [ɣ] to around 1400 in Kent, but as early as *c.* 1200 in Worcester (§186); cf. *KS daghen, laghe, seghen*, etc., and cf. *Proc1258 muȝe*; in *O&N*, however, [ɣ] is not preserved: 414 *wowe* < OE *woh:snowe*.

21. Monosyllabic verbs keep *-n* in infin.: 7 *quen:ben*, 1520 *quene:bene* OL; the OE *-ian* verbs are retained: 1385 *werie* (OE *werian*):*merye* OL. The ppl. has *-(e)n* in *Horn:(i)born* 10, 138, 510,:*forlor(e)n* 479 (C), :*iorne* 1146 (COL); *icume* 161 is ambiguous,:*gumes* C, but 161 in O is *grome:ycome*, and in L *gomen:ycomen*. The pres. 2 sg. ends in *-es*, e.g., 537 *dedes:sedes* and pres. pl. ends in *-e*: *stonde:londe* sb.

22. There is no glide before ȝ after back vowels in the spelling of 250 *poȝte* C, *þohte* L (contrast *þoute* O), etc.; C 755 *iȝe* is *eyȝen* in L (but see 6 above); cf. *VV þoht, noht, besohten*, etc., but *eiȝe, þeih* 'though', *Proc1258 eȝtetenþe, KA seiȝe, heiȝe, EPPs seiȝen* (beside *seȝe(n), heiȝe. Samuels dates this *u*-glide early 13c (*Linguistic Evolution*, 159).

The phonology of *KH* considered so far is not incompatible with a London provenance, but establishes nothing more specific on the date of composition than the general period some time after the end of the twelfth century. This evidence for date and provenance from rhyme is of course negated if the poet did not rhyme carefully. Here again, the corrupt state of the tradition creates difficulties. It is likely that an editor will regard a faulty rhyme shared by all manuscripts as evidence of archetypal error, for editing cannot function if the original was itself weak in sense and metrics, the very features by which scribal error is normally to be identified. The reading

> 275   þe stuard was in herte wo,
> For he nuste what to do   COL

---

[31] Karl Luick, *Historische Grammatik der Englischen Sprache*, 2 vols. (1914–40; Oxford, 1964), §402, Anm. 1.

may be such an archetypal error, or may exhibit raising of *o:* after *w*; since the metre and sense are weak, I assume e.c.a. error. Usually, however, a faulty rhyme in one MS appears correctly – or corrected – in another, and here one is forced to assume that the 'error' is in fact the weaker rhyme, rather than that the poet erred and was 'improved' by his scribes. Such improvement is not impossible, however, and probably frequently occurred in the scribal tradition of Middle English romances, but does not seem to have happened with *KH*. For example:

> 277 *þohte:þuhte* C (*bysohte:þohte* L; *wroute:þoute* O); 411 *biþohte: mihte* CO (*ohte* L).

Although in these and similar cases none of the variants may acutally present the right reading, they indicate attempts to repair corruption at a deep level, rather than independent attempts to improve on a poor original. In *flete:wepe* (159 L, 161 O, om. C) the rhyme is immediately restored by emending to the harder form *grete*, while 497 *yfere:luþere* C is probably not corrupt but a form of rhyme (see example under ii below) on the secondary syllable. Occasionally an alternative form of a word will secure a rhyme: 166 *verrade* (OE *gefēr* + *rǣden*, with *ā* for *ǣ²*):*makede*, where the syncopated form *made* will rhyme, but *⋆verrede* (*ē̆*) would not rhyme with *ĕ* in *makede*, but contrast *KA* 30056 (MS B) *Mede* 'Medes':*felaurede*.

On the other hand, there are instances where the poet does not seem to have been meticulously precise: he rhymes OF loan words with only approximately similar ME phonemes:

> 879 *compaynye:hiʒe* (possibly corrupt); 325 *bur:mesauentur* (325, 642)/ *couerture* (695), but cf. *Orfeo* 21, 46, etc., *auentoures*, on which Bliss remarks that this is a characteristic of North Normandy, and of parts of England where magnates from N Normandy settled, especially the SE Midlands;[32] 1267 *houe* (OE *hofe*):*proue(d)*; 313 *iliche* (OE *gelic*): *riche* (OF *riche*? or OE *rice* with short vowel or OAS lengthening); 403 *chere:swere* COL; 1111 *ber* 'beer':*squier*; 1185 *deide:preide* C (*deʒe: preʒe* L, *ded:bed* O); 1251 *bitraie:laie* (but cf. O *bywreyen:leyen*, probably only a minor grammatical corruption).

Some rhymes are products of C's dialect, e.g., 755f. *iʒe* 'eye':*siʒe* 'saw' (? pl.), and *diþe:iþe* (OE *deaþ, eaþe*).

It may be that 391 *sixe:nixte* C (*syxe:nexte* O, L sophisticates) is a corruption: the original seems to have had the form *sexe* 'six', twice confused by C or an antecedent scribe with *seue* (lines 96, 918), but there are other cases where final consonants do not rhyme exactly, and these seem to be original. They fall into three categories: (i) the cluster *-rst:rt/st*; (ii) 'rhymes' involving non-identical spirants, notably [*f*,˙*χ*], stops, or nasals; (iii) rhymes of *v:w*.

---

[32] A. J. Bliss, ed., *Sir Orfeo*, 2nd ed. (Oxford, 1966), xxiii, n. 2.

(iv) A fourth category seems to comprise rhyme between *e*:*er*. (v) Plurals seem to be irregular, as in many ME texts. (vi) Lowering of *i* seems to have taken place either after *w*, or before *l*. The following exemplify each category.

(i) 27f. *beste*:*werste* [Jordan, §166, dates this assimilation of *r* 'about 1300'; Dobson, *Pronunciation* 2: 966, §401 (c): 'early']; (cf. 724, 824 *beste*: *strengeste*, *faireste*, with rhyme on final unstressed syllable). Loss of *s*: 885f. L (904f. O) *furste*:*h(u)erte* (om. C); 927 *schorte*:*dorste* CO (*sherte*:*derste* L); 945 *biweste*:*Westernesse* C. *Belsetters Lane* > *Belliter Lane* (Stowe, cited in *StNLdn*, 58) shows loss of *s*, but not in the *-rst* cluster, while *Foster* < *St Vedast* shows the common AN intrusive *r* after *-st* (*StNLdn*, 161, n. 1). These must be eye-rhymes.

(ii) 145 *doster*:*poȝte* C; 389 *softe*:*dohter* LO (C corrupts); 697 *doȝter*: *ofte*; 903 *doȝter*:*lofte*, cf. *O&N*, 277 *foȝle*:*puuele*, ibid. 63 *vuele*:*fuȝele*. (Jordan, §196 Anm., thinks that *f*:*γ* is assonance; Dobson claims that ȝ and *v* grew more similar in ME (*Pronunciation* 1:128), and that [γ] > [f] (§§89, 371).) Probably assonantal: 51f. *gripe*:*smite*, cf. *O&N* 987 *wepen*:*forleten*; 501 *whit*:*ilik* C is an error, but shows C's tolerance of this kind of assonance; 21f. *sones*:*gomes*; 787f. *man*:*cam*; 1446 *sone*: *icome*; cf. *Hav* 1102f. *shop*:*ok*, 739f. *erde*:*erpe*.

(iii) 545 *proue*:*wowe* OL (*woȝe* C); 561 *trewe*:*leue* 'believe' CO; 793 *wowen*:*glouen* OL (*woȝe* C). There is perhaps a parallel in *Dowgate Hill* (City), prob. from OE *dufe* (?*dufena*, 'dove', *StNLdn*, 191). Cf. Reaney, 'London in Thirteenth Century', 19: *v*/*v* < *f* > [*u*], a sound change also noted in *PNEsx*, xxxvii, as a common Essex sound-change, e.g., *Warish* < *St Valery sur Somme*, (Ballivus) *Sancti Walerici*, 1236, to which foundation it was given by William I, *Whipp's Cross* < *Phypp(y)s Cross* 1517, and the frequent interchange in Essex between *ford*/*worth*, *werth*/*wood* in place-names. Dobson (*Pronunciation*, 2:984, §423) refers (in discussing preconsonantal [v] > [w]) to the South-Eastern dialectal change of inter-vocalic [v] to [w], but Jordan (§300) dates this to late 14c; (Zachrisson, 348, lists *w* for *v* as a characteristic of 15c standard taken from 'Eastern dialects', identified with Essex (353).

(iv) 145 *moder*:*gode*; 249f. *dohter*:*pohte* L (*douter*:*poute* O, *doster*:*poȝte* C, cf. (ii) above); 389 *softe*:*dohter* (LO); 697 *doȝter*:*ofte*; 903f. *doȝter*: *lofte* (CO). Interchange and loss of *l*, *n*, *r* are 'a characteristic of the later Essex dialect' (*PNEsx*, xxxviii), but not finally.

(v) Plurals seem to be especially irregular: *-es*/*en* seem to rhyme with each other or with *-e*, or perhaps *-e* plurals were regular in the original, e.g. 161f. *gumes*:*icume* C (*gomen*:*ycomen* L, *grome*:*ycome* O); 1059 *clopes*:*lope* COL; 1260 (O) *gestes*:*feste* (*geste*:*feste* C, *gestes*:*festes* L). In *KA* *-e*:*ep*, 7528 *afongep*:*long*, 7586 *sire*:*desirep*, which shows a similar disregard of final, unstressed, syllable.

(vi) Rhymes of *-ille*: *-elle* may signify a genuine dialectal variant, e.g., 365, 943 *wille*: *telle* (all MSS, perhaps lowering of *-e-* after *w-*, but contrast 943 *telle*: *spelle* L, *felle*: *telle* O); 373 *stille*: *duelle* CO, cf. *snelle*: *wille* 1463 C, contrast 999 *stille*: *wille* C; 1414 *pelte*: *hilte* C (*pylte* L, *pulte* O: the rhyme may be on OF *helte*). There may be a genuine lowering before *l*, cf. *Delewiȝe* 1199, *Delewyssh* 1350, Dulwich, < OE *dile* (*PNSur*, 19). (Zachrisson, 348: *e* for *i* is an E dialect characteristic adopted in 15c standard; cf. Luick, 543, Anm. 1, Dobson, *Pronunciation*, 2:570, §80; but contrast Jordan, §34, *e* raised to *i* before *l* (e.g., *fill* 'fell' in Chaucer, *sily* < *sely* in *SS*), dated from *c.* 1200).

The near-rhymes 479 *forloren*: *Horn*, 509 *iboren*: *Horn* resemble the paragogic vowel *e*, as in *O&N* 1260 *harem*, 1161 *hareme* 'harm', but probably show S lack of syncope between *r* and *n* (although in S loss of final *n* in ppl. might be expected, Jordan, §142b); Dölle regards the ppl. in *-en* as evidence of Midland influence in London dialect (*Zur Sprache Londons*, 89). 119 *drof*: *þerof* COL must depend on shift of stress into the normally unstressed syllable *-of*; 575 *þeran*: *lemman* CL is probably not *a* + *n* > *o* but weakened stress in *lemman*.

Evidence seems to show, therefore, that the poet of *KH* rhymed his work carefully, or at least as carefully as the poet of *O&N*, *pace* Stanley's strictures on that poet's rhyming;[33] apart from a few assonances, his rhymes were apparently exact in his own dialect. Where that dialect is to be located is suggested by features listed above: it must have been a border area inviting constrained usage of dialect features from some contiguous area such as Middlesex, replacing more habitual forms from further east, e.g., Essex and Kent; the antecedent OE dialect seems to lack many typical WS features.

(b) Relict Forms

The scribe of C himself came from an area of WS dialect forms; it is therefore instructive to examine C for instances of relict forms which have been retained in that MS from previous layers of copying and which do not correspond to the scribe's habitual usage. The form *sede* 688 C (cf. 19 above): *leide* (=*lede*) may be such an instance. 583 *kesse*: *blesse* (*kusse* / *cusse* OL) and similar rhymes are not valid evidence here, for while scribes of antecedent MSS in the C tradition might have preserved the rhyme for the very reason that only *kesse* would rhyme, C might have restored the rhyme, as L often seems to have done. Yet C so frequently spoils rhymes with [ɣ], which was still phonemic in his dialect, in contrast to the poet's, that 669 *þinowe*: *knowe* C may perhaps be considered a relict form. Similarly, to find the Essex form *late*: *gate* 'gate' at 1473 and the SE *kenne*: *Suddenne* at 1518, both very near the end of the poem,

---

[33] E. G. Stanley, ed., *The Owl and the Nightingale* (London, 1960), iiif.

when C had had plenty of time in which to perfect his translation of the dialect of his exemplar, is surprising, and perhaps evidence that, through fatigue, C was no longer translating efficiently: if so, his exemplar itself was in a SE dialect, and had not diffused far from the area of composition, which may explain why C is the most accurate MS of *KH* (though neither the earliest nor most complete).

The most significant relict forms, obviously, will be those within the line. Here 1231 *arnde* 'ran' C (cf. *ernde*: *bernde* L) matches *KA* (MS B) 4349 *barnd*: *beþ arnd*, cf. *KH* 689 *warne*: *berne* (probably OE *warnian*: OE *bærnan*), and *Brandewode* (Brentwood, Essex), 'burnt wood', 1279 (it is *Brendewode* in the 1319 Subsidy Roll (Ekwall, *Subsidy Rolls*, 224). C also has *ar(e)* (OE *ǣr*) twice, cf. 554 *arrer* O (Hall prints *aire*); *VV* has *ær* / *ar* (*arrer*, *ærrer*, *arst*, etc.) regularly. Samuels identifies *ar* as the 14c London form for 'ere'.[34] The Kt spelling *ss* occurs at 1144 *disse* CO, and 1142, 1143, 1134 *fiss(e)*, *fissere* C. But C has far fewer relicts than O, whose translation of his exemplar is less complete. For instance, although O has *kyrke* in rhyme at 932f., a couplet he himself seems to have composed, within the line he uses the SE form *cherches* at 63, and his retention of *cherchen*: *werche* (instead of *⋆kirke*: *wirke*) at 1380 may be a relict London form (Samuels identifies *werche* as an E London form), or at least a part of his passive repertoire, as are probably 1120 *of þerste* (*afurste* L, *ofþurste* C): *furste*, and 1191 *ferste*: *berste* (*furste* CO). O has *biforn* twice in mid-line (O 244, O 870); at 520 *biforn*: *Horn*, and Samuels identifies *biforn* as typical of Auchinleck Hand I. Similarly, O has the Essex *swiche* (cf. *VV swilch*) and *michel* three times (Essex, cf. *VV michel*, *muchel*) and S Essex *miche* twice; *dede* 'did', Kt / Essex occurs at O 354, cf. *VV*, *KS*, *AI dede* (cf. Campbell, *OE Grammar*, 348: the vowel in OE was short). All three MSS have *þar(e)* / *þore* sporadically, O four, C five and L six times (three of these fifteen instances are in rhyme): *þar* / *þær* is regular in *VV*. Forms for the 3 sg. fem. pers. pron. show probable relict forms in both L and O: *hy* 'she' occurs at 73 L (where Samuels identifies it as a Kt form ('Dialect of Harley Scribe', 41), 1125 O, *hye* at 262 O, 1237 O, and *he* at 71 C, 73 O, 308 L, 1202 O (with the reverse spelling *heo* for *he* at 649 C, 651 C, 779 C indicating confusion caused by an exemplar with *he* = 'she'); *hy* is the form found in the *KS*. Many of the past participles with *y-* prefix in O must have a similar source in the exemplar of this or an antecedent scribe (e.g., 186 *ycomen*, 172 *ycome*; 1170, 1176, 1180 *hycome*; cf. 541, 797 *comen*, 140, 1495 *come*; 583 *hy graue*). But O seems to have been derived from a tradition which had also passed through the hands of a western copyist, since this MS twice presents the form *dude* 'did' (beside *dede*, which occurs also in *Hav*) and in addition to *ferste* (beside *first*) also has *furste* at 1154, 679, and 904, in each instance in rhyme on *-e-*. This western element may in part account for the genetic relationship between

---

[34] 'Chaucer's Spelling', 31.

O and L, despite the fact that scribes L and C derive from geographically closer areas.[35]

The evidence so far examined explains why *KH* has so often been described as Western or South-Western. There are few relict forms which indicate undisputed SE origin, and some extant rhymes apparently reflect scribal repair rather than archetypally inherited forms. Paradoxically the 'non-rhymes' in (*a*, iii) are more indicative of dialect origin than obvious true-rhymes. Evidence does seem to support the SE, and more particularly, the London region, as the area in which *KH* was composed. When the dialect survey for the thirteenth century is published a more complete picture may emerge.

The dating, however, was not firmly established by the preceding assessment of the language of the original. Evidence that $\bar{a} > \bar{\varrho}$ and that OAS has probably taken place in the dialect of the original does not establish date, since the forms *ifoan* and *moare* in *Proc1258* seem to prove that in this mid-13c London text *a* has already been rounded, while on the other hand OAS lengthening may not have been fully worked out in the late 14c in Gower's Kentish (Gradon, 20, n. 3). Moreover, both *KS* and *AI* preserve grammatical gender (Bennett and Smithers, 392, Gradon, 85–97, esp. 95–7), *KS* more fully than *AI*; and cf. *Proc1258 ouer al þære kuneriche, of þan . . . redesmen*. In *KH* grammatical gender is sporadically preserved in the definite article: e.g., 674 *at þare truþe* C (*here* O, *þilke* L), dat. sg. fem.?; 624 *at þan orde* (*þen* L, *þe* O), dat. sg. masc.?; 1441 *þene castel* L (*þe* CO); 147 *þene heþene kyng* L dat. sg.? (*þe* C, *þat* O). These forms, like the use of *he* ref. sb. *ring* in 580 O, and eight other instances in the three MSS where 'he' refers to inanimate objects, may be scribal errors (147 L is a case in point); if not, they are relicts from earlier layers of copying, and probably original: metre requires a dissyllable at 674, for instance.

Similarly, vocabulary provides little clue to dating. At first sight it might seem that *KH* must be early because of the relative paucity of OF loan words other than those covering common-place objects, nouns of social relationship or function, and abstract nouns of administration, feudal service, or values.[36] OF derived nouns for abstract qualities in *KH* do not occur for the first time

---

[35] Sometimes L is closer to the original because fortuitously his dialect contains forms identical with those of the SE; e.g., 1155 *felle* (:*telle*), which must have been the poet's form, is shown on Samuels's map of *felle* to occur (if rarely) in an area which must just touch on the L scribe's region of Leominster–Ludlow (*Linguistic Evolution*, 122). In other cases, L may be emending, e.g., 1137 L *hende*:*pende* (? < *pyndan*), 1240 *nycke* 'neck':*þicke*, and 1315 L *on slape*:*yshape*.

[36] The total of OFr loans in *KH* is 107 of the 900 in the language before 1250. These words may possibly be derived from literary contexts, but are not abstruse and need not all have been derived via the Anglo-Norman *HR*, *pace* Christmann, 'Über das Verhältnis zwischen dem Anglo-Normannischen und dem Mittelenglischen "Horn"', *ZFSL*, 70 (1963), 166–81.

in ME in this poem, even on the traditional 1225 dating. It must be pure accident that *cosin* and *colur* 'complexion' are not recorded before *KH*. Most of the words from OF in *KH* appear in *Ancrene Riwle* and Katherine Group texts and must have formed part of the everyday vocabulary of the middle and upper classes. It may be significant that, in a poem of swift and vigorous action, only nineteen of the many verbs are OF loans and these all cover actions relating to feudalism or armed warfare.[37] There are two unusual loans: *preie* 'troop' and *bleine* (discussed below). One other loan, ON *ille* (lines 675, 1316), is significant in a S text, but it is not evidence of late date since it occurs in *O&N*.[38] Obsolescent native words such as *ac*, *nim* 'take', and *mid* (proved by the rhyme 628 *mitte* (*mid þe*):*sitte*), which are regular in *KH*, are also attested in the fourteenth century in some authors and hence no guide to date: all three occur throughout *AI*, Langland has *ac*, and Chaucer uses *nim* twice. It is also impossible to date *KH* precisely on the basis of its regular preservation of prefixed verbs, since there is no way of knowing whether the prefixes are all still formative, and the absence of the periphrastic subjunctive (esp. in vb. *to be*) is probably a metrical convenience in the short trimeter line: an archaism adopted for practical reasons.

Certain stylistic idiosyncrasies in *KH* do give the impression that the poem is 'early', but probably merely reflect the way the words were adjusted to a musical score of some kind. These include the postpositing of possessive adjectives and personal pronouns in the genitive case: L 881 *fader his*; 538 *wille þine*:*pine*; 1053 *cloþes myne*:*sclauyne*. This feature probably occurred far more in the original but has been modernised by scribes. Likewise the use of the full form of the possessive adj. before consonants as well as vowels (144 *of myne kenne*, 770 *mine beste*) is probably also metrically convenient (*min* only occurs before a vowel, *h* or hiatus in *AI*, but is regularly used before consonants in *KS*: *into mine wynyarde*, *inte mine beleaue*). The inversion of object and verb, together with emphatic word order where an adverb occupies the head position, look 'archaic' to us, because they are common in earlier stages of the language, but may again be metrical conveniences, or even perhaps vestigial survivors of some earlier version of the poem: 930 *A writ he dude deuise*; 1300 *& vp he ȝede to londe*. These inversions seem also to have occurred more frequently in the original, and are only sporadically preserved in the extant MSS (e.g., 1414 *Wolde vp to londe* C, *swymme wolde to londe* L, *Wolde suemme to londe* O, probably for *vp wolde to londe* in original). This is also the case with the absence of an article, where later usage, including that of the scribes of *KH*, would employ the def. or indef. art. (1201 *To herte knif heo*

---

[37] E.g., *adute, ariue, assaille, bigile, bitraie, chaungi, devise, dubbe, faille, fine, giled, graunt, lace, scaped, serue, spuse, strive* (and sb.), *tuche* and *turne*.

[38] *O&N*, 421, 1536; the word is not found in Chaucer, except in the Northernisms of the *Reeve's Tale*, and does not occur in *AI*. See Dobson, 'New Edition', 385.

sette; 1144 *Drink to me of disse* / *Drink to horn of horne* (O: *of þy disse*); 1261 *Horn sat on chaere* (*on his chaere* O). All these features look to me like the typical syntax of a song or ballad,[39] rather than evidence of early composition. *KH* is considerably less inflected than Essex *VV* (*c.* 1200), for example, but employs articles far less than *KS* (dated 1275 in *MED*). Evidence of provenance is not incompatible with early Type II London dialect; the relatively few Essex forms seem to point to a date nearer to the early 14c Type II London texts (Auchinleck MS, hands I and III, Pepysian Gospel Harmony, Earliest Prose Psalter) than to the earlier Essex type of London dialect.[40]

If the date and dialect of *KH* are fixed more firmly than this in the future, a question of editorial procedure may arise. Normal editorial practice involves selecting the MS which is most complete, most consistent in dialect, and, if possible, closest to the poet's own dialect. It is clear that the MS which most closely matches the SE dialect of the poet is the SE Midland MS O, early but incomplete, often incompetent. The other two MSS give a misleading impression of western origins; C, however, is comparatively accurate (albeit in a wildly inaccurate tradition) and less subject to rewriting. Should *KH* be edited in such a way that the original dialect forms are restored? This seems to have been the partial intention of one of its medieval editors (L). Although Kane and Donaldson were content to opt for a B version MS of *Piers Plowman* (TCC MS B.15.17) in the language of a London scribe of about 1400 of exceptionally 'consistent spelling and systematic grammar' (Kane–Donaldson, 220), their uncertainty about Langland's linguistic habits has since been dispelled by Samuels, who has shown that Langland did indeed retain much of his Worcestershire dialect into adulthood after migration to London and has detected relict forms in the extant MSS of *PPl*.[41] Such identification poses the question of whether the editor should regularly restore original forms, especially those which are occasionally present as relics in the extant MS tradition.

In the case of *KH* there are two reasons for hesitating to restore the dialect of the original in an edition. The first is that the poem seems not to have been copied under supervised and controlled conditions, and, as far as we can tell, was apparently modified orally, perhaps at several stages in the transmission. Although in my opinion this amounted to no more than memory failure remedied by some patching of text, often through a certain amount of memorial contamination from one part of the poem into another, some would consider that any oral transmission of a work inevitably involves re-composition; and, further, that for popular works such as romances there is

---

[39] Cf. Dobson, 'New Edition', 376.
[40] Samuels, *Linguistic Evolution*, 166f.; id. 'Chaucer's Spelling', 22f.
[41] *MÆ*, 54 (1985), 232–47.

rewriting with scribal transmission also.[42] It follows that if a popular work is 're-composed' in a dialect even slightly removed from the author's, the resulting work, especially if such reworking is repeated, will resemble the *mischsprache* successive scribes might produce. While it may be possible for a skilled editor to determine such layers of composition, and their relevant dialects, the effort would be arduous, and the results not meaningful, for each 'rewriter' would have worked over the existing parts of the poem, translating into his own dialect wherever feasible: the open display of all the excavated strata would not present the poem as any contemporary would have experienced it.

But the second problem in relation to *KH* is that in any case the original seems to have been written in a border dialect, where alternative forms were available to the poet: in self-rhymes we have no means of knowing which dialect variant he may have used. What is more, if *KH* really is a London poem, it was written at a time when immigration into the City was creating a change in prevailing linguistic patterns in that dialect, opening up the poet's own active repertoire of available forms and providing a valuable resource in the exigencies of rhyming. Even when the poet's dialect is established, the best recourse with *KH* seems to be to retain the grammatical and phonological features of the copy text, while restoring such rhymes as have been damaged by scribal translation if their original forms are undisputable. The result will

---

[42] A. C. Baugh, 'Improvisation in the Middle English Romance', *PAPS*, 103 (1959), 440: 'some of the Middle English romances owe their final form in part to improvisation'. S. T. Knight, 'The Oral Transmission of *Sir Launfal*', *MÆ*, 38 (1969), 164–70, shows that Chestre's *Sir Launfal* is derived from an orally known version of *Sir Laundevale*. W. E. Holland, 'Formulaic Diction and the Descent of a Middle English Romance', *Speculum*, 48 (1973), 89–109, questions the reliability of traditional means of textual editing where scribes substituted formulas, wrote from memory, or took down dictated performances, and reckons it unlikely 'that any unbroken chain of written texts connects the existing manuscripts' of *Arthour and Merlin*. D. Pearsall, 'The English Romance in the Fifteenth Century', *E&S*, n.s., 29 (1976), 59 states that 'the process of change continues after the poem is written down', following M. Mills, 'A Medieval Reviser at Work', *MÆ*, 32 (1963), 22: 'quite complex distortions of the original can have been produced by a single act of writing down the text'. In 'Middle English Romance and Its Audiences', *Historical and Editorial Studies in Medieval and Early Modern English*, ed. M-J. Arn and H. Wirtjes (Groningen, 1985), Pearsall says: 'The surviving manuscripts of poems like *King Horn* or *Beves of Hamtoun* show a range of textual variation within the individual romance which it is difficult to attribute to the normal processes of scribal transmission' (41). John Hirsh, however, in '*Havelok* 2933', *NM*, 78 (1977), 346f., suggests that romances were transmitted in written rather than oral form, on the evidence of four codices which he has examined; and J. R. Hurt, 'The Texts of *King Horn*', *Journal of the Folklore Institute*, 7 (1970), 47–59, welds the two views by concluding that *KH* began as an oral-formulaic poem which was taken down from dictation and transmitted subsequently by scribes familiar with the oral-formulaic method. See also Quinn and Hall, *Jongleur*. My own view of *KH* is given in my edition, *King Horn* (New York, 1984), 24–33.

be a '*mischsprache*', but in this case not much more so than the contemporary audiences will have encountered.

If *KH* was indeed written in or near London, its first audience must have consisted of London citizens, probably the merchants of the City, familiar with Anglo-Norman for business purposes and perhaps engaged in some official business with court dignitaries, but less interested in the socially and culturally prestigious Anglo-Norman literature. *KH* is conventionally feudal in tone, but the poet was not concerned with the elaboration of courtly detail and etiquette. Long, often formal and dignified conversations occur in *KH*,[43] but there is a confident *insouciance* about how the aristocracy really conduct their lives. Horn is handed over to the steward for instruction in musicianship and in serving at table,[44] but there is no mention of martial training,[45] which scribe O found incredible, and inserted a line (perhaps from the A-N *HR*) describing Horn's education in riding with shield (O 241); moreover, Horn is given no scholarly education that we hear of (though interestingly both he and Aþulf can write, whereas Rimenhild uses Aþulf as her amanuensis). In apparent contrast to the aristocracy, at least in the fourteenth century, London citizens were not interested in education beyond the requirements of business and actually blocked the licensing of schools.[46] When Horn is out hunting he is apparently out 'shooting' alone; there is no mention of companions, nor of the elaborate etiquette of the hunt, such as occurs in *Sir Gawain*, details which an audience of gentry or nobility would have found indispensable. Merchants certainly did copy the country gentry, into whose ranks they married quite frequently, but their idea of hunting seems to have been limited to the small-scale: one London citizen enclosed two hundred acres for hunting,[47] hardly enough for an organised hunting-party of the kind

---

[43] The significance of conversation in *KH* is shown by the amount of direct speech in the narrative: 692 lines, against 838 of narrative, as has been pointed out by Mary Hynes-Berry, 'Cohesion in *King Horn* and *Sir Orfeo*', *Speculum*, 50 (1975), 652.

[44] The term *stiward* for Aþelbrus's rôle could be significant. By 1293 or earlier there was only one Steward of the Royal Household (by 1274 he was Hugh Fitz Otto) who had the important rôle of mediating between Court and the clerics and barons who assisted in running the country. Fitz Otto had Custody of the Tower of London after the Battle of Evesham and had been with Edward on Crusade, becoming Steward of the Royal Household before Edward's return in 1274. See F. M. Powicke, *The Thirteenth Century, 1216–1307* (Oxford, 1953), 323, citing Foedera 1.2.585; also S. L. Thrupp, *The Merchant Class of Medieval London [1300–1500]*, (Chicago, 1948), 261.

[45] *KH*, lines 229–40.

[46] Thrupp, 158. There were only three approved church schools from the twelfth century to the fifteenth: several were closed in 1393 because their masters lacked the proper degree, and schools were forced to close in 1446 and 1447; another could not continue; a 15c bequest to found a school in the Leadenhall market chapel was never implemented. Schooling seems to have been 'limited to a grounding in the three R's' at the time of apprenticeship (Thrupp, 159).

[47] Thrupp, 145.

described in *Sir Gawain* or *The Awntyrs off Arthure*. There are similar omissions in *KH* in the scenes of feasting, and in the arming, dubbing, and coronation motifs: these romance themes are included cursorily, the detail is always omitted.[48] It is this omission of detail which makes loans from OF so sparse, for the terminology and epithets in any detailed courtly and chivalric episodes would have been OF derived. The selectivity of the narrative presentation also contributes to the terse, ballad-like mode of the poem: the 'primitive' feel of the poem is an illusion. The poem may have been reworked from traditional matter to present a straightforward political message.

In some ways *KH* is analogous to the political events of the 1270s: Edward I had taken the cross in June 1268, landing at Acre in 1271, and was abroad on his crusade when his father, Henry III, died in 1272. Edward returned in 1274 and was crowned on 18 August of that year. An old tale of a prince returning to claim his kingdom after fighting Saracens would have a particular poignancy in the mid-1270s. Moreover, Edward already had a close connection with the City, having been commissioned by his father to restore their full liberties to the citizens, with the election of mayor and sheriffs, in 1270.[49] London had received de Montfort in 1263 and been deprived of its privileges as a reprisal, with the Tower and custody of the City being placed by Henry III in the hands of his son, the Lord Edward. After 1270 the City was at peace, and the supremacy of the leading families (who had anyway remained loyal to the Crown) was again assured, and when a handful of Simon's supporters, who had fled the City, tried to return, they were expelled at Christmas 1269.[50] Londoners had no reason not to be royalist in sentiment by 1274.

Who first commissioned the poem *KH* with its celebration of the triumphs of kingship must remain a speculation. There are two possible clues: when Horn blackens his face to disguise himself as a beggar *And al bicolmede his swere* (1064), he acquires a **colmie** snute (1082). *Culm* is a word which seems to have been used more often of sea-coal dust, rather than charcoal,[51] and the sea-coal trade from Newcastle to London developed during the thirteenth

---

[48] In *HR* the battle scenes are extensive and detailed. In the second third of the poem 57 laisses are devoted to fighting, and in all a quarter of the poem deals with battle episodes, nearly 700 lines with actual fighting: see M. K. Pope, 'The *Romance of Horn* and *King Horn*', *MÆ*, 25 (1956–7), 164–7. By contrast only 50 lines in *KH* describe actual fighting.

[49] F. M. Powicke, *King Henry III and the Lord Edward. The Community of the Realm in the Thirteenth Century*, 2 vols. (Oxford, 1947), 549f.

[50] Powicke, *King Henry III*, 550.

[51] S.v. *colme*. The sb. is only recorded for the 14c and 15c. *MED* and *OED* cite a record for Nottingham 1348, 'illam partem minerae carbonum marinorum et culmorum', where association with sea-coal may imply that coal-dust and not charcoal fragments were meant. There is one quotation in *OED* (s.v. *coom*), from John Evelyn (1664), which refers to charcoal.

century; perhaps these expressions would have especial point to a London audience in this period. The other clue is the unusual word *bleine*, preserved only in O, < OF *baleine*, 'large fish, whale', this being Horn's rationalisation of the monster of Rimenhild's prophetic dream. The only other entries in *MED* for this word are 14c and 15c accounts of the capture and import of large fish and the decorative use of whale ivory;[52] *b(a)leine* seems to be a technical term, doubly unusual in *KH* with its low incidence of OF loans; it must have meant most to those whose business it was to catch or vend such large fish, or claim them as crown property when stranded. The officers responsible for such claims would be the King's sheriff, the escheator and perhaps the coroner; fishmongers might well have disposed of the whale meat and blubber. A whale did come up river as far as the City in February 1309.[53] There is another reference to fishing in *KH*, when Horn returns in disguise to rescue Rimenhild from marriage to Mody; announcing his identity to her in riddle, he declares that he is a fisherman:

> 1134 *ihc am fissere*; 1143 *Ihc am icome to fisse*.

In *HR* this episode lacks point: Horn makes the declaration to his betrayer Wikele (Fikenhild) as Wikele escorts Horn's rival Modin to his marriage with Rigmel; there it is not an echo of foregoing narrative, but in *KH* the fishing reference is to Rimenhild's dream.[54] If the A-N version is that of the original Horn story,[55] then the English poet not only showed intelligence in providing Rimenhild with a dream to match the disclosure episode, but may also have done so to give his version added relevance for an audience involved in the fish trade. The Fish Merchants were a powerful guild, based in the Bridge Ward. The sea is a prominent feature in the tale of Horn, and in *KH* the sea-voyage motif is used to mark narrative divisions which chart the stages in the hero's self-realisation. This inherited narrative feature is made prominent in *KH* by highlighting the perils of navigation, pirates, sickness at sea, and drowning, all relevant to a merchant community.[56] At the opening of the

---

[52] S.v. *baleine*; there are also two comparisons of skin texture to whale ivory.

[53] *Annales londonienses and Annales paulini*, *Chronicles of the Reigns of Edward I and Edward II*, ed. W. Stubbs, 2 vols., Rolls Series, 76 (London, 1882–3), 1. 157, 1. 267. I owe this reference to Dr Derek Keene of the Museum of London.

[54] In *HR* Horn's declaration to Rigmel takes the form of a riddle of a Goshawk which he left in mew seven years before; he has returned to see if it is still undamaged (*HR*, 4257–68).

[55] The existence of an 'Ur-Horn' is refuted by Christmann, 'Verhältnis', 181.

[56] Further maritime details are found in the two sea-dreams (see Hynes-Berry, 'Cohesion', 661), and in the six loan-words from OFr relating to river and sea: *galeie*, *grauel*, *i(s)le*, *passage* 'sea strait', *river* (and *ariue*), and *roche*. Perhaps significant too is the use of *sture* in *KH* 695 and 1471 apparently as a generic term for 'river'; there are five River Stours in Southern England, and Ekwall notes one instance in an Assize Roll of such apparent generic usage, where the River Test at Romsey is called *Swansture* in 1280: see *English River Names* (1928; Oxford, 1968), 381.

poem, Horn's father Murry challenges the pagan invaders to declare their trade interest:

40 He axede what isoȝte
Oþer to londe broȝte

much as a London alderman might do.

Merchants did not adopt the luxuries of Norman aristocratic life-style until the fifteenth century, living in houses used for the storage, offices, and workshops of their trade and the lodging of apprentices.[57] They were stoutly loyal to the Crown and to civil authority.[58] This sparse, utilitarian, and practical world matches that of *KH*, where little note is made of courtly etiquette: Horn actually eliminates his rival, whereas he finds him a bride in *HR*. Perhaps it is merely a coincidence that there was a family, prominent among the City Fishmongers' Guild over several generations in the thirteenth and early fourteenth centuries, whose surname was Horn.[59] Their most famous member was Andrew Horn, a fishmonger and lawyer; *KH*, however, probably derives from the time of his father or grandfather. Unfortunately, we cannot be sure that Richard and John Horn of the records were related to Andrew the fishmonger, but it seems likely that they too were fishmongers, and that Richard's father was the John Horn who was Sheriff of London during the 1270s; John was alderman of Bridge Ward, again perhaps indicating that he was a fishmonger.[60] Ekwall claims that the earliest reference to the Horns dates from 1248, with a reference to Henry Horn, whose brother

[57] Thrupp, Ch. 3, esp. 131–6.
[58] Thrupp 87; Edward I took £1,000 'as a "courtesy" in !289' and 2,000 marks for restoring the city's liberties in 1299. Such gifts were traditional, and often expedient.
[59] This was first noted by Heuser, *Altlondon*, 62.
[60] Details of Andrew Horn and three other family members are found in R. R. Sharpe, ed., *Calendar of Letter Books of the City of London: Letter Book C* (London, 1901), 157. The Richard Horn in this entry is perhaps the same John Horn's son, Richard, who in 1298 was made to answer to a jury from Bridge and Billingsgate Wards for moneys received by John while the latter was sheriff of London in the 1270s: see *Calendar of Early Mayor's Court Rolls*, ed. A. H. Thomas (Cambridge, 1924), 1. 49. If this is Richard Horn, fishmonger, then John is also likely to have been a fishmonger, for John was alderman of Bridge Ward, the Fishmongers' district: see M. Weinbaum, ed., *The London Eyre of 1276*, London Record Society, 12 (Leicester, 1976), Index. I am much indebted to Dr Brand for these references.
Nine Horns figure in Ekwall, *Two Early London Subsidy Rolls*. In 1292 John's widow Auice was assessed at vj.s viij.d (146, entry 92), and Walter and Richard, fishmongers, at xx.s each. Edmund, warden of Bridge and presumably a fishmonger, was assessed at xxvj.s viij.d (entry 55). Also in Bridge Ward are two Horns in the wine trade, Richard (entry 71) and Walter (entry 98). In the 1319 Roll, Richard, fishmonger, appears again with Andrew (214, entry 47). Stephen, warden of fishmongers, appears in 1307 (he died 1325). Two Johns appear in 1319: one surnamed 'de Suthwark' in documents of 1324, 1332, and 1342; one from Queenhithe (336, entry 48). Perhaps neither is related to Richard, Andrew, and Stephen.

John he identifies as the John who was Sheriff in 1272–3 and 1275–6, and alderman of Bridge from 1274 (or earlier) to 1282. The name was common (Ekwall cites Martin, Nicholas, and Edmund Horn for the period 1271–96) and probably all were from the same family.[61]

Connection of *KH* with the Horn family must remain conjectural, at least for the present. Nevertheless, it is in this kind of social context, perhaps in the setting of a banquet to celebrate the appointment of a sheriff or alderman and in the London of the 1270s, that *KH* seems to have had its original performance.

Queen Mary College

---

[61] *PersN*, 154f.; Andrew probably compiled *Liber Horn*, 1311 (155), but probably not *The Mirror of Justices*. Powicke attributes the *Mirror*, written *c*. 1285–90, to Andrew or his circle and suggests that it may have been 'a fantasy of his youth' (*Henry III*, 702, n. 1); but F. W. Maitland, ed., *The Mirror of Justices*, Selden Society, 7 (London, 1895), thought it not certain that Andrew Horn was its author, an opinion confirmed by E. F. J. Tucker, '*The Mirror of Justices*: Its Author and Preoccupations', *The Irish Jurist*, n.s., 9 (1974), 99–109. In 1327 Andrew Horn, as Chamberlain of the City, explained in English to the citizens assembled in the Guildhall the privileges confirmed by Edward II: see A. C. Baugh, *A History of the English Language*, 2nd ed. (Englewood Cliffs, N.J., 1957), 176, citing Stubbs, ed., *Chronicles of the Reigns of Edward I and Edward II*, 1. 325.

Patterns in Middle English Dialogues

W. A. DAVENPORT

Plato, Cicero, and Lucian are the founding fathers of the literary dialogue. Few Middle English works in dialogue form bear comparison with the ancient examples, but, grouped together, they form a substantial body of writing and display as wide a variety of purposes as their classical ancestors. At least eight vernacular works classifiable as dialogues, including *The Owl and the Nightingale* and *The Debate of the Body and the Soul*, survive from the twelfth or thirteenth century (plus one or two others with a major dialogue element). From the fourteenth century there are about twenty, including types as varied as *Winner and Waster*, *The Testament of Love*, and the religious dialogues in the Vernon MS, plus a strong dialogue element in other major works, including *Pearl*, *Piers Plowman*, and *Confessio Amantis*. From the fifteenth century there are over forty, ranging from short carols, through *chansons d'aventure*, bird-debates, semi-dramatic allegorical exchanges, and lengthy instructional catechisms to humanist explorations of the classical texts and traditions from which most of them originally stem. Despite the variations of date, length, and quality among these works, some interesting things emerge from an overall survey.[1] Utley, following Wells, divided them into debates and catechisms (with some sub-classes and extras).[2] Others have separated them into 'horizontal' and 'vertical' dialogues,[3] or into works with and without settings.[4] I propose to concentrate on two main ideas, the 'equal' contest and

---

[1] A complete survey was attempted in Elizabeth Merrill, *The Dialogue in English Literature* (New York, 1911).

[2] *A Manual of the Writings in Middle English 1050–1500*, vol. 3, ed. A. E. Hartung (New Haven, 1972). Chapter 7 by F. L. Utley lists debates, dialogues, and catechisms.

[3] Distinction made by Stephen Gilman, *The Art of La Celestina* (Madison, Wisconsin, 1956) and quoted by others.

[4] B. R. Voss, *Der Dialog in der frühchristlichen Literatur* (Munich, 1970), divides Augustine's dialogues into 'szenisch' (varying number of speakers, physical locus) and 'nichtszenisch' (only 2 speakers, usually a student/teacher colloquy). Quoted by Seth Lerer, *Boethius and Dialogue* (Princeton, N.J., 1985), 47; I am indebted to Lerer in general for the late classical background to dialogue. Voss's distinction could be adapted to distinguish between dialogue and drama.

the 'unequal' teacher/pupil dialogue, with some briefer references to the 'parliament',[5] a variant form of the contest. I am not attempting a history of these forms and they do not correspond to the Platonic, Ciceronian, and Lucianic dialogues, but it is appropriate to recognise that they have distant relationships with classical examples, as well as, in many cases, being translations or adaptations of medieval Latin texts.[6]

Through French court-of-love poems, in the form of bird-parliaments or assemblies of courtiers (plus Latin examples such as *The Council of Remiremont*), and allegorical assemblies such as the council of virtues in Alain de Lille's *Anticlaudianus* the English parliaments absorb the idea of the dialogue as a natural product of intellectual inquiry among equals. The inquiry is usually a narrow pragmatic or dogmatic one for medieval writers rather than an open, philosophical one as, in theory, it was in the Platonic symposium; but, just as Cicero retained the setting of Plato's *Phaedrus* in the *De Oratore*[7] while employing his own preferred dialogue technique of *disputatio in utramque partem*,[8] and as Macrobius set Servius, his custodian of educational tradition, in a group of grammarians in the *Saturnalia*,[9] so medieval English writers can use a group of three or more voices to create the illusion of freedom and comprehensiveness, even if the actual argument is rigged and selective.

The contest and the teacher/pupil dialogue show their Latin ancestry more directly, through Cicero's influence on medieval rhetoric and literary theory and on the pedagogical and forensic uses of disputation in medieval schools and law-courts in particular, through the development of debate as a favourite form for medieval Latin lyric poets, and through the use of dialogue as a text-book method of splitting up knowledge into sections. Cicero's interest in the theory of debate is clear in several places[10] and it is particularly interesting for the student of medieval dialogues that in the *Tusculan Disputations* Cicero showed himself aware of the tension between *disputatio* and *oratio* and tried to counteract the tendency of dialogue to deteriorate into monologue by developing debate with himself as a conscious variation.[11] Both the 'equal' and the

---

[5] On parliaments see W. Pieper, 'Das parlament in der m.e. Literatur', *Archiv*, 146 (1923), 187–212; D. S. Brewer, 'The Genre of *The Parliament of Fowls*', *MLR*, 53 (1958), 321–6; J. Wimsatt, *Chaucer and the French Love-Poets* (Chapel Hill, N. Carolina, 1968), Ch. 3.

[6] J. H. Hanford and J. M. Steadman, Jr, '*Death and Liffe*: An Alliterative Poem', *SP*, 15 (1918), 223–94, give a useful account of debate poetry.

[7] A point made by Joel B. Altman, *The Tudor Play of Mind* (Berkeley, 1978), 70, and the whole discussion of Platonic and Ciceronian dialogue in Ch. 3.

[8] See the excellent discussion of this method and of 'Cicero and Fiction' in Wesley Trimpi, 'The Quality of Fiction: the Rhetorical Transmission of Literary Theory', *Traditio*, 30 (1974), 1–118.

[9] Lerer, 19.

[10] Cicero, *De natura deorum*, 1.12, and *Academica*, 2.3.7; quoted by Lerer, 35.

[11] Lerer, 37–45.

'unequal' dialogues thus have points of contact with Cicero, one through the debating method of arguing alternately the sides of the question until by rhetorical skill a sufficient degree of probability had been established to permit choice, and the other through dialogue's usefulness to the teacher and its possibilities for exploring internal conflict and uncertainty. Such possibilities were, of course, explored by subsequent Latin writers who became authorities and sources in their turn: Augustine's externalisation of the process of mental debate in the *Soliloquia* and the combination of teaching dialogue with his son and of higher inner dialogue with Christ in *De Magistro*[12] are closer than Cicero to the derived experiences encountered in medieval dreams, allegories, and fictional presentations of wisdom, as is Boethius, who, like Augustine, combined in *De Consolatione Philosophiae* mental debate with the student's progress through a syllabus of study. Equally, with other forms, cross-currents are visible: Walther saw the classical eclogue and the methods of the monastic schools as explaining the impulse behind the medieval Latin debate-poems between winter/summer, wine/water, soul/ body, knight/ clerk as lovers, etc.,[13] and Raby suggests popular song as an additional factor in these lively and varied clerical pieces.[14] The exact literary history of the forms (except for some specific relationships between text and source) is too complex a matter to be dealt with in a short space; I want merely to register that the use of dialogue by Middle English writers could not but belong to the art of variation of existing patterns and that the creativity of the writers is visible in the ingenuity with which these variations were developed.

Direct influence sometimes seems to explain less than the vaguer one of pattern and formula. This I find to be the case with the relationship between dialogues and the history of disputation in the medieval schools. J. J. Murphy suggests that 'outside the classroom the methodology was translated directly into a pattern for writing' but it is in learned Latin works that he finds his examples.[15] True, the method sounds adaptable and seems to ensure balance:

> The disputation as practised in the thirteenth century is a discussion of a scientific question between two or more disputants, of whom one undertakes the role of defender of a particular opinion, while the other or others raise objections and difficulties against this opinion.[16]

But there were four or five different kinds of public disputation, depending on the function of the particular dispute, and in addition the private dis-

---

[12] Lerer, 46–56.

[13] H. Walther, *Das Streitgedicht in der lateinischen Literatur des Mittelalten* (Munich, 1920).

[14] F. J. E. Raby, *A History of Secular Latin Poetry in the Middle Ages*, 2 vols. (Oxford, 1957), vol. 2, Ch. 14, 5, 'The Poetical Debate'.

[15] J. J. Murphy, *Rhetoric in the Middle Ages* (Berkeley, 1974), 103.

[16] A. G. Little and F. Pelster, *Oxford Theology and Theologians, c. AD 1282–1302* (Oxford, 1934), 29.

putation, held by the master in the school for his own students; even the preliminary *quaestio in scolis*, where the student attempts to answer the teacher's question, might serve as a model. The disputatio therefore offers several possible patterns for use in fictional dialogue: master and student, with master summing up; student and respondent with master as declarer of the *quaestio* and pronouncer of the *determinatio*; the public dispute with a candidate for a degree faced by several senior masters, and so on. Evidence suggests that these outline patterns were more use in vernacular fictions than the detailed processes of dispute. Only *The Owl and the Nightingale* makes extended use of the terminology and stratagems of debate and of the law-court as a technique;[17] the two opponents are characterised in terms of their skill and cunning in escaping from the tight corners of argument; there is no positive 'right' answer to the argument, which distinguishes the poem from the medieval religious and moral debates where the 'right' speaker has to defend his beliefs against the tempting or scornful attacks of the wicked or mistaken opponent. But in other vernacular works what one finds is either piecemeal use of the terms and attitudes of debate, as with Will and the friars ('"*Contra!*" quod I as a clerc and comsed to disputen') and again with Scripture ('"*Contra!*" quod I, "by crist! þat kan I [wiþseye]"'),[18] or more extended argument of issues or presentation of opposing viewpoints without much use of the technical terms, let alone the logical rigour, of formal disputation.

The process of simplifying debate in vernacular poetry is observable in the Middle English versions of the Soul/Body debate. The Old English *Address of the Soul to the Body*, dialogue only in that the soul makes a series of antitheses, already shows the direction to be taken by the later English poets: theological precision and orthodoxy are sacrificed to dramatic and emotional expression of the universal theme of the conflict between impulse and conscience. The Middle English versions are based on different sources, two Latin poems of the twelfth and early thirteenth centuries, the Royal Debate, and the widely circulated *Dialogus inter Corpus et Animam* (the *Visio Philiberti*).[19] The thirteenth-century English *Debate of the Body and the Soul* retains the dialogue structure of the latter, but gives one extra speech to each antagonist; many lines are literal renderings of the Latin; others are suggested by it, but the English is livelier, more emotional in effect, more pungent in idiom. Ackerman

---

[17] See J. J. Murphy, 'Rhetoric and Dialectic in *The Owl and the Nightingale*', *Medieval Eloquence*, ed. J. J. Murphy (Berkeley, 1978), 198–230.

[18] Kane–Donaldson, Passus 8.20 and Passus 10.349. The same examples are used in the analysis of debate techniques by Myra Stokes, '*Sir Gawain and the Green Knight*: Fitt III as Debate', *NMS*, 25 (1981), 35–51.

[19] T. Wright, ed., *The Latin Poems commonly attributed to Walter Mapes*, Camden Society Old Series 16 (London, 1841), 95–106 for the Latin, 334–9 for the thirteenth-century English version, and 346–9 for a later treatment.

convincingly analysed the differences to show that the English writer has reduced the theological element and has infused into the work the spirit of parochial vernacular preaching and popular treatises;[20] it seems possible that popular preachers did not see the heresy of dualism lurking in the attribution of the active principle of evil to the body, nor grasp the theologians' conception of the soul as the incorporeal principle of life and the seat of the reason and the will. Other popular features identified by Ackerman are the use of the two figures as representatives of common humanity, the introduction of images from popular works and folk beliefs, and the consistent simplification of the argument.

The directions indicated of a reduction of the level of argument from balanced reasoning to simple didactic antithesis and a movement towards emotional contrast (plus introduction of 'local' references, new material, popular images, etc.) are ones which other 'equal' debates of the Middle English period confirm.

The thirteenth-century *Vices and Virtues* shares with the *Debate of the Body and the Soul* the assignment of a separate will to the body and so belongs to the same tradition of popular theology. But more significant as a sign of literary intention, particularly given its date, is its combination of the body/soul debate with a dialogue of personifications. Despite the theological and dialectical simplicity of the work, there is some sophistication of literary structure: within a religious confession-dialogue between Soul and Reason the text includes both the Soul/Body conflict and, inset into Reason's exposition of Virtues, a dialogue of the Daughters of God. The author rounds off the piece by thanking God for the knowledge and wisdom he has culled from so many writers (and Cicero, Boethius, Isidore, and Hugh of St Victor have been suggested as influences, among others), but it is not a mere compilation; without profundity or analytical precision the distinctions between the natures of body and soul are nevertheless intelligently placed between the opening exposition of Vice and the closing one of Virtue, so that the debate focuses the opposition between the two states and the didactic frame creates perspective for the central lament of the body, which effects the transition from reproof of evil to praise of good:

> Ic am heui, al so he ðe is imaked of ierðe; and hie is liht alswo ðe left, ðat is icleped *spiraculum uite*, ðat is, 'ðe blast of liue'. Hie is gost, and ic am dust; hie is heuenlich, and ich ie[r]ðlich; hie is of heiʒe kenne al swo hie ðe is godes aʒen anlicnesse, ic ham ðes forʒeltes Adames anlicnesse, þurh hwam ic am on muchele aruednesses, on hungre and on ðurste[s], on wacches and on swinkes, and on maniʒe[s] kennes wrecchades, sori and sorhfull, woninde and wepinde.[21]

[20] Robert W. Ackerman, 'The Debate of the Body and the Soul and Parochial Christianity', *Speculum*, 37 (1962), 541–65.

[21] *Vices and Virtues*, ed. F. Holthausen, EETS, 89 and 159 (London, 1888, 1921), 95.

In *Sawles Warde* one can see a similar process at work. The author's free adaptation of Chapters XIII, XIV, and XV of *De Anima* has created from part of a longer work a coherent literary structure of frame (the allegorical narrative of the house with its master Wit and its mistress Will) and included 'morality' dialogue.[22] This dialogue section itself has a symmetrical form, with the debate of the Daughters of God set between the arrival of *Fearlac*, messenger of Death, who describes the terrors of Hell, and the appearance of the contrary messenger *Liues luue* (*desiderium vitae aeternae* in the Latin) who makes the house shine with his light and describes the brilliance of God in Heaven, with Mary, the angels, patriarchs, martyrs, confessors, and the holy maidens. So the dialogue reaches resolution in putting fear to flight before the author reverts to third-person narration to complete the fable of the lord and lady and their household. Dialogue creates variety of effect but its inclusion is probably for its demonstrative and focusing power. The larger context is the representation of man's life and the theme of governing that life; the dramatic portion defines the contrary forces through spokesfigures who reveal visionary knowledge from beyond worldly experience (the fiction thus resembles dream-poems) and presents the argument about the governance of man's soul in an antiphonal pattern. The work goes in literary ingenuity beyond vivid illustration, which is where the main vernacular additions to the actual content lie.

The pattern of the combination of literary forms to create a 'framed contest' visible in these prose treatises is the design used by most of the longer debate poems in Middle English. Though not in dialogue form the fragments of *The Conflict of Wit and Will*[23] suggest that, while the poet's main energies were devoted to the verbal violence of alliterative battle poetry, the *psychomachia* was contained within a framework of moral purpose:

> By þis long' geste,
> Alle were bot' winde-lorne bot' ȝhef Witte follues.
>   By Witte þe wise kyng' wele mai we trow
> Ilk ane wey in þe werlde þat wilnes þe right,
> Þat bothe leute and loue louies with herte
> And leues on þer lefte hoende alle lither redes.
>   By Wille þe wick' wele mai we leue
> Alle þis manshedemen [*excommunicates*] als mani eren in toune,
> Þat haues oende and euste til þar euen-cristen.   (Fragment G)

The allegory of moral conflict within the human being is overtaken by the desire for broader social application: crude though the poem is, it is more

---

[22] *Sawles Warde*, ed. R. M. Wilson (Leeds, 1938). The resemblance to later morality plays results from the use by dramatists of *De Anima* as a source; the general question of the influence of dialogues on drama is one I have chosen to leave aside in this essay, though it is often implicit in what follows.
[23] *The Conflict of Wit and Will*, ed. Bruce Dickins (Leeds, 1937).

evidence of interest in combining literary strands – here Germanic battle poetry with religious allegory.

Winner and Waster[24] is a cleverer example of a similar poetic idea. Here the battle is verbal, not physical, but the setting and presentation arouse similar audience interest in the pageantry of armies, nobles in the field, heraldic colours and devices. The poem is not closely structured in its argument but has a loose symmetry of four speeches for each of the antagonists framed by long speeches for the Prince at the beginning and the King at the end, preceded by the poet's prologue of complaint of the times and entry into the dream (and perhaps, if the poem were complete, to be rounded off by a return). The effect is not so much of a debate of an issue as an antithesis of two equal personifications, a ritualised opposition dramatising the contrary aspects of worldly life. The vigorous expression of the opposite polarities of hoarders and enjoyers of the fruits of the earth is set between the formal speeches of Prince as herald and King as judge; they function to create the thematic context of the realm and its government as well as to act as officers controlling the contest, which becomes a mixture of dispute and tournament.

Again, in *Death and Life*[25] the opening passage (termed Prologue by Gollancz) defines the perspective of the poem by a prayer to Christ, which reminds the reader of values beyond death, and the contrasting transitoriness of earthly things:

> . . . all wasteth away & worthes to nought,
> When Death driueth att the doere with his darts keene.
>
> (9–10)

So the poet's voice, speaking for all men in general, defines the parameters of the poem before the elaborate scene-painting of the spring-time landscape (predisposing the reader towards the values of life), and then, in the dream, the transformation of the world into a diagram. Here, in parallel passages, the green-clad, laughing Life comes from the shimmering east, and Death, the foul, half-naked ghost from the north, to confront each other in formal exchanges of speech before Life's raising of the dead and the Dreamer's arousal from sleep assert the triumph of life and return the poem to the prayer from which it began. The debate pattern with its dream frame is deftly used as a device for retelling the narrative of Fall, Crucifixion, and Harrowing of Hell; New Testament history is thus refracted through allegorical fable which combines vivid physical detail with strong eschatological themes and familiar images (the Crucifixion as tournament, Death as bringer-down of great heroes). The pattern of dialogue is of five speeches which divide into two pairs separated by a brief middle speech which simply affirms what Life has already said in her opening accusation; Life thus enjoys both strong positions,

[24] *Winner and Waster*, ed. I. Gollancz (1921; Cambridge, 1974).
[25] *Death and Liffe*, ed. I. Gollancz (London, 1930).

like the master who issued the *quaestio* for debate and also pronounced the *determinatio* at the end. One could summarise the design of the whole as: (a) perspective in prologue; (b) amplification in tableau; (c) values analysed in debate; (d) outcome fused with affirmation of the opening. *Mutatis mutandis* this could stand as a blueprint for the other English debates, particularly those in the form of dreams.

It is this pattern which Langland applies in Passus 3 of *Piers Plowman* to focus the issue of the moral acceptability of financial reward. Although this debate before a judge with use of law-court terms of charge and counter-charge can be read as an instance of Langland's gift for endowing allegory with immediacy, that is as purely local vividness, it too is a 'framed contest'; the six alternating speeches of Mede and Conscience bring to a head the slowly festering discomforts established bit by bit in the contrasts of the Prologue, the identification of government and the relationship of worldly and spiritual as themes, the physical differences between Holy Church and Mede, and so on; after the trial the temporary resolution closes the perspective. Whereas other writers combine an ostensibly open (but, in fact, limited) argument with a moral frame which effectively confines and sometimes even settles the dispute, Langland uses the 'equality' of debate with greater intellectual purpose. He has absorbed the idea of welding the equal dialogue to a moral framework to create a double perspective; but in using the power of debate locally to focus issues he has not over-simplified, but allows the unsettling complexity of the issues to recur.

Some of the 'equal' contests in Middle English are, of course, simple antitheses after the manner of the Latin *altercacio* and the French and Anglo-Norman *estrif*. Both *pastourelles* among the Harley Lyrics, 'De Clerico et Puella' and 'The Meeting in the Wood' put up a brief show of opposition and then make a sudden, unjustified reversal.[26] Compared to Passus 3 of *Piers Plowman* the dialogue 'Mede and Much Thank'[27] is a trivial treatment of the same theme, an antithesis, supposedly overheard, between flatterer and faithful servitor, but the touches of satire and didacticism are applied with a light hand and its eleven rhyming stanzas present a pleasant enough exchange. The eight lines of 'The Saved and the Damned',[28] on the other hand, hardly get beyond doggerel labels which might accompany two drawings on a wall. The debates of heart and eye are more interesting, partly because, as with the body/soul debates which they resemble, one can see the relationship of Latin, French, and English versions and there are two English types, religious and secular. Carleton Brown points out that the transition from a literary,

[26] *The Harley Lyrics*, ed. G. L. Brook (Manchester, 1948), 39, 62.
[27] From MS Digby 102 in *Twenty-Six Political and Other Poems*, ed. J. Kail, EETS, 124 (London, 1904), 6–9.
[28] From MS Harley 7322 in *Political, Religious and Love Poems*, ed. F. J. Furnivall, EETS, 15 (1866; London, 1903), 269.

philosophical treatment of the theme to a homiletic one can already be seen in the differences between the Latin poem *Disputatio inter Cor et Oculum* and the Latin prose version in Merton College MS 248, which is the source of the brief French and English translations of the religious version in the same MS and of the slightly different version of the English in John Grimestone's Commonplace Book (1372).[29] There is no doubt in either version that the poem represents the process of reduction of witty game to moral demonstration. The secular English poem (based on a French *Débat du Cuer et de l'Oeil* which shows the familiar loosening and blurring of motive from the starting point of this courtly theme in Chrétien's *Cligès*), consists of over 800 lines of fifteenth-century courtly commonplaces in which, after a prologue of hunting and dalliance, the lamenting poet hears in sleep the contrary complaints of his heart and eye. The debate occupies a mere fifth of the poem, though it is more vital than the elaborate tournament between the two which follows and the flaccid rehearsal of the argument before Venus, who delegates the decision to all her servants and sends out a letter, carefully keeping a duplicate, to which we are all bidden, if we 'of trewe loue be set in the wey', to send in a reply; the 'openness' of debate endings could hardly be more democratically expressed. Hanford's brutal summing-up of the poem ('thanks to the joint efforts of the author, the translator and the scribe the poem is something worse than pedestrian')[30] confirms the reader's general feeling that medieval English writers had a heavy hand with courtly persiflage and that they tend to prefer the moral versions of debate.[31] The poem illustrates, however, the tendency to fit debate into the framework of dream-prologue and concluding judgement scene which seems as characteristic of the longer 'equal' dialogue poems as is the simplification of argument towards homiletic assertion of the debate treatment of religious and moral themes.

The tendency to set debate in narrative and/or moral frameworks (or, to put it more positively, the tendency to use dialogue within a larger work to focus the antithetical issues) is even more apparent with the 'parliaments' or dialogues for three or more voices. Chaucer's *The Parliament of Fowls* insets a particularly lively example but beneath the individuality of Chaucer's brio is a characteristic parliament pattern of speeches allotted to a number of spokespersons who together comprehensively represent a community (of human

---

[29] Carleton Brown, 'A Homiletical Debate between Heart and Eye', *MLN*, 30 (1915), 197–8. The Latin and the fifteenth-century French version are in T. Wright, 93–5 and 310–21. The secular English version is in E. P. Hammond, 'The Eye and the Heart', *Anglia*, 34 (1911), 235–65.

[30] J. H. Hanford, 'The Debate of Heart and Eye', *MLN*, 26 (1911), 161–5.

[31] The serious version of the soldier/clerk debate is more substantially represented in English than the courtly through Trevisa's translation of *Dialogus inter Militem et Clericum*: A Dialogue . . . concernynge the power spiritual and temporall. *John Trevisa Dialogus*, ed. A. J. Perry, EETS, 167 (London, 1925).

beings *qua* lovers in this case); their function is to argue out the theme established by the narrative parts of the work.[32] The personified figures of Youth, Middle Age, and Old Age in *The Parliament of the Three Ages*[33] comprehensively represent human life (though in fewer stages than in many medieval treatments of the Ages of Man) set within a dream frame which obliquely acts out the themes of heedless youthful enjoyment and middle-aged acquisitiveness needing the lesson of elderly detachment. The loose structure allows the parliament to dissolve into a teacher/pupil dialogue which fuses the time of man's life with historical time in its own comprehensive scheme of the Nine Worthies; the result is rather a hotch-potch. More carefully structured, though less vividly written, is another treatment of the Ages of Man which is largely in dialogue for a multitude of speakers, *The Mirror of the Periods of Man's Life*.[34] This may be grouped with the brief dialogue contention among the parts of man's body in 'The Description of Man's Limbs'[35] and the curious *Debate of the Carpenter's Tools*.[36] All three illustrate the use of the parliament mode to register the nature of division and disharmony in man's life (and in the social fabric of which he is microcosm) and the quest for its resolution (a pretty hopeless one in the carpenter's case!). As with the 'equal' dialogues between two speakers, medieval poets are keen enough to set the voices in lively exchange but their sense of form has the effect of limiting the extent of the parliamentary exchange to the exemplification of a homiletic theme; only Chaucer's parliament takes risks.[37]

The parliament is a recognised variant of the debate; it can suggest that conflict is being explored and judged in a more inclusive way. The major poets of the period, Chaucer and Langland, find more possibilities in the form than their contemporaries and successors; they see how useful it can be in a longer work to be able to shift from monologue to duologue to a company of voices. One way of seeing *The Canterbury Tales* is as the most ambitious of medieval parliament poems and one which includes other kinds of debate and dialogue within it. Langland uses the parliament as one of the several dialogue techniques by means of which he shifts the perspective in *Piers Plowman*.

The other main mode used in Middle English dialogues is the teacher/pupil

[32] Other bird parliaments include 'Birds' Praise of Love', Brown-Robbins no. 1506 and *The Parliament of Birds* in M. Andrew, ed., *Two Early Renaissance Bird Poems* (London, 1984).

[33] *The Parlement of the Thre Ages*, ed. M. Y. Offord, EETS, 246 (London, 1959).

[34] From MS Lambeth 853 (*c*. 1430) in *Hymns to the Virgin and Christ*, ed. F. J. Furnivall, EETS, 24 (London, 1867), 58–78.

[35] From MS Digby 102 in Kail, *Twenty-Six*, 64–9.

[36] From MS Ashmole 61 in W. Carew Hazlitt, *Remains of the Early Popular Poetry of England*, vol. 1 (London, 1864), 79–90.

[37] Despite the title in MS Lambeth 853, *Þe Deuelis Perlament* uses the mode in only one or two passages where various devils speak; it is mainly a narration of the duel between Christ and Satan: See Furnivall, *Hymns*, 41–57.

dialogue. Although most dialogues are removed from the context of the schoolroom (educational works such as Pecock's *Donet* excepted), writers inherited the attitudes of pedagogy with Latin works which they probably first met in the course of their own education and linked them with contemporary vernacular teaching, particularly religious instruction. The adaptation of 'school' approaches to different purposes is variously identifiable in Gower's use of the confessional dialogue as a process of moral discipline and of narrative classification, in Trevisa's turning of question/answer and statement/objection to the function of a literary preface to his translation of the *Polychronicon*, in the teaching dialogues in *Piers Plowman*, and in the mockery of the teacher/pupil relationship in Book 2 of *The House of Fame*. The teacher/pupil idea is often metaphorical; authors assume that man's rôle is that of learner and insist on the inferiority of the pupil not only in dialogue between man and Christ but in other confrontations such as those in dreams where the dreamer's rôle is associated with ignorance and bewilderment.

Some of the dialogues are examples of encyclopaedic instruction; a great sage's learning or a sequence of lessons in some branch of knowledge is arranged in question and answer form. Others are dialogues between human and superhuman figures where the human being is either being taught or tested or reformed. One of the earliest English examples, the Old English *Solomon and Saturn II*, displays characteristic patterns and problems, despite its strangeness in some respects. The two wise men here begin with a kind of debate in the form of riddles, but Saturn, a Chaldee, friend of Philistines and thus linked with enemies of God, moves from near-equality to increasing subordination and his rôle is thus modified from that of challenger for supremacy to that of sincere questioner and joyful recipient of new knowledge. The dialogue is thus a contest in which one contestant triumphs through knowledge. The knowledge given is sometimes obvious, sometimes esoteric; as Shippey points out, the more precise the information presented in 'wisdom' poems, the weaker now seems the effect.[38] He goes on to suggest that *Solomon and Saturn* may offer a clue to other Old English wisdom poems in its repeated condemnation of grumblers: the sages argue that the purpose of books and knowledge is to strengthen in adversity and to cheer people up. Such poems make us aware of the state of the world and encourage us not to be overwhelmed by it, either by offering religious hope or by calling on innate strength of mind.

The idea is applicable to a number of Middle English teacher/pupil dialogues, though some of these have limited theoretical, let alone literary, intent. The early twelfth-century Latin prose *Elucidarium*, attributed to Honorius of Autun, with Augustine and Anselm as authorities for its doctrine,

---

[38] T. A. Shippey, *Poems of Wisdom and Learning in Old English* (Cambridge, 1976), 21–8 (introduction) and 86–103 (text).

achieved wide circulation in Latin and produced two or three English prose versions, one from the twelfth century and another from the late fourteenth. In the original the three books of questions and answers for pupil and master cover God, Creation, Fall, Incarnation, Passion, Redemption, Eucharist, sin and piety, the afterlife, together with aspects of the Christian Church. Vernacular versions with some literary intention tended to select from this mass (as even the English prose translations do) and turn the dialogue into a matter of moral instruction as much as the communication of facts and ideas. One of the two fifteenth-century Winchester Dialogues, *Lucidus and Dubius*, turns selected portions of the *Elucidarium* into verse.[39] Without altering the basic instructional limitation of the exchange, the author has created some conflict of temperament between pupil and master, making Dubius rather truculent and Lucidus at first boastful and then needing to be long-suffering in the face of persistent questioning. There is a sense that the imparting of knowledge is being valued not only for its own sake but as a strengthening of character. The use of dialogue was in itself a device intended to present scientific or theological material in a progressive and readable manner and the literary uses of teacher/pupil dialogues consist of a variety of ways of developing that idea to increase the reader's involvement in the exposition. One way was to follow the example of Augustine and Boethius, by offering instruction as an answer to inner trouble of the mind and spirit; the sufferer's need can be a poignant interpretation of the pupil's ignorance. The closest Middle English attempt at an original Boethian (or Chaucerian–Boethian) dialogue is Thomas Usk's prose work *The Testament of Love*.[40]

It is Usk's noble intention to teach the nature of love and, through allegory, to illuminate the continuity between human and divine love. His prologues indicate his absorption of the medieval literary theory of scholastic commentators[41] and the likelihood is that Usk, stimulated by Chaucer, is using the teacher/pupil dialogue with full intellectual intention to exploit its combination of the autobiographical and theoretical, that is, to combine the troubles of his own times and society with the transcendent philosophy of charity. Usk, like Gower in *Confessio Amantis*, is taught to be a lover and to be virtuous. At the beginning the voice we hear is the sufferer's and the dialogue that of the self answering its own questions:

> O, where art thou now, frendship, that som-tyme, with laughande chere, madest bothe face and countenance to me-wardes? Truely, now art thou went out of towne. (Bk 1, Ch. 1)

[39] *Non-Cycle Plays and the Winchester Dialogues*, with Introduction by N. Davis (Leeds, 1979). See B. S. Lee, 'Lucidus and Dubius: a Fifteenth-Century Theological Debate and its Sources', *MÆ*, 45 (1976), 79–96.

[40] *Chaucerian and Other Pieces*. Supplement to the Works of Geoffrey Chaucer, ed. W. W. Skeat (Oxford, 1897).

[41] See A. J. Minnis, *Medieval Theory of Authorship* (London, 1984), 162–4.

Once Love appears Usk gives to the dialogue the decorum of the school-room:

> 'Sothly,' quod I, 'my wit is leude and I am ryht blynd, and that
> mater depe. How shulde I than haue waded? Lightly might I haue
> drenched, and spilt ther my-selfe!'
> 'Ye,' quod she, 'I shal helpe thee to swimme.' (Bk 3, Ch. 2)

He allows long speeches freely to take over from duologue but these are not
always for the teacher and they are split up by passages of briefer exchange. At
the end it is, surprisingly, the voice of the inadequate pupil which remains, as
Love 'starts' into his heart and ceases to be a separate voice. Love has taught
him what she can; Usk stays in character, the light of his knowledge blurred
by the 'cloude of unconning'. And so ought he to seem to us as a writer – no
great transformer of a literary genre perhaps, but one sensitive to its nature
and its possibilities.

The obviously much less ambitious *Mercy Passeth Righteousness*,[42] a dialogue
in twenty stanzas, also manages to convert instruction into the experience of
the growth of understanding. Here the pupil is a despairing, devil-taught
sinner who slowly learns the way to earn mercy and the extent of God's
generosity; in mid-poem the sinner moderates his despair, determines to serve
God, prays, confesses, and is given penance. The teaching process is made
interesting by the initial rejection of comfort, the drawing in of the Devil
as opposing tutor and the modification of the sinner's negation towards
acceptance of Christian discipline. The teacher/pupil dialogue of God and
man is ingeniously joined to the body/soul debate in 'How man's flesh
complained to God against Christ',[43] a long lament of the alienation between
body and soul followed by God's reproof. Other Christian dialogues take the
opportunity of reversing the emotional balance so that the teacher is the
sufferer and the pupil the unfeeling and unresponsive clay into which the
mould has to be impressed. Several Middle English poems initiate the
instructional process by means of impassioned complaint from Christ: 'This is
goddis owne compleynt', eleven stanzas based on the Reproaches, is not far
removed from monologue, but William of Lichfield's *Complaint of God or
Christ* is a substantial debate showing carefully structured tension in Christ's
charges and man's responses.[44]

The use of the Devil as pseudo-instructor is another way of turning
teacher/pupil dialogue into conflict. The defeat of the demonic attempt to
outwit turns the teaching process inside out and is neatly used by several
Middle English poets. The riddle as a 'wisdom' dialogue provides the

---

[42] From MS Lambeth 853 in Furnivall, *Hymns*, 95–100.
[43] From MS Digby 102 in Kail, *Twenty-Six*, 89–95.
[44] Both in MS Lambeth 853, in Furnivall, *Poems*, 190–232.

structure of the short *Inter Diabolus et Virgo*,[45] where the Devil's series of questions ('What is heyer þan is the tre?', etc.) are followed by the God-provided answers. A much longer use of the idea is *A Disputison between a God Man and the Devil*,[46] in which 'þe wikked gost' tries to persuade the good man to ignore the priest's teaching by urging the appeal of each of the Seven Deadly Sins in turn. The good man's rejecting speeches each begin with a refrain (or a variant of it):

> Þe goode mon wel vnderstod
> Þat he seide was not good.

Eventually the handsome beguiler is recognised as the Devil and forced to show his real ugliness. Thus the poet creates a double dialogue: the devil teaches the good man with false lore and this elicits the true teaching for the reader; the apparently vulnerable pupil proves the stronger and the false teacher is exposed. In another short poem, 'Of the Seven Ages',[47] good and bad teacher are both present: man is represented at each of seven stages accompanied by good angel and fiend; the unheeding pupil rejects virtue until his last speech of reversal and repentance leaves the frustrated Devil to report his salvation. A related type of twisting of the pupil/teacher relationship is visible also in a better known dialogue, *Pearl*.[48]

In *Pearl* there is a double use of dialogue: the main 'debate' between the Dreamer and the Maiden and the use of direct speech in the included parable. If one approaches this latter passage from the point of view of form, then as striking as the effects of mimetic realism introduced into the retelling of Scripture is the building up of the dialogue within the narrative. The source-text (Matthew 20:1–16) uses direct speech simply for the words of the householder and the labourers; only the final speech of those who murmur against equal pay and the longer reply of the goodman of the house have the effect of exchange. One way a vernacular poet could interpret this is seen in the English version of the story in MS Harley 2253, 'The Labourers in the Vineyard',[49] where the poet retains speech in only one stanza (out of five) for the householder's reproof; otherwise reported speech reduces dramatic narrative to summarised instance. In contrast the poet in *Pearl* lengthens each of the speech occasions in Matthew. The hiring of the labourers at the third hour turns one speech by the goodman into two questions, an order and an offer from the lord separated by the labourers' replies; the speech to the reeve,

---

[45] From MS Rawlinson 328, ed. F. J. Furnivall, *EStn*, 23 (1897), 444–5.

[46] *The Minor Poems of the Vernon MS* Part I, ed. C. Horstmann, EETS, 98 (London, 1892), 329–54.

[47] Edited in E. C. York, 'Dramatic Form in a late Middle English Narrative', *MLN*, 72 (1957), 484–5.

[48] *Pearl*, ed. E. V. Gordon (Oxford, 1953).

[49] *The Harley Lyrics*, 42.

the grumbles of the workers and the lord's reply are all lengthened so that each becomes a statement of a point of view rather than (as all but the goodman's final speech are in the original) natural-sounding conversation. When the labourers say 'More haf we serued, vus þynk so', the insistence on their right to an opinion is not just a touch of realistic comedy but a response to the lord's own sense of asserting his view in his concern 'þat non me may reprené'. Debating points are being made within the story, as well as by Christ in his use of the parable (the whole passage 501–72 is presented as spoken by Christ and the reader is reminded of his speaking presence at line 569), and, of course, by Matthew in his retelling (and so the passage is also expressed as something which 'Mathew melez in your messe'), and, most importantly for the theme of the poem, by the Pearl-Maiden herself in employing the Scriptural text for a particular didactic purpose; the perspective of the disputing exegete is clear in the subsequent application of the parable to her own case. The complexity of the several layers (which force Gordon to use three sets of inverted commas within one another to punctuate the passage and, strictly speaking, it should be four sets) illustrates the flexibility of dialogue; effects of lifelikeness are combined with illustrative function and its being imagined or recalled by an actual speaker puts it into a new contest. Chaucer demonstrates a similar virtuoso command when he has the Wife of Bath re-enact for the supposed audience of pilgrims her 'dialogues' with her first three husbands.

The new contest in the dialogue section of *Pearl* is itself a clever combination of the Boethian consolation dialogue and the form of teacher/pupil dialogue associated with the tradition of the 'wise child'. This tradition is well attested in Middle English versions. The main example, *Ypotis*, with the Emperor Hadrian as questioner and the child Ypotis (Epictetus) as answerer, seems to have been a popular text. It survives in fifteen manuscripts and early prints from the first half of the fourteenth century onwards and its manner is that of popular romances. ('Lestneþ to me & ʒe mowe here/ Off a tale of holy writte.') But though the manner is popular the material has a complex, learned ancestry, going back to Latin texts of the second and third centuries and producing versions in Latin, Welsh, French, Provençal, and other European tongues between the tenth and fifteenth centuries. *Ypotis* attempts to present Christian dogma in a simple narrative frame; it proceeds by question and answer and deals with the number of heavens, the dimensions of hell and the universe, the orders of angels, the days of creation, the number of Adam's sins, the three deaths of man, and the thirteen Fridays which provide reasons for fasting on that day (plus a few other things). It comes nearest to *Pearl* in such moments as the child's description of the heavens:

> The þrydde heuen shyneth as cristall,
> Full of Joye & swete smelle;

> For confessores þat place ys dyȝt;
> Ther euur ys day & neuur nyȝt.
> The fourþe heuen ys gold lych,
> Full of precyous stones rych;
> For Innocentes þat place ys sette,
> And euur yn Joye wythouten lette.
>
> (67–74 in MS Cotton Caligula A. II)[50]

It is one of the Pearl-Maiden's functions to provide the Dreamer with answers to just such questions as are given to the Emperor in *Ypotis*, who 'became a good man' as a result of his lessons.[51]

Ypotis is an example of wisdom literature reversed and given piquancy by the knowledge being put in the mouth of a supposedly innocent child. The element of reversal of expectation plays its part in a number of other dialogues. The child Ypotis is, in the Middle English versions, identified as Christ at the end of the poem and the tradition of Christ amazing the Doctors in the Temple was the core of medieval interpretations of the Wise Child motif, either implicitly, as for most of *Ypotis*, or explicitly as in another Vernon dialogue, the *Disputison betwene child Jhesu & Maistres of þe lawe of Jewus*.[52] The authors of the medieval mystery cycles found it difficult to develop a very convincing discussion for the pageant dealing with Christ and the Doctors; Christ's exposition of the Ten Commandments in the York, Towneley, and Chester versions is too simple to convey any sense of the wonder of the child's knowledge; the N-Town Cycle has a better stab at it with an exposition of the Trinity, the Virgin Birth, and the Incarnation, together with development in the character of the Doctors from boastful and colloquial scorn to sober humility.[53] The Vernon dialogue shows a similar joining of the pattern of arrogant adults disconcerted by the child and Jesus's use of prophecy and emblematic imagery to explain the Christian mystery. Before their eventual marvelling the masters repeatedly reprove Jesus for his presumption:

> Þow schuldest lerne A.b.c.,
> For þe fayleþ a foundement;
> Þou tellest tales of Trinite!
> In wonderwyse þi wit is went.   (25–8)

---

[50] There is a lot of minor variation among the MSS; quotations are from C. Horstmann, *Altenglische Legenden*, Neue Folge (Heilbronn, 1881), 511ff. See J. D. Sutton, 'Hitherto Unprinted Manuscripts of the Middle English *Ipotis*', *PMLA*, 31 (1916), 114–60.

[51] Another link is the attribution of the work to John the Evangelist.

[52] *The Minor Poems of the Vernon MS*, Part II, ed. F. J. Furnivall, EETS, 117 (London, 1901), 479–84.

[53] See W. A. Davenport, *Fifteenth-Century English Drama* (Woodbridge, Suffolk, 1982), 97.

Vigorously Jesus rejects their lore ('Þi Bok is blynt, and þou art blent!') and gives them the letter A as symbol of the Trinity and the mystery of light as the image of the Incarnation:

> ʒif þou take wel good ʒeem
> Hou þe sonne-Beem euere is set
> Vndeparted, so is þe strem
> Of crist with God mid knottes knet.   (129–32)

The use of child/father reversal and of the imagery of light and nature in *Pearl* seem to me to draw on the material and the technique of such instructional dialogues.

The pattern of disconcerting the over-confident figure in authority occurs in other dialogues. The powerful figure of Alexander is subjected to unflattering comparison in his dialogue (in the form of letters) with Dindimus, King of the Brahmans.[54] Here exchange of encyclopaedic information (from Vincent of Beauvais) is combined with teaching material drawing on the Desert fathers to produce a contrast between two philosophies of life; the virtues of simplicity and sobriety, supported by attacks on the Greek gods, inevitably from a medieval Christian writer expose the active life of the conquering Greeks. The David and Goliath aspect of the dialogue engages the reader's sympathies in the ethical distinctions between enjoyment and asceticism. The incomplete text of the alliterative poem blunts the effect of reversal, but the conclusion of the episode in the *Speculum Historiale* (and its derivatives such as the *Polychronicon*) completes Alexander's submission in a meeting between the two and a ceremonial offering to God. Similarly the early fifteenth-century prose dialogue *Dives and Pauper*[55] begins with a debate on poverty in which the rich layman Dives is at first condescending, seeing Pauper, 'a well-read mendicant preacher', as a fool who does not use his intellect to make money. Pauper, in robust response, sees Dives as a different kind of fool who risks his chance of heavenly bliss by pursuing worldly gain. Dives is soon chastised and the relationship becomes that of the ignorant doubter and the knowledgeable expositor. The editor suggests[56] that Dives personifies the intended audience of literate but worldly and credulous laymen of pious leaning, while Pauper, for whom the author uses a style consistent with the practices of the teaching friars, is given the rôle of the poor preacher: so poverty and teaching authority oppose worldly wealth and ignorance. As in *Pearl*, once the reversal is effected, the figure who had falsely claimed authority is reduced to humble learner and the exposition of the Commandments proceeds by brief question and long reply, though the

---

[54] *Alexander and Dindimus*, ed. W. W. Skeat, EETS ES, 31 (London, 1878).
[55] *Dives and Pauper*, ed. Priscilla Heath Barnum, 2 vols., Part I, EETS, 275 (London, 1976), and Part II, EETS, 280 (London, 1980).
[56] *Dives and Pauper*, 1:x.

debating manner is kept up for much of the time. Such works show that the familiar didactic motif of bringing down pride, to create a sense of development as well as to produce contrasting tones of voice, was found as useful in literary dialogues as it was in drama.

The fictional uses that could be made of teacher/pupil dialogue are demonstrated most fully in *Piers Plowman*, where substantial instances of such exchange are introduced for the Dreamer with Holy Church, Thought, Wit, Clergy and Scripture, Imaginatif, Anima and Conscience and for Haukyn with Patience. The first striking feature of Langland's handling of the idea is the frequent change of teacher, which is as invigorating a difference from the single teacher/pupil pattern in, say, *The Testament of Love* as the difference between Chaucer's shifts of style in *The Canterbury Tales* and the consistency of manner of other tale-collections. Will's process of learning is not allowed to settle for long and the second striking aspect of Langland's use of dialogue is his mixing teacher/pupil dialogues with one-to-one contests (Passus 3, 6, and 7 are instances) and with passages in the mode of a 'parliament' (Prologue, Passus 5, 6, 13, 18) and with long authoritative monologues. Such flexibility with patterns of speech draws, I suggest, on the variation in the patterns of debate and instructional dialogue developed by other English writers of the period.

I have tried in this essay simply to suggest that the range of Middle English dialogues is wider than is often implied in comments on debate, and that the body of writing illustrates some general aspects of literary composition and adaptation. Middle English writing tends to aspire to the condition of speech and exploits the relationship between speaker and hearer; in some works dialogue becomes a state of being. As with classical dialogues associated with the state of leisured withdrawal from worldly occupation, so medieval dialogues often imply some suspension of normal life – in dream, or in special assembly, or in isolated setting. Wesley Trimpi distinguishes between the literary dialogue and acts of public oratory in terms of setting and suggests a metaphor for medieval writings: rhetorical exercises can remain in cool halls and gardens while practical oratory bears the dust and heat of the forum; the leisurely settings of fictional debates recognise the element of intellectual play and the withdrawal from practical concerns involved in fiction; the *quaestiones* of fictional debate 'offer shaded amenities to the excursions of wit', he argues, and correspond to the entrance into the walled garden or the dream-vision or even to the departure on quest or pilgrimage – a 'period of artistic immunity before return to the moral realities of the listener's world'.[57] Debate becomes fiction by leaving its logical rigour and its forensic purpose behind and by becoming a demonstration – of the poet's relationship with his audience or of the common human conflicts and of tensions in belief and thought. Middle

[57] Trimpi, 'Quality of Fiction'; quotations are from page 82.

English writers point the illumination of dialogue in different directions and its sharpening and polarising effect is as vivid in short pieces such as the Holly and Ivy carols as in long narratives such as *Troilus and Criseyde* (Chaucer's use of dialogue therein deserving an essay in itself). That ancient master Lucian personified Dialogue when describing his own treatment of the form:

> When I first took him in hand he was regarded by the world as one whose interminable discussions had soured his temper and exhausted his vitality. . . . My first step was to accustom him to walk upon the common ground like the rest of mankind . . . next teaching him to smile.[58]

No Middle English writer has such consciously expressed intent but now and again the tones of Menippus are heard, even if only from that simpleton dreamer Geoffrey in an unwelcome pupil/teacher dialogue with an Eagle or faced like Lucian with evidence that 'human life is a vast sort of pageant organised by Chance'.

Royal Holloway and Bedford New College

---

[58] *The Double Indictment*, quoted by Merrill, *Dialogue*, Ch. 1. See Lucian, *Satirical Sketches*, translated by Paul Turner (Harmondsworth, 1961); the final quotation is from *Menippus Goes to Hell*.

The Miller's Tale, *line 3325:*
'Merry Maid and Gallant Groom'?

J. M. COWEN

When Absolon is introduced in *The Miller's Tale* he is called *A myrie child* (line 3325).[1] Editors who have given a specific gloss for this occurrence of the word *child* have usually chosen either the neutral 'young man', 'youth',[2] or the more colloquial sounding 'lad',[3] a translation favoured also by some modernised versions of the text.[4] Other attempts to impart a colloquial flavour to the phrase have been the translations 'young fellow',[5] 'the very fellow . . . The merry chap',[6] 'knave',[7] and 'a merry devil'.[8]

The meanings of *child*, other than transferred or figurative meanings, given in *OED* with examples from the Middle English period are:

1. The unborn or newly born human being; foetus, infant. 2. A young person of either sex below the age of puberty; a boy or girl. b. In the Bible, as

---

[1] References are to *The Complete Works of Geoffrey Chaucer*, ed. F. N. Robinson, 2nd ed. (Cambridge, Mass., 1957).

[2] A. C. Baugh, ed., *Chaucer's Major Poetry* (New York, 1964); N. F. Blake, ed., *The Canterbury Tales by Geoffrey Chaucer Edited from the Hengwrt Manuscript* (London, 1980); John Cunningham, ed., *The Miller's Tale* (Harmondsworth, 1985); John H. Fisher, ed., *The Complete Poetry and Prose of Geoffrey Chaucer* (New York, 1977); Constance B. Hieatt, ed., *The Miller's Tale* (New York, 1970); Robert A. Pratt, ed., *The Tales of Canterbury* (Boston, 1966); W. W. Skeat, ed., *The Works of Geoffrey Chaucer*, vol. 6 (Oxford, 1894); *The Riverside Chaucer* (Boston, 1987).

[3] A. C. Cawley, ed., *Canterbury Tales* (London, 1958); E. T. Donaldson, ed., *Chaucer's Poetry: an anthology for the modern reader* (New York, 1958); A. Kent Hieatt and Constance Hieatt, ed., *Canterbury Tales* (New York, 1964); J. P. Tatlock and P. Mackaye, ed., *The Modern Reader's Chaucer* (1912; New York, 1966).

[4] Frank Ernest Hill, *The Canterbury Tales rendered into modern English verse* (London, 1934); *The Canterbury Tales done into Modern English Verse* (New York, 1946); David Wright, trans. (prose), *Geoffrey Chaucer: The Canterbury Tales* (London, 1964); (verse), *Geoffrey Chaucer: The Canterbury Tales* (Oxford, 1986).

[5] William Frost, ed., *The Age of Chaucer* (Englewood Cliffs, N.J., 1961); R. M. Lumiansky, trans., *The Canterbury Tales of Geoffrey Chaucer* (New York, 1961).

[6] W. Van Wyck, ed., *The Canterbury Tales of Geoffrey Chaucer Together with a version in Modern English Verse* (New York, 1930).

[7] Nevill Coghill, trans., *Canterbury Tales* (Harmondsworth, 1951).

[8] Theodore Morrison, ed., *The Portable Chaucer* (Harmondsworth, 1977).

rendering Heb. *yeled* 'child', 'bairn', extended to youths approaching or entering upon manhood. 4. Formerly applied to all pupils at school, esp. to those at charity schools. 5. A youth of gentle birth: used in ballads, and the like, as a kind of title. 6. A lad or 'boy' in service; a page attendant, etc. 8. The offspring, male or female, of human parents; a son or daughter.[9] The example of *The Miller's Tale*, line 3325, is not quoted under any heading in *OED*.

Absolon's age is not specified. He is old enough to take an interest in the opposite sex, and old enough to be a parish clerk.[10] Clearly the tale represents him as an adolescent or young adult, albeit one very inexperienced in the love matter he is trying to prove, hence the modernisations 'youth', 'young man', etc. If we look again at the *OED* examples from the Middle English period which denote a wider age range than that covered in senses 1 and 2, it is notable that there is no general equivalent to the sense of Modern English 'young man'. When we exclude sense 8, denoting a person in relation to their parents, and the specialised senses 2b and 4, we find that the remaining senses exemplified in Middle English, 5 and 6, have a much more limited application than Modern English 'young man': specifically, they are not neutral as to social station.

MED, on the other hand, does list a socially neutral meaning, sense 5a, 'A young man; youth, lad',[11] including here the example of *The Miller's Tale*, line 3325. But when the other examples under this heading antedating or contemporary with Chaucer (nine in all) are examined, some of them seem to be based on mistaken translations or questionable interpretations of their contexts. The quotation from Lay. *Brut*, 297, *Pat child was ihaten Brutus* occurs in a narrative context in which Brutus is newly born, and can simply be taken to mean a baby. The quotations from Lay. *Brut*, 255, and *SLeg. Becket* (Ld), 217, occur in contexts in which a person just referred to as an infant has grown up. In both cases the temporal conjunction *Pa/Po* implies 'Then (when the child had grown up)'. The *child* is now an adult, but the meaning of the word *child* in the sentence is not 'young man': the sentence as a whole relates the transition from childhood to adulthood. Three other examples, which are references to or translations from the first chapter of the Book of Daniel, are instances of the specialised sense given above under *OED* sense 2b. In two other cases, *WBible (1)*, Wisdom 8: 19 and Trev. *Higd.* 4. 81, there is no

---

[9] See *OED*, Child, sb.

[10] Given that the usual requirement in the fourteenth century was that the holders of this office should be in minor orders (see, e.g., W. R. W. Stephens and W. Hunt, ed., *A History of the English Church*, 8 vols. [London, 1899–1924], 3, *The English Church in the Fourteenth and Fifteenth Centuries*, 275), Absolon might be imagined as being as young as fourteen, the usual age for the giving of minor orders; he seems, however, to be rather more than a novice in his job. I am indebted to Professor Rosalind Hill for advice on this point.

[11] See *MED*, child n.

indication of age, and no reason to assume that these might not equally well, or more probably, be examples of the meaning given under *OED* sense 2 (*MED* sense 3a). This leaves two examples: *Miller's Tale* 3325, and *Horn Child* 310, referring to Horn and Rimnild when they fall in love: *Loued neuer childer mare,/ Bot tristrem or ysoud it ware.*

Perhaps a socially and tonally neutral meaning 'youth', 'young man' as given in the *MED* entry and assumed by some modern translators of *The Miller's Tale* is not as widely attested as has been supposed. It is certainly not a usual meaning in Chaucer. Indeed, it is arguable whether Chaucer ever uses the word in this sense at all. Of the entries given in the Chaucer concordance,[12] some 160, the large majority, are clearly determinable from the narrative context as examples of *OED* senses 1, 2, or 8. Of the rest, two are examples of the specialised sense *OED* 2b, referring to the young Israelite captives of the Book of Daniel (*Monk's Tale* 2151, 2155). Others are examples of the theological sense 'child of God' (*OED* sense 10), extended in some cases to Christ and the Virgin Mary: *PrT* 667; *Mel* 1679; *ParsT* 135, 221, 461, 660, 790. Other figurative senses (cf. *OED* sense 12) are: *WBProl* 697 (children of Mercury and Venus); *SqT* 272 (children of Venus); *ParsT* 612, 629 (children of the devil). *OED* sense 4 (a schoolchild) is found in *PrT* 497, 519, and *OED* sense 11 (a transferred sense applied to disciples of a teacher) in *ParsT* 669–71. *PardT* 686 is probably best taken as an example of *OED* sense 6, a serving boy (cf. line 666, *his knave*). *OED* sense 5 is found in *The Tale of Sir Thopas* 810, 817, 830, where it is part of the parody of romance idiom (cf. the reference to 'Horn child' later in the tale, line 898), an uncharacteristic usage for special effect which is consciously or unconsciously normalised by some scribes (cf. manuscript variants to line 830). In *The Clerk's Tale* 982 and 1103, Chaucer uses *children* to include a person about to be married (Walter's daughter), the girl's age being specified as twelve (line 736). Here, however, the narrative context serves to emphasise the filial relationship, which, although not specified in these particular lines, is continually present in the reader's mind throughout the episode. These two examples need not, therefore, be taken as exceptions to Chaucer's normal usage, but as contextual extensions of *OED* sense 8.

Two other examples are debatable. The first is *Boece*, 2, Prose 4, 42–5: *What schal I seyn eek of thi two sones conseylours, of whiche, as of children of hir age, ther shyneth the liknesse of the wit of hir fadir or of hir eldefader!*. Clearly the two sons are adults. The thrust of the remark, which emphasises the reappearance of personal characteristics in successive generations, may suggest that the sense of *children* here is that of *OED* sense 8, but there is a question

---

[12] See John S. P. Tatlock and Arthur G. Kennedy, *A Concordance to the Complete Works of Geoffrey Chaucer and to the Romaunt of the Rose* (Washington, 1927). I refer here to all examples under the headings *child*, *childs*, *children*, and *childhood* except those from *The Romaunt of the Rose*, Fragments B and C.

whether *as of children of hir age* should be translated 'as in the case of children (i.e., offspring) when they reach the age these have arrived at now', or 'as far as possible in young people of that age'.[13] The Latin is *ut in id aetatis pueris*. *Puer* can be used of young men after the seventeenth year and can also be used for 'son'.[14] If Chaucer is departing from his normal usage and using *children* to mean adult young men, it may be under the influence of the first of these two possible senses of Latin *puer*, but the case is unclear.

The second debatable case is one which raises a question about the effect Chaucer wished to create in the particular narrative context. This is the use of *child* to refer several times to Custance's son Maurice in the last part of *The Man of Law's Tale*. It is notable that Chaucer has made the time references in this part of the tale much less specific than those in his source, perhaps because he wished to move the tale from the world of chronicle towards that of romance. Chaucer says that Custance's ship floats *Fyve yeer and moore* (line 902) before coming to land at the heathen castle, and then sails on until it is met by the senator from Rome, in whose house Custance then stays *longe tyme* (line 979). Trevet says that Constaunce was rescued by the senator in the fifth year of her exile and then stayed with him twelve years, and he says further that when Alle arrived in Rome Moris had entered his eighteenth year, a comment for which Chaucer has no equivalent.[15] Chaucer's indefinite time reference is such that the reader is not obliged to imagine Maurice as a young man by the time of the family reconciliation with which the tale ends. There is, furthermore, one detail in Chaucer's text which has no equivalent in the source and which suggests that Chaucer wishes to retain a sense of Maurice as a person of tender years. The narrator reports that, as *Som men wolde seyn* (line 1086), it was Maurice who took the message when, at Custance's request, Alla invited the Emperor to dine. The narrator does not himself credit this account, saying he does not believe that Alla was *so nyce* as to send *any child* on such an errand, but that he went himself (lines 1088–92). The comment is an intrusive one, emphasising an inappropriateness avoided, and the inappropriateness is presumably the greater the younger the messenger is imagined to be. Either Chaucer is using the word *child* in this part of the tale in a way which is unusual for him, or he has made use of a loose chronology which allows the reader to retain the earlier image of Maurice at the concluding scene of reconciliation, an image which helps to maintain the tale's dominant strain

[13] See Norman Davis *et al.*, *A Chaucer Glossary* (Oxford, 1979), *as* adv., conj., for *as of* in the meaning 'touching', and Tauno F. Mustanoja, *A Middle English Syntax*, Part 1 (Helsinki, 1960), 332 for *as* with a preposition in the meaning 'having regard to the particular time or other circumstance mentioned' (neither cites this example).

[14] See Charlton T. Lewis and Charles Short, *A Latin Dictionary*, and for the latter sense see also Charles du Fresne Du Cange, *Glossarium mediae et infimae Latinitatis*.

[15] See W. F. Bryan and Germaine Dempster, ed., *Sources and Analogues of Chaucer's Canterbury Tales* (New York, 1958), 177–9.

of pathos to the end. Given Chaucer's general handling of the tale, the second of these explanations seems the more probable.

It seems, then, that evidence for the meaning 'youth', 'young man' for the word *child* is not easy to find in Chaucer. Should we then assume that in the example under discussion from *The Miller's Tale* the word is used in a transferred sense, and is used to give tonal colouring, as a lightly scornful indication of Absolon's immaturity? Such a use seems natural enough to modern ears, and fits the narrative context well enough.[16] The relevant *OED* definition would then be that of sense 3, 'One who has (or is considered to have) the character, manners, or attainments of a child; esp. a person of immature experience or judgement; a childish person' (cf. *MED* sense 4b). Most of the ME examples cited in the dictionaries are in serious contexts and do not have the jocularly patronising tone which we must assume if we accept such a transferred meaning for this example in *The Miller's Tale*, but it is of interest that the one example with such a tone is *The Reeve's Tale* 4098, cited in *MED*. Such a meaning in *The Miller's Tale* context seems easier to account for in terms of Chaucerian usage than the meaning 'young man' would be.

But there is one more possibility which remains to be considered, that is, whether we should try to identify the tonal colouring of the word not simply in terms of semantic definition and register, but in terms of literary allusion. There is one further example of the word *child* in Chaucer's work which is itself unusual and which bears an intriguing similarity to the reference to Absolon. It is in *The Romaunt of the Rose*, Fragment A, where Narcissus, spurning the love of Echo, looks into the fountain and sees his reflection as that of *a child of gret beaute* (line 1522). While it is easy to suggest ways in which Absolon could be seen as another manifestation of Narcissus, it would be to pursue source study too curiously to suggest that Chaucer had in mind this particular reference to Narcissus in his creation of Absolon. Nevertheless, the coincidence of idiom may not be insignificant. *Child* in this line of *The Romaunt of the Rose* must be taken in the sense of *OED* 5, 'a youth of gentle birth', its use reflecting the source *enfant*, which can have a similar meaning:

> Qu'il cuida veoir la figure
> D'un enfant bel a desmesure.[17]

---

[16] A recent commentator has made a good deal of Absolon's 'childishness': see John Cunningham, *Miller's Tale*, notes to lines 578, 590–6, 643–5, 651, though he does not relate these comments specifically to the line under discussion. See also Earl Birney, 'The Inhibited and the Uninhibited: Ironic Structure in the *Miller's Tale*', *Neophil*, 44 (1960), 333–8.

[17] *Le Roman de la Rose*, ed. Ernest Langlois, SATF, 5 vols. (Paris, 1914–24), 2: 1487–8. Cf. Frédéric Godefroy, *Dictionnaire de L'Ancienne Langue Française* (Paris, 1880–1902): '*ENFANT*, s.m., jeune homme noble non encore adoubé chevalier.'

Donaldson's work on the vocabulary of *The Miller's Tale*[18] has shown certain verbal affinities between *The Romaunt of the Rose*, Fragment A, *The Miller's Tale*, and *The Tale of Sir Thopas*, certain allusive and otherwise non-Chaucerian items of vocabulary being used in the two tales for a parodic purpose which differs in its total effect in each case. Should we add *child* to the list of words which Donaldson discusses, and so add another allusive link to those which already connect Absolon and Thopas and distinguish them from other Chaucerian heroes (their *rode*, their affliction by *love-longynge*, as pointed out by Donaldson, and also, one might add, their yellow hair, of the head in the case of Absolon, of the chin in the case of Thopas)? If so, then we would be adding also to the list of details by means of which Chaucer pairs and yet distinguishes Absolon and Nicholas within the tale. As Donaldson has pointed out, both have some of the stylistic accoutrements of the hero of vernacular romance. If Absolon shares an epithet with *child Thopas*, then he advances slightly in idiomatic ranking beside his rival *hende* Nicholas. In a tale so notable for its allusiveness and word-play the sense 'a childish person' (*OED* sense 3) need not be excluded from the phrase in question, but can be taken as an added irony. And if an allusion to the idiom of vernacular romance is admitted into this phrase, then the subsequent descent into bathos is the steeper when the would-be hero turns cry-baby:

> Ful ofte paramours he gan deffie,
> And weep as dooth a child that is ybete.   (3758–9)

One might also suggest, more tentatively, that if the epithet *child* links Absolon with heroes such as Horn, then the adjective *myrie* may link him with heroines such as Rimnild. The word *myrie* has, of course, a wide range of meanings in Middle English, most of which are attested in Chaucer, but it may be worth noting in the context of the present discussion that *MED* sense 6a, 'Of persons or their features: fair, comely, handsome' (this example), which fits the present context very well even if other connotations are also present, is illustrated by a cluster of examples from vernacular romance and lyric in which the word collocates with *mai*.[19]

King's College, London

---

[18] E. Talbot Donaldson, 'Idiom of Popular Poetry in the Miller's Tale', *English Institute Essays 1950*, ed. A. S. Downer (New York, 1951), reprinted in E. Talbot Donaldson, *Speaking of Chaucer* (New York, 1970), 13–29.

[19] To the examples there cited can be added *Horn Childe*, ed. J. Hall (Oxford, 1901), 313, 325, 364: *miri(e) maiden*.

Chaucer's Host

S. S. HUSSEY

It is rather surprising that the impressive figure of Chaucer's Host has not produced more investigative criticism. Alan Gaylord's article seeks for a principle of unity in the apparently disparate collection of stories in Group VII of *The Canterbury Tales*. He finds it in 'the art of story-telling' and contrasts the Host's literalism and his disdain for what he cannot understand with 'the marvellously varied responses created by Chaucer the artist'. Barbara Page considers the Host as social and psychological type. C. C. Richardson and Walter Scheps are also primarily concerned with Harry's characterisation by Chaucer and how it develops from the description in the *General Prologue*. For Richardson, the Host's comments on the tales are those of 'a rather ordinary listener'. She, like other critics, notices his obsession with the passing of time. Scheps also speculates on which pilgrim would have won the tale-telling competition (his favoured candidate is the Nun's Priest).[1]

Two more recent articles take a somewhat broader view. D. R. Pichaske and L. Sweetland, whilst recognising the complexity of the character, investigate the nature of his 'governance' from the standpoint of late medieval political theory. He passes from the initial tyrant misgoverning a disordered society to a much greater wisdom and understanding. L. M. Leitch also sees a progression, a growing tension between Harry's desire for pleasure and the competing wish of some of the pilgrims for edification rather than for mere entertainment (*sentence* rather than *solaas*). She believes that several of the pilgrims are also concerned for the taste, interests, and spans of attention of their fellows and provide 'Harry-like' criticism of the tales (hence the plural in her title). However, in discussing the teller's relationship to his audience, she gives no weight to such features as oral delivery, the modesty topos or other

---

[1] A. Gaylord, '*Sentence* and *Solaas* in Fragment VII of the *Canterbury Tales*: Harry Bailly as Horseback Editor', *PMLA*, 82 (1967), 226–35; B. Page, 'Concerning the Host', *ChauR*, 4 (1970), 1–13; C. C. Richardson, 'The Function of the Host in *The Canterbury Tales*', *TSLL*, 12 (1971), 325–44; W. Scheps, '"Up Roos Oure Hoost, And Was Oure Aller Cok": Harry Bailly's Tale-Telling Competition', *ChauR*, 10 (1975), 113–28.

rhetorical practices.[2] Both articles argue that the Host progressively loses his domination over the pilgrims and therefore his editorial power. Clearly he finally gives place to the Parson, although neither so willingly nor so obviously as is suggested. *Beth fructuous, and that in litel space* has a somewhat grudging ring. Surely this change is a decision of Chaucer the poet, not of the Host or even Chaucer the pilgrim: the Host has simply outlived his usefulness.

Both Harry Bailly and Chauntecleer measure the height of the sun (the one by learning, the other by instinct) and so does Chaucer the pilgrim at the opening of the Parson's Prologue:

> If these lines [X. 1–9] are intended to remind us of Chauntecleer – a rooster who does not have control over himself, much less over his flock – and of Harry Bailly – a figurative rooster who governs his flock of pilgrims with indifferent success – perhaps we should see here the introduction of another figurative rooster, the Parson. This rooster is a better one than Harry and is to be the true, spiritual leader of the flock. He is linked with the other metaphorical roosters by the device of time-telling in order to demonstrate his categorical similarity and his individual difference. In the General Prologue the Parson was several times described as a shepherd with a flock of sheep, and it surely requires no stretching of the imagination to perceive the obvious similarities between the shepherd of a flock and a rooster of a flock. Moreover, there is a Latin poem from about 1300 comparing priests to the roosters on weather vanes.[3]

Or, alternatively:

> Harry Bailly takes his charges on a trip for his own profit, with a supper at the end; *oure Hoost* is a parody of the true Host and offers a parody of the Last Supper.[4]

Allegory and parody can be marvellously sudden and dainty devices. How easy is a bush supposed a bear! If the Canterbury pilgrimage too quickly becomes the pilgrimage celestial, the consequence is so to diminish the Host as almost to remove him altogether. Which would be a great pity.

Although parts of Germaine Dempster's earlier article[5] try to cast *Melibeus* as a kind of trailer for the Marriage group which is her chief concern, her

---

[2] D. R. Pichaske and L. Sweetland, 'Chaucer on the Medieval Monarchy: Harry Bailly in the Canterbury Tales', *ChauR*, 11 (1977), 179–200; L. M. Leitch, '*Sentence and Solaas*: The Function of the Hosts in *The Canterbury Tales*', *ChauR*, 17 (1982), 5–20.

[3] C. Wood, *Chaucer and the Country of the Stars* (Princeton, 1970), 275.

[4] J. Leyerle, 'Thematic Interlace in "The Canterbury Tales"', *E&S*, 29 (1976), 116.

[5] G. Dempster, 'A Period in the Development of *The Canterbury Tales* Marriage Group and of Blocks B and C', *PMLA*, 68 (1953), 1142–59. I quote from *The Works of Geoffrey Chaucer*, ed. F. N. Robinson, 2nd ed. (1957).

careful investigation of textual revisions, revisions which do not altogether remove inconsistencies, is closer to my own interest here. I hope to show that what is said about the Host reflects Chaucer's changing conception of the character, not only in one or two blocks of tales but throughout the poem, so that the Host, like the Wife of Bath, if on a smaller scale, becomes a unifying feature of the whole pilgrimage fiction.

As he is described in the *General Prologue* the Host is undoubtedly impressive: large, with prominent eyes, virile, and above all *right merye*. He is indeed *Boold of his speche*, and perhaps *wys* (in the sense of appraising people quickly and decisively, if sometimes wrongly), but *wel ytaught* he certainly is not. The tale-telling competition provides him with the hope of future profit on the pilgrims' return to the Tabard, but whether *by aventure, or sort or cas* or the task of producing some one hundred and twenty stories – Lydgate or Gower might have managed it – the return is not referred to again after Group I. Already by I. 847, *his tale* is firmly in the singular and that is the way it stays. We do not learn the Host's name at once. It is left to the Cook to call him *Herry Bailly* at I. 4358, but this delay need not be particularly significant, even if the Friar is already *Huberd* in the *General Prologue* and the Miller and Reeve *Robyn* and *Osewald* respectively in the first of the Links. The Cook himself is identified as *Hogge* (Roger) *of Ware* at I. 4336, and we have to wait until later still to be able to call the Monk Daun Piers and the Wife of Bath Alison. Perhaps the figure of the Host really did suggest to a London audience the real-life Henri Bayliff of the Southwark Subsidy Rolls and/or the Henry Bailey who held several public offices between 1377 and 1394,[6] but speculation of this kind has now become unfashionable, well on the way to joining that about Lady Macbeth's children or the girlhood of Shakespeare's heroines, dark ladies and second-best beds. Fiction is all, and the text must either mean what it unambiguously says or, increasingly and ironically, the direct opposite of what it says, but apparently nowhere between the two.

Two things in the initial description of the Host become more interesting in the light of the Links. The pilgrims ask him

> . . . . that he wolde been oure governour,
> And of oure tales juge and reportour.   I. 813–14

Reportour is difficult for the glossators. Is it simply a synonym for *juge*? It can hardly mean, as has been suggested, 'foreman of the jury'; not even Bottom the Weaver would have thought of combining that office with judge. If, however, *juge* is 'umpire', 'arbitrator', the sense of reporting the verdict back to us (pilgrims or readers) is, I suppose, possible. The *Chaucer Glossary* settles for 'chairman', 'umpire' for *reportour*, but the *OED* gives this reference as its illustration for 'narrator'. The *Concordance* cites the line as the only use of the

---

[6] J. M. Manly, *Some New Light on Chaucer* (New York, 1926), 78–83.

agent noun in Chaucer. The *MED*, however, may help us further. True, its entry for *reportour*, sense (b), glosses 'judge; ? also an umpire' and cites only one other and rather dubious use of the word in this sense. But two fifteenth-century quotations under sense (a), 'One who reports what was said or done by another' are more illuminating. In his *Dialogue* (*c.* 1422, edited EETS, 73), lines 760–2, Hoccleve denies responsibility for having abused women in the *Epistle of Cupid*:

> Considereth ther-of was I noon Auctour;
> I nas in þat cas but a reportour
> Of folkes tales; as they seide I wroot.

Scrope, in his translation of *Othea* (*c.* 1440, EETS, 264), 60/27, speaks of a *reportoure or a contreuour of wordis*, curiously enough in a comment on the story of Phoebus the crow which Chaucer had told as the *Manciple's Tale*. The entries in both the *Concordance* and the *MED* for *report* (v.) recognise only the sense 'narrate' and for the noun *MED* also has 'account' or 'rumour', although the latter sense is usually preceded by *good* or *fals*.[7]

I suspect that the difficulty for later readers lies in reconciling 813–14 with the earlier remark of the Narrator, Chaucer the pilgrim:

> And after wol I telle of our viage
> And al the remenaunt of oure pilgrimage.   (723–4)

Assuming that Chaucer's earliest conception of *The Canterbury Tales* envisaged some kind of pilgrimage framework – and this assumption is not universal[8] – his original plan may have been to cast the Host as both umpire and narrator and his second (and better) idea to separate these functions. Whatever may have been said about him by later critics, the new Chaucerian narrator needs very little *condicioun, degree, or array* beyond the disclaimer that his wit is short, for his reporting is the significant thing about him. He consequently makes much, in the *General Prologue* and again in the *Miller's Prologue* (for the Miller and Reeve both told *harlotrie*) about his faithfulness to his material, but he is seldom so directly involved as the Host. Some support for my theory comes at VII. 2803–4 (B. 3993–4):

> And wel I woot the substance is in me,
> If any thyng shal wel reported be.

Once again there is an alternative explanation. The Host may be saying he is a good listener to what has been accurately reported by someone else, although if so the meaning of *substance* is a little vague. Yet, as will appear later, it is

---

[7] *A Chaucer Glossary*, ed. N. Davis *et al.* (1979); J. S. P. Tatlock and A. G. Kennedy, *A Concordance to the Complete Works of Geoffrey Chaucer* (Washington, 1927); *OED*; *MED* R3.
[8] N. F. Blake, *The Textual Tradition of the Canterbury Tales* (London, 1985), 47–8.

evident that Chaucer was revising around this point at which the names *Daun Piers* for the Monk and *Sir John* for the Nun's Priest (unless that is a nickname) make their appearance.

The second, and less contentious, element in the *General Prologue* description is that the Host is not only *semely* but remarkably *myrie*. He *spak of myrthe*; he is delighted to discover *so myrie a compaignye* and would fain *doon [them] myrthe* in return. In the very next line a *myrthe* strikes him: naturally, the pilgrims will wish *to talen and to pleye* for there can be no *confort ne myrthe* in riding along in silence. So, lest they should not be *myrie*, his competition will give them both *disport* and *confort*. He even offers to accompany them himself *for to make yow the moore mury*. Even the Knight is seized with the general air of good-fellowship and begins (a little inappropriately?) his tale with *right a myrie cheere*.[9]

This desire for entertainment is usually, and correctly, seen as the *solaas* or *murthe* of the two constituents of a good tale:

> And which of yow that bereth hym best of alle,
> That is to seyn, that telleth in this caas
> Tales of *best sentence and moost solaas*,
> Shal have a soper at oure aller cost
> Heere in this place, sittynge by this post,
> Whan that we come agayn fro Caunterbury. (I. 796–801)

and, after the interruption of Sir *Thopas*:

> Lat se wher thou kanst tellen aught in geeste,
> Or telle in prose somwhat, at the leeste,
> In which ther be *som murthe or som doctryne*.
> (VII. 933–5 (B. 2123–5))

In the Host's mind, however, these qualities are by no means equal. It is interesting that *and* in the first quotation becomes *or* in the second. Can the two qualities be found in the same tale? But perhaps when, in the *General Prologue*, it was still a question of four tales per pilgrim, a balance might be struck. As things are, or as they *become, doctrine* is almost a non-starter. When the *Reeve's Prologue* threatens to disintegrate into *sermonyng*, the Host reminds the pilgrims that they must get on (here's Deptford and there's Greenwich, and only two stories told). He can essay a short 'sermon' of his own to the Man of Law and, moreover, couch it in legal language:

> Ye been submytted, thurgh youre free assent,
> To stonden in this cas at my juggement.
> Acquiteth yow now of youre biheeste;
> Thanne have ye do youre devoir atte leeste.   (II. 35–8)

---

[9] *myrie* need not mean 'cheerful', e.g., *m. day*, I, 1499, *Troilus* III, 1061; *m. citee*, VII, 3071; *m. site* (of a house) *Boece* II, m. 4. But the great majority of instances in Chaucer attest to the usual sense.

but no one else is to be allowed to compete, and at the close of the *thrifty* tale of Constance (the word is used also by the Man of Law himself at its beginning), no pilgrim, Parson or whoever, is going to be permitted a *predicacioun* (the polysyllabic French loan-word making it sound even longer). The Friar is a man after the Host's own heart, even though he may simply be trying to score a point off the Wife of Bath:

> Us nedeth nat to speken but of game,
> And lete auctoritees, on Goddes name,
> To prechyng and to scole eek of clergye. (III. 1275–7)

The Clerk, too, is advised to

> Telle us som myrie tale, by youre fey!
> For what man that is entred in a pley,
> He nedes moot unto the pley assente.
> But precheth nat, as freres doon in Lente,
> To make us for oure olde synnes wepe,
> Ne that thy tale make us nat to slepe.
> Telle us som murie thyng of aventures. (IV. 9–15)

Clearly, one pennyworth of doctrine to a very tolerable deal of mirth will be most satisfactory.

At the close of the *Physician's Tale* the Host is much affected and outraged at the circumstances of Virginia's death, but it was, after all, a *pitous* story and it is consequently time for a *myrie* tale, some *myrthe or japes*, from the Pardoner. The latter promises the Host his amusement but also *som moral thyng* for the *gentils* who seem apprehensive at the mention of *japes*; perhaps the Pardoner alone really can combine *sentence* and *solaas*, *murthe* and *doctrine*? The *Shipman's Tale*, a double jape, is very much to the Host's taste, even if he is incapable of seeing that anyone except the Monk can be at fault. He begins to *japen* himself to counteract the reverent silence at the close of the *Prioress's Tale*. He asks Chaucer for *a tale of myrthe, som deyntee thyng*, and is rewarded by *Sir Thopas* which takes *solaas* to its ridiculous extreme. We might have been happier if the Host had instead interrupted the *Melibeus* which is Chaucer's answer to the request for *som murthe or som doctryne*, the only request the Host ever makes for *doctrine* and even then it comes significantly after *murthe*. Chaucer's offer of *a litel thyng in prose*, a third best to rhyme or alliterative verse (*geeste*), promises, as Professor Norton-Smith points out,[10] to be chock-full of *sentence* (mentioned five times between 946 and 963) and then fully lives up to its promise. Bored by all the tragedies of the *Monk's Tale* in which there had been *no desport ne game*, Harry suggests a hunting story but the Monk replies that he has *no lust to pleye*. The Nun's Priest, however, agrees to be *myrie* and in the probably spurious Epilogue is praised for *a murie*

---

[10] J. Norton-Smith, *Geoffrey Chaucer* (London, 1974), 147.

tale. A myrie tale or tweye is what the Host would have liked from the Yeoman's Canon, but the *Canon's Yeoman's Tale* is something quite other. And, finally, since even the Host realises that a fable would be inappropriate for the concluding tale of the series, he accepts the *meditacioun* the Parson offers. As Chaucer's conception of his Host moves further and further away from the possibility of both *sentence* and *solaas*, so *sentence* becomes a medicine to be taken under protest and in small doses only and *solaas* all that he will willingly accept. He can appreciate, for instance, Chauntecleer's virility as being the *solaas* of the *Nun's Priest's Tale* but hardly the double *sentence* to which its teller directs his audience.

Just how much the Host says in the Links, and to whom, will depend on the editor's view of four passages which, because of their overlapping subject-matter, are likely to represent successive stages in revision of *The Canterbury Tales*. At the close of the *Man of Law's Tale* the Host first simply praises it as *thrifty* and calls on the Parson for the next story. The Shipman, however, is prepared to offer something much more entertaining, and in view of the remarks between Host and Parson might well have been allowed to proceed. What we have now, however, is a break between groups II and III.[11] But if, as is often thought, the *Tale of Melibeus* had been the original choice for the Man of Law, *thrifty* says nothing about either the impulsiveness of Melibeus or the wisdom of Prudence. When *Melibeus* was given to Chaucer the pilgrim, a new link was necessary to connect it with the *Monk's Tale* which then followed. This in turn incorporates some lines from what may have been the original ending of the *Clerk's Tale*. Whether that ending had followed the Envoy or the close of the story proper in both Petrarch and the French version (i.e., l. 1162 in Chaucer), it cannot now intervene between the last line of the Envoy and the first line of the *Merchant's Tale* which echoes it. Furthermore, the Host's remarks in this possibly cancelled link are almost unbelievably mild and vague: he merely wishes that his (unnamed) wife at home had heard such a *gentil* tale. So the new link connecting *Melibeus* and the *Monk's Tale* is both revised and longer. In it the Host wishes that *Goodelief my wyf* had heard the preceding tale since she has nothing of the *pacience* of Prudence. *Pacience* fits either Griselda or Prudence; it depends on whether the irony of the praise of Prudence (who in fact exhibits 'sovereignty' of a kind)[12] is intentional. The extra lines in the link between *Melibeus* and the *Monk's Tale* develop the earlier single remark into a one-sided picture of the aggressive wife who dominates and terrifies her husband. But the Host knows better than to tangle with the Wife of Bath, a termagant who is not conveniently at home but here among the pilgrims, and so, as always, he keeps his distance.

[11] J. H. Fisher, *The Complete Poetry and Prose of Geoffrey Chaucer* (New York, 1977), emends 1179 conjecturally to read *Wif of Bath* to allow the passage to remain as a link to Group III.

[12] R. M. Lumiansky, *Of Sondry Folk* (Austin, Texas, 1955), 95.

So far so good, but the new link ('Monk's Prologue') continues with a request to the Monk for the following tale. Not only does this make no mention of the much earlier choice of the Monk to follow the Knight (I. 3118–19) which had been frustrated by the drunken Miller, but it professes not to know the Monk's name (given as Daun Piers, VII. 2792) nor his monastic office, whereas the *General Prologue* calls him an *outridere*. It repeats and develops the joke about the *tredefowel*, the square peg in the religious round hole, which appears also in the Endlink ('Epilogue') to the *Nun's Priest's Tale*. Although the mention of Chauntecleer and the hens ties the remark to the *Nun's Priest's Tale*, it surely fits better the *manly* Monk. The word *another* in the final line of the earlier form of this passage suggests an early stage of composition, so that most editors agree that it was meant to be cancelled from the close of the *Nun's Priest's Tale*. It appears in ten manuscripts in all, but not in Ellesmere or in Hengwrt which is now recognised as the most valuable of the early manuscripts, perhaps even based on Chaucer's own papers.[13] The *Nun's Priest's Tale* is followed by the *Second Nun's Tale* in thirteen manuscripts (seven of which have the Endlink) but there is no direct connection and the *Manicple's Tale* comes next in thirty-three others. The *Nun's Priest's Tale* is now preceded by the Link which interrupts the *Monk's Tale*. This occurs in both a short and a long form. Most of the manuscripts of the short form (Hengwrt and nine others) have the Knight as interrupter, but three manuscripts give this opening to the Host. In most of the manuscripts of the long form the Knight interrupts the Monk and is later supported by the Host (*'Ye', quod oure Hooste . . .*). It would be tempting to think that the Host was Chaucer's original choice as initial interrupter, but a more likely explanation is that the three manuscripts show over-careful editorial revision, extrapolating from line 2780. The sequence *Monk's Tale* – Monk–Nun's Priest Link (in the longer form) – *Nun's Priest's Tale* would seem to be what Chaucer finally intended.[14] My point, however, is that these important revisions all involve the character of the Host.

One part of this development pictures the Host as henpecked husband. He is discomfited too at several other places in the Links. The drunken Miller insists on telling the second story to *quite* the *Knight's Tale* and the Host forgoes his own choice of the Monk in the interests of peace and quiet. The Host–Franklin dialogue after the interruption of the *Squire's Tale* is more subtle. *Straw for youre gentillesse!* exclaims the Host, and the Franklin has indeed repeated the word (*gentilly, gentil, gentillesse*) and will again in both his Prologue and his Tale. Is it that the Host does not understand the concept?

[13] Blake, *passim*. He believes that the Nun's Priest Endlink is not by Chaucer but was first added in Cambridge University Library Dd 4 24, possibly the earliest manuscript of Manly and Rickert's group a. It does not occur in Ellesmere.
[14] D. Pearsall, ed., *The Nun's Priest's Tale, A Variorum Edition of the Works of Geoffrey Chaucer*, 2 (London, 1983), 85–91.

Does he fail to see through the Franklin's excessive politeness (*sire . . . yow . . . your . . . yow . . . yow*) and the irony of the latter's reply to his gruff '*Telle on thy tale withouten wordes mo*'?

> I prey to God that it may plesen yow;
> Thanne woot I wel that it is good ynow.   (V. 707–8)

Chaucer's own remark in offering *Melibeus*, a story which has been the rounds (*in sondry wyse/ Of sondry folk*) and which should satisfy the Host unless he is *to daungerous* ('impossibly difficult to please'), may well be of the same ironic kind. The Host manages, not without difficulty, to handle the quarrelling Friar and Summoner. He thinks he can make a joke at the expense of the Cook, but is silenced by the threat of a tale about a *hostileer* which will quit *him*. The same verb is used by both Miller and Reeve earlier, and it may be significant, in the development of the Host-figure, that his name, *Herry Bailly*, is revealed at this point. The Prologue to the *Manciple's Tale*, lacking in several manuscripts, gives hints first of a continuation of the Host–Cook quarrel and then of an incipient confrontation between the Cook and the Manciple. The latter takes over from the Host as the Cook's tormenter, but the Host is not finished yet. He hints of the Cook's likely knowledge of shortcomings in the Manciple's own *rekenynges* which one day might be used as yet another 'quitting'. The greatest threat to the Host's authority as *governour* comes, of course, from the Pardoner's offer that he should be the first to kiss the relics since he is so *envoluped in synne*. For perhaps the first time the Host sees the danger of someone else taking control and addressing him as unceremoniously as he himself addresses some of the pilgrims. His furious and crude outburst is only quietened by the good offices of the Knight.

I have spoken regularly of 'revisions', but we cannot know the sequence of these revisions or even if they were all authorial. The important thing is that revisions there were and that in many manuscripts inconsistencies remain, suggesting that the revisions were still in progress. That so many of them concern the Host who gradually emerges as a *semely* man who is terrified of his wife, a self-appointed master of ceremonies (but no longer a *reportour*) who nevertheless cannot keep complete control of his charges, a man who calls for *murthe or doctrine* but who really wants only the first of these, suggests the growth of the Host-figure not only as a realistic character but also as an important structural device. For this Chaucer's second thoughts in shifting some tales from one pilgrim to another provided not only the necessity but also the opportunity.

University of Lancaster

'Look Out for the Little Words'

C. A. LADD

When George Kane was my professor, more years ago than I care to remember, I learned the lesson of the importance of precision and accuracy in detail and the necessity of impressing this on those I taught. 'When translating,' I used to tell them, 'always look out for the little words' – the little words and small phrases, often, no doubt, colloquialisms, which it is easy to pass over in translation, but which (I assured them) make all the difference to the emphasis and tone of a passage. Unfortunately, when pressed to explain the precise meaning of these words and phrases, I often found, and still find, great difficulty in providing any plausible answer. What, for instance, is the exact force of *as* before an imperative in Middle English? The *MED* says 'Usually without lexical equivalent in MnE',[1] but I could hardly say that when I had just told them that every word counted. Presumably the word would have conveyed some difference of flavour in the fourteenth century – but what? A greater note of entreaty, perhaps? It would be nice to be sure.

Some years ago I had a student who was adept at facing me with such problems. 'What does *let see* mean in *The House of Fame*, 1623?' he asked. 'Let's see,' I replied. 'Yes, but what does it mean in that context?' he asked. 'Let's see,' I said. I found the passage; it ran:

> 'And thou, dan Eolus, let see,
> Tak forth thy trumpe anon,' quod she.

Did it mean 'And you, Master Aeolus – let's see (what we shall do) – take your trumpet . . .', or 'And (as for) you, Master Aeolus, let's see (what you can do); take your trumpet . . .'? I couldn't be sure. Neither Skeat nor Robinson gave any help.[2] The student went away unsatisfied.

---

[1] s.v. **also 1d**. The *MED* does not make matters clearer by confusing this *as* with the accusative singular feminine and accusative plural pronoun *as*. The examples given under **1d** (c) should surely go under **his** pron. (3) and (4) in the *Dictionary*.

[2] There is some doubt over the reading in this passage, but the variants do not make the translation any easier; so in the parallel passage, *HF*, 1765. My colleague Mr W. A. Davenport, to whom I owe many thanks, suggests the meaning 'Let it be seen, publish it to the world', but elsewhere in Chaucer *let see* seems always to mean 'let us see'.

I had similar difficulties with *The Book of the Duchess*, 1085:

> She was as good, and nothyng lyk.

Pace Helen Phillips,[3] surely not the Modern English meaning of 'nothing like'. Does it mean, as Skeat hesitatingly suggests: 'She was as good (as they), and (there was) nothing like (her)'? If so, the change of subject is awkward.[4] Could it possibly mean: 'She was not just similar to these heroines, but exactly as good as they'? Perhaps to a fourteenth-century reader this was a colloquial phrase that would be instantly recognisable.[5] But not to me!

Sometimes, however, there is a glimmer of light. The same student wanted to know the meaning of *God toforn* in *Troilus and Criseyde*, V, 960ff.:

> That Grekis wolde hir wrath on Troie wreke,
> If that they myght, I knowe it wel, iwis.
> But it shal naught byfallen as ye speke,
> And God toforn!

The matter seemed clear enough; the editors agreed that this was an inversion of preposition and noun and that the phrase meant 'before God, in God's sight, I call God to witness'. The *MED*, under the heading 'In oaths and exclamations', rendered it 'By God, for God's sake, etc.'.[6] The *Chaucer Glossary* gave 'In God's sight (I swear).'[7] But what about the *and*? I looked at other examples; they all began with *and*.[8] Surely, I thought, the meaning must

---

[3] *Chaucer, Book of the Duchess*, ed. Helen Phillips (Durham and St Andrews, 1982), n. ad loc.

[4] Admittedly, similar awkwardnesses are not unknown in Middle English and may have seemed more natural to the fourteenth century ear; e.g., *BD*, 932f.:

> As for her was al harm hyd –
> Ne lasse flaterynge in hir word.

The passage has caused difficulty, but from what follows seems to mean 'On her part, all that could be detrimental (to another) was concealed, nor (on the other hand was there any woman) less given to flattery in her speech'.

[5] In the same way, a fourteenth-century reader would no doubt have known at once whether *leve* meant 'believe' or 'leave' in *BD*, 691:

> For nothyng I leve hyt noght.

The editors list *leve* here under 'believe'. Do they intend the meaning to be 'It is not for nothing that I believe this', with the two negatives cancelling one another out? Or is the meaning 'I will not leave it (my intent) for anything'?

[6] s.v. **God** 6 (b).

[7] Norman Davis *et al.*, *A Chaucer Glossary* (Oxford, 1979), s.v. *toforn*.

[8] A typical example is *TC*, III, 1639ff.:

> Quod Troilus, 'I hope, and God toforn,
> My deere frend, that I shal so me beere,
> That in my gylt ther shal nothyng be lorn'.

The Chaucerian references are all from *Troilus*, curiously, except from one in the presumably non-Chaucerian portion of *The Romaunt of the Rose*, *RR* 7196. Apart from those already mentioned, they are as follows: *TC* I, 1049; II, 431, 992, 1363, 1409; III, 335, 849, 1326.

be 'If God (go) before, with God as guide, God willing'. This meaning fitted the contexts as well or better than the other. The difference in tone between 'I swear by God' and 'God willing' is not unimportant; Criseyde is a timorous creature. I had made a discovery – something that could be the substance of a learned note. I then thought to look the phrase up in the *OED* under *God* instead of under *tofore*. Here the meaning is given plainly as 'with God's guidance' and examples of this and similar phrases are listed up to the beginning of the seventeenth century – including one from Shakespeare.[9]

So it was not such a great discovery after all. But I still hold to the lesson that I had learned. Precision and accuracy are important; what may seem trivial is ignored at one's peril – and the authorities are not always beyond reproach. These are not principles that it is always easy to live by – but, *and God toforn*, we can but try!

Royal Holloway and Bedford New College

---

[9] s.v. **God III 9c**, thus contradicting the entry under **Tofore A 1c**. The Shakespearean example, in the form *God before*, is *Henry 5* I, ii, 307. It should be mentioned that in John Warrington's lightly modernised *Everyman* version of *Troilus* (rev. Maldwyn Mills, London and New York, 1974) the phrase is translated in most passages as 'by God', etc., but in *TC* II, 1363, and III, 335, as 'with God's help'.

Poverty and Poor People in Piers Plowman

DEREK PEARSALL

'On exorcise la misère par son image idéale, la pauvreté'[1]

The persistence of Langland's concern for the sufferings of poor people is remarkable, as many of his readers have recognised,[2] and seems unusual for a medieval writer. It is a concern that is announced in the A version of *Piers Plowman*, developed extensively, and towards some sort of resolution, in the B version, and then returned to, with renewed intensity and at some length, in the C version. An exceptionally large proportion of the new material in C has to do with questions of poverty, and it is clear that to the end of his life Langland was still painfully conscious of the actual sufferings of poor people, and of the rebuke that they constituted to himself, to his fellow human beings, and to the notion of good government. The revisiting in C of problems apparently resolved in B is characteristic of Langland, and of the anxious movement of his social conscience.

Whether he was as unusual in his concern for poor people as he seems to us it is hard to say. There is, it is true, a large literature of poverty in the Middle Ages, but it is rarely concerned with 'the poor', with the actual lives of those who suffer and do not choose penury and destitution. There is the classical praise of voluntary poverty as a form of moral and philosophical exercise, found in Virgil, Horace, and above all in Seneca (Epistles 18 and 20), and

---

[1] Roland Barthes, *Mythologies* (Paris, 1957), p. 51. Quoted in Claus Uhlig, *Chaucer und die Armut: Zum Prinzip der kontextuellen Wahrheit in den Canterbury Tales*, Akademie der Wissenschaften und der Literatur (Mainz), Abhandlungen der Geistes- und Sozial-wissenschaftlichen Klasse, no. 14 (Wiesbaden, 1973), p. 46.

[2] Two recent essays worthy of particular remark are those of David Aers, '*Piers Plowman* and Problems in the Perception of Poverty: A Culture in Transition', in *LeedsSE*, new series 14: Essays in Memory of Elizabeth Salter (1983), 5–25, and Geoffrey Shepherd, 'Poverty in *Piers Plowman*', in *Social Relations and Ideas: Essays in Honour of R. H. Hilton*, ed. T. H. Aston, P. R. Coss, Christopher Dyer, Joan Thirsk (Cambridge, 1983), pp. 169–89.

coming down to the Middle Ages in a wealth of proverbial and sententious lore.[3] 'Poverty' here usually means the lowest level of subsistence commensurate with comfort, rather than with survival, and since comfort is a relative term, where survival is not, the estate of life recommended is difficult to define. No doubt the philosopher's poverty would have seemed riches to many poor folk. There was also the loftier ideal of spiritual poverty, inspired by the first Beatitude (Matthew 5: 3, cf. Luke 6: 20), and most powerfully embodied in the person of St Francis of Assisi, whose marriage to Lady Poverty is celebrated in Dante's *Paradiso* (XI. 57–81). Here the goal is not sufficiency in little and the avoidance of excess, as it was in the classical ideal of poverty, but renunciation of all wealth and possession – indeed, of all exploitative use of one's fellow men or of one's fellow creatures – on the model of Christ and of the injunctions of Christ in Matthew 6: 25–34 (cf. Luke 12: 27) and Matthew 10: 9–10 (cf. Luke 9: 3). The nobility and immense spiritual force of this ideal is a fact of great importance in thirteenth- and fourteenth-century European history, but it will be readily apparent that the message of spiritual poverty is chiefly powerful when renunciation is practised by former middle-class consumers, like St Francis, with a high spiritual profile.[4] There is also much in the thirteenth- and fourteenth-century debate about poverty, within the Franciscan order and between the mendicant orders and the rest of the Church, which is of only remote interest to society at large.[5]

The extensive medieval literature of poverty, therefore, is marked by its pursuit of philosophical and ideological issues: it rarely touches on the lives of poor people, except in a conventional way for purposes of demonstration. When poor people, or issues of poverty, are present in other kinds of writing there is usually some similar purpose that they are brought in to serve: as a means to attack the ostentation of wealth, for instance, in the Judgement Day sermons cited by Owst, or to criticise certain kinds of economic measure (*The*

[3] There is a useful summary of the classical texts and their medieval derivatives in Uhlig, *Chaucer und die Armut*, pp. 17–25. The traditional idealisation of poverty is well represented in Chaucer in the Wife of Bath's Tale (*Canterbury Tales*, III. 1177–1206) and in Langland in the discourse of Patience (*Piers Plowman*, C. XVI. 115–56). Langland's poem is generally cited in this paper from the C-text, in Pearsall. The A version is cited from Kane, and the B version from Kane–Donaldson.

[4] Compare the pre-Franciscan lay groups of people dedicated to poverty, like the Humiliati of Lombardy: see Brenda M. Bolton, 'The Poverty of the Humiliati', in *Poverty in the Middle Ages*, ed. David Flood, Franziskanische Forschungen, 27 (Werl, Westf., 1975), pp. 52–9; also Lester K. Little, *Religious Poverty and the Profit Economy in Medieval Europe* (Ithaca, 1978), p. 113.

[5] For full discussion, see M. D. Lambert, *Franciscan Poverty* (London, 1961).

Song of the Husbandman), or to reveal the hypocrisy of the so-called poor friars (*Pierce the Ploughman's Crede*).[6] When the chronicler Henry Knighton describes children crying from hunger on the streets of Leicester in 1390, it is not because he has had a sudden rush of compassion but because he wants to demonstrate the consequences of a policy which prohibits the export of wool.[7] It might seem that the literature of poverty represents it as a theme for argumentation, as well as a very relative matter of perception, and certainly medieval historians find themselves somewhat nonplussed when they come to look for the documents that will tell them about the realities of poverty. 'Most obscure of all', says one historian, 'in late medieval England were the really poor and those, relatively few, who remained tied with the yoke of legal bondage'. He goes on: 'To find out how the poor themselves felt we have to search many kinds of literature'.[8] But the search, as we have seen, except in rare instances (of which Langland himself is the most notable),[9] will be likely to turn up not the feelings of the poor but the views and opinions of their various spokesmen. Other historians hardly mention the poor. Economic historians, perhaps understandably, have tended not to be interested in the non-productive poor: an economic history of indigence might seem to them something of a contradiction in terms. The most authoritative general historian of late-fourteenth-century England speculates on whether there was much poverty in the countryside, quotes Chaucer and Langland, and concludes reassuringly that 'unrelieved misery can hardly have been general'.[10] And then again, she says, there were the consolations of religion; landlords could be quite kind; and there were lots of opportunities. 'Society as a whole was mobile, active, and fundamentally healthy. No power known to medieval man

---

[6] See G. R. Owst, *Literature and Pulpit in Medieval England* (Cambridge, 1933), pp. 290–307. *The Song of the Husbandman* is edited in *Historical Poems of the XIVth and XVth Centuries*, ed. R. H. Robbins (London, 1959), pp. 7–9, and *Pierce the Ploughmans Crede* by W. W. Skeat, EETS, OS, 30 (1867).

[7] Henry Knighton, *Chronicon*, ed. J. R. Lumby, Rolls series (London, 1895), II. 314–15, quoted in F. R. H. du Boulay, *An Age of Ambition: English Society in the Later Middle Ages* (London, 1970), p. 37.

[8] Du Boulay, *An Age of Ambition*, pp. 59, 77.

[9] So G. G. Coulton, *Chaucer and his England* (1908; 3rd edn. London, 1921), p. 268, commenting on Chaucer's Nun's Priest's Tale: 'For glimpses of the real poor, the poor poor, we must go to "Piers Plowman"'.

[10] May McKisack, *The Fourteenth Century 1307–1399* (Oxford, 1959), p. 343. Cf. J. E. Thorold Rogers, *Six Centuries of Work and Wages* (1884), p. 415: 'The grinding, hopeless poverty under which existence may be just continued, but when nothing is won beyond bare existence, did not, I am convinced, characterise or even belong to mediaeval life'.

could have prevented the able and enterprising peasant from going up, the slack, the feeble, and the unlucky from going down' (p. 346).

Langland's conscience was by no means so easily pacified, and it is fortunate that, in the absence of English work on the subject, there are the researches of continental scholars, particularly those schooled by Michel Mollat at the Sorbonne, to provide some sort of background for Langland's exploration of the problems of poverty.[11] What is clear from these researches is that there was a substantial increase in the late thirteenth century (somewhat earlier in developed and industrialised societies, somewhat later in more backward economies like that of England) in the number of the poor and, more or less simultaneously, the beginnings of a radical shift in attitudes towards poverty. Conditions in the twelfth and thirteenth centuries had been such as to allow some idealisation of poverty, along with the opportunity to relieve most of its more conspicuous distresses within a network of ecclesiastical and civic structures of almsgiving.[12] Periodically, at times of bad harvest, there would be more widespread starvation, and the programmes of charity would buckle and collapse under the strain, but generally the extremest forms of indigence were contained and, indeed, ideologically 'institutionalised'. Almsgiving acted to relieve suffering, but it also acted to preserve the established social order, its aim being to mitigate the misery of the poor without denying the inevitability of poverty. The manifestation of poverty is an important incentive to charity: the rich help the poor, and the poor thus serve the rich.[13]

The first half of the fourteenth century was however a time of economic depression, especially after the fierce winters and bad harvests of 1314–17. The existence of the poorest classes of society had been a precarious subsistence at best: a large proportion, perhaps as much as half, of the rural population had always lived 'at or even under subsistence minima', and had always had to eke out a living by supplementing the produce of their tiny plots with the most menial wage-labour.[14] Now those who had been living on the

[11] See the general synthesis of the work of the school by Michel Mollat, *Les Pauvres au Moyen Age: Etude Sociale* (Paris, 1978); the collaborative volume of essays by his followers and pupils, *Etudes sur l'Histoire de la Pauvreté*, ed. Michel Mollat, Publications de la Sorbonne, Etudes 8, 2 vols. paginated consecutively (Paris, 1974); and the more general survey of Mollat's work by Jean-Louis Goglin, *Les Misérables dans l'Occident médiéval* (Paris, 1976). A wider survey, using some of the results of the researches of the Sorbonne school, and employing also some evidence from England, is Catharina Lis and Hugo Soly, *Poverty and Capitalism in Pre-Industrial Europe* (Hassocks, 1979).

[12] Michel Mollat, 'Hospitalité et assistance au début du XIIIe siècle', in *Poverty in the Middle Ages*, ed. Flood, pp. 37–51 (p. 49).

[13] Mollat, *Les Pauvres*, p. 94.

[14] Lis and Soly, *Poverty and Capitalism*, p. 11.

starvation line fell below it, and comparatively minor accidents of fire, flood, theft, or injury could undo many lives.[15] As always, pauperism had its roots in the rural economy, but its most devastating effects are now seen in the towns, especially after the Black Death of 1347–9 created a tide of immigration from the country into the towns.[16] Urban poverty is not like traditional poverty: it is not spread through a community which is economically able and socially prepared to sustain and relieve the poor. There is now, in the towns, a depressed class of part-time, casual and unemployed workers, many of them unqualified, many recently immigrated. In Lille, it is a steady, grinding, unspectacular, mostly secret, chronic poverty, a life of those who are poorly fed, poorly clothed, poorly housed, and without access to the aid traditionally given to the 'marginaux'.[17] Many turn to begging (sometimes simulating disablement to improve their prospects), or to vagabondage, or prostitution, or crime. The passage from poverty to criminality is an easy one, and the records frequently attribute the cause of crime to poverty, and specially to being 'chargé de femme et de petitz enfantz'.[18] Examples from Florence in the same period from 1340 onwards show small artisans and textile workers falling below the poverty line. In the past there had usually been some special cause for poverty – age, infirmity, accident – but now a low-paid worker can be one of 'the poor', and earn insufficient to maintain a proper diet. The poor begin to settle in segregated areas, in ghettoes, or in the new 'suburbs'. It is 'la nouvelle pauvreté urbaine'.[19]

The textile industry, it may be noted, was a particular breeding-ground for the new poverty. Since it happens that the industry is one which employs so many poorly paid workers at the lowest level (so many women 'to carde and to kembe', as Langland puts it, C. IX. 80), it is inevitable that the contrasts between rich and poor should there be starkest. Large numbers of part-time, home-based, piece-workers were engaged in the thirty or so operations involved in the wool industry (sorting, beating, washing, combing or carding, spinning, warping, spooling, weaving, fulling, tentering, raising, shearing, and so on): they worked at home, and thus kept the employer's overheads down; they produced little and made little money, and remained directly dependent on the merchant-employer, who supplied them with work in small quantities. 'It meant the proletarianization of a steadily increasing number of people alienated from the land', and since there was a continuous supply of labour as a result of urban immigration there was no great incentive for

---

[15] Mollat, *Les Pauvres*, p. 198; Goglin, *Les Misérables*, p. 54.
[16] Mollat, *Les Pauvres*, p. 242; Little, *Religious Poverty*, p. 28. McKisack (*The Fourteenth Century*, p. 337) comments that 'there was a steady drain of villeins to London' from Barnet in the aftermath of the Black Death.
[17] Mollat, *Les Pauvres*, p. 296.
[18] Mollat, *Les Pauvres*, p. 298.
[19] Mollat, *Les Pauvres*, p. 200.

employers to increase wages or to organise the industry in a more rational way.[20] At Bruges, from a tax raised in 1396–7, '87% of textile workers fell into the lowest tax division'.[21] It is women of Lille in the ill-paid professions of 'lingère' and 'fileuse' who are found most commonly turning to prostitution. The poorest paid textile workers played a large part in popular uprisings in the Italian towns and in Flanders.[22] The development in the rural wool industry in the years after the Black Death, in England especially, ironically contributed to the plight of the urban workers, who found themselves in a declining industry and forced to accept lower wages.[23]

From many European sources, therefore, there is evidence of an increase in real poverty in the fourteenth century, an increase in the number of poor people who lived close to starvation and lacked the necessities to life of clothing and housing. It may be that there was some temporary alleviation of the worsening situation in the years of full employment following the Black Death, and there was certainly a time of comparative prosperity in Florence in the decades 1350–69, but the passing of this era would leave a more bitter legacy of realisation.[24] The increase in the number of the poor is only one factor in the new situation: more and more people are now chronically poor and concentrated in urban centres, where they constitute an anonymous and rootless class, more and more perceived as a threat to the social order. Poor people had once had the advantage of being a small and uncomplaining group, manageable, even desirable, as the recipients of private and organised charity. Now, by their numbers, and above all by their conspicuousness, they have become a source of disquiet and irritation.[25] Where Dante spoke of poverty as a value which it is necessary to affirm and defend against worldliness, and of the poor as the possessors of a spiritual riches which makes them specially pleasing to God, his near-contemporary, Francesco de Barberino, speaks of poverty as a social evil which should be eradicated or at least opposed, and of the poor as a scourge and a menace.[26]

It was in the terms of the latter that a new response was made in the fourteenth century to the increasing problem of poverty, as it was perceived

---

[20] Lis and Soly, *Poverty and Capitalism*, pp. 10–11.

[21] Lis and Soly, *Poverty and Capitalism*, p. 45.

[22] See Mollat, *Les Pauvres*, pp. 128, 237, 253, 261, 272–3; also his citation from the *Ménagier de Paris* (*Les Pauvres*, p. 237); and, for a much earlier period, from Chrétien's *Yvain*, lines 5298–324, in 'Hospitalité et assistance', in *Poverty in the Middle Ages*, ed. Flood, p. 43.

[23] Lis and Soly, *Poverty and Capitalism*, pp. 36–7.

[24] Mollat, *Les Pauvres*, p. 244.

[25] Jean Batany, 'Les pauvres et la pauvreté dans les revues des "estats du monde"', in *Etudes sur l'Histoire de la Pauvreté*, ed. Mollat, pp. 469–86 (p. 484); Mollat, *Les Pauvres*, p. 304.

[26] Raoul Manselli, 'De Dante à Coluccio Salutati: Discussions sur la pauvreté à Florence au XIVe siècle', in *Etudes*, ed. Mollat, pp. 637–59 (p. 645).

by the governing classes. In the towns of Poitou and Anjou, what had once been the transient poor, adequately catered for by ecclesiastical charity, was by the late fourteenth century a large, local, permanent class.[27] The town authorities see their task now as one, above all, of discrimination in charity, and what they try to do is to separate those classes of the poor that are endorsed by the gospels as the traditional recipients of charity (widows, orphans, the sick and disabled, those made poor by some accident) from the new classes of professional beggars and vagabonds (as they are perceived) who constitute a public nuisance and a threat to law and order.[28] The thing to do with these, the undeserving poor, is to run them out of town. Statutes of 1351 in Paris give sturdy beggars the choice of finding work immediately or of leaving the city within three days; citizens were forbidden to give alms to any but the sick, lame, and aged.[29]

The denial of the Franciscan principle of the absolute poverty of Christ, in the papal bull *Cum inter nonnullos* of 1323,[30] was in part the product of an anti-mendicant move within the Church, but it was a sign of the times. The great debate about Franciscan poverty had acted in a way to obscure the social realities of poverty and to divert attention to more intellectually manageable issues. Instead of adding an edge to concern about poverty, it actually deflected it,[31] and one of the effects of the bull *Cum inter nonnullos* was to make it easier for an anti-mendicant writer like Richard FitzRalph to downgrade poverty as an absolute value, to advocate discrimination in charity, even to argue that Christ's invitation to the poor (Luke 14: 12–14) excludes the 'stalworþe and stronge' poor who might work.[32] Meanwhile the friars, the representatives of the traditional ethos of poverty, found themselves justifying the financial activities of the urban rich, from whom they obtained most of their endowments and support, on the grounds that profit was the necessary prerequisite of philanthropy.[33] The friars' further recommendation to dis-

---

[27] Robert Favreau, 'La pauvreté en Poitou et en Anjou à la fin du Moyen Age', in *Etudes*, ed. Mollat, pp. 589–619 (p. 608).

[28] Favreau, 'La pauvreté en Poitou et en Anjou', p. 607; Jacqueline Misraki, 'Criminalité et pauvreté en France à l'époque de la guerre de Cent Ans', in *Etudes*, ed. Mollat, pp. 535–46.

[29] Lis and Soly, *Poverty and Capitalism*, p. 49. Similarly, Ordinance VII of the Statute of Labourers (1349) forbade, on pain of imprisonment, the giving of alms to any beggar who might work, 'so that thereby they may be compelled to labour for their necessary Living' (*Statutes of the Realm*, vol. 1, London, 1830, p. 308).

[30] Lambert, *Franciscan Poverty*, p. 234.

[31] Mollat, *Les Pauvres*, p. 222.

[32] Cited by Aers, '*Piers Plowman* and Problems in the Perception of Poverty' (note 2, above), p. 9. Aers places much emphasis on the 'materialism' of the new ethic of discrimination.

[33] Little, *Religious Poverty*, pp. 203, 213.

crimination in charity was more precise and pointed: it should go to them.[34]

Self-interest was as always at work, but one should not see in all this a deliberate policy, any more than one would think that Langland, in his more traditional moments, is 'offering easy speeches to comfort cruel men'.[35] In mid-fourteenth-century Florence, poverty is often a subject of discussion, but almost always in the language set aside by centuries of ecclesiastical tradition: the *pauperes Christi* are constantly mentioned, but rarely described as real people.[36] Where they are described, they are the 'safe' traditional poor – widows, orphans, the sick and disabled. In this structure of mental attitudes the perception of the reality of indigence is filtered through a conceptual understanding of poverty as a religious virtue. Sermons and other writings are full of models and types of poverty that are part of a centuries-old rhetoric and have little relation to current realities: the image of the poor is sweetened, idealised, abstracted, and the daily reality of the labouring poor is absent. The tendency is to think of the poor – and to get them to think of themselves – as undergoing some moral and spiritual strengthening through which they will attain the more readily to heavenly reward. Poverty for us may be a wound in society, a reproof to human dignity, but in this understanding it was a positive and permanent *institution*, and a part of the providential order. It was preserved so, in the face of social change, by the blocking out of non-traditional types of indigence from the concept of poverty: poorly paid workers, the unemployed, rebellious vagabonds, are not perceived as 'poor':

> Il y a là une sorte de relecture spirituelle de l'indigence a la lumière de la pauvreté.[37]

This is not due to hard-heartedness or lack of compassion, suggests La Roncière, but to the insensible structuring of traditional expectation (as also the usual identification of clerics, who do most of the writing about poverty, with the views of the well-off).

These European evidences, and the writings of these European scholars, provide an apt and suggestive context for the understanding of Langland's approach to the problem of poverty, as we see him moving uneasily between the old and the new values, between what he sees and what, perhaps, he wishes to believe. Langland's response to the social realities he perceives is as always that of a devout Christian, who sees all change and transformation as a form of decay, and who struggles to comprehend the nature of change within

---

[34] Chaucer, Summoner's Tale, *Canterbury Tales*, III, 1954–73.

[35] Shepherd, 'Poverty in *Piers Plowman*' (note 2, above), p. 174.

[36] Charles-M. de la Roncière, 'Pauvres et pauvreté à Florence au XIVe siècle', in *Etudes*, ed. Mollat, pp. 661–745 (pp. 685–8). This is an exceptionally valuable essay.

[37] Roncière, 'Pauvres et pauvreté à Florence', p. 741.

the structures of a traditional mode of thought. But it is also the response of an individual and a poet, whose power of imagination, allied to an implacable honesty and urgent personal sense of impending disaster, enables him to see more penetratingly than other men. He shows himself, in the particular context of the present discussion of poverty, keenly aware of and deeply engaged with the problems of traditional rural society in the aftermath of agricultural depression and the Black Death, and with the threat posed to its stability by the landless and workless labourers who have left their villages in search of better-paid wage-labour and now drift the country as vagrants and beggars. Langland has no sympathy for the labourers who demand higher wages and prefer fresh meat and fish, properly cooked, to salt bacon and warmed-up vegetables (C. VIII. 330–2):[38] like those who framed the Statutes of Labourers, he regards wage-claims as selfish and wilful wickedness on the part of labourers, and an attempt to disturb a divinely ordained hierarchy.[39] Likewise, in his vision of the Ploughing of the Half-Acre, the allegory of the setting up of the ideal social and economic order, he sees the class of unemployed labourers, whom he personifies in *Wastour*, as the threat to the new order. Their idleness and insolence drive even Piers Plowman to anger and violence: his response to their refusal to work is to call in Hunger (as we might say, to administer a sharp dose of deflation to the economy) so as to coerce them into submission. The scene in which scores of 'faitours' scatter their crutches and fall eagerly to work is an ugly as well as a comic one (C. VIII. 179–96).

At the same time, Langland faces squarely the problem of the chronic poor, not only those who are poor through misfortune (the 'safe' traditional poor) but also the able-bodied unemployed, or 'sturdy beggars', as they came later to be called. The question is not, and never is in the Middle Ages, how to eliminate poverty, but how to discriminate between the deserving and the undeserving poor, and then what to do with the latter. The difference here, between Langland's view of the matter and the contemporary move towards discrimination in charity, is the continued scrupulous concern that Langland has for the 'undeserving' poor, and the debate that he enters concerning their entitlement to personal or organised charity. The government, by contrast,

[38] Langland echoes here a theme of European complaint: the Italian Matteo Villani speaks similarly of the way the common people in the years after the Plague have come to demand expensive and delicate food, and refuse their customary labour (Mollat, *Les Pauvres*, p. 241).
[39] The opening preamble of the Statute of Labourers, as re-enacted in 1351, speaks of 'la malice de servantz, queux furent preciouses et nient voillantz servir apres la pestilence sanz trop outrageouses lowers prendre', and of the way they have no regard to the earlier ordinance, 'mes a lour eses et singulers covetises' (*Statutes of the Realm*, I. 311).

had no interest in any such debate. A Commons petition of 1376 speaks thus of itinerant labourers:

> Plusours de les avaun ditz Laboreres corores devenont mendinantz beggeres, pur mesner ocious vie, & soi trient hors de lours pays comement as Citees, Burghwes, & as autres bones Villes, pur begger; & lesquels sont fort de corps, & bien purroient eser la Commune pur vivre sour lour labour & service, si ils voudroient.[40]

Another petition of the same year speaks of the 'fortz Ribauds mendinent' who pretend to be out-of-work soldiers (perhaps the braggart Breton of C. VIII. 152 is one of these).[41] The government's answer was imprisonment, though this was an empty threat and not a practical solution, and clearly the bureaucracy of the day was incapable of distinguishing between the relief of poverty and the suppression of vagrancy.

Nor could the Church do any better. The problem for a Christian community was in the conflict between economic realism, to which were allied the Biblical texts recommending discrimination in charity ('If any would not work, neither should he eat', 2 Thess. 3: 10, cf. Gen. 3: 19) and the clear exhortation of the gospels ('Give to every man that asketh of thee', Luke 6: 30, cf. 2 Cor. 9: 7, 1 John 3: 17). This conflict was not reconciled in the debates on the subject in canon law. What was needed, says Tierney, was 'a kind of scholastic critique of employability in able-bodied vagrants', but it was not forthcoming from a canon law which was by now hardened into rigidity and incapable of adaptation to change.[42]

It was to these problems that Langland addressed himself. At one point Piers had suggested in a fit of exasperation, 'in puyre tene', that idlers should be left to starve:

> 'But ȝe aryse þe rather and rape ȝow to worche
> Shal no grayn þat here groweth gladyen ȝow at nede,
> And thow ȝe deye for deul, þe deuel haue þat reche!'
>
> (VIII. 125–7)

A more characteristic compassion makes him ask later, of Hunger:

> 'Of beggares and biddares what beste be to done? . . .
> . . . hit are my blody bretherne, for god bouhte vs alle.
> Treuthe tauhte me ones to louye hem vchone
> And to helpe hem of alle thynges ay as hem nedeth.'
>
> (VIII. 210, 217–19)

---

[40] *Rotuli Parliamentorum* (Rolls of Parliament), 6 vols. (London, 1783), II. 340.
[41] *Rot. Parl.*, II. 332.
[42] Brian Tierney, *Medieval Poor Law: A sketch of canonical theory and its application in England* (Berkeley, 1959), p. 119.

Hunger argues that Piers, as manager of the economy, has a responsibility to ensure that no one should starve, though no responsibility to maintain life beyond the meanest level (VIII. 223–35). Similar thinking concerning the 'dole', of course, produced the Elizabethan poor law and the workhouse, and Piers evidently has his reservations:

> 'Y wolde nat greue god', quod Peres, 'for al þe good on erthe!
> Myhte y synneles do as thow sayst?' sayde Peres þe plouhman.
>
> (VIII. 236–7)

Yet the many reservations one might have about such a system of administering poor relief should not encourage a belief that Hunger's solution is implicitly rejected by Langland.

There might be here a useful warning, to digress for a moment, against the danger of looking too hard for what one wishes to find, in this case Langland the radical reformer. He may be this at times, but not here. A well-known essay by Coghill argues persuasively that Langland in the B-text, discussing the urgent question of what to do with the able-bodied unemployed, has Hunger put forward without qualification a recommendation of universal welfare provision:[43]

> 'And alle maner of men that thow myȝte asspye
> That nedy ben, and nauȝty, helpe hem with thi godis.'
>
> (B. VI. 225–6)[44]

Thus Langland responded to the full, as we might wish him to, to the gospel injunction to give to all who ask, including the wicked or 'nauȝty', and sets charity higher than economic expediency or social justice. But the reading *nauȝty* is shown by Kane and Donaldson, in their edition of the B-text, to be the product of an error in scribal transmission, and Langland's argument, here at any rate, somewhat less simple than Coghill thought. The Athlone Press editors restore the text thus, on the model of the corresponding lines in the A-text (A. VII. 208–10):

> 'And alle manere of men þat þow myȝt aspie,
> That nedy ben [or naked, and nouȝt han to spende,
> Wiþ mete or wiþ mone lat make hem fare þe bettre]'.
>
> (B. VI. 222–4)[45]

They point out further how Langland, working on the C-text revision with a

---

[43] N. K. Coghill, 'Langland, the "Naket", the "Nauȝty", and the Dole', *RES*, 8 (1932), 303–9.

[44] *The Vision of William concerning Piers the Plowman*, in three parallel texts, ed. W. W. Skeat, 2 vols. (London, 1886, repr. 1954), B. VI. 225–6.

[45] See Kane–Donaldson, Introduction, pp. 103–4, 108–9; also C. VIII. 232–4.

bad copy of B, instinctively gropes back through the misreading in the copy before him to what he knew he had meant (C. VIII. 232–4). The editors of the *OED*, incidentally, working on the basis of ideological presuppositions apparently closer to those of Langland than those of Coghill, solved the problem by creating a 'ghost' meaning for *nauȝty*. Trying to avoid the usual sense 'wicked' for *nauȝty* (itself first evidenced in 1526), which Coghill bravely accepted, they proffered a signification 'having naught, needy' based solely on Skeat's text of B. VI. 226 and on a reading of MS R in B. VII. 72 which may well have been generated by the earlier error.[46]

There is no sentimentalisation of the poor in Langland's analysis of the problem of poverty in the Ploughing of the Half-Acre. He is rigorous as well as compassionate, conscious both of the reality of need and of the need for realism, as well as for justice and charity. As he returns to the question in the next passus, describing those who are to receive Truth's pardon, his first reaction, in offering a spiritual analysis of the social and economic order, is to affirm the orthodoxy of his day: mercantile profit is legitimate so long as the surplus (beyond what is 'needed') is dedicated to almsgiving and charitable works (C. IX. 22–42),[47] and beggary is condemned:

> Beggares and biddares beth nat in þat bulle
> Bote the sugestioun be soth þat shapeth hym to begge.
>
> (IX. 61–2)

The account of professional beggary (IX. 153–74), of those who make a trade out of poverty, is, as Geoffrey Shepherd says, 'as hateful a passage as any in the poem'.[48] It is notable, too, how insistent Langland is on the distinction between those beggars who go forth, like the apostles, 'withoute bagge and bred' (IX. 120), who 'bereth none bagges ne boteles vnder clokes' (IX. 139), and the 'beggares with bagges' (IX. 98), the professional beggar who goes about

> With a bagge at his bak in begyneld wyse.   (IX. 154)

Langland is referring here to a dominant theme in the Franciscan idealisation of poverty: to have a bag is to betray Christ (Judas 'was a thief, and had a bag', John 12: 6); to renounce it is to join him. Judas's bag is an image of all care for the world: *tanto magis sibi loculos ad periculum anime componunt*.[49]

But the power of Langland's imaginative vision and loving compassion does not permit him to rest content with these assertions of the offensiveness of beggary. He adds in the C-text a prolonged meditation upon the opposed injunctions of Cato, *Cui des videto*, and of the gospels in relation to alms-

---

[46] *OED*, s.v. *naughty*, sign. 1.
[47] See Little, *Religious Poverty*, pp. 178–9.
[48] Shepherd, 'Poverty in *Piers Plowman*', p. 171.
[49] Lambert, *Franciscan Poverty*, p. 63. Cf. also C. V. 52.

giving. The meditation is pursued with characteristic tenacity, probing, questioning, objecting, qualifying, so that one has the liveliest sense that Langland is working at the problem, 'ruminating' upon it, as Coghill puts it, rather than presenting in a rhetorically persuasive manner a conclusion he has already arrived at.[50] In one particularly moving passage, he turns aside from the condemnation of beggary and the question 'Who is worthy to have?' to a contemplation of the needs of the real poor, those who never ask, who are ashamed to beg, who try to make ends meet by taking on all the most menial jobs that society allows them – washing and patching clothes, scraping flax, winding yarn, peeling rushes to make tapers:

> Woet no man, as y wene, who is worthy to haue;
> Ac þat most neden aren oure neyhebores, and we nyme gode hede,
> As prisones in puttes and pore folk in cotes,
> Charged with childrene and chief lordes rente;
> Pat they with spynnyng may spare, spenen hit on hous-hyre,
> Bothe in mylke and in mele, to make with papelotes
> To aglotye with here gurles that greden aftur fode.
> And hemsulue also soffre muche hunger,
> And wo in wynter-tymes, and wakynge on nyhtes
> To rise to þe reule to rokke þe cradel,
> Bothe to carde and to kembe, to cloute and to wasche,
> And to rybbe and to rele, rusches to pylie,
> That reuthe is to rede or in ryme shewe
> The wo of this wommen þat wonyeth in cotes;
> And of monye oþer men þat moche wo soffren,
> Bothe afyngred and afurste, to turne þe fayre outward,
> And ben abasched for to begge and wolle nat be aknowe
> What hem nedeth at here neyhebores at noon and at eue.
>
> (IX. 70–87)

The revelation that Langland is writing about women, 'this wommen þat wonyeth in cotes', is a gradual one, and it might seem that women (presumably widowed), being members of the 'safe' traditional poor, are an easy choice for the exercise of social compassion. Yet the focus is not exclusively on women; and furthermore the specificity of detail is such as to identify the reality of this class of women in relation to the European context we sketched in earlier. These are women in part-time or casual employment, often in the most poorly paid jobs in the textile trade, widowed or otherwise responsible for their families ('charged with childrene' poignantly recalls the phrase in the Lille records). It is, I would have thought, specifically an urban class that Langland is describing, and the reality and extent of this class is indicated by

---

[50] N. K. Coghill, 'The Character of Piers Plowman considered from the B text', *MÆ*, 2 (1933), 108–35 (p. 128).

Gwyn Williams, who, though he deals only with the period of London history up to 1337, speaks of 'the submerged population of non-citizens and paupers', working in shops that 'measured as little as five or six feet by ten, with a living-room above; thousands lived, worked, ate and slept in an airless solar in some alley tenement'.[51] It is a class for which Langland has on many previous occasions shown concern. An example is his attack on those traders who exploit the economic weakness of the poor people who must buy in small quantities, 'parselmele' (C. III. 86), and who are specially vulnerable to even small price-rises.

The passage stands out from its surroundings in Langland's poem, and stands out too in the history of the representation of poor people, remarkable both for its unsentimental loving compassion and for its raw truth. Geoffrey Shepherd has said that it is 'probably the earliest passage in English which conveys the felt and inner bitterness of poverty', and adds: '[Langland] is precocious in that he often presents the inner life of the unvocal unassertive people who live in powerlessness and poverty and he draws them into the cultural reality of his time'.[52] It is a class of people that makes little enough appearance in our literature, except in romantically deodorised form, and it may be that we should need to turn to writers like Crabbe to find any comparably systematic contemplation of poverty. Blake, describing the women working in the brick-kilns of North London, as the industrial revolution got under way, is closest of all, in spirit, to Langland.[53] Chaucer's portrayal of the poor widow at the beginning of the Nun's Priest's Tale is like something from a different world – a genre-portrait of rural poverty, and a masterpiece of patrician condescension.

The rawness of Langland's honesty stands in sharp contrast. What he records with such unwavering accuracy, furthermore, is what he would not wish to see, something that constitutes itself an objection to his own passionate orthodoxy. There is no sense that the contemplation of the miseries and indignities suffered by poor people provides the fuel for indignation at economic oppression and for programmes for reform (the 'chief lordes' are a cipher in this account). It is not at all like *The Road to Wigan Pier*, nor indeed, in the end, like Blake, for Langland has no proposals to make, no plans for reform which will remove the problem. The question remains, 'Who is worthy to have?', and, having spoken earlier of a discriminating charity, Langland now insists that charity must actively seek out the needy in order to

[51] Gwyn A. Williams, *Medieval London: From Commune to Capital* (London, 1963), p. 24.
[52] Shepherd, 'Poverty in *Piers Plowman*', pp. 172, 175.
[53] William Blake, *Complete Writings*, ed. Geoffrey Keynes (London, 1966): *Vala, or The Four Zoas*, II. 214–28 (p. 285); cf. *Jerusalem*, IV. 17 (p. 735).

fulfil the promise that God will provide whilst accepting the ban on beggary. Those who have must give so that those who have not need not ask.

Beyond that, Langland cannot go, and a characteristic pattern emerges in this great passus IX of the C-text in which the pressure of poetic and compassionate imagination, moving against an equally powerful and passionately felt orthodoxy of belief, finds release eventually only in the reinstatement of the traditional spiritual ideal of poverty, and the appeal to posthumous rewards:

> Ac olde and hore, þat helples ben and nedy,
> And wymmen with childe þat worche ne mowe,
> Blynde and bedredne and broken in here membres,
> And alle pore pacient, apayed of goddes sonde,
> As mesels and mendenantes, men yfalle in meschief,
> As prisones and pilgrimes and parauntur men yrobbed
> Or bylowe thorw luther men and lost here catel after,
> Or thorw fuyr or thorw floed yfalle into pouerte,
> That taketh thise meschiefes mekeliche and myldeliche at herte,
> For loue of here lowe hertes oure lord hath hem ygraunted
> Here penaunce and here purgatorye vppon this puyre erthe
> And pardon with the plouhman *a pena et a culpa.*
>
> (IX. 175–86)

This passage is a 'full and careful list' that 'identifies and consolidates almost with legal precision a class with a role and status in society'.[54] But whatever the function of poor people in society (as they approximate more and more as a social class to the abstraction 'poverty'), the essential point of emphasis is now that it is the patience and humility with which the distresses of poverty are endured that makes of it a form of spiritual purgation. The movement is from the outer to the inner, not because Langland is retreating in the face of an insoluble and painful social dilemma, but because in the structure of mental process upon which his perceptions are dependent, and which he shares with the French and Italian commentators whose views were briefly referred to earlier, every question about the outer life turns out in the end to be a question about the inner life. As R. H. Tawney puts it:

> The distinctive feature of medieval thought is that contrasts which later were to be presented as irreconcilable antitheses appear in it as differences within a larger unity, and that the world of social organization, originating in physical necessities, passes by insensible gradations into that of the spirit.[55]

---

[54] Shepherd, 'Poverty in *Piers Plowman*', p. 174.
[55] R. H. Tawney, *Religion and the Rise of Capitalism* (New York, 1926), p. 20.

Langland returns on a number of occasions in the *Vita* to the theme of poverty, but it is now always patient poverty that he writes about – not poverty as a social evil and human indignity, but poverty as a means to the strengthening and purifying of the moral and spiritual life. Poor people slip out of focus and grow blurred in the imaginative vision, as they are subsumed among the *pauperes Christi* and into the rich imagery of voluntary poverty. The image of Christ as a poor man has all its traditional resonance:

> [For] oure Ioye and oure [Iuel], Iesu Crist of heuene,
> In a pouere mannes apparaille pursue[þ] vs euere,
> And lokeþ on vs in hir liknesse and þat wiþ louely chere . . .
> (B. XI. 185–7)

Langland may be affected by certain considerations not present in the *Visio*, such as the complications that have entered into any simple eulogy of poverty as a result of the Franciscan debate about the absolute poverty of Christ and the Wycliffite insistence on the poverty of the priesthood, but the pattern of spiritualised interpretation is now set, and it is recurrently exemplified.

In C. XII–XIII, for instance, Langland draws on Biblical sources to provide a vision of patient poverty as the tempering of the moral life of the individual, the hard shell which holds the coveted kernel of salvation (XII. 143–8), the winter-sown seed which endures the frosts and promises a good harvest (XII. 185–96).[56] There is no loss of honesty and integrity in the vision, but it is clear that there has been a shift of focus: poverty, from being a great evil, has become a great good; from being a problem to be solved, it has become the solution to the problem. It may be that Langland has deliberately over-simplified his idealisation of poverty in putting it into the mouth of Rechelesnesse, and in the little exemplum of the merchant and the messenger that follows (XIII. 32–97) there is something to make us think that Langland is characterising the views of Rechelesnesse as 'recklessly' easy. It is as if Rechelesnesse, in his recommendation of poverty, settles for 'sinlessness for want of opportunity', and refuses a certain necessary strenuousness in the moral life.[57] His general recommendation of a poor priesthood –

> Vch a parfit prest to pouerte sholde drawe
> (XIII. 98)

may also seem rather incautious.

Yet, whatever impression we have of Rechelesnesse, it is still true that the same themes are taken up by Patience in his great discourse on patient poverty in C. XV. 279–XVI. 156. Much of this discourse is made up from the

---

[56] Mollat, *Les Pauvres au Moyen Age*, p. 231, refers to the development of a similar theme in *Le Roman de Sidrach*.

[57] See Britton J. Harwood, ' "Clergye" and the Action of the Third Vision in *Piers Plowman*', *MP*, 70 (1972–3), 279–90 (p. 289).

traditional commonplaces of the discussion of poverty, including the well-known aphoristic commendation of poverty that begins 'Paupertas est odibile bonum' (XVI. 115a), and there is also an extensive demonstration that poverty is the best protection against the seven deadly sins.[58] The demonstration is dry, witty, comic, and full of that vitality and specificity that was equally the mark of Langland's deeply compassionate account of the sufferings of the poor: those sufferings are now the styptic to sin. So the temptation to gluttony is the less when misery follows so soon after:

> And thogh his glotonye be of gode ale he goth to a colde beddynge
> And his heued vnheled, vnesylyche ywrye,
> For when he streyneth hym to strecche the strawe is his shetes.
> So for his glotonye and his grete synne he hath a greuous penaunce,
> Þat is welowow when he awaketh and wepeth for colde;
> So he is neuere merye, so meschief hym folleweth.
>
> (XVI. 74–9)

In the same way, poverty removes the opportunities for lechery:

> A straw for the stuyues! hit stoed nat hadde they noen haunt bote of
>   pore!   (XVI. 93)

'I cannot', said Milton in the *Areopagitica*, 'praise a fugitive and cloistered virtue', but it is clear that Patience could, and there is no easily credible way in which his views can be separated from Langland's.[59]

If we look elsewhere, we shall find that the discourse of Patience has lost none of that earlier vivid realisation of the sufferings of poor people, even though the mitigation may be offered exclusively in terms of the hereafter:

> Ac poore peple, þi prisoners, lord, in þe put of meschief,
> Conforte þo creatures þat muche care suffren
> Thoruȝ derþe, thoruȝ droghte, alle hir dayes here,
> Wo in wynter tymes for wantynge of cloþes,

---

[58] There are striking resemblances between this passage and the exposition of the virtues associated with poverty, and the corresponding sins associated with wealth, in the 8th *quaestio* of Peter Olivi's *Quaestiones de perfectione evangelica*, as cited in David Burr, 'Poverty as a Constituent Element in Olivi's Thought', in *Poverty in the Middle Ages*, ed. Flood, pp. 71–8.

[59] This is the technique by which David Aers, in his discussion of other parts of Patience's discourse, in *Chaucer, Langland and the Creative Imagination* (London, 1980), pp. 25–30, separates Patience's 'spiritual ideology' from the 'striking specificity of the imagination's loving engagement with the material conditions under which life had to develop' (p. 27). Elsewhere, he says 'Poetic imagination does not sanction this part of Patience's claim' (p. 25). He puts forward a different opinion in discussing another part of Patience's discourse in the later article, 'Problems in the Perception of Poverty': 'The speaker is Patience, and certainly not subjected to critical undermining by Langland' (p. 18).

And in somer tyme selde soupen to þe fulle.
Conforte þi carefulle, crist, in þi rich[e],
For how þow confortest alle creatures clerkes bere witnesse.

(B. XIV. 174–80)

The physical reality in this passage of 'summer' and 'winter' is now, however, more usually commuted into figurative language: the winter of purgatorial suffering here which is to be endured in the hope of the summer of heavenly joy hereafter:[60]

Muche murthe is in May amonge wilde bestes
And so forth whiles somur laste here solace duyreth,
And moche murthe among ryche men is þat han meble ynow and
    hele.
Ac beggares aboute myssomur bredles they soupe,
And ȝut is wynter for hem worse, for weet-shoed þey gone,
Afurste and afyngered and foule rebuked
Of this world-ryche men, þat reuthe is to here.
Now lord, sende hem somur somtyme to solace and to ioye
That al here lyf leden in lownesse and in pouerte!   (XVI. 10–18)

Humble acceptance of poverty as a manifestation of divine will –

For al myhtest þou haue ymad men of grete welthe
And yliche witty and wys and lyue withoute nede –
Ac for þe beste, as y hope, aren som pore and ryche.   (XVI. 19–21)

makes of it a spiritual benefit. The rich lack the opportunity for this exercise, and the assertion of the poem's now firmly established priorities is made clearest in the sorrowing over their deprivation:

Allas! þat rychesse shal reue and robbe mannes soule
Fro þe loue of oure lord at his laste ende.   (XVI. 1–2)

'Rychesse', like 'pouerte', has been totally abstracted from the economic context in which it exists, in which rich people are visible, and in which they are the cause that there are poor people.

This, then, finally, is the way in which Langland, conscious as he is of every suffering and every harrowing indignity to which poor people are subject, springs open the trap of economic circumstance. It is a traditional enough solution, but Langland has arrived at it, as is his custom, by his own

---

[60] So Gautier de Coincy, in his sermon *De la misere d'omme et de fame*, speaks of the rich having their summer here, their winter in hell, while 'Li boen povre qui en povrece,/ Em maladie et en tristrece/ En ceste vie aront esté,/ Après yver aront esté' (lines 487–90), in *Miracles de Gautier de Coincy*, ed. A. Langfors, Annales Academiae Scientiarium Fennicae, B, 34 (Helsinki, 1937), pp. 207–92 (cited in *Etudes*, ed. Mollat, pp. 479–80).

personal and painfully honest route. There is nothing of which he forces himself to become oblivious, no wilful obscuring of uncomfortable realities, and the frankly outspoken personification Need appears at the beginning of the very last passus to reassert the primacy of the claim of the indigent upon society:

> So nede at greet nede may nyme as for his owne
> Withouten consail of Consience or cardinale vertues,
> So þat he sewe and saue *Spiritus temperancie.*
>
> (XXII. 20–2)[61]

But the scrupulousness of Langland's record of reality can end only, for him, in the necessity of raising the eyes to a higher reality.

Harvard University

---

[61] On the right of the poor, in extreme need, to seize what is needed to maintain life, see the note in Pearsall (ed.) to C. XXII. 15; Mollat, *Les Pauvres*, p. 139; Little, *Religious Poverty*, pp. 178–9. For an important discussion of the Need passage, putting forward views very different from those advanced in this paper, see Robert Adams, 'The Nature of Need in "Piers Plowman" XX', *Traditio*, 34 (1978), 273–301. Adams does not believe that Langland endorses the views of Need at this point (p. 288), and, more generally, argues that 'Langland never shifts his basic principles on the issues associated with poverty' (p. 289). The appearance of self-contradiction is not due to any ruminative process of lived experience, such as I have argued for, but to the extraordinary effort Langland makes to give fair representation to a great wealth and complexity of 'legitimately canonical views' (p. 290).

The Character Hunger in Piers Plowman*

R. E. KASKE

In the B-text of *Piers Plowman*,[1] following the confessions of the Deadly Sins
and the abortive pilgrimage to Truth, Piers himself emerges suddenly
(generated, I suspect, by the newly awakened good will of the Field of Folk at
large), tells the throng that he knows the way to Truth, and offers to guide
them once a particular half-acre of his has been ploughed and sown; the point,
I take it, is that the needs of natural man must be met before the pilgrimage to
Christian perfection can be properly undertaken. In a passage clearly reflecting
the obligations of the various classes in a well-ordered society, Piers assigns
each group its duties – the women to sew, the ploughmen to till the earth, the
knights to defend them, and so on. For a time all goes well, but then certain
'wasters' refuse to work, defying the warnings of both Piers and the Knight
(6. 115–70). In retaliation Piers summons Hunger, who cruelly punishes the
miscreants (174–80), at Piers's own request instructs him at length about the
proper distribution of food (202–74), and finally, after devouring everything
that is given him, falls asleep (278–301). With the threat of Hunger elimin-
ated, the workers relapse into their slothful ways (302–18); and Passus 6 ends
with a grim warning of future famine (321–31).
    Let us begin with the final lines of this warning:

> Thanne shal deeþ wiþdrawe and derþe be Iustice,
> And Dawe þe dykere deye for hunger
> But [if] god of his goodnesse graunte vs a trewe. (329–31)

*This study was undertaken as part of my National Endowment for the Humanities
Summer Seminar, 'Latin Christian Tradition in Medieval Literature', held at Cornell
University in 1986, and was presented before that group in essentially its present form.
[1] Citations and quotations, unless otherwise noted, are from Kane–Donaldson; all
brackets and italics are those of the edition. Though my interpretation is based on the
B-text, its main lines are intended to apply also to A and C.

It seems obvious that this *trewe*, or truce, must anticipate the pardon which Truth immediately sends Piers in the opening lines of the following passus:

> TReuþe herde telle herof, and to Piers sente
> To [t]aken his teme and tilien þe erþe,
> And purchaced hym a pardoun *a pena & a culpa*
> For hym and for hyse heires eueremoore after.   (7. 1–4)

So far as I know, this pardon has been generally understood as the Atonement – or perhaps, more precisely, the conditions for salvation brought into being by the Atonement. If this is so, the *trewe* in the final line of Passus 6 must also allude to the Atonement; and since its literal context is as a relief from the physical hunger presented in Passus 6, one might reasonably expect that this 'hunger' will also carry both literal and spiritual meaning.

This expectation is borne out particularly in Piers's three questions to the personification Hunger (202–11, 229–30, 253–6) and Hunger's extended replies:

> 'I am wel awroke of wastours þoruȝ þy myȝte.
> Ac I preie þee, er þow passe', quod Piers to hunger,
> 'Of beggeris and bidderis what best be to doone.
> For I woot wel, be þow went þei wol werche ille;
> Meschief it makeþ þei be so meke nouþe,   205
> And for defaute of foode þis folk is at my wille.
> [And it] are my blody breþeren for god bouȝte vs alle;
> Truþe tauȝte me ones to louen hem ech one,
> And helpen hem of alle þyng [after þat] hem nedeþ.
> Now wolde I wite, [if þow wistest], what were þe beste,   210
> And how I myȝte amaistren hem and make hem to werche.'
> 'Here now', quod hunger, 'and hoold it for a wisdom:
> Bolde beggeris and bigge þat mowe hir breed biswynke,
> Wiþ houndes breed and horse breed hoold vp hir hertes,
> [And] aba[u]e hem wiþ benes for bollynge of hir womb[e];   215
> And if þe gomes grucche bidde hem go [and] swynke
> And he shal soupe swetter whan he it haþ deserued.
> A[c] if þow fynde any freke þat Fortune haþ apeired
> [Wiþ fir or wiþ] false men, fonde swiche to knowe.
> Conforte h[e]m wiþ þi catel for cristes loue of heuene;   220
> Loue hem and lene hem [and] so [þe] lawe of [kynde wolde]:
> *Alter alterius onera portate.*
> And alle manere of men þat þow myȝt aspie
> That nedy ben [or naked, and nouȝt han to spende,
> Wiþ mete or wiþ mone lat make hem fare þe bettre].
> Loue hem and lakke hem noȝt; lat god take þe vengeaunce;   225
> Theiȝ þei doon yuele lat [þow] god yworþe:
> *Michi vindictam & ego retribuam.*
> And if þow wilt be gracious to god do as þe gospel techeþ

And biloue þee amonges [lowe] men: so shaltow lacche *grace.*'
Facite vo[bis] amicos de mammona iniquitatis.
'I wolde noȝt greue god', quod Piers, 'for al þe good on grounde!
Miȝte I synnelees do as þow seist?' seide Piers þanne.   230
'Ye I [h]ote þee', quod hunger, 'or ellis þe bible lieþ.
Go to Genesis þe geaunt, engendrour of vs alle:
In sudore and swynk þow shalt þi mete tilie
And laboure for þi liflode, and so oure lord hiȝte.
And Sapience seiþ þe same – I seiȝ it in þe bible: 235
Piger [propter frigus] no feeld [w]olde tilie;
He shal [go] begge and bidde and no man bete his hunger.
Mathew wiþ mannes face mouþe[þ] þise wordes:
Seruus nequam hadde a Mnam and for he [n]olde [it vse]
He hadde maugree of his maister eueremoore after,   240
And bynam hym his Mnam for he [n]olde werche
And yaf [it hym in haste þat hadde ten bifore];
And [siþen] he seide – [hise seruauntȝ] it herde –
"He þat haþ shal haue and helpe þere [nede is]
And he þat noȝt haþ shal noȝt haue and no man hym helpe,   245
And þat he weneþ wel to haue I wole it hym bireue".
Kynde wit wolde þat ech wiȝt wroȝte,
Or [wiþ tech]ynge or [tell]ynge or *trauaill*ynge [of hondes],
Contemplatif lif or Actif lif; crist wolde [it als].
The Sauter seiþ, in þe psalme of *Beati omnes,*   250
The freke þat fedeþ hymself wiþ his feiþful labour
He is blessed by þe book in body and in soule:
Labores manuum tuarum &c.'
'Yet I preie [þee]', quod Piers, '*p[u]r charite,* and [þow] konne
Any leef of lechecraft lere it me, my deere;   255
For some of my seruauntȝ and myself boþe
Of al a wike werche noȝt, so oure wombe akeþ.'
'I woot wel', quod hunger, 'what siknesse yow eyleþ
Ye han manged ouer muche; þat makeþ yow grone.
Ac I hote þee', quod hunger, 'as þow þyn hele wilnest,
That þow drynke no day er þow dyne somwhat.   260
Ete noȝt, I hote þee, er hunger þee take
And sende þee of his Sauce to sauore þi lippes,
And keep som til soper tyme and sitte noȝt to longe;
[A]rys vp er Appetit haue eten his fille.
Lat noȝt sire Surfet sitten at þi borde;   265
L[o]ue hym noȝt for he is [a] lech[our] and likerous of tunge,
And after many maner metes his mawe is [alonged].
And if þow diete þee þus I dar legge myne [armes]
That Phisik shal hi[s] furred ho[od] for his fode selle,
And his cloke of Calabre [and] þe knappes of golde,   270
And be fayn, by my feiþ, his Phisik to lete,
And lerne to laboure wiþ lond [lest] liflode [hym faille].

[Ther are mo lieres þan] leches; lord hem amende!
They do men deye þoruȝ hir drynkes er destynee it wolde.'
'By Seint [Pernele]', quod Piers, 'þise arn profitable wordes!   275
[Th]is is a louely lesson; lord it þee foryelde.
Wend now whan [þi wil is], þat wel be þow euere.'   (201–77)

Though some of these questions and instructions are credible as lessons to be learned from physical hunger, others are not – for example, Piers's remark about the people of the field being his 'blody breþeren' (207–9), Hunger's answer that he should be generous to the truly unfortunate and trust God for ultimate justice (218–28), and Piers's further question about whether he may do so without grieving God (229–30).

My suggestion is that in the passage quoted above, Hunger takes on overtones of the fourth Beatitude in the Sermon on the Mount as reported in Matthew 5: 6: 'Beati qui esuriunt et sitiunt iustitiam, quoniam ipsi saturabuntur.'[2] Hunger, that is, represents not only the famine that results from not working but also this biblical 'hunger and thirst after justice', exerting a compulsion in the spiritual realm parallel to that exerted by bodily hunger in the physical. He enters the poem, to be sure, as physical hunger (176–201), and later leaves as physical hunger (278–301); but within this literal frame (in 202–77) he takes on the added spiritual significance that accounts for his instructions to Piers. It is of course a truism that figures with tag-names do not usually have multiple meanings, having presumably been created to embody the meanings epitomised in the names themselves. The rule, however, is surely not an inflexible one (witness, as a single example, the evident overtones relating Lady Meed to Alice Perrers and the Whore of Babylon); and in any case, the tag-name here would refer with equal accuracy to both physical hunger and the *esuries iustitiae*.

There is, first of all, a cluster of traditional associations that would speak strongly for the plausibility of such a significance. Among the countless numerical structures invented to codify and interrelate the commonplaces of medieval Christian doctrine, one of the most popular is the *septenarium* or 'septenary' – an elaborate scheme in which various familiar groups of seven are connected to or set off against one another, item by item: the seven Gifts of the Holy Ghost, the seven Virtues, the seven Deadly Sins, the seven Petitions of the *Pater noster*, seven of the eight Beatitudes from the Sermon on the Mount, seven faculties of the soul, and so on. Though there is of course great variation, what appears to be the most typical septenarian design opposes the fourth Beatitude, 'Beati qui esuriunt et sitiunt iustitiam', to *acedia* among the

---

[2] The parallel in Luke 6: 21, 'Beati qui nunc esuritis quia saturabimini', is irrelevant for present purposes. A different interpretation of Hunger, which seems to me less convincing, is presented by Katherine B. Trower, 'The Figure of Hunger in *Piers Plowman*', *ABR*, 24 (1973), 238–60.

Deadly Sins, and associates it with 'Panem nostrum quotidianum da nobis hodie' among the Petitions of the *Pater noster*, with *fortitudo* among the Gifts of the Holy Ghost, and with *fortitudo* among the seven Virtues. The pattern, except for the Virtue *fortitudo*, is summarised concisely by Bonaventura: '*Panem nostrum quotidianum. Petitio*, panem dari; *donum*, fortitudo; *virtus*, esuries iustitiae; . . . *vitium*, contra quod, acedia.'³ The late Middle English treatise *A Mirror to Lewed Men* includes all our correspondences:

> *Panem nostrum quotidianum da nobis hodie.* In þis askynge we prayeþ of
> þe holy goost þe ȝifte of strengþe þat putteþ awey þe synne of sleuthe
> and settiþ in þat stede þe vertu of prowes, þat lediþ a man to þe
> blessidhede of hunger and þirst of rightwisnes and to þe mede þat
> longeþ þerto, þat is gostliche ful of endeles ioye and likynge.⁴

The configuration is given pictorial form in a popular diagram of human

---

³ *Expositio Orationis Dominicae*, 9, in *Opera omnia* (Quaracchi, 1882–1902), 7. 654; see also his *Collationes de septem donis Spiritus Sancti*, 2. 2–5, *Opera* 5, 463. The fivefold pattern described above appears in an elaborate septenary table drawn from the works of Bonaventura by J.-Fr. Bonnefoy, *Le Saint-Esprit et ses dons selon Saint Bonaventure*, Études de philosophie médiévale, 10 (Paris, 1929), 220–1; and in the tables drawn from the *Summa* of Simon of Hinton and its extracts, by A. Dondaine, 'La Somme de Simon de Hinton', *RTAM*, 9 (1937), 11, and P. A. Walz, 'The "Exceptiones" from the "Summa" of Simon of Hinton', *Angelicum*, 13 (1936), 368. The *esuries iustitiae* is also opposed to *acedia/tristitia* and associated with the Petition *Panem nostrum* and the Gift *fortitudo* by Hugh of St Victor, *De quinque septenis seu septenariis* (*PL*, 175: 409); and Innocent III, *De sacro altaris mysterio*, 5. 23 (*PL*, 217: 903). It is opposed to *acedia* and associated with the Petition *Panem nostrum* by Hugh of St Victor in an apparently authentic *Pater noster* printed as part of the inauthentic *Allegoriae in Novum Testamentum* 2. 11 (*PL*, 175: 782). It is opposed to *acedia* by Edmund of Canterbury, *Speculum ecclesiae*, 9, ed. Marguerin de La Bigne, *Maxima bibliotheca patrum* (Lyon, 1677), 25. 319, and the Vernon text of the ME translation of the *Speculum*, ed. C. Horstmann, *Yorkshire Writers: Richard Rolle of Hampole . . . and His Followers* (London, 1895), 1. 247. And it is associated with the Petition *Panem nostrum* and the Gift *fortitudo* by Augustine, *De sermone Domini in monte*, 2. 9, 38, ed. Helmut Mutzenbecher, CCL, 35 (Turnhout, 1967), 129; a homily on the Beatitudes perhaps by Anselm of Laon, printed as Homily 2 by Anselm of Canterbury (*PL*, 158: 596); and Honorius Augustodunensis, *Speculum ecclesiae*, 'De omnibus sanctis' (*PL*, 172: 1021). These various connections, especially that between the *esuries iustitiae* and the Petition *Panem nostrum*, also appear sporadically in commentaries and sermons on Matt. 5: 6.

⁴ Quoted from MS London, BL Harley 45, fo. 34v, by Siegfried Wenzel, *The Sin of Sloth: Acedia in Medieval Thought and Literature* (Chapel Hill, 1967), 74. Wenzel adds (226, n. 29) that substantially the same passage appears in the metrical *Speculum vitae* attributed to William Nassyngton; and that in the *Summa brevis* by Richard Wethershed, 'Acedia . . . corresponds with the prayer for daily bread, the gift and the virtue of fortitude, and the blessing of those that hunger and thirst for righteousness' (74). *The Book of Vices and Virtues*, ed. W. Nelson Francis, EETS, 217 (London, 1942), 162–3, relates the *hunger and þrist of riȝtwisnesse* to the Gift of *strenkþe* and the Virtue of *prowesse*, which combat *accide and slowþe*.

history which sometimes accompanies the *De quinque septenis* by Hugh of St Victor or the *Compendium historiale* by Peter of Poitiers, besides appearing independently. A good example, preserved in an early fourteenth-century roll-manuscript, is an elaborate wheel which bears on its outer circle eight medallions picturing the Deadly Sins (the conventional seven plus *inanis gloria*), and on its next three inner circles medallions enumerating in turn the Petitions of the *Pater noster*, the Gifts, and the virtues of the Beatitudes. The bottom medallion of the outer circle, labelled 'Accidia', shows a young man asleep; the first three of the four medallions which run from it to form one spoke of the wheel are 'Panem nostrum cotidianum da nobis hodie', 'Fortitudo', and 'Esuries iusticie'.[5] An accompanying brief exposition *De oracione dominica* explains:

> *Panem nostrum cotidianum da nobis hodie*. . . . Hoc est: da spiritum fortitudinis qui roborat animam sicut panis roborat corpus. Quo habito esurimus iusticiam. Justicia enim uie non est nisi esuries patrie comparacione iusticie, ut sic in futuro saturemus plena iusticia. Quod manifeste est contra accidiam, quam expulit spiritus fortitudinis et indeficiens esuries iusticie.[6]

Each of these relations between the *esuries iustitiae* and other items in the septenaries seems potentially relevant for the scene on the half-acre in *Piers Plowman*. Most obvious is the opposition between the *esuries iustitiae* and *acedia*, since it is sloth in its most blatant form that is the root of the trouble on the half-acre. This prominence of *acedia* in the episode is emphasised also by the word *Sleuþe* (143) in Piers's accusation of the wasters, and especially by the four biblical texts cited in Hunger's answer to Piers's second question (229–30): Genesis 3: 19, 'In sudore vultus tui vesceris pane . . .' (232–4);[7]

[5] MS London, BL Royal 14.B.ix, beginning of second-last sheet of roll; an outline sketch is printed by Jeanne Krochalis and Edward Peters, *The World of Piers Plowman* (Philadelphia, 1975), 172–3. Other possible examples, which I have not examined, are cited by F. Saxl, 'A Spiritual Encyclopedia of the Later Middle Ages', *JWCI*, 5 (1942), 82–134; and Albinia de La Mare, *Catalogue of the Collection of Medieval Manuscripts Bequeathed to the Bodleian Library, Oxford, by James P. R. Lyell* (Oxford, 1971), 254–6.

[6] MS London, BL Royal 14.B.ix, last sheet of roll; I am grateful to my colleague James J. John for checking my transcription of this passage. A rather erratic translation appears in Krochalis and Peters, *World of Piers Plowman*, 178.

[7] I add, without much confidence, a suggestion about line 232, 'Go to Genesis þe geaunt, engendrour of vs alle', which on the face of it seems a striking impressionistic personification of the Book of Genesis as a giant. There are in fact some additional arguments to support such a meaning: the quotation which follows is of course from Genesis; the word γένεσις itself does mean 'origin'; and a somewhat similar figurative characterisation of a biblical author – though this time a highly traditional one – occurs a few lines later in 'Mathew wiþ mannes face' (238). On the other hand, while there seems to be no tradition associating Genesis with a giant, the gigantic stature of Adam is common in Jewish legend and elsewhere. See for example Louis

Proverbs 20: 4, 'Propter frigus piger arare noluit;/ mendicabit ergo aestate, et non dabitur illi' (236–7); Matthew 25: 14–30, the parable of the talents (238–46); and Psalm 127: 2, 'Labores manuum tuarum quia manducabis,/ beatus es, et bene tibi erit' (250–2). As Wenzel and Bowers have pointed out, all four are commonly invoked in condemnations of *acedia*; a further example appears in Peraldus's treatment of *acedia* in the *Summa vitiorum*, where they are quoted (along with other biblical passages) in the space of two rather small pages.[8] In addition, this whole part of Hunger's instructions reads like a dramatisation of several familiar biblical denunciations of *acedia*, like for example 2 Thessalonians 3: 10, '. . . si quis non vult operari, nec manducet'. Again, the relevant Petition from the *Pater noster*, 'Panem nostrum quo-tidianum da nobis hodie', refers to exactly what Piers's followers are working for – or are supposed to be working for – on the half-acre. And while the relevance of *fortitudo* as one of the Gifts or Virtues will in itself be less persuasive, it seems that the forceful opposition of the wasters to Piers (152–8), the failure of the knight's courteous approach (159–70), and especially Hunger's slam-bang solution (174–80), all speak for *fortitudo* as at least one element of the remedy.[9]

Ginzberg, *The Legends of the Jews*, trans. Henrietta Szold (Philadelphia, 1946–64), 1. 59, 76 and 5. 79, 86; Augustin Calmet, *De gigantibus*, in J.-P. Migne, *Scripturae Sacrae cursus completus* (Paris, 1853), 7. 771–2; Ernst H. Kantorowicz, *The King's Two Bodies: A Study in Mediaeval Political Theology* (Princeton, 1957), 70 and n. 62; and *The Prose Solomon and Saturn and Adrian and Ritheus*, ed. James E. Cross and Thomas D. Hill, McMaster Old English Studies and Texts, 1 (Toronto, 1982), 27 and 72. I wonder, then, whether our line might involve a wildly elliptical bit of syntax, to be rendered, 'Go to Genesis [concerning] the giant [Adam], engenderer of us all' (or, removing Kane–Donaldson's comma and construing *geaunt* as an adjective, '. . . the giant engenderer of us all'; or, accepting the reading *þe geaunt þe* found in nearly all manuscripts, '. . . the giant, the engenderer of us all'). Such an ellipsis, if it existed, would presumably be the ancestor of modern expressions like 'Look at today's *Times* – the damned administration . . .', followed by a quotation from the *Times* about the administration just as the quotation following line 232 is about Adam. I must emphasise, however, that I know of no precise syntactic parallels in *Piers Plowman* or elsewhere in ME; that the corresponding passage in C. 8, 239–42 (Pearsall, 156), might be thought, if anything, to support the idea of Genesis as 'engendrour of vs alle'; and that in any case, as John Livingston Lowes remarked long ago, 'Original genius sometimes does originate.'
[8] Wenzel, *Sin of Sloth*, 142; John M. Bowers, *The Crisis of Will in Piers Plowman* (Washington, DC, 1986) 87, 125–6. Guilielmus Peraldus, *Summae virtutum ac vitiorum*, 2.5.1.2–3 (Cologne, 1629), 2. 134–5.
[9] An illustration of the opposition between the virtue *Proesse* (*fortitudo*) and the vice *Peresce* (*acedia*), employing precisely the imagery of Passus 6, appears in an early fourteenth-century manuscript of the *Somme le Roi* (BL Add. 28162, fo. 8v), repro-duced by Rosemund Tuve, *Allegorical Imagery: Some Mediaeval Books and Their Posterity* (Princeton, 1966), 96, fig. 19: *Proesse* (upper left) is opposed to *Peresce* (upper right), represented by a man sitting idle while the plough stands; and *Peresce* is in turn contrasted with *Labor* (lower right), represented by a man busily sowing seed.

This pattern in the septenaries, while certainly relevant for my argument, seems to me to provide only circumstantial evidence, establishing a context that would favour an interpretation of Hunger as the *esuries iustitiae* if more specific correspondences can be found; for such correspondences we must turn to commentaries and sermons on Matthew 5: 6, concerning the fourth Beatitude itself. An extremely common exposition begins with the Classical definition of *iustitia* as the virtue 'quae tribuit unicuique quod suum est' – the virtue that renders to each what is his own, or what is due him. This obligation is then divided into three main categories: what we owe to God, what we owe to our neighbour, and what we owe to ourselves. The interpretation is expressed by a number of commentators from the ninth century through the twelfth – Paschasius Radbertus, Peter Damian, Raoul Ardent, Anselm of Canterbury, and Anselm of Laon – and is incorporated into the *Glossa ordinaria* and the *Summa virtutum* of Peraldus.[10] I quote the development of it that appears in the great thirteenth-century commentary by Hugh of St Cher:

> Non autem dicit, Beati qui esuriunt prudentiam vel temperantiam vel fortitudinem sed iustitiam, quia iustitia est virtus communis ad omnes alias, quae tribuit cuilibet quod suum est. Deo enim tria debemus: Reuerentiam cultus inquantum Dominus, timorem inquantum iudex, amorem inquantum homo incarnatus. Proximis similiter tria: Paribus auxilium, maioribus obedientiam, inferioribus consilium. Nobis tria: Cordis munditiam, carnis substantiam, vtrique sollicitudinem. . . .[11]

And in the fourteenth century, Ludolf of Saxony's *De vita Jesu Christi* produces the following version:

> Et haec est justitia, quae tribuit unicuique quod suum est: Deo, proximo, et sibi. Deo tria: scilicet honorem Creatori, amorem Redemptori, timorem Judici. Proximo tria: obedientiam superiori, concordiam pari, beneficentiam inferiori. Sibi tria: munditiam cordi, custodiam ori, disciplinam carni.[12]

If we now look back at Piers's questions to Hunger and Hunger's replies (quoted above), we will find that they are on precisely this large subject: how

---

[10] Paschasius, *Expositio in Evangelium Matthaei*, 3. 5 (*PL*, 120: 220); Damian, *Sermo 55* (*PL*, 144: 813); Raoul, *Homilia 42 de tempore* (*PL*, 155: 1479); Anselm of Canterbury, *Homilia 2* (*PL*, 158: 595); Anselm of Laon, *Enarrationes in Matthaeum*, 5 (*PL*, 162: 1286); *Glossa*, in *Biblia Sacra cum glossa interlineari, ordinaria* . . . (Venice, 1588), 5: fo. 18v, marginal gloss; Peraldus, *Summae virtutum ac vitiorum*, 1. 5, Tractatus de beatitudinibus, 8 (1. 394). For the Classical definition of *iustitia* as giving each man his due, see for example Cicero, *De officiis* 1.5.15.

[11] *Opera omnia in universum Vetus et Novum Testamentum* (Lyon, 1645), 6: fo. 16r. Hugh then proceeds to associate the *esuries iustitiae* with *fortitudo* as a Gift of the Holy Ghost and with the Petition *Panem nostrum*, just as in the septenaries.

[12] *Vita Jesu Christi*, 1. 33 (Paris, 1865), 149.

to render to each what is due him. More specifically, they are made up entirely – though not in quite the same order -- of the exegetes' three classes of duties: those to God, one's neighbour, and oneself. Piers's first question, asking how he is to handle those who do no work (202–11), and Hunger's answer, telling him how to deal with the undeserving and the deserving hungry (212–28), clearly concern his duty to his 'neighbour' in the generally accepted Christian sense. The last few lines in this first speech of Hunger (225–8) introduce the further subject of his duty to God in this respect, prompting Piers's second question about whether he can do as Hunger says without offending God (229–30); and Hunger expands on this subject of what is owed to God by way of the four biblical pronouncements against *acedia* discussed earlier (231–52). Piers's final question, asking how he and his servants can stay well (253–6), and Hunger's answering dietary prescriptions (257–74), can without difficulty be seen as covering his duty to himself.[13]

This broad pattern of correspondences can be developed in various ways. For example, Piers's reference to the Atonement (207) may relate to Ludolf's *amorem Redemptori* (above); Piers's question about grieving God (229–30) bears an inevitable connection with Hugh's *timorem [Deo] inquantum iudex* and Ludolf's *timorem Judici*; and Hunger's instructions on the care of oneself (257–74) seem to go in the same direction as Hugh's *cordis munditiam, carnis substantiam, vtrique sollicitudinem* and Ludolf's *disciplinam carni*. Again, Piers's strenuous earlier efforts to reform the wasters (117–44) and Hunger's endorsement of a like severity towards them (212–17) accord with comments like that of Ludolf on the *esuries iustitiae*: 'hanc iustitiam et vitae rectitudinem, non solum in nobis, sed et in omnibus aliis appetere debemus'.[14] Hunger's harsh treatment of the wasters (174–80) seems to dramatise part of Peraldus's analysis of Matthew 5: 6: 'potest sumi [iustitia] prout attenditur in inflictione poenarum. . . .'[15] And Piers's merciful qualification of his initial judgement (207–9), also supported by Hunger (218–26), finds agreement in the *Glossa ordinaria*, commenting on Matthew 5: 6 and the following verse, 'Beati misericordes':

> [On 5: 6:] Iusticiae lumen est misericordia; misericordie virtus iusticia. Hec misericordia eget spiritu consilij, sine quo nemo circumspecte miseretur. . . . [On 5: 7:] *Beati misericordes*: Misericordia nascitur de precedentibus quia si precesserit vera humilitas & animas mansuescat,

---

[13] It is perhaps worth noting that in A.7.239, ed. George Kane, *Piers Plowman: The A Version, Will's Visions of Piers Plowman and Do-Well* (London, 1960), 339, Piers's question refers simply to 'summe of my seruauntis'; one suspects that in B. 6. 255, the words 'and myself boþe' may have been added to create or sharpen the correspondence I am proposing.

[14] *Vita Jesu Christi*, 1. 33 (149).

[15] *Summae*, 1. 5, Tract. de beat., 8 (1. 394).

& suos & aliorum casus fleat, & iusticiam esuriat, post nascitur uera misericordia. Tunc enim miserias alienas faciet suas & pro viribus iuuabit; & si iuuandi facultas deest, compassio non deerit.[16]

If this interpretation is convincing in itself, we may observe that *iustitia* in its most inclusive sense – the virtue by which things are ordered as they ought to be – lies at the heart also of various other climactic pronouncements in *Piers Plowman*, like for example the tag '*Nullum malum þe man mette wiþ inpunitum/* And bad *Nullum bonum be irremuneratum*' (4. 143–4), which apparently sums up the lesson of the Lady Meed episode; the lines from the Athanasian Creed, '*Et qui bona egerunt ibunt in vitam eternam;/ Qui vero mala in ignem eternum*' (7. 113–14), epitomising the Pardon; and the insistent refrain *Redde quod debes* in the final two passus (19. 187, 193, 259, 390; 20. 308).[17] But even so, we are left with the question of why the *esuries iustitiae* should emerge for special emphasis in Passus 6. Some years ago I suggested that the broad organisation of *Piers Plowman* grows in large part from the speech of Lady Holy Church in Passus 1; that Passus 2–6 deal with the problems of natural man, and Passus 8–20 with those of specifically Christian man; that within the treatment of natural man, Passus 2–4 are concerned with artificially contrived goods (wealth), and Passus 6 with natural goods; and that the scene on the half-acre is, accordingly, an unsuccessful attempt to reform man's most basic appetites – represented by gluttony, which appears second-last in three of Langland's four enumerations of the Deadly Sins, and especially sloth, which appears last in all of them.[18] In the light of this pattern, it is not difficult to recognise *acedia* (considered not only as physical laziness but as a flaccidity of the whole person, embracing qualities like inertia, indifference, and lack of commitment) as a kind of root-sin in *Piers Plowman*, the flaw most deeply ingrained in man's nature and therefore the most difficult to eradicate.[19] If so, I would suggest that its root-antidote in the poem is the *esuries iustitiae* – its direct opposite, by which one is inflamed not merely to be just, not merely to seek justice where the opportunity presents itself, but to *hunger and thirst* after a proper order of things. As Jerome puts it, in a passage often repeated by later exegetes, 'Non nobis sufficit velle

---

[16] *Glossa*, 5: fo. 18v, marginal gloss.

[17] Possible relations of *Nullum malum inpunitum* and *Redde quod debes* to the *esuries iustitiae* are offered by Peraldus, *Summae*, 1. 5, Tract. de beat., 8 (1. 394), commenting on Matt. 5: 6: 'Vel potest sumi iustitia, prout ad eam pertinet reddere vnicuique quod suum est. . . . Item qui esuriunt iustitiam tertio modo tunc saturabuntur, quia tunc nullum malum relinquetur impunitum.'

[18] 'Holy Church's Speech and the Structure of *Piers Plowman*', *Chaucer and Middle English Studies in Honour of Rossell Hope Robbins*, ed. Beryl Rowland (London, 1974), 320–7. For Langland's enumerations of the Deadly Sins, see 2. 79–101; 5. 296–460; 13. 271–420; and 14. 218–57.

[19] See the valuable recent study by Bowers, *Crisis of Will*, especially 61–96.

justitiam, nisi justitiae patiamur famem, ut sub hoc exemplo nunquam nos satis justos, sed semper esurire justitiae opera intelligamus.'[20] To even their dutiful work on the half-acre, Piers and his faithful followers must add an active longing that things be set right and a will to expend themselves in that effort. This, I take it, would be in human terms the only real antidote to the hard core of *acedia* that has made the reform an indifferent success; and the end of the passus seems to add the ironic reflection that man is not easily brought to hunger for justice with the same intensity that he hungers for food and repose. The unending battle between human inertia and the hunger for reform surfaces again in the final passus, where Sleuþe appears prominently among the attackers of Holy Church (20. 156–64, 217, 373–4), Contrition is drugged by the friars (377–9), and Conscience declares that he will search the world for Piers Plowman to put an end to the universal torpor:

> 'By crist!' quod Conscience þo, 'I wole bicome a pilgrym,
> And [wenden] as wide as þe world [renneþ]
> To seken Piers þe Plowman, þat pryde [my3te] destruye. . . .'
>
> (380–2)

Cornell University

---

[20] *Commentarii in Evangelium Matthaei*, 1. 5 (*PL*, 26: 35); repeated for example by Ludolf, *Vita Jesu Christi*, 1. 33 (149). Cf. Albertus Magnus, *Enarrationes in evangelium Matthaei*, ed. August Borgnet, Vivès *Opera omnia*, vol. 20 (Paris, 1893), 135: '. . . esurire et sitire iustitiam est non quiescere nisi operando iustitiam, et affligi si non fiat iustitia, et refici sicut in sagina et conuiuio, quando iustitia fit per eum.'

The Idea of Reason in Piers Plowman

JOHN A. ALFORD

In one of his numerous articles on the poem, George Kane warns that translators of *Piers Plowman* 'will be well advised to adopt as a working principle that historical differentiation by meaning between a fourteenth-century word and its twentieth-century descendant is as likely as not, and never guess'.[1] We are, in fact, more likely to be misled by the familiar than by the unfamiliar word. *Caurimaury, herne, lordein, maynprise, roynouse, saulee?* We look them up. *Allow, disgise, gerl, harlot, take, tower, venyson?* We tend to assume — many scholars *have assumed* with often disastrous results[2] — that their meanings are evident.

The caveat is to be taken all the more seriously when the word in question is crucial to the interpretation of *Piers Plowman* as a whole. The poem affords a handful of such words. The most important is *treuthe* — the Middle English translation of both *veritas*, 'a true statement or account, that which is in accord with the fact', and *fidelitas*, 'loyalty, honesty, righteousnes'[3] — and around this central word revolves a constellation of related concepts, such as *mesure, law, love, lewte,* and *resoun.*

Resoun is the focus of this essay. Although it is both an essential aspect of truth and the name of a major personification, it has received scant attention.

---

[1] 'Poetry and Lexicography in the Translation of *Piers Plowman*', *Medieval and Renaissance Studies*, 9 (1982), 48.

[2] Robertson and Huppé's misunderstanding of disgise (B. Prol. 24) as 'to pretend or dissemble' (*Piers Plowman and Scriptural Tradition* [Princeton, 1951], 17) is probably the most notorious example of an ahistorical reading. George Kane cites others (e.g., harlot, venyson) in 'Poetry and Lexicography'. The rendering of Middle English *tower* into the rather meaningless Modern English 'tower' (instead of the more accurate and socially significant 'castle') is endemic in critical interpretations of the poem.

[3] The most thorough analysis of *treuthe* in Langland's day is George Kane's 'The Liberating Truth: The Concept of Integrity in Chaucer's Writings', The John Coffin Memorial Lecture 1979 (London, 1980). For a discussion of truth as the central theme of *Piers Plowman*, see my chapter, 'The Design of the Poem', *A Companion to Piers Plowman*, ed. John A. Alford (Berkeley, 1988), 29–65.

The incidental remarks to be found in articles and books on the poem reveal pretty clearly the assumption that modern readers should have little difficulty with the term. *Resoun* is taken to be primarily the mental faculty: 'understanding',[4] 'reasonableness',[5] one of the few 'personifications . . . traceable to human process of mind',[6] 'the way in which something already known is known to determine something coming afterward'.[7] More often than not, critics have failed to adopt as a 'working principle' the likelihood that *resoun* has undergone significant semantic change. Instead they have guessed.

In the following pages I shall explore a variety of meanings contained in the word *resoun*. The best equivalent is not modern English *reason* (although it will be spelled thus for the sake of convenience) but Latin *ratio*. We find repeatedly in Langland's use of *resoun* the evidence of 'print-through', that is, the surfacing of a traditional network of meanings – legal, mathematical, epistemological, and philosophical – that had developed around the word's Latin progenitor. Here, as in many other instances, the poet thought in one language and wrote in another.

I

Let us begin with the legal context of the word. Historically, definitions of law have always turned on the question, 'Is law an act of will or intellect?' 'Nowadays', observes Ewart Lewis, 'most people think of law as the command of a definite will or group of wills endowed with legislative authority'.[8] Most people in the Middle Ages thought otherwise. They started from the assumption that law is an act of the intellect, an expression of immutable truth, a norm of right completely independent of the will. In the *Year Books 18–19 Edward III*, we find the following exchange:

> R. Thorpe (pleader): 'You will do as others have done in the same case; otherwise we shall not know what the law is.'
> Hillary: 'Law is volunte des Justices.'
> Stonore: 'Nanyl; ley es resoun.'[9]

---

[4] Barbara Raw, 'Piers and the Image of God in Man', *Piers Plowman: Critical Approaches*, ed. S. S. Hussey (London, 1969), 173.
[5] Priscilla Martin, *Piers Plowman: The Field and the Tower* (London, 1979), 25ff.
[6] John Norton-Smith, *William Langland* (Leiden, 1983), 103.
[7] Britton J. Harwood, '*Piers Plowman*: Fourteenth-Century Skepticism and the Theology of Suffering', *Bucknell Review*, 19 (1971), 132.
[8] 'The Idea of Law', *Medieval Political Ideas*, 2 vols. (1954; New York, 1974), 1. 1.
[9] Quoted in *Early Registers of Writs*, ed. Elsa de Haas and G. D. G. Hall, Publications of the Selden Society, 87 (London, 1970), xi. In opposition to the rationalist view, the voluntarist or will theory of law 'is seen clearly for the first time in Hobbes, the founder of "legal positivism"', A. Passerin d'Entrèves, *Natural Law*, 2nd rev. ed. (London, 1970), 122.

Where Langland stood in this dispute is hardly open to question. In fact, his whole poem is an argument for the subordination of *volunte* to *resoun.*

The 'rational' view of law has its roots in classical thought. In his *De legibus,* for example, Cicero dismisses as 'foolish' the idea that anyone could derive a science of law from the praetor's edict or from the Twelve Tables – which is precisely where a proponent of the will theory of law would begin – but proposes instead to 'seek the origin of Justice itself at its fountain-head. For when that is discovered we shall undoubtedly have a standard by which the things we are seeking may be tested' (I. 6. 20).[10] Cicero finds this standard in Reason, conceived by the Stoics as innate, everywhere the same, and 'the first possession of man and God'. He likens the universe to a commonwealth, in which Reason is sovereign and delegates its authority by means of particular laws and commands. To obey any reasonable command, therefore, is to 'obey this celestial system, the divine mind, and the God of transcendent power' (I. 7. 23). In short, he says, 'I find that it has been the opinion of the wisest men that Law is not a product of human thought, nor is it any enactment of peoples, but something eternal which rules the whole universe by its wisdom in command and prohibition. Thus they have been accustomed to say that Law is the primal and ultimate mind of God, whose reason (*ratio*) directs all things either by compulsion or restraint' (II. 4. 8).

This vision of an orderly universe, regulated in every detail by an eternal law, made an extraordinary impression upon St Augustine and, through him, upon the entire Middle Ages.[11] He was thrilled to imagine that 'an immutable law governs all mutable things in a most beautiful manner'.[12] Quoting Cicero almost verbatim, he defined the eternal law as 'reason dwelling within the mind of God, whereby all things are directed to their proper ends'.[13] Taking his theory from Stoic philosophy, chiefly by way of Cicero, Augustine developed a specifically Christian concept of eternal law, which became his point of departure for explaining the nature not only of law but also of sin, penance, and redemption. Whatever we desire or do in conformity with the eternal law belongs to virtue; whatever we desire or do against the eternal law belongs to sin.[14]

Especially pertinent to our understanding of *Piers Plowman* is the name

---

[10] Trans. Clinton Walker Keyes, Loeb Classical Library (1928; Cambridge, Mass., 1970), 319.
[11] See A. H. Chroust, 'The Philosophy of Law from St Augustine to St Thomas Aquinas', *The New Scholasticism,* 20 (1946), 26–71.
[12] *De diversis quaestionibus LXXXIII,* Q. 27 ('De providentia'), *PL,* 40: 18.
[13] *De libero arbitrio,* 1. 6 (*PL,* 32: 1221–1303), quoted by Aquinas 1. 2, Q. 93, A. 4, 5. Cf. *Contra Faustum Manichaeum,* 22. 27, 'And the eternal law is the divine order [*ratio*] or will of God, which requires the preservation of natural order, and forbids the breach of it'; trans., *A Select Library of the Nicene and Post-Nicene Fathers,* 4: 283.
[14] *Contra Faustum,* 22. 27; trans., *A Select Library,* 4: 283.

given to the eternal law. 'Transcending our minds a law appears,' Augustine says in *De vera religione*, 'and this is called Truth.'[15] In another famous passage, from *De baptismo, contra Donatistes*, he contrasts the eternal law of truth to the ephemeral law of custom: 'He who, despising truth, presumes to follow custom, is either envious or evil-disposed towards the brethren to whom the truth is revealed. . . . The Lord says in the Gospel, "I am the Truth". He does not say, "I am custom". Therefore, when the truth is made manifest, custom must give way to truth. . . . Since Christ is the Truth, we ought to follow truth rather than custom.'[16] Augustine's interpretation of 'ego sum veritas' (John 14: 6) as referring to justice, an absolute norm of conduct, and not to intellectual truth alone, became standard. We see it again in the letters of Gregory VII and Urban II.[17] It has a prominent place in Gratian's *Decretum* (Prima Pars, Dist. 8. 4 and 5) and thus in the writings of canon law in general.[18] It receives a slightly different twist at the hands of Andreas de Isernia: 'Ad veritatem semper oculum debet habere judex, quia verum amamus . . . et Christus dominus noster dixit, "ego sum veritas", non dixit, "ego sum sententia."'[19] Jean Gerson explicitly identifies the truth which is Christ and the Ciceronian concept of justice: 'Qui clot ses oreilles a verité . . . ne attend salut ne amendement. . . . Ceste verité congneu bien Tulle quant il dit que le droit ne venoit mie des escriptures des juges, comme des XII tables, maiz [de] la raison.'[20]

Why Augustine called the eternal law 'Truth' – and why medieval writers adopted the same usage – is not hard to understand. For one thing, there is the authoritative precedent of the Bible itself, where *veritas* is frequently put to signify justice (e.g., 'Scimus enim quoniam iudicium Dei est secundum veritatem in eos qui talia agunt', Romans 2: 2) and where the formulaic phrase *via veritatis* is used to refer not to knowledge but to righteousness (cf. John 8: 44). For another, to give the name of truth to law is to emphasise its integrity in the strongest possible terms. Like truth, justice is one. It is not this in Rome and that in London, not one thing under Caesar and another

---

[15] *PL*, 34: 147. The passage is quoted in Aquinas, *ST*, 1. 2, Q. 93, A. 1, where the equation of truth and eternal law is explicit: '*We see a law above our minds, which is called truth.* But the law which is above our minds is the eternal law. Therefore truth is the eternal law'; trans. Fathers of the English Dominican Province, 2nd ed. (London, 1927), 8: 28.

[16] Trans., *A Select Library*, 4: 438–9.

[17] Gregory is quoted in Gratian's *Decretum*, Prima Pars, Dist. VIII, C. 5; see *Corpus Iuris Canonici*, ed. Aemilius Friedberg, 2 vols. (1879; Graz, 1955), 1. 14; for Urban II's statement, see his letters, *PL*, 151: 356.

[18] *Corpus Iuris Canonici*, 1: 14.

[19] From his commentaries on Frederick II's *Constitutiones*, 1. 28, quoted by Walter Ullmann, *The Medieval Idea of Law as Represented by Lucas de Penna: A Study in Fourteenth-Century Legal Scholarship* (1946; New York, 1969), 122 n.

[20] Louis Mourin, *Jean Gerson* (Bruges, 1952), 369–70 n.

under Richard. It is everywhere and at all times the same.[21] But above all, the ultimate standard of law must be called truth if, like knowledge, law is a discovery of the intellect rather than a command of the will.

This last point deserves further elaboration. Thomas Aquinas, perhaps the foremost exponent of the intellectual approach to law, explains how the human mind is able to apprehend and thus participate in that absolute truth which is the eternal law.

> A thing may be known in two ways: first, in itself; secondly, in its effect, wherein some likeness of that thing is found: thus someone not seeing the sun in its substance, may know it by its rays. So then no one can know the eternal law, as it is in itself, except the blessed who see God in His Essence. But every rational creature knows it in its reflection, greater or less. For every knowledge of truth is a kind of reflection and participation of the eternal law, which is the unchangeable truth, as Augustine says (*De Vera Relig.* xxxi). Now all men know the truth to a certain extent, at least as to the common principles of the natural law: and as to the others, they partake of the knowledge of truth, some more, some less; and in this respect are more or less cognisant of the eternal law.[22]

That part of truth or the eternal law brought within the scope of human psychology is called the natural law, which is 'an imprint on us of the Divine Light' and 'the rational creature's participation of the eternal law [*participatio legis aeternae in rationabili creatura*]' (*ST*, 1.2 Q. 91, A. 2). Every person of sound mind, whether pagan, Jew, or Christian, has an innate knowledge of the first principles of the law (that is, God is to be honoured, good pursued, evil avoided, and so on). This was the received opinion throughout the Middle Ages. Its sanction was biblical. The *locus classicus* is Romans 2: 14–15, where Paul speaks of the Gentiles, 'who have not the law' but nevertheless 'shew the

---

[21] The notion of *unity* is a central tenet of natural law theory. In a famous passage from *De re publica*, Cicero asserts, 'True law is right reason in agreement with nature; it is of universal application, unchanging and everlasting. . . . And there will be not different laws at Rome and at Athens, or different laws now and in the future, but one eternal and unchangeable law will be valid for all nations and all times, and there will be one master and ruler, that is, God, over us all, for he is the author of this law, its promulgator, and its enforcing judge' (3. 22. 33), trans. Keyes, 211. For a discussion of the passage, see d'Entrèves, 25ff., and *The Cambridge History of Later Medieval Philosophy*, ed. Norman Kretzmann et al. (Cambridge, 1982), 705. The Ciceronian ideal is echoed in the prophecy of Conscience (B. 3. 284–324):

> I, Conscience, knowe þis for kynde wit me tauȝte
> That Reson shal regne and Reaumes gouerne . . .
> Kynges Court and commune Court, Consistorie and Chapitle,
> Al shal be but oon court, and oon burn be Iustice.

[22] *ST*, 1. 2, Q. 93, A. 2; trans. 30.

work of the law *written in their hearts*.[23] When Lady Holy Church tells Will that the knowledge of truth is our natural heritage – 'a kynde knowyng þat kenneþ in þyn herte' (B. 1. 142) – she is simply reminding him of what everyone believed already.

As the manifestation of the supreme truth, then, law reveals itself primarily to reason. In the words of the fourteenth-century jurist, quoted earlier, *Ley est resoun*; or in the words of the philosophers, *Lex est ratio*.[24] Because this formula was the starting point for most medieval speculation on the nature of law, a correct understanding of terms is essential. 'Reason' was often used equivocally. For instance, when Isidore of Seville (a main source for medieval definitions of law) says that 'law consists in reason', he is referring to a principle; but when he concludes from this that 'everything made known through reason will be law', he is referring to a faculty of the mind.[25] *Ratio* is both that which is apprehended and that which apprehends. The distinction is extremely important. In identifying the eternal law as *ratio summa*, the Stoics (and, through Augustine, medieval writers in general) were thinking of an objective order that would exist even if there were no creatures to perceive it. It is the 'reason behind' all things. However, a partial image of *ratio* in this sense of the word has been imprinted on the minds of all rational beings. It is ours by nature. Hence that part of the intellect by which this order is apprehended is called 'natural reason'. As the representative of divine *ratio* in man, it hands down those first principles of thought which the lower faculties (conscience, for example) then apply to particular circumstances. It alone is infallible. As Aquinas states, 'The intellect does not err in the case of first principles; it errs at times in the case of conclusions at which it arrives by reasoning from first principles'.[26]

These two meanings of *ratio* explain the authority of reason in *Piers Plowman* and its relation to the central concept of truth. Among critics of the

---

[23] Italics added. On the important place of this verse in natural law theory, see Chroust, 47, 65, and *passim*, and d'Entrèves, 39, and *passim*. In quoting the verse, Thomas Aquinas cites the following comment: 'Although they have no written law, yet they have the natural law, whereby each one knows, and is conscious of, what is good and what is evil' (*ST*, 1. 2, Q. 91, A. 2).

[24] The formula derives, again, from Cicero; for example, 'lex est ratio summa insita in natura', *De legibus* (1. 5. 18), Keyes, 316. Cf. Lucas de Penna, 'Lex est ratio summa insita in natura' (Ullmann, p. 16); Aquinas, *ST*, 1. 2, Q. 93, A. 1, 'Utrum lex aeterna sit ratio summa'. Sir Edward Coke and others referred to the English Common Law as *ratio summa* and 'the perfection of reason'; see Henri Levy-Ullmann, *The English Legal Tradition* (London, 1935), 55; for a broader discussion of the formula in the context of natural law in general, see d'Entrèves, esp. Ch. 3.

[25] 'Porro si ratione lex consistat, lex erit omne iam quod ratione constiterit', *Etymologiae*, 2. 10. 3, ed. W. M. Lindsay (Oxford, 1911).

[26] *Summa contra Gentiles*, 1: 61; trans. Anton C. Pegis (1955; Notre Dame, 1975), 205. See also *ST*, 1. 2, Q. 94, A. 4 (trans. 47–8).

poem, Daniel Murtaugh is one of the few to have appreciated both meanings: 'Reason has a dual aspect in medieval thought. On the one hand it is the power of the individual rational intellect. On the other, it is the transcendent order by which God created the world.'[27] It should be noted, however, that when Langland wishes to indicate 'the power of the individual rational intellect', he generally prefers the native English *wit* or *kynd wit*, reserving his use of the word *resoun* for those contexts in which the idea of 'transcendent order' predominates.

The most obvious example of the latter usage is the recurring phrase 'reason and right' – an extremely common doublet in the literature of the period. Conscience says that heaven is reserved for those who 'han ywroght werkes wiþ right and wiþ reson' (B. 3. 239), that it is 'nother resoun ne ryhte ne in no rewme lawe/ That eny man mede toke but he hit myhte deserue' (C. 3. 293–4), and that it 'is nat resonable ne rect to refuse my syre name' (C. 3. 366); Imaginatif, that 'It were neiþer reson ne riȝt to rewarde boþe [saint and sinner] yliche' (B. 12. 209); Lucifer, that he holds 'by right and by reson þe renkes þat ben here' (B. 18. 278); a lord, that he takes from his reeve by 'riȝt and reson' (B. 19. 460), and so forth.[28] Like most legal doublets, the phrase is clearly pleonastic: reason is right, and right is reason.

Included in the idea of reason as transcendent order is a strong numerical component. One meaning of the word *ratio* is 'a reckoning, account, calculation' (cf. C. 9. 274, '*Redde racionem villicacionis* or in arrerage fall').[29] There is a hint of this definition in the examples just given: it is neither reason nor right 'that eny man mede toke but he hit myhte deserue' or to reward saint and sinner alike. But elsewhere the imagery of accounting is quite explicit. Several times Langland puns on the sense of *ratio* as 'a reckoning'. Holy Church, speaking of the necessities of life, will 'rekene hem by reson' (B. 1. 22); the king threatens Wrong, 'Ac Reson shal rekene wiþ yow' (B. 4. 177); Rechelesnesse says that merchants and messengers must all 'rikene byfore resoun a resonable acounte' (C. 13. 34); the Dreamer observes of the 'reneyed caityf', 'Ac reson shal rekene wiþ hym and rebuken hym at þe laste,/ And conscience acounte wiþ hym and casten hym in arerage' (B. 11. 131–2). The same pattern of reason, reckoning, and arrearages occurs again in the following speech by Patience:

> Thouȝ men rede of richesse riȝt to þe worldes ende,
> I wiste neuere renk þat riche was, þat whan he rekene sholde,

---

[27] *Piers Plowman and the Image of God* (Gainesville, 1978), 89.

[28] All quotations of the B version are taken from Kane–Donaldson; the C version is quoted from Pearsall.

[29] See Charlton T. Lewis and Charles Short, *A Latin Dictionary* (1879; Oxford, 1966). John Conley has pointed out that *reson* and *acownte* are used as synonyms in the morality play *Mankind*: ' "Reson" in "Mankind", 173', *N&Q*, 23 (1976), 447–8.

Whan he drogh to his deeþ day þat he ne dredde hym soore,
And þat at þe rekenyng in Arrerage fel raþer þan out of dette.
Ther þe poore dar plede and preue by pure reson
To haue allowaunce of his lord; by þe lawe he it cleymeþ.

(B. 14. 105–10)

Although *resoun* may be taken here to refer to the intellectual process, it is nevertheless a process dominated by the idea of compensatory justice – as if the poor man might appeal to reason as to an accountant whose records would indicate clearly that he was, indeed, owed 'some allowaunce of his lorde'. On many estates, of course, the task of reckoning the accounts fell to the reeve (cf. B. 5. 420, 'a Reues rekenyng'). Thus reason is cast in this rôle in C. 3. 308–9:

And ther is resoun as a reue rewardynge treuthe
That bothe the lord and the laborer be leely yserued.

Reason is not the actual source of the wages given for true labour any more than a reeve is. He is an administrative official – a bookkeeper, a paymaster, someone who reckons precisely what is owed each worker. The reference is less to the faculty of reason than to that eternal and inviolable *ratio* according to which, as Truth's pardon has it, 'Qui bona egerunt, ibunt in vitam eternum; qui vero mala, in ignem eternum'.[30]

II

It is because the eternal law of Truth consists *in* reason (order) and reveals itself *to* reason (the faculty) that Reason figures as a major personification in the poem. The idea of order dominates, however, and this is increasingly so as the poem progresses. Let us examine just the three major appearances of Reason, first as an adviser to the king in the trial of Wrong and Lady Meed, next as a preacher on the field of folk, and finally as Will's instructor on 'a mountaigne þat myddelerþe hiʒte'. As we shall see, each appearance tends to strengthen the notion of reason as a moral absolute.

Having summoned Reason to the trial of Lady Meed, the king seats him beside himself 'on benche' and the two then 'wordeden a gret while wel wisely togideres' (B. 4. 46). We might interpret this to mean simply that the king consults his own reason in the case. Yet this allegorical action also underscores an important legal doctrine. In his office as judge, the medieval king functions primarily as an agent of reason. Law is reason (*lex est ratio*), and

---

[30] On the semi-pelagian 'justice' of salvation, see Robert Adams, 'Langland's Theology', *A Companion to Piers Plowman*, ed. John A. Alford (Berkeley, 1988), 87–114. The position seems to be rejected by the *Pearl*-poet (see especially lines 701–4). The two poets may represent opposing points of view in the contemporary controversy on works versus grace.

whatever is not reason is not law. 'Human law has the nature of law in so far as it partakes of right reason. . . . But in so far as it deviates from reason, it is called an unjust law, and has the nature, not of law but of violence' (Aquinas); and 'When the will of the prince deviates from equity, justice and reason, it is not law' (Lucas de Penna).[31]

The king's behaviour is exemplary, therefore, and the sudden appearance of Wrong in the courtroom serves to dramatise its opposite – to distinguish in action between reason and will, right and might. As a purveyor of the king, Wrong has abused his position. He is charged with maintenance, forestalling, breaking and entering, robbery, rape, and murder – all technically defined as crimes 'against the king's peace'.[32] His behaviour in court is really no better, for he remains contemptuous of the law. Unable to enforce his will by violent means, he resorts to the power of the purse, enlisting the help of Lady Meed and others. His friends Wisdom and Sire Waryn þe Witty set about 'To ouercomen þe kyng wiþ catel if þei myȝte' (B. 4. 82). They offer him a disguised bribe in the form of bail money: if Wrong 'amendes mowe make lat maynprise hym haue'. On the other front, Lady Meed attempts to buy off the plaintiff, Peace, with 'a present al of pured golde'. Although Peace is willing enough to drop the charges – 'For he haþ waged me wel as wisdom hym tauȝte/ I forgyue hym þat gilt wiþ a good wille' – he cannot. He is no longer the true plaintiff in the case. By law, an offence against the king's peace is an offence against the king himself. The king, in turn, refers the matter to Reason: 'But Reson haue ruþe on hym he shal reste in þe stokkes'; and immediately Wrong's supporters 'radde Reson to haue ruþe on þat shrewe'.

Reason is implacable, of course, as by definition he must be:

> 'Reed me noȝt', quod Reson, 'no ruþe to haue
> Til lordes and ladies louen alle truþe
> And haten alle harlotrie to heren or to mouþen it;
> Til pernelles purfill be put in hire hucche,
> And childrene cherissynge be chastised wiþ yerdes,
> And harlottes holynesse be holden for an heþyng;
> Til clerkene coueitise be to cloþe þe pouere and fede,
> And Religiouse Romeris *Recordare* in hir cloistres
> As Seynt Beneyt hem bad, Bernard and Fraunceis;
> And til prechours prechynge be preued on hemselue;
> Til þe kynges counseil be þe commune profit;

---

[31] *ST*, 1. 2, Q. 93, A. 3 (trans. 32); Ullmann, 55. As noted above (note 24), even English common law was held to be the perfection of reason: 'what is not reason is not law'. One of the main questions confronting legal philosophers was 'how reason is transmuted into law' (Lewis, 1: 6). The actual place of reason in judicial practice is problematic; see, for example, Alan Harding, *A Social History of English Law* (Harmondsworth, 1966), 134.

[32] Anna P. Baldwin, *The Theme of Government in Piers Plowman* (Cambridge, 1981), 40–5.

Til Bisshopes Bayardes ben beggeris Chaumbres,
Hire haukes and hire houndes help to pouere Religious;
And til Seint Iames be souȝt þere I shal assigne. . . .'

(B. 4. 113–26)

Two things should be noted about this response. It identifies Reason with the social doctrine that order depends on truth, each individual performing the duties of his estate. It also serves to reveal his uncompromising nature. As the principle of order, Reason will have no 'ruþe' on those who deliberately flout it. He will not because he cannot. To forgive – if I may invoke once again the meaning of *ratio* as 'a reckoning' – is tantamount to juggling the books. It is simply not his prerogative.

Lest anyone doubt his meaning, Reason goes on to affirm the iron-clad principle of *nullum malum inpunitum*. If he were 'kynge with crowne to kepen a rewme', he says,

Sholde neuere wrong in þis world þat I wite myȝte
Ben vnpunysshed at my power for peril of my soule,
Ne gete my grace þoruȝ giftes, so me god helpe!
Ne for no Mede haue mercy but mekenesse it made,
For *Nullum malum* þe man mette wiþ *inpunitum*
And bad *Nullum bonum* be *irremuneratum*.   (B. 4. 139–44)

Earlier we saw Reason 'as a reue rewardynge treuthe'; now we see him as a judge meting out punishment for the lack of it. In both cases Reason stands for the same principle, the principle of *retributive justice*, which is expressed most succinctly – as noted above – in the words of Truth's pardon. In order to safeguard this principle, the king appoints Reason as 'cheef chaunceller in cheker and in parlement' and, only a step lower, Conscience as 'a kynges iustice' in all his courts (C. 4. 185–6).[33] As the first vision of the poem comes to a close, then, we see the triumph, at least temporarily, of reason over meed and wrong, justice over injustice.

The figure of Reason reappears at the beginning of the next vision (in B and C), which is a 'showing' of the pilgrimage to Truth. He has exchanged his judicial robes, however, for the vestments of the Church ('yreuestede ryht as a pope' [C. 5. 112]). His audience is also different: he is now back on the 'fair field full of folk'. Yet, as many readers have noticed, the message is the same. It is an effective way of stressing the universality of *ratio* as idea. The same

[33] Although the subordination of Conscience to Reason has been denied by a few critics, it is clearly established in the C version by the legal analogy; see Baldwin, 40. The superiority of Reason can also be argued from the perspective of Scholastic psychology; see Charles Whitworth, 'Changes in the Roles of Reason and Conscience in the Revisions of "Piers Plowman" ', *N&Q*, 19 (1972), 4–7. The pairing of Reason and Conscience as a literary theme is explored (though superficially) by A. L. Hench, 'The Allegorical Motif of Conscience and Reason, Counsellors', *English Studies in Honor of James Southall Wilson*, University of Virginia Studies (Charlottesville, 1951), 193–201.

principle that rules in the courtroom ought to govern *ecclesia* and society as a whole.

Although other critics have observed that Reason's sermon is mainly a replication of his words before the king, I should like to call attention here to certain specific similarities. First, there is the matter of repeated words and phrases. In his earlier speech – to cite only a few examples – Reason advises that 'pernelles purfill be put in hire hucche' and now 'Pernele hir purfil to leue/ And kepe it in hire cofre for catel at nede' (B. 5. 26–7); earlier that 'Religiouse Romeris *Recordare* in hir cloistres' and now 'Religion hir rule to holde'; earlier, that 'prechours prechynge be preued on hemselue' and now 'prelates and preestes togideres,/ "That ye prechen þe peple, preue it yowselue"'. More significantly, the structure of his sermon reveals the same respect for social hierarchy: he addresses each estate in turn, admonishing all to fulfil their special obligations, and he returns to his earlier injunction that 'Seint Iames be souȝt þere I shal assigne':

> And ye þat seke Seynt Iames and Seyntes at Rome,
> Sekeþ Seynt Truþe, for he may saue yow alle.　　(B. 5. 56–7)

Finally, Reason affirms once again the rule of *nullum malum inpunitum*. The theme of punishment runs throughout the sermon:

> Tomme Stowue he tauȝte to take two staues
> And fecche Felice hom fro wyuen pyne. . .
> He bad Bette kutte a bouȝ ouþer tweye
> And bete Beton þerwith but if she wolde werche.
> He chargede Chapmen to chastiȝen hir children
>
> . · . · . · . · . · . · . · . · . · .
>
> And siþen he radde Religion hir rule to holde
> 'Lest þe kyng and his conseil youre comunes apeire
> And be Styward of youre stede til ye be stewed bettre'.
> 　　　　　　　　　　　　　　　　　　　　(B. 5. 28–47)

The emphasis on punishment is even greater in the C text, where the sermon is expanded by additional material from B. 10. 292–320. In a warning to Religious, for example, Reason says:

> Ac þer shal come a kyng and confesse ȝow alle
> And bete ȝow, as þe bible telleth, for brekynge of ȝoure reule
> And amende ȝowe monkes, bothe moniales and chanons,
> And potte ȝowe to ȝoure penaunce, *Ad pristinum statum ire*,
> And barones and here barnes blame ȝow and repreue.
>
> . · . · . · . · . · . · . · . · . · .
>
> For þe abbot of Engelonde and the abbesse his nese
> Shal haue a knok yppon here crounes and incurable þe wounde.
> 　　　　　　　　　　　　　　　　　　　　(C. 5. 168–77)

As a result of this revision in the C text, the poet was able to bring together in one place numerous illustrations of the idea of *nullum malum inpunitum* and to connect that idea even more forcefully with the figure of Reason.

In both speeches, therefore, Reason aligns himself with the principle of order, manifested primarily in the rigid structure of feudal society and in the invincible workings of retributive justice. Although associated with the king in Passus 4, he is clearly not the 'reason' of any particular individual. He is the *idea* of reason, by which we know that obligations are to be kept, debts paid, sins punished, good deeds rewarded, and the standard by which our every act will be judged ultimately as either true or untrue. [34]

The identification of Reason with transcendent order – the eternal law as manifest in the *lex naturalis* – is clearer still in his third major appearance (B. 11. 324–404, C. 13. 128–213). From 'a mountaigne þat myddelerþe hiзte' (B. 11. 324) or 'in þe myrour of Mydelerthe' (C. 13. 131), the Dreamer is given a panoramic view of nature:

> Resoun y sey sothly sewe alle bestes
> In etynge and drynkyng, in engendrure of kynde
>
> . . . .
>
> Saue man and his make; and þerof me wondrede,
> For out of resoun they ryde and rechelesliche taken on,
> As in derne dedes, bothe in drynkyng and elles.
>
> (C. 13. 142–54)

The contrast between animal behaviour, which conforms to natural law, and human behaviour, which doesn't, is a literary *topos*. In a Vernon lyric, for example, the poet observes:

> For Beestes and foules, more & leeste,
> þe cours of kynde alle þei suwe;
> And whonne we breken Godes heste,
> Aзeynes kuynde we ben vn-trewe. [35]

The issue was very much alive as late as the eighteenth century. In the first chapter of his treatise, the *Esprit des Lois*, Montesquieu enquires why it is that while animals obey 'the law of their nature', man does not but falls into sin. [36]

The *topos* derives, ultimately, from a well-known passage in Roman juris-

---

[34] The specific obligations dictated by reason or natural law are treated by Chroust. Of particular relevance to Reason's sermon is St Bonaventure's 'justification by natural law of the existing social stratification and man's duty to obey his superiors' (61).

[35] Carleton Brown, ed., *Religious Lyrics of the XIVth Century*, 2nd ed. (Oxford, 1957), 129.

[36] See H. L. A. Hart, *The Concept of Law* (Oxford, 1961), 182.

prudence, Ulpian's definition of *ius naturale* as *quod natura omnia animalia docuit*. In full, the passage runs as follows:

> The law of nature is that law which nature teaches to all animals. For this law does not belong exclusively to the human race, but belongs to all animals, whether of the air, the earth, or the sea. Hence comes that yoking together of male and female, which we term matrimony; hence the procreation and bringing up of children. We see, indeed, that all the other animals besides man are considered as having knowledge of this law.[37]

This is the germ of Will's vision of 'Mydelerthe'. He beholds, in detail, 'þe sonne and þe see and þe sond . . . where þat briddes and bestis by here make þei зeden . . . in engendrure of kynde'. (The failure to appreciate that Langland's focus is not natural history but rather natural law has led to numerous misinterpretations of the scene, perhaps none more trivialising than the criticism that the poet was 'a little too preoccupied with reproductive functions'.[38])

Reconciling the two definitions of natural law as *ratio* and as *quod natura omnia animalia docuit* was one of the major tasks confronting the schoolmen.[39] William of Auxerre posits a hierarchy of natural laws: '*ius naturale speciale* is natural right taken in its strictest sense, and this is found only in those beings possessing reason; *ius naturale universalius* [*quod natura omnia animalia docuit*] pertains to the whole realm of animal nature; finally, *ius naturale universalissimum* is nothing else than the law and harmony of all creation, inanimate as well as animate'.[40] Albertus Magnus rejects the solution: 'We do not agree with that distinction posed by some,' he writes, 'namely that natural right may be spoken of in many ways, and that in one way it is common to us and the beasts. . . . Although training and nutrition and procreation are common to animal nature in general, they do not fall within the compass of natural right unless in some way they participate in reason and are morally virtuous acts.'[41] It remained for Thomas Aquinas to explain in what way animals may be said to 'participate in reason'. Both men and beasts, he argues, obey the *ratio divina* through fidelity to their proper ends. 'Now just as man . . . impresses a kind of inward principle of action on the man that is subject to him, so God imprints on the whole of nature the principles of its proper actions' (*ST*, 1. 2, Q. 93, A. 5). Thus, speaking analogically, 'Even

---

[37] Thomas Collett Sandars, *The Institutes of Justinian* (London, 1962), 7.
[38] Norton-Smith, 113.
[39] See O. Lottin, *Le droit naturel chez Saint Thomas d'Aquin et ses prédécesseurs*, 2nd ed. (Bruges, 1931).
[40] Stanley B. Cunningham, 'Albertus Magnus on Natural Law', *JHI*, 28 (1967), 494.
[41] Cunningham, 496.

irrational animals partake in their own way of the Eternal Reason, just as the rational creature does' (Q. 91, A. 2).

The Thomistic synthesis, clearly indebted to the Stoic tradition described above, can be summarised in a word as teleological. According to this view, as H. L. A. Hart explains, '[E]very nameable kind of existing thing, human, animate, and inanimate, is conceived not only as tending to maintain itself in existence but as proceeding towards a definite optimum state which is the specific good – or the *end* (*telos, finis*) appropriate for it'.[42] It is *natural* for animals to mate, and for human beings to love God and neighbour; any behaviour that frustrates the attainment of one's proper end (for example, sin or injustice) is *unnatural*. This is the logic behind the Dreamer's vision of Mydelerthe:

> I was fet forþ by forbisenes to knowe
> Thorugh ech a creature kynde my creatour to louye.
>
> (B. 11. 325–6)

To love one's Creator, here identified with *Kynde* ('Natura, id est, deus'), is itself a *kyndeliche* act, a basic precept of natural law, a movement towards the realisation of one's own 'inward principle of action'.[43]

Why, then, do rational beings go against their own nature? When Will sees how *unkyndeliche* they behave, 'how men token Mede and Mercy refused', how 'No Reson hem ruled, neiþer riche ne pouere', his immediate reaction is to fault Reason itself:

> Thenne y resonede Resoun and ryht til hym y sayde:
> 'Y haue wonder in my wit, so wys as thow art holden,
> Wherefore and why, as wyde as thow regneste,
> That thow ne reuledest rather renkes then other bestes?
> Y se non so ofte sorfeten, sothly, so mankynde;
> In mete out of mesure and mony tymes in drynke,
> In wommen, in wedes, and in wordes bothe,
> They ouerdoen hit day and nyhte and so doth nat oþer bestes;
> They reule hem al by resoun, ac renkes ful fewe.
> And þerfore merueileth me, for man is moste yliche the of wit and of
>   werkes,
> Why he ne loueth thy lore and leueth as þou techest?'
>
> (C. 13. 182–92)

The absurdity of Will's position is betrayed by his own words, 'Thenne y

---

[42] Hart, 184.

[43] On the decretists' formula 'Natura, id est, deus', Gaines Post comments, 'If God can be called *natura*, it is only a way of saying that God is the ultimate source of the laws of nature', *Studies in Medieval Legal Thought* (Princeton, 1964), 522. Langland exploits the rich polysemy of *kyndenesse*, including the notion of love of one's Creator and fellow creatures, most fully in B. 17. 206–98.

resonede Resoun'. He rebukes or – to treat 'resonede' as a pun – 'reasons against' Reason.[44] In behaving thus, he in effect answers his own question. Why does man alone of God's creatures not live in harmony with reason? Because man alone is endowed with a free will, capable of – and since the Fall, bent on – asserting its independence from the *ratio divina*. The error in Will's rebuke of Reason is not primarily to criticise the mental faculty by which we catch a glimpse of the divine order; it is to criticise that order itself. It is, in the words of Murtaugh, 'to call into doubt the existence of Reason as a stable, objective entity, as a divine idea corresponding to our subjective reason and securing its stability' (89).

That the Dreamer regards Reason as something more than our 'subjective reason' is clear from his own words. He opposes Reason and 'wit' to each other ('Y haue wonder in my wit, so wys as thow art holden') and says explicitly that the former is the model or idea for the latter ('for man is moste yliche the of wit'). Most obviously, of course, if beasts 'reule hem al by resoun, ac renkes ful fewe', then Reason cannot be simply the intellectual faculty that distinguishes man from the animals.[45] It is the principle of *ratio* in which both share, man by virtue of 'wit' and animals by virtue of instinct, which Langland sees as a less developed form of the same thing (Nature gave to all beasts a 'cantel of kynde wyt here kynde to saue' [C. 14. 163]). In the above passage, *ratio* manifests itself primarily in the form of moderation. While animals observe order and proportion in all their behaviour, men 'sorfeten', they are 'out of mesure', they 'ouerdoen hit day and nyhte', 'out of resoun they ryde'. This association of reason and 'mesure', of course, is established from the very beginning of the poem in Lady Holy Church's lecture to Will.[46] Truth, she states, has provided the necessities of life 'in mesurable manere to make yow at ese':

> That oon is vesture from chele þee to saue;
> That oþer is mete at meel for mysese of þiselue;
> And drynke whan þee drieþ, ac do it noȝt out of reson
>
> . . . .
>
> For riȝtfully reson sholde rule yow alle,
> And kynde wit be wardeyn youre welþe to kepe
> And tutour of youre tresor, and take it yow at nede.
>
> (B. 1. 23–56)

---

[44] Cf. 'To reason with hym that made reason our reasonȝ are but wyld', Carleton Brown, ed., *Religious Lyrics of the XVth Century* (Oxford, 1939), 184.

[45] I cannot accept Pearsall's explanation, which defines *resoun* far more narrowly than the poem requires: 'The dreamer is confusing the issue; animals are not ruled by reason, but by natural instinct. Man alone has the power of reason, and the power of choice to follow its law' (230).

[46] The association is common. 'In Chaucer it [reason] quite frequently translates *mesura* ('Chaucer and Reason', *MLR*, 21 [1926], 18).

Whatever violates the law of reason, as safeguarded by *kynde wit*, may be called 'unreasonable'. This is the sense, for example, in which Piers means the word when he declares, 'it is an vnresonable Religion þat haþ riȝt noȝt of certein' (B. 6. 151). Most attempts to render the meaning of *unreasonable* in this context have been wide of the mark. A. V. C. Schmidt glosses the line as follows: 'For it would not be reasonable to expect members of any religious order to possess absolutely no source of sure sustenance'.[47] Expansion of the word *unreasonable* – 'not be reasonable to expect' – is unnecessary. The referent is not some implied mental process but simply, as the syntax declares, *religioun*, which, if it 'haþ riȝt noȝt of certein', is unreasonable *in and of itself*, lacking the essential quality of measure, proportion, justice.

In his reply to Will's challenge, Reason identifies himself once again with the existing order, the cosmic *status quo*, 'the way things are'. Just as in his earlier appearances, where he stresses the idea of degree and the various obligations thereof, so now he reminds Will of his proper place in the scheme of things, telling him in effect to mind his own business: 'Reche þe neuere/ Why y soffre or nat soffre . . . *De re que te non molestat, noli te certare* [Strive not in a matter which does not concern you]' (C. 13. 193–4a). It is not for the will to question reason – taken either as transcendent order or as the faculty perceiving it – but simply to submit, to 'soffre'. After all, God 'myhte amende in a mynte-while al þat amys standeth,/ Ac he soffreth, in ensaumple þat we sholde soffren alle' (C. 13. 197–8). This seems to be the main lesson of the dream.[48] At least Will takes it to be. Awakened by his own acute embarrassment ('Tho cauhte y colour anoen and comesede to ben aschamed'), he is now able to formulate a definition of Dowel – 'To se moche and soffre al', that is, to recognise and accept the divine order, especially as it dictates one's own place and behaviour.

In its three major appearances, then, Reason functions primarily as a moral absolute. It is identified first with secular power, then with ecclesiastical authority, and finally with nature itself, all delegates of the *ratio divina*. Coupled with its other, numerous manifestations as a common noun – associated, as we have seen, with 'right', 'law', and 'order' – Reason emerges as far more crucial to the poem than previous criticism has allowed: it is an essential component of *treuthe*. To 'do well' means to subordinate one's will to the *ordo* of reason, apprehended in its general principles by Kynde Wit and applied in specific cases by Conscience. As *The Book of Virtues and Vices*

[47] *The Vision of Piers Plowman* (London, 1978), 71.
[48] The dream is actually a dream-within-a-dream. As Joseph Wittig argues, it marks a turning point in the Dreamer's progress towards truth: the will must be engaged both intellectually and *affectively*, that is, 'to se moche and soffre al', '*Piers Plowman* B, Passus IX–XII: Elements in the Design of the Inward Journey', *Traditio*, 28 (1972), 211–80.

states, quoting St Bernard, '"Vertue is non oþer þing but assent bitwixe resoun and wille", þat is whan wille wole wiþoute grucchynge or countre-pledyng speke and do and put to worke þat þat resoun seiþ and scheweþ and techeþ'.[49]

Michigan State University

[49] Ed. W. Nelson Francis, EETS, 217 (London, 1942), 152.

Mede and Mercede: the Evolution of the Economics of Grace in the Piers Plowman B and C Versions

ROBERT ADAMS

Early in the B version of *Piers Plowman*, Langland offers us a mordant description of contemporary economic corruption dominated by Lady Meed. Somewhat later, by contrast, he contrives an idealistic vision of a reformed society of grace where Meed 'Shal na moore . . . be maister on erþe' (3. 290).[1] Yet the relatively simple dichotomy that this summary suggests does not suffice to describe the complexity of Langland's initial perspective on the world of Mammon in the B version; for Langland is nowhere so utopian as to imagine a world freed from some of the most basic economic impulses, e.g., the desire to reward good work and the wish to have one's just deserts. In fact, Langland recognises in these impulses something fundamentally holy; the innate desire of the human heart to please God (1. 142–4), a desire that motivates all fruitful human endeavours. It is this perception that causes Theology to insist on the theoretical goodness of Meed (2. 119–33), even in the teeth of all the evidence that tends to incriminate her as a socially demoralising force in the actual economic life of fourteenth-century England.

Hence the B version seeks to express the paradox of an essential, indeed sacred, human impulse distorted through sin by insisting on there being 'two manere of Medes' (3. 231ff.), the first being God's gift of salvation to the virtuous soul and the second being earthly bribery. Though the stark contrast of these two categories appears to leave little room for ordinary, permissible human economic behaviour, Langland is careful to classify wage labour and trade as falling beyond the bounds of any sort of reward situation since a clear *quid pro quo* is always involved in these latter activities. They are, for Langland, examples of *marchaundise* or *mesurable hire*, not of *mede*.

One may easily object that such a theology of economic motives is considerably oversimplified (the same could be said of most medieval treatments of

---

[1] Unless otherwise noted, all citations of B are from Kane–Donaldson. Citations of C are from Pearsall.

economics),[2] but it would be difficult to describe it as less than comprehensive. And yet, when Langland encounters this passage during the revision of B to C, he subjects it to one of the most complete re-workings of any segment of the poem. Seemingly dissatisfied with his earlier scheme, the author now offers a more complex description of human economic relationships and their figurative connection to divine grace, introducing in the process a completely new term for certain reward situations, *mercede*.

Of course the real puzzle in all of this, the one that caused the Reverend Skeat to despair of a solution, is the relationship between *mede*, which is still present in Passus 3 of C, and the new term, *mercede*. And a major cause of the obscurity of this passage – Langland's final attempt to grapple with the theology of economics – is the seemingly muddled grammatical analogy through which he sought to clarify the significance of his two key terms. Hence, as part of my contribution, I wish to present a close paraphrase of the passage in question. But first we must review the philological status of these two terms prior to Langland's use of them, interpret his discussion of *mede* in B, and describe how that discussion, the reactions it appears to have evoked, and mere changes in the times seem to have altered his aproach to the same issues in C.

The previous philological status of *mede* and *mercede* is relatively easy to summarise. There appears to be no etymological relationship between the two words, at least none in historical times; and Langland is apparently the only English author ever to attempt anglicising the Latin term, *mercede*, whose nominative is *merces*. *Mede*, on the other hand, is as old as the English language itself and, in Langland's day, covered exactly the same semantic range as Latin *merces*, viz., wages, payment, material reward, bribe, profit, just desert, special favour, and, of course, theological grace or merit. In the Vulgate *merces* is favoured overwhelmingly as the means to express most of these concepts (the exception is 'bribery'), far more often than the combined usages of such obvious rivals as *stipendium*, *remuneratio*, and *praemium*. And the translators of both the earlier and later versions of the Wyclifite Bible show a strong preference for *mede* as the means to render this generalised term into English. Indeed, *mede* is employed approximately 150 times and over a much broader range than its only rival, *hire*, which is used about fifty times to render *merces* in contexts involving a specific *quid pro quo*.

Therefore, when in B Langland chooses to define *mede* so as to exclude all situations concerned with wages and trade, he is artificially delimiting the term to suit the argument he wishes to develop. He is not so much acting lexicographically as he is acting philosophically. Still, if the evidence of the

---

[2] Cf. Jean Ibanès, *La doctrine de l'église et les réalités économiques au XIIIe siècle* (Paris, 1967), and John W. Baldwin, *The Medieval Theories of the Just Price* (Philadelphia, 1959).

Wyclifite Bible is given due weight, one must admit that Langland's stipulative definition is perceptive; for *mede*'s centre of semantic gravity seems to have shifted noticeably in the late fourteenth century, moving away from 'wages' and towards 'pure reward' or 'gift'. Furthermore, when in C Langland employs these English and Latin equivalents *mede* and *mercede* to describe evil and good recompense respectively, it seems clear that he is once more imposing his own philosophical distinctions on the lexicographical reality and that he has not, in truth, moved very far away from his assertion in B that there are 'two manere of Medes'. Also, it should come as no surprise that Langland has reserved the Latin term, sanctified by its use in Holy Scripture (though it there describes Balac's reward to Balaam as well as God's to Abraham!), to cover recompense rendered in proper circumstances, while leaving the English word, with its smell of the marketplace, to cover less reputable dealings.

As for Langland's motives in introducing these doublets to enforce a novel semantic distinction, we must return briefly to B. There, it will be recalled, we were introduced to a distinction between two kinds of *mede*, the one earthly and immoderate, openly equated with graft (3. 246–54); the other heavenly, seemingly proportionate to merit, and implicitly equivalent to grace, beatitude, or both. No allowance is made for any other sort of *mede* situation, and, as was noted previously, wages and trade are set to one side.

Judging from the nature of changes made both here and elsewhere throughout the poem, one may assume that Conscience's definition of *mede* in B occasioned at least three types of response from the original readers of the poem: (1) Like certain other features in the dramatised dialectic of the B version (e.g., the tearing of the pardon), the introduction of two almost antithetical forms of *mede* seemed to some readers too troubling and confusing to be edifying. Especially problematic here is the fact that Lady Meed, the allegorical character who provokes this philosophical distinction, seems so onesidedly sluttish as to undercut the point Langland wishes to make about the holy origins of the impulse to give and receive rewards. (2) Also, several major revisions from B, including this one, seem to be seeking to defuse criticisms of Langland's theology of grace. Hence, he eliminates B's implication that the hallmark of God's grace is its correlation with the previous good deeds and merit of the recipient ('god of his grace gyueþ in his blisse/ *To hem þat werchen wel while þei ben here* [3. 232–3]). Apparently someone has complained to him that zealous Augustinians of Bradwardine's ilk believe precisely that divine grace has *no relationship whatsoever* to preceding human 'good works' or merits. Thus, from their viewpoint, B's entire discussion of this subject made it sound as though God either agreed with Pelagius or else that He practised bribery on a cosmic scale. (3) Finally, someone seems to have pointed out that the poet's insistence on equating all earthly *mede* with corruption was needlessly inflammatory. Especially in the aftermath of the

Peasants' Revolt, such remarks could be construed as a repudiation of the whole feudal order, based, as it was, on what most people would have called *mede*.

In response to the first of these criticisms, Langland attempts to simplify (though of course he ends by making matters worse). He will grant the uniform blackness of *mede*, a situation which his own portrait of Lady Meed has done so much to foster. And he will offer as an alternative a morally proper form of recompense with a distinctive Latin name, *mercede*.

In answer to the second objection, which for Langland must have seemed the most serious since he had no intention of modifying his basic positions on ethics, the provocative distinction based on *mesure* or lack of *mesure* ('Ther is a Mede *mesurelees* þat maistres desireþ;/ To mayntene mysdoers Mede þei take' [3. 246–7]) is deleted. By having criticised human *mede* as 'immoderate' or 'lacking in measure', Langland appears in B to have been inviting the conclusion that God's *mede*, by contrast, is good because it is measured to fit the deserts of its recipient ('*Qui ingreditur sine macula & operatur Iusticiam*' [3. 237]). In its C version, however, *Piers Plowman* will no longer be quite so easy a target for those heresy hunters eager to sniff out any sentimental suggestion of a correlation between natural merit and divine reward. Instead, Langland substitutes two fresh distinctions. The first of these judges propriety of recompense by looking at the chronological sequence between the deed and the reward. The second, offered in the infamous grammatical analogy, sees propriety as depending on an existing relationship of permanent and complete congruity or fidelity between giver and recipient.

With the introduction of the first of these new distinctions, which defines improper rewards as those paid before performance and proper ones as those paid afterwards, Langland has not retreated a single inch from the semi-Pelagian convictions of the B version. Much of the issue, after all, revolved around this question of the proper chronological order between human deeds and divine grace. Nevertheless, he manages to offer a lower profile to critics by seeming, at this stage (where *mercede* is being defined as a kind of outright debt that must be paid), to be focusing exclusively on issues of *human* recompense. As for the second distinction, Langland here gains an even greater rhetorical advantage over his critics because of the total absence of any explicit chronological order between deed and reward. Now good rewards are those issuing from proper, congruent relationships; with bad ones, the reverse is true. Who could quarrel with this sort of moral commonplace?

Finally, to the charge of social radicalism Langland manages a brilliant (albeit rather unrealistic) reply by introducing yet another new distinction. In B he had begun by contrasting two forms of *mede* and had concluded by explaining briefly, in a sort of postscript, that trade and wages are completely different phenomena from *mede* since neither involves the gratuity or gift-quality that he *then* considered essential to that concept. Similarly, in C he begins by defining good and bad recompense in contrast with each other (though the whole basis for the comparison has shifted) and seems to be following the outline of B's argument (of approximately the same length), where he had concluded with a list of two exceptions. But where the two previous exceptions had been trade and wages, wages has now been assimilated (necessarily) into the category of *mercede* ('a manere dewe dette' [3. 304]) and the new exceptions are trade and feudal 'fees', as they were called. The essence of Langland's defence, therefore, against the accusation that B had slandered the feudal system is to point out that feudal fees do not qualify as wages or gifts outright and thus are not examples of *mede* or *mercede*. Instead, title (*dominium directum*) remains with the giver and his heirs perpetually and such endowments are always – at least in theory – conditional and revocable.[3] Any medieval English lawyer could have vouched for the accuracy of Langland's description of these fees and their proprietary status. Retention of title and revocability contingent on infidelity are, Langland is arguing, sufficient to exempt these feudal rewards from the charges of bribery in B and from the strictures of C against rewards offered in advance.

At this point the parallel argument of B had ended: two forms of reward and two exceptions. Evidently, however, Langland felt the need to add another kind of illustration. One factor may have been the realisation that his earlier distinction, based on chronological sequence, claimed too much for itself and failed the test of universality. After all, a villain who waits patiently for his bribe until after his mischief has been perpetrated still receives only a bribe, a *mede*, and not a due debt, a *mercede*. On the other hand, Langland may have pursued the issue further because he had not yet rendered sufficiently explicit the connection between his theory of rewards and his theology. To spell out that connection in terms of his earlier distinction about the proper chronology of rewards would merely invite more criticism of his theology. So he develops a new analogy from one of his favourite sources – Latin grammar.

Before following Langland through this most difficult passage in C, however, we should notice several factors that have prevented some readers from successfully applying the analogy.

First, it is not likely to be so elaborate an analogy as some have thought. Thus certain readers, including Pearsall, have mistakenly supposed that *mede*

---

[3] Cf. John Critchley, *Feudalism* (London, 1978), 11–37; F. L. Ganshof, *Feudalism*, trans. Philip Grierson (1952; New York, 1964), 69–149; and S. F. C. Milsom, *The Legal Framework of English Feudalism* (Cambridge, 1976), 36–102. Langland's answer, while technically correct, is unrealistic because – even before his time – legal procedures had begun to alter the realities of power in regard to ownership of land, eventually investing tenants with rights of domain far easier to exercise effectively than were the theoretically superior rights of their lords. See, for example, Milsom and Ganshof, 131–2.

and *mercede* were here being compared, in different ways, to both of the relative pronoun relationships (known to Latin grammarians as *direct* and *indirect*) as well as to the relationship between adjective and substantive.[4] Some fifteen years ago Amassian and Sadowsky, in their highly influential study of the grammatical analogy, propagated this unnecessarily complicated solution, apparently because their studies convinced them that most elementary Latin grammars treat these two kinds of relationship as discrete phenomena;[5] more recently, Overstreet endorsed the same conclusion, though he felt obliged to concede that Langland's actual references to these categories sometimes tend to be so casual as to overlap them.[6]

Hence, it is quite inconvenient for such interpreters that Langland uses the word *sustantif* in connection with *relatio*: 'hardy relacoun/ Seketh and seweth his sustantif sauacioun' (3. 351–2). If Langland's purpose was truly, as Overstreet believes, to preserve a distinction between the two sorts of grammatical categories (i.e., relative pronouns and their antecedents versus the adjective–substantive relationship) rather than to exploit the features that they share, one can only lament the poet's carelessness! But it scarcely seems an example of carelessness when, some ten lines later, Langland reiterates the similarity between relative pronoun relationships and those of adjective and substantive: 'This is relacion rect, ryht as adiectyf and sustantyf/ Acordeth in alle kyndes with his antecedent' (3. 360–1). Faced with two such awkward passages as these, Overstreet holds his ground, insisting that Langland is usually more careful and that 'such a way of speaking has no basis in elementary instruction'.[7] Nevertheless, as he also admits, 'it does reflect the tendency of speculative grammarians (e.g., Radulphus Brito) sometimes to define relative and antecedent *as a variety of adjective and substantive*' (my italics).[8] Overstreet's concession, rather than his thesis, appears more adequate as an account of what Langland is doing in this analogy: *mede* and *mercede* are like indirect and direct relation respectively, and both of these are like (because they are instances of) the relationship of adjective to substantive.

---

[4] Pearsall, note to 332–405; cf. Lavinia Griffiths, *Personification in* Piers Plowman (Cambridge, 1985), 35–6, where the same assumption generates a confused and halting analysis. More persuasive and less intricate hypotheses (ones which, nevertheless, I cannot endorse without some reservations) are offered by Janet Coleman, Piers Plowman *and the Moderni* (Rome, 1981), 88–94, and by A. G. Mitchell, 'Lady Meed and the Art of *Piers Plowman*', *Style and Symbolism in* Piers Plowman, ed. Robert J. Blanch (Knoxville, Tenn., 1969), 183–7.

[5] Margaret Amassian and James Sadowsky, 'Mede and Mercede. A Study of the Grammatical Metaphor in "Piers Plowman" C. IV. 335–409', *NM*, 72 (1971), 457–76, esp. 463.

[6] Samuel Overstreet, 'Grammaticus Ludens': Theological Aspects of Langland's Grammatical Allegory,' *Traditio*, 40 (1984), 251–96, esp. 263–5.

[7] Overstreet, 265.

[8] Overstreet, 265.

In sum, it seems probable that Langland is talking about one set of grammatical facts, not several.

Second, because indirect relation is a legitimate pattern in Latin grammar, readers have wrongly assumed that Langland must be incorporating that fact into the developed moral analogy. The truth seems to be that Langland is playing with the moral associations of the words *direct* and *indirect* in order to praise one sort of human relationship and criticise another; but some readers, forgetting that an analogy is rarely complete and is usually selective, demand of this one more than it offers. Thus, despite the absence of any explicit evidence, they think they must find in these lines both a good example of *indirect relation* and a bad example of *direct relation* in order to complement the bad *indirect* and good *direct* ones overtly referred to. Having such expectations, looking for the kind of intricate metaphysical conceit one might expect from Donne, they manage to make a muddle of something relatively simple and then blame it on Langland! In actuality, his only fault is a stylistic one: an occasional tendency (most apparent when he waxes philosophical) towards a loose, disjointed syntax that blurs his focus and renders his statements patient of such overreading.

But what about the fact that in C. 2, as in B. 2, Theology defends Meed as the Daughter of Amends and as being betrothed to Truth? Doesn't that entitle us to look for four entities in the grammar analogy rather than merely two? That is, a good form of *mede* and a bad *mercede* in addition to the more obvious pair? The answer to this objection is that the passage referred to in C. 2 (2. 116–26) plainly contradicts the discussion in C. 3 and amounts to an oversight of a type fairly common in this incompletely revised, final version of *Piers*. Evidently Langland rethought the whole problem of *mede* between C. 2 and C. 3, because when he begins Conscience's speech in C. 3 (3. 285ff.), he deliberately departs from the opening lines of B.3 about two types of *mede* (lines which had been intended to amplify on Theology's point in B. 2/ C. 2). So, where Conscience had in B insisted on both a good and a bad form of *mede*, now he begins, in direct contradiction to Theology's speech in both versions, by saying ' . . . clerkes witeth þe soþe,/ That Mede is *euermore* a mayntenour of gyle'. The purpose of this universal negative is, of course, to withdraw the notion of the double-sided *mede* presented in B. 2–3 and C. 2 and to present instead a *mede* thoroughly evil, for whom there are no redemptive qualities or family relationships, even in forced inferences from overextended analogies.

In the light of these points, I now propose the following paraphrase of the opening of the passage in question:

'No', said Conscience to the king, 'scholars know the truth,
That Meed is always a supporter of deceit.
As the Psalter says concerning those who give meed:

"Those who live unlawfully have large hands
For giving men small or great sums of meed."
But there is not only meed; there is also merced, and men see
    both
As a reward for doing something, either secretly or otherwise.
Many times men give meed before the deed.
And it is neither reasonable nor right nor allowed by any realm's law
That anyone should take such a reward unless he deserved it;
But it is also unreasonable for a man to undertake a job for someone
    else
And never know for certain whether he will live long enough
Nor have the good fortune to deserve a reward.
I consider him presumptuous or else dishonest
Who either asks for or is paid his reward in advance.
Scoundrels and whores and also quack doctors
Demand their wages before they have deserved them,
And deceivers pay in advance but good men at the end,
When the deed is done and the day concluded.
And that isn't meed but merced, a kind of due debt.'

Here I must pause to concede that the possibility of a good *mede* seems
inferable from line 294 ('That eny man mede toke but he hit myhte deserue')
because this line appears to acknowledge that one may, in some unspecified
instance, deserve a *mede*. But Langland is here departing momentarily from
his specialised, stipulative usage and is employing the term as a generic one
for 'reward'. This is made clear by the progression of his thought, for when he
comes to speak of the circumstances that qualify one for such a reward, he
clearly states that this can only be after performance and that one's reward is
then a matter of simple equity or justice and must be termed a *mercede*
(3. 298–304).

    To continue our paraphrase:

And unless this merced is paid promptly, the payer is at fault.
As may be seen in the Book, which demands that nobody
Withhold the hire of his servant beyond evening:
    non morabitur opus mersenarii.
And in this verse there is Reason acting as a reeve to reward truth
So that both the lord and the labourer may be faithfully treated.
On the other hand, the meed that many priests take for the masses
    that they sing,
Amen, amen, says Matthew, *mercedem suam recipiunt.*
In trade there is no meed, I can well avow,
Because it is mere permutation, one pennyworth for another.
    And although the king, for courtesy, or the emperor or the pope,
May give lands or lordship or large gifts

To their loyal retainers, love is the motive;
And if the loyal should prove to be wicked men afterwards,
Both the king, the emperor, and the tonsured pope
May revoke their gift and endow another with it.
They may snatch it from them immediately and never afterwards
Can any of their heirs be so bold as to argue
That the king or emperor gave them property or income.
For God gave Solomon grace here on earth,
Wealth and wisdom while he lived righteously.
And as soon as God saw that he failed to follow His will,
He took from him his wealth and wisdom
And allowed him to live in error – I think he's probably in Hell.
Thus God never gives anything unconditionally.
And similarly the king and pope may truly
Both give and grant wherever they like
And yet reclaim it again from those who do ill.
   Thus meed and merced are like two sorts of grammatical relation,
Direct and indirect, both of which require
Something firm and stable resembling themselves,
As an adjective and substantive require unity
And agreement in gender, case, and number –
Each one supporting the other. From this kind of unity comes a
    reward,
And that is the gift that God gives to those who live loyally:
Grace of a good death, and great joy thereafter.
Retribuere dignare, domine deus.

Here I must pause once more to note that, though each is said to depend on something fixed and stable as an antecedent ('reninde bothe/ On a sad and a siker semblable to hemseluen' [3. 333–4]), there is no intention to imply that both forms of pronoun relation actually involve all of these same kinds of agreement with the antecedent. In grammar they do not, and, in fact, the whole point of the moral analogy is that while both sorts of people (those who take *mede* and those who wait for their *mercede*) are totally dependent on the same divine Antecedent, they do not both achieve perfect congruity with that Antecedent. This perfect congruity, illustrated in the lines about adjective and substantive, is what brings the divine reward to human beings who have achieved *rect relacioun*.

   To continue:

   Direct relation is a record of truth,
Quia ante late rei recordativum est,
Pursuing and seeking out the foundation of a strength,
And stoutly standing to support that foundation
In gender and case and number.

As a loyal labourer believes that his master,
In his pleasure and his mercy and his mere honesty
Will pay him if he does the job and have pity if he fails
And give him for his effort everything that fairness requires;
Thus from a holy heart comes hope, and a courageous relative pronoun
Seeks and pursues its proper substantive, salvation,
And that is God, the basis for everything, a gracious antecedent.
And man is like a relative pronoun in direct relation if he lives truly:
He accords with Christ in gender, *Verbum caro factum est*;
In case, *Credere in ecclesia*, by believing in Holy Church;
In number, to die and rise again and have remission
Of our deadly sins, to be absolved and cleansed,
And to live, as our Creed teaches us, with Christ eternally.
This is direct relation, just as an adjective and substantive
Agree in all respects with each other.
  On the other hand, indirect relation is like someone who desired
To follow and have knowledge of all genders
And without reason tried to obtain and arrive at both singular and
    plural,
Mixing good and evil and satisfying neither's will.
And that is neither reasonable nor correct – to disown my Sire's
    name
When I am His son and make claims on his servant for His rights.
For anyone who wishes to marry my daughter
I would endow with the sum total of both her fair and foul qualities.
Therefore, indirect relation is to covet inwardly
To agree with all genders and numbers,
Without having the cost [pun on 'case']⁹ and care and all the labour.
  But direct relation is a proper custom,
As when a king requires the commons at his command
To follow him and provide for him, and offer him advice,
So that their love may accord with his law throughout the land.
Similarly, the commons requires of a king three sorts of things,
Law, love, and faithfulness, and that he act as lord antecedent,
Both the head and their king, taking sides with no clique
But standing as a stake embedded on a property line
Between two lords to serve as a true boundary marker.
  But most people today seem totally indirect.
For they want only what is best for themselves,
Though the king and the commons have all the cost [pun on 'case'].
All reason rebukes such imperfect people
And regards them as disloyal because they lack case [i.e., proper
    relationship].
Just like indirect pronoun relations, they never care

---

⁹ I owe this observation to Overstreet, 267.

About the outcome of a case so long as they make money from it.
Though others may complain, if the money has been paid
He who can snatch some meed cares not a whit.
So long as he makes a number of nobles or shillings,
Meed cares little how the clients may accord.
  But adjective and substantive are as I have already explained,
That is, unified in accord in case and gender and number;
And that means, in our mouth, neither more nor less
But that all sorts of men, women, and children
Should conform themselves to one nature by believing in Holy Church
And should desire, when they may understand, the opportunity [pun
    on 'case']
To bewail their sins and suffer harsh penances
For the love of that Lord who died for our love
And who sought out our nature and was called by our name,
    Deus homo,
And who betook Himself into our number, now and evermore.
    Qui in caritate manet in deo manet et deus in eo.
Thus He is man, and mankind now, acting as a substantive
(As *hic et hec homo*), requires an adjective
Drawn from three true terminations, *trinitas unus deus;*
    Nominativo, pater et filius et spiritus sanctus.

Several final points remain to be made. First, it must be conceded that nowhere in this grammatical analogy does Langland clearly and unambiguously stipulate the equation he wishes us to derive from it. Also, it seems fair to observe that none of the offered solutions, including this one, is entirely free of difficulties. Nevertheless, I consider this reading of the analogy preferable to many others on two scores: (1) it requires fewer unsupported assumptions; and (2) certain contextual clues scattered throughout this passage from C. 3 appear to confirm it.

For example, in the earlier passage on *mede* and *mercede* (3. 290–331), Langland nowhere gives a bad example of *mercede* nor a good one of *mede*. In an effort to support their more complicated, and less plausible, conclusions both Amassian–Sadowsky and Overstreet are forced to misread lines 310–11 ('The mede þat many prest taken for masses þat thei singen/ *Amen Amen*, Matheu seyth, *mercedem suam recipiunt*) so as to make an example of evil 'mede' into an example of evil 'mercede'. Their rationale for this misreading is Langland's use of the aforementioned citation from the Sermon on the Mount, in which the term *merces* is employed for 'reward': 'Amen I say to you, they have received their reward.' While grasping desperately at the Latin word here, they overlook the fact that Langland has already labelled the reward of such priests as a *mede* in line 310 (in English!) and that he applies the Matthew 6: 5 text for the obvious purpose of pointing out that men of this sort, like others who accept payment in advance (here, presumably, for a set of commemorative masses),[10] have already had all the reward that they will ever receive.

The same sort of mistake is involved in the effort of such scholars to read the passage about feudal endowments as though it offered examples of good *mede*.[11] Here the mistake is more pardonable since Langland does, at one point, refer to such items as 'large ʒeftes' (3. 315); nevertheless, as I have explained above, the structure of the entire argument as well as what Langland actually says about these 'fees' and their peculiar retention of title indicates that he saw them, like *marchaundise*, as an exception rather than an example.

Similarly, in the later sections of the text paraphrased above one may search in vain for any bad examples of *rect relacoun* or any good ones of *relacoynes indirect*. There are simply none to be found. Even Amassian and Sadowsky concede this point, though they misunderstand its significance. As they see it, Langland shifts the rules of the game halfway through:

> It is . . . essential to note that, up to now, Langland has meant nothing pejorative when he refers to the indirect grammatical relationship. As

[10] To argue that priests are entitled by canon law to their mass stipends and that therefore the payments referred to by Langland must be an example of *mercede* (i.e., 'a manere dewe dette') is to ignore context and tone completely. The whole point of the invocation of Matthew 6: 5 is to assert the presence of hypocritical motives. Motive is the essence of much simony (cf. *The New Catholic Encyclopedia*, 13, 228–9, and Thomas Aquinas, *ST*, 2. 2, Q. 100, A. 1–3), and it seems clear that Langland, like many of his contemporaries, regarded trafficking in masses as invariably betraying simoniacal motives. Though simony is not a central complaint of the Lollards, it sometimes functions as a leitmotif in their polemics (e.g., *Selections from English Wycliffite Writings*, ed. Anne Hudson (Cambridge, 1978), 77–8; also see John A. F. Thomson, *The Later Lollards, 1414–1520* (Oxford, 1965), 247, who records the complaint of Lollards that 'the priests buy thirty hosts for 1*d*. and sell them at 2*d*. each . . .'

The position of Aquinas (a standard one for the late Middle Ages on this issue) is that, while one is entitled to receive both voluntary contributions and gratuities established by custom, and while it is even (on occasion) permissible to extract such payments as are necessary for the support of the clergy from those who are able but unwilling to pay for sacramental offices, nevertheless, any demand for such payments from those unable to pay or any demand that goes beyond custom or necessity is simoniacal. To substantiate his position, Aquinas quotes 'a gloss of Augustine' on 1 Tim. 5: 17, which advises priests to 'look to the people for a supply to their need, but to the Lord for the *reward* of their ministry' (2. 2, Q. 100, A. 2). In this context, it seems clear that, for Langland, it is irrelevant whether the priest in question celebrates a series of private masses or applies their benefits *before* or *after* receiving money for them. The only assumption that makes sense of the passage is the one broached here by Aquinas, viz., that taking at any time more than the mere cost of such services invariably involves one in receiving *now* from man what one should *wait* to receive from God – one's reward.

[11] Cf. Amassian and Sadowsky, 461, and Overstreet, 269–70.

we have seen, he uses it, in lines 335–7 [Skeat], simply to distinguish Mercede from Mede, the 'two manere relacions', both of them reward, both of them good to receive. But, from line 365 [Skeat] to the end of the C-text passage at line 409 [Skeat], we are to scorn the 'indirect thyng', with all its dangers and its potential perversions of good.[12]

The reason why this comes as such a shock to Amassian and Sadowsky is that they have not only reshuffled Langland's examples in the earlier passage (so as to produce good examples of meed and bad ones of merced) but they have also misread what are arguably the two most crucial lines of the entire passage: 'Thus is mede and mercede as two maner relacions,/ Rect and indirect . . .' (3. 332–3a). Rather than allowing the context to define for them the pairs in this analogy, Amassian and Sadowsky proceed on the unfounded assumption that Middle English syntax will treat such a structure with the same ironclad rules as Modern English, i.e., they merely take for granted that the first member of the second pair is being compared to the first member of the first and so forth. Hence they conclude that meed = direct relation and merced = indirect.

But if we limit ourselves to nothing but those examples where Langland clearly names his terms, and allow them to dictate our understanding of this equation, our conclusion will be precisely the opposite (meed = indirect and merced = direct); and then we will have nothing to explain away when we reach the later discussion of direct and indirect relations. We will not be surprised when we note that, in discussing *rect relacoun*, Langland uses the same example (a labourer and his lord) that he had used previously to describe how *mercede* works (cf. 3. 304–9 and 3. 347–50). Nor will we have something awkward to explain when, near the end of the last passage (in the analysis of *relacoynes indirect*), Langland connects such relationships with *mede*:

> Ac þe moste partie of peple now puyr indirect semeth,
> For they wilnen and wolden as beste were for hemsulue
> Thow the kyng and þe comune al the coest hadde.
> Such inparfit peple repreueth alle resoun
> And halt hem vnstedefast for hem lakketh case.
> As relacoynes indirect reccheth thei neuere
> Of the cours of case so thei cache suluer.
> Be the peccunie ypaied, thow parties chyde,
> He þat mede may lacche maketh litel tale.
> Nyme he a noumbre of nobles or of shillynges,
> How þat cliauntes acorde acounteth mede litel.   (3. 382–90)

---

[12] Amassian and Sadowsky, 468.

So what has changed from B to C? In B we had a single semantic entity, *mede* = 'reward', with a polarised set of offspring, *bribery* and *beatitude*. In C. after rethinking his position, Langland has decided to surrender the shared and highly paradoxical parent. The offspring were so mutually hostile that the bond between them has dissolved. Apparently the poet is now reasoning that 'rewards' are either merited or unmerited. If unmerited, they are not true rewards but merely bribes. If merited, they are not simply rewards but, more properly, one's just deserts.

In thus describing Langland's apparent reasoning, I may seem to be stretching the tolerable limits of paradox; nevertheless, as I noted briefly in the opening of this essay, the C version of *Piers Plowman* has not truly moved very far from the opinions expressed in B with regard to 'reward'. We must recall that, in the world of B, the idea of good rewards *in hac vita* has *already* been repudiated. Only bad rewards, earthly meeds, are available here. Theology laments that this is so and insists that, ideally, it ought not to be. But so it is, and Conscience is steadfast in his refusal to marry Lady Meed here on earth.

The only apparent compensation for this lacuna is the availability of rewards in heaven, but they are reserved exclusively, in B, for those who 'worked well while they were here'. Such rewards, tailored to the merits or deserts of those who will receive them, have been made the subject of debate recently by Overstreet, who questions my inference (in an earlier article) that this form of meed is here being offered as the implicitly *mesurable* counterpart to the explicitly *mesurelees* meed of bribery.[13] Readers must, of course, make

---

[13] Cf. my remarks in 'Piers's Pardon and Langland's Semi-Pelagianism', *Traditio*, 39 (1983), 398–401, with Overstreet, 285, n. 92. Overstreet there misrepresents my position on the heavenly (implicitly *mesurable*) meed of the B version, suggesting that I identify it with 'eternal life merited *de congruo*'. Nothing so technical is intended, either by me or, I hope, by Langland. Instead, by implying a *mesurable* meed as the reward of the virtuous in heaven, Langland is, I believe, merely asserting the paradox of simultaneous equity and gratuity that lies at the heart of Nominalist grace theology. Because man in a state of grace may merit beatitude, the saved do truly get 'what is coming to them'. In this sense there is *mesure*. But because the entire system that offers such rewards is contingent upon God's merciful and free ordaining, equity is surrounded and supported by abundant grace.

As for my inference about Langland's intention (i.e., does he really mean to imply that heavenly meed is *mesurable?*), that is a question that cannot be resolved by mere appeals to the immediate context: see, for example, the discussion of Myra Stokes, *Justice and Mercy in* Piers Plowman (London, 1984), 127–9. Rather, one's judgement here must be harmonised with one's assessment of the entire poem's theology, as I have tried to do in fitting this crux into the pattern of what seems to me a pervasive semi-Pelagianism. By contrast, Overstreet wishes us to see his solution as simpler and more elegant, viz., that both meeds are *mesurelees* and that Langland merely 'distinguishes the two meeds by the uses to which they are put' (286, n. 92); however, if this were correct there would be no reason for Langland to distinguish two meeds at all

their own judgements about the exact meaning of *mesurelees* in this context and about the interpretation to be placed upon the passage in question (B. 3. 231–47); but the fact remains that the interpretation offered here (and in the aforementioned article) is consonant with a sizeable body of evidence drawn from the rest of the poem that points towards a semi-Pelagian outlook: what Judson Allen was fond of terming 'Langland's theology of entitlement'.

Furthermore, it seems clear that, as late as the time of the composition of C. 2, Langland's thinking on this issue had changed very little, for in describing the attitude of St Lawrence on his gridiron, Langland gives the saint these very revealing words: 'God of thy grace heuene gates opene/ For y, man, of thy mercy *mede haue diserued*' (2. 132–3; my italics). No phrase, perhaps, in any of the three versions of *Piers Plowman* more vividly encapsulates the essence of the Nominalist dialectic whereby God, in an act of consummate mercy, creates a contingent order of justice in which rewards can be *earned*, and *demanded* (as Lawrence does here) as one's right![14] Hence the

since their difference would then have shrivelled to the status of a logical accident. One could, moreover, point out that Aquinas explicitly denies that created grace can ever be *mesurelees* or infinite (*ST*, 3, Q. 7, A. 11). In issuing this denial, Aquinas cites a well-known proof text that tends to prejudice medieval thinkers against most forms of infinitude, Wisdom 11: 21: 'Thou hast ordered all things in measure and number and weight.' Langland is reflecting the same bias (and alluding to the same text) when, near the end of his poem, Conscience upbraids the friars for not limiting their numbers:

> 'And yf ʒe coueiteth cure, *Kynde wol ʒow telle*
> *That in mesure god made alle manere thynges*
> *And sette hit at a serteyne and at a syker nombre*
> And nempned hem names and nombred þe sterres.
> *Qui numerat multitudinem stellarum.*
> Kynges and knyhtes, þat kepen and defenden,
> Haen officerys vnder hem and vch of hem a certeyne.
> And yf thei wage men to werre thei writen hem in nombre;
>
> . . . .
>
> Monkes and monyales and alle men of religioun,
> Here ordre and here reule wol to haue a certeyne nombre.
> Of lewed and of lered the lawe wol and asketh
> A certeyne for a certeyne – saue oenliche of freres!
> Forthy', quod Conscience, 'bi Crist, kynde wit me telleth
> Hit is wikked to wage ʒow, ʒe wexeth out of nombre;
> *Heuen hath euen nombre and helle ys withouten nombre*'
>
> (C. 22. 253–9, 264–70; my italics).

I remain satisfied that the viewpoint expressed by Conscience here, in which heaven is identified with finitude of measure and number while hell is associated with infinitude, is that of his earlier speech about Lady Meed as well.

[14] The best discussion of this outlook remains Heiko Oberman, *The Harvest of Medieval Theology. Gabriel Biel and Late Medieval Nominalism*, 2nd ed. (Grand Rapids, Mich., 1967).

paradox of a meed – a free gift – which, nevertheless, by the time of its actual bestowal, may be seen as deserved and required both by the *viator*'s deeds and by the divine guarantee behind the system. Man in a state of grace may truly merit beatitude. But if that is so, then salvation itself, 'þe gyft þat god gyueth to alle lele lyuynge' (3. 338) can also be regarded as a kind of wage earned by the righteous:

> As a leel laborer byleueth þat his maister
> In his pay and in his pite and in his puyr treuthe
> To pay hym yf he parforme and haue pite yf he faileth
> And take hym for his trauaile al þat treuthe wolde;
> So of holy herte cometh hope, and hardy relacoun
> Seketh and seweth his sustantif sauacioun,
> That is god the ground of al, a gracious antecedent.

> (3. 347–53)

According to the common scholastic doctrine of *facere quod in se est* that appears to govern this passage, God is *self-obligated* to respond favourably to any person who makes his best effort to please Him: 'To pay hym yf he parforme and haue pite yf he faileth.'[15] When the deed has been done and the day has ended, as it has for St Lawrence, this reward has become 'a manere dewe dette'.[16] Thus the logic of the *mede | mercede* dichotomy has been implicit in Langland's earlier formulations and has gradually evolved so as to emphasise the difference in equity between heavenly and worldly recompense (wage versus fraud) at the very point where B had tended to emphasise their common roots in shared gratuity (good gift versus bad). The change of terminology that occurs between C. 2 and C. 3 aims to highlight not a complete alteration in the poet's theology but an important shift of nuance.

Sam Houston State University

---

[15] Oberman, 132–45; see also Arthur M. Landgraf, *Dogmengeschichte der Früh-scholastik* (Regensburg, 1952–4) 1. 1. 249–64.

[16] If we take seriously the analogy that Langland draws at C. 3. 323ff., viz., that God's grace to Solomon (and hence to all *viatores*) is akin to a feudal fee in its conditionality and revocability, then neither such preliminary 'gifts' of God nor the final 'gift' of salvation itself are 'gifts' in the same sense as earthly meed. Meed carries with it a definite ownership but very dubious entitlement in equity. On the other hand, where grace *in via* is concerned, we have no secure proprietary interest of the sort that would allow us to defend a mere *mede* from confiscation; and where salvation is concerned – by the time we are endowed with it, we have earned it as a wage and need fear no forfeiture.

The Imperative of Revision in the C Version
of Piers Plowman

G. H. RUSSELL

Among all his distinguished writings across a range of medieval themes, George Kane's examination, either alone or with Talbot Donaldson, of the interrelationships between the three versions of *Piers Plowman* is of conspicuous interest and value. He rightly sees the fact and nature of revision and the complex relationships of the surviving texts as central to the discussion and evaluation of all three versions and their by-products. A very large number of editorial, and hence exegetical, decisions are seen to turn upon the reading of the respective archetypal traditions, and the magisterial treatment of the question of the C poet's B manuscript offered by him and Talbot Donaldson in the introduction to their B edition constitutes a definitive statement of the general pattern of that relationship.

Such an acknowledgement must be an essential prelude to any discussion of the process of revision which produced the three versions of the poem. While this must finally be both tentative and incomplete, there exists an obligation to set out what appears to be the strategy of the process and even, on occasion, its dynamic, and to seek to understand what light the evidence of the existing documents casts on the nature and direction of the process of revision.

In their analysis, space did not allow, nor did the nature of their task require, that the question of the revision of B to C be examined in detail. That is the task of the C editor, a difficult and complex task since, by definition, it seeks to grasp and characterise a phenomenon that must often be impenetrable and so deeply integral to the creative process which is the C poem that no mind or sensibility other than that of the poet himself can hope to gain access to the fullness of its realisation.

Such a discussion might address itself to almost any part of Prologue, Passus I–XX. But it may be most useful to select a short passage in which the poet's attention is notably engaged with his original. Passus IX of the C version, which corresponds to A. VIII and B. VII, is among the most heavily reworked passages of the poem, containing as it does the last part of Piers's first intervention, with an exploration of the nature and operation of pardon, a meditation on the manifestations of poverty, the revelation of the text of the pardon bestowed on Piers by Truth and the sequel to this in the dispute between Piers and the priest in AB, and the reworking of this episode in C, concluding with a reflection on the significance of dreams and an admonition to those who deal in pardons.[1]

In important ways, the handling of this passus by the revising poet is exemplary, displaying as it does the variety of approaches to his B text that characterises his methods throughout the poem as far as the end of Passus XX. To generalise and, more, to rationalise the working of a creative mind as large, as subtle, and as obliquely allusive as that of Langland is clearly so hazardous as to constitute an impertinence. No kind of summation or discussion can confidently or adequately identify the strategy of the poem or expose the dynamic of its realisation. This is to be clearly asserted at the outset and the reservations that are implied in the statement qualify both the total concept and the individual discriminations of what follows.

The evidence offered by the archetypal tradition of the C version appears to require that we give assent to two propositions: the first, that the poet, for whatever reason, revised against a B text which, although demonstrably superior to that which supplies the tradition of the extant B manuscripts, was nevertheless a scribally produced manuscript which contained a substantial body of error, and that the poet seemingly had no access to a better text, much less to what one might be permitted to call a final draft of B; the second, that the revision was not carried through in a manner that subjected all parts of the poem to a detailed, consecutive, and orderly scrutiny from beginning to end, line by line, but that, rather, the process was sporadic in its operation, allowing some parts of the text to stand without correction, perhaps even without examination, others to be subjected to intense scrutiny, issuing in radical alteration in either their small detail, their strategy, their dimension, or all three.

These propositions seem consistent with the testimony of the archetypal traditions, yet neither of them can be used as an editorial or exegetical tool in any routine or mechanical discrimination between B and C. The reality which is the transmitted poem identified as the C version is necessarily various and elusive in its rendering of the earlier form.

One further important reservation is to be advanced: in particular cases it is not possible to distinguish with certainty between restoration of damaged readings as part of a revising process and the undisturbed preservation of authentic readings lost or damaged in the archetypal B tradition. A decision as

---

[1] References to the A version are to Kane; those to the B version to Kane–Donaldson; those to the C version to Pearsall.

between the two possibilities must often be subjective and can, at best, represent a judgement based upon what appears to be the probable status of each individual reading as the context declares. Clearly, the revising poet will carry with him a uniquely authoritative sense of the shape and detail of the text which is not accessible to any reader, and a shape appearing in A as original and reappearing in C may be present by uncorrupted transmission to the revising poet's manuscript or may be restored by him as the precisely recalled form of his original which he wishes to retain. It is, of course, to be remembered that the same corruption of A can arise independently in B and C. If a corrupt B reading appears in C it is by no means certain that it will have been transmitted and retained. It may be generated anew, and the fact that the corruption has occurred once necessarily means that it may be independently generated.

In either case, the readings judged as original which offer an AC identity over a B variation are to be accepted as representing an authentic form of the poem even though the rationale of their reappearance in C must remain undetermined. But, while this is to be conceded, there is also to be attached to this the further observation that the evidence also suggests that the poet's recall of the uncorrupted B original was by no means certain or unfailing, and that dissatisfaction with the shape of the line available to him did not inevitably result in restoration of the obscured or lost reading as it had appeared in A. There is a large number of places where the B reading, putatively corrupted over A, is allowed to stand or is replaced by a correction which repairs the context but does not restore the A reading. Again a determination of the reason for the change is a hazardous undertaking. At least two possibilities emerge: the first, clearly, must be the poet's decision to alter what he had written earlier – that is, that the mere restoration of the A reading, even if it is accessible to him, no longer satisfies him; the second is that he simply cannot recall the lost A reading or that he declines the effort of recall and determines to adopt a new form. He is under no obligation to return to A. Indeed, if neither A nor an uncorrupted B is accessible to him, he will not necessarily weigh the matter beyond the immediate task of required repair. We need to remember that the writing of the A version was most likely now a distant experience and that the B version was the evolved shape of the poem which realised his most recent, perhaps very recent, creative endeavour. These and other attendant complexities appear throughout Passus IX and by way of exemplification we may turn to the first part of that passus.

Passus VIII in C, it will be recalled, had ended with a piece of recasting, a restatement of the riddling and necessarily obscure prophecy of impending hardship and destruction. While it is to be conceded that such a passage is vulnerable, it is also true that the kind of recasting involved is characteristic of the poet's treatment of Passus VIII where, although there are no large-scale alterations, the text has clearly been exposed to persistently close examination and where alterations, perhaps small in scale but significant in their import, are very frequent.[2]

In this sense Passus IX appears in a context of close reassessment and enters upon the crucially important revelation of Truth's mandate to Piers. Passus VIII had demonstrated the poet's keen sense of the significance of the fine detail of the poem's subtle and sensitive exploration of the complex social and political relationships exposed during the ploughing of the half-acre. Much of the text had been extensively reworked and while the lineaments and dimensions were not greatly altered, the text revealed the revising poet with his attention keenly aroused. What follows is a context which will show us the poet as the uniquely engaged scrutiniser of the transmitted text of the lines that enact highly sensitive issues.

And we are reminded of this by the opening lines. The revising activity of the end of Passus VIII is not immediately resumed. But the attentive reading persists and as early as line 4 we encounter the first revision. The poet's manuscript seems likely to have read *for euere* against what appears to be the original reading of A, *euere*. This change is allowed to stand but the latter part of the line is distinctly strengthened with what we must accept as an authentic reading: *for euere to be asoiled*, where the B reading is still visible but decisively strengthened. Line 6 in B reads as scribally emphatic as against the spare A line, but the change is accepted by C. There is perhaps not a great deal at stake here; the copy can stand. At line 7 C, in reading *manere*, is clearly correct against *ooþer* of B; the unmetrical B reading must be replaced and *manere* is an obvious reading by way of repair. But it is more reasonable to assume that the poet's manuscript in fact contained the reading, subsequently lost in B. That he was allowing his manuscript to stand might also be suggested by his retention of the more emphatic *auayle* against *helpen* of A, but, if so, he did not stay with his manuscript; instead he rewrote the latter part of the following line, a regular line quite firmly attested in AB, but in very different forms. B had removed the reference to the pope as the agent of transmission of the pardon and had totally recast the line so that Truth communicates the pardon without an intermediary. C preserves this, but offers a much more emphatic form of the line which yet must be accepted as genuinely revised: *perpetuelly he graunteth*. This is a very sensitive area. The rewriting extends into the next line, again firmly attested, and this time unanimously, in AB, where the equivocal *kepen* is replaced by the unambiguous *defenden*, to accommodate which the line is reorganised and, as is common practice with the poet, the alternative spelling *kyrke* is adopted to

---

[2] A rough characterisation may be offered: VIII 1–33 are lightly revised; 34–66 are persistently reworked; 67–83 stand largely unrevised; 84–91 are new, perhaps unfinished, lines; 96–134 are close to B; 135–40 are heavily revised; further substantial revision appears at 187–205; 213–16; 232–55; 259–65; 278–89; 349–53.

respond to the reshaping. The same attention to small but significant change persists in the following line where *peple* of the AB traditions appears in C as *comune* although *reumes* retains the less convincing plural form against the harder singular of A as, again, in line 11 C remains faithful to the weaker *ful liȝtly* of B which had replaced *wel sone* of A. This tolerance, however, seems not to persist in line 12 where B had both inflated A and replaced the attractive reading *pleiȝe þereaftir* with the much flatter *to be felawe*; while the expanded shape of the line is retained, the substituted reading is rejected and replaced by *to sitton*. This may suggest that A was out of mind, and if we are tempted to regard the phrase as a limp filler, the *NED* article will recall to us the very full sense of this verb in the context of paradise, as, indeed, A. 39 reminds us.

At this point B departs from A with a complete rewriting of A. 13–8 (B. 13–6), in which the A original is only occasionally glimpsed. For whatever reason B has greatly diluted the passage into a form which C does not accept. The rewritten section (C. 13–20) in turn retains little of the B version but at 19–20 the poet seems to recall readings which he had replaced in B. 9–10, and, much later in the passus (256–80), there is a piece of bitter recrimination directed at delinquent bishops which develops the scabbed sheep image here removed by B from A. Perhaps this is coincidental; the shepherd and his neglected sheep is, after all, a common image. In all of this there is no evidence that the archetypal B tradition was corrupt and that the poet was abandoning a deformed original. Hence we cannot judge whether the revision at C. 21 formed part of this ungenerated rewriting or was a response to the substitution in B of *hiȝe* for *hire*, which seems clearly to be a corruption.

This spell of heavy revision is followed by a return to B in C. 22–9 with only minor variation: the consistent alteration of *pope* to *Treuthe* at 23, a sharpening of 26 (B. 22) and preservation or restoration of A at 28 (B. 24). This stability is disturbed at 30 (B. 26) where the poet seems to have received a corrupt form of the line in which the B archetype has apparently picked up *amende* from the following line and lost the sense of the latter part of the line. Both the doubtful readings are allowed to stand in C but the presence of *men fynde* as an alternative to *folk helpe* may suggest a sense that the reading has gone awry. Another, perhaps less easily explicable, revision, one certainly not generated by any B corruption since he retains the unoriginal *And*, follows in the next, short, line where *wightly* of AB is replaced by *with here goed*. While it is not easily represented as an improvement on the AB reading and is perhaps suspect as a scribal expansion in face of the short line, it is, nevertheless, to be retained as consonant with the perceived proceeding of the poet in this part of the poem and in the absence of any generating collocation.

B. 28 appears to stumble over a hard reading of A. 30, *And bynde brugges aboute* . . . , which had also offered difficulty to the A scribes. Whether the B reading *do boote to brugges* is accepted as genuine or not – and it is a remarkably limp alteration of A – the C poet was not prepared to allow it to stand. He did not, for whatever reason, return even remotely to A but offers a line which preserves the concept of the broken bridges but postpones the verb, fills the latter part of the line with a convenient, if not convincing, phrase *by the heye wayes* and completes the sense of the immediate context by recasting the following line (32), which is firmly attested in AB, and offering what must be regarded as a weak line: *Amende in som manere wyse and maydones helpe*, which reads as expedient both in terms of the flaccid sense and structure, in its reuse of *Amende* and in its retrieval of *helpe*, removed from line 30. In the B lines that follow (B. 30–2), the tradition of the B archetype must be called into question as a genuine revision of A. Certainly the revising poet did not accept them. His version runs: *Pore peple bedredene and prisones in stokkes/ Fynde hem for goddes loue and fauntkynes to scole*. These lines are clearly based upon B, not A. They are consonant with B in removing the reference to widowhood, more readily perhaps because the preceding C line had excluded the question of marriage and celibacy. But these B lines are patently unsatisfactory and it seems likely that they result from a telescoping of three original lines into two, as the AC forms seem to suggest. The rewriting of C is firm but is not a return to A although the reappearance of *for goddes loue* is clearly a reminiscence of A, and it may not be entirely fanciful to associate the appearance of the form *fauntkynes* with the lost *skynes* of A.

This revision does not take the poet away from B for the two following lines, B. 33, 34 (C. 35, 36) appear without change, including the explicit *ʒow* reading of B. 34. However, this compliance does not issue in endorsement of the shape offered by B. 35 which has an irregular, and unacceptable, metrical pattern. There is no return to A; B is still visible but the metre is restored by a distinctly original-looking reading – *ne despeyre in ʒoure deynge* – which compresses into a single, authoritative half-line the sense of B. 36, which then disappears. B had rewritten 37 over A. 38, 39; the revision was apparently still not to the poet's satisfaction and C. 39, 40, although restoring the two-line version, represent no return to A; the B shape is again to be seen beneath the total revision. In contrast, C. 41, 42 offer no change over their B counterparts, if we assume that at 42 the C archetype is corrupt in reading *preyde for* and *hem* as, respectively, easier and less appropriate and more explicit readings.

But C. 43 is quite new and appears to represent the beginning of a passage of revision which leads to a rejection of the archetypal shape of the latter part of B. 40 which offers a decidedly weak version of the by no means easy or obvious A reading and is followed by a thorough revision of A. 46–8 (B. 41–6). While this B revision is clearly before him and there is no attempt at reversion to A, as the retention of the emphasis on the venality of lawyers suggests, the C poet is not prepared to sustain the B reworking and it is not unreasonable to guess that the unsatisfactory shape of B. 40 directed his attention to the text and led to the recasting which involves removal of the new material and a persistent scrutiny of what follows. B. 47 survives untouched, but 48 has been reworked over the AB shape and 49, 50 preserve a rendering of the A form as against B, with, in the one case, a slight variation, in the other, a substantial alteration, followed in C. 50 by a complete replacement of the AB line.

These are interesting cases. B. 49, 50 are reasonably to be suspected of corruption and the simplest explanation for the C form would be that the poet's B manuscript preserved the original form of the lines lost in the B archetypal tradition, and this may be suggested by the shape of the C lines, but, if so, it is not easy to see why the poet did not retain the taut A form; instead, he modified it substantially and one suspects that the revising process imposed upon him by the need to alter pronouns to meet the new context was extended to cover the larger matter of the form of the two lines and that of B. 51 which he totally rejects, perhaps because of its near resemblance to B. 35 at which he had already been forced to look closely. Such a passage reminds us that we are not dealing with a repaired poem but with a different poem.

This view seems to be confirmed in what follows. B. 52–5 are removed from the C poem and their removal perhaps merely represents a dissatisfaction with their rewriting of the A form which he either does not recall or does not wish to resurrect. He does, however, retain the new material of B. 57, 58, including the archetypal *ful* for *wel* in 58; he offers a slightly sparer version of 59 but then encounters the confusion of 60 with its corruption and its intruded spurious line. Of the two, the latter does not appear; the former is rewritten in a form quite different from the damaged B and with no recall of A; a new version of the omitted B. 52–5 is attached and, while 61 is retained, preserving *with* as against *by*, the lines that follow (B. 62–4), firmly attested in AB, are rewritten as C. 59–60 in a shape that resolutely recalls the earlier change in C. 8.

After this reworking, C. 61, 62 returns to AB and follows B. 65–7. But the imperative of revision is clearly upon the poet, not now dictated by the state of his original, but apparently by the demand for an exploration of the social and personal cost of poverty. B had already revised A by way of a substantial expansion of the text (B. 70–89) and the first part of this addition is clearly before the poet as he writes and B. 70–3 and 78 make a shadowy appearance. While it is true that B. 70 and 71 appear to contain corruptions, the nature of these corruptions scarcely prepares a reader for the shape of the lines offered by C, for this transformation is the prelude to a massive addition (C. 72–161), the first of three great C interventions in this passus, the others being the addition of 187–280 and the omission of B. VII, 119–43.

Such an analysis might be carried through to the end of the passus. But the pattern is established by this example and it remains constant through this heavily worked piece of text which is passus IX. Clearly, this was for the poet an area of his poem where his revising activity was urgently required, at times as repair, but conspicuously as recreation.[3]

If we may generalise, the procedure which is illustrated by Passus IX is not unlike that encountered in the Prologue. There is no sense of mere line by line scrutiny designed to remove the slips, indiscretions, and impertinences of scribes or even to rephrase the poet's own infelicities and inadequacies. These are, of course, often dealt with, profitably or otherwise, and may, on occasion, be seen to generate a more extensive review of the text than the immediate process of repair demands. But it is a centrally important passus within the strategy of the poem, as critical discussion has long attested. The pardon scene, its preliminaries and its enactment have been seen to offer acute problems of interpretation and to be central to the reading of the poem. The C poet clearly shared this concern and attempted by close attention to his text to clarify the social and moral dilemmas posed by Truth's intervention and his dealings with Piers. The solution is, of course, radical and, as such, was judged to require the most alert response even to the small detail of the line or the readiness to reshape the poem by extensive rewriting, by large additions or the removal of equally large sections of text now judged to be variously unsatisfactory.

It is the urgency of this task of reshaping this climactic encounter rather than the leisurely and minute reworking of individual lines that engages the poet's attention. The latter process could perhaps wait; the former could not. To put the matter crudely: the tearing of the pardon was to be removed and the context refashioned; the intruded conjunction at the head of the line could wait – or could stand. If scribal error was of a kind to deform a line it was attended to, but larger issues were at hand and one senses that the meditation on the social and theological dimensions of poverty thrust itself forward as a central preoccupation while incidental repair and even refinement had to be of secondary concern.

All of this is a crude characterisation of an immensely complex and intense enterprise, but even such a brief and necessarily inadequate reading of the opening lines of the passus leaves us with two conclusions, the one clear and unequivocal, the other, of its nature, less comprehensible and less easily characterised. The first is that a single mind and sensibility, of a remarkable but identifiable kind, produced all three forms of the poem and that the alterations of the one over the other represent uniquely authoritative inter-

---

[3] In summary, the remainder of the passus may be characterised thus: 162–75 consistent revision; 178–82 new material; 186–281 a large addition preceded by B corruption; 282–92 left undisturbed; after 293 omission of a substantial section of B; 294–303 largely unrevised; 304–9 sporadic revision with omission; 310–16 unrevised; 317–28 heavily revised; 328α–41 largely unrevised; 342–9 substantial revision; 350–3 unrevised.

ventions designed to realise more intensely the vision of which the Prologue is the adumbration.

However these revisions are judged, there remains one substantial reservation to be advanced: that is, that the surviving evidence suggests that this third version has come to us in a form that does not fully represent a final shape or stage of the revision and that there are, sporadically through the poem and comprehensively in the two final passus, signs of revision not completed. Whether this shape offered by the manuscripts is an accident of transmission or a genuine record of an unfinished enterprise is not under discussion here. But the question is germane to any understanding of the C version.

Even if our evidence is, in important ways, ambiguous, the design of the C version is so clearly revealed that we can, with due circumspection, examine the manner in which the poet undertook his revision. The simple analysis given above suggests that instead of identifying a single imperative we should rather acknowledge two imperatives. The first is that of the poet-craftsman exercising his right to retouch, rephrase, or reorder on a small scale. This we see operate frequently in the replacement of single words, the changes of order within a line, the alteration of small syntactic structures and the like. These are of the poet's free choice and perhaps the notion of an imperative is inappropriate since they do not carry a sense of urgency. There are other places, however, where, although the process appears to be of the same kind, it is, in fact, very different, places which seem to proclaim a dissatisfaction even with small detail, a determination to refine response which may involve minor relocation, restructuring, addition or omission. This is more than mere tinkering or emergency repair: it is the exercise of the creator's right to attempt a more satisfying shape of his creation without abandoning its original design. Such places are *sui generis*; no generalisation is safe. The alteration of a single word, the relocation of a single line may signal a dramatically different reading; the dimension of the change is no indicator of its resonance, either immediately or subsequently in the larger perspective.

And there are other places, several of them in the present passus, where there can be no mistaking the significance of the changes. These may be large or they may be relatively small, but they represent unmistakably decisive transformations of the nature of the poem. The meditations on poverty and beggary and the dispute over the pardon are of this kind: they carry no sense of the ad hoc or accidental, in so far as we are able to judge such matters. They have a weight, a magnitude and a depth accessible only to the revising poet and must be assumed to represent new initiatives.

The other great category of revision seems less autonomous in its operation. This is the response to detected error in an unsatisfactorily transmitted original. Here the ground is more treacherous and judgement more hazardous. One obvious difficulty appears in our inability to be certain of the exact shape of the text upon which the poet was working. We find many corruptions appearing in B which are absent from A and C. Some of these cases, of their nature, seem clearly to represent an original reading lost in the archetypal B tradition but preserved in that shape of the B tradition to which the poet had access.

But one cannot be certain: in many cases it is, even at this distance, not impossible to identify the nature of a corruption and to reconstruct the original that has been lost or damaged – substitution of similars with loss of alliteration is an obvious example. The sensibility of the revising poet would easily and confidently reconstruct contexts of some complexity. Indeed we would, in the nature of things, have to concede to him a unique sense of the form which the line had originally assumed but had subsequently lost through scribal interference. To this sensibility the restoration of the A form might, on occasion, come almost automatically since the shape of his poem is uniquely present to him.

While this important reservation is to be maintained, it is also true that, confronted by a corruption, the poet will not necessarily or invariably wish to restore the lost original or that he will always be able to do so. That lost original will often be merely one of a number of verbalisations that were available to him: of this number the original A will not necessarily return or, even if it does so, it will not necessarily now – years later and in a new context – appear as the inevitably acceptable shape.

If this is true, it would also seem to be the case that the revising poet did not – for whatever reason – always concern himself with what we may venture to call the detail of the line. What may appear to a modern hypercritical eye as more explicit, more emphatic, easier, or accidental seems not always to have concerned the revising poet. We cannot, however, conclude that this observed phenomenon necessarily denotes acceptance or indifference; we must also recall that certain lines, and presumably certain longer passages, seem to have received no scrutiny at all and that urgency to give new shape to the larger design of the poem and also closely to rework sensitive areas did not necessarily extend across the fullness of the detailed working of the poem. The reason for this is obviously not accessible to us, but the most likely explanation must remain that of the incompleteness of the revision, whatever the reason for that may be. It may have been incapacity or death; it may have been the physical circumstances of the revision, even the state of the documents available to him. One can do no more than guess, and the best guess would seem to be the former, for this, too, may account for the sense of urgency, even haste, felt in certain parts of the poem. Nor is it inconsistent with the testimony of John But.

University of Melbourne

Making a Good End: John But as a
Reader of Piers Plowman

ANNE MIDDLETON

This exercise in the archaeology of literary intention declares George Kane's presence as a tutelary spirit even more openly than must any general consideration of the text of *Piers Plowman* since the appearance of his magisterial editions. It is indebted specifically to his two complementary studies of the problem of authorial identity in the poem. On the surface, they had two quite distinct purposes. The one, *Piers Plowman: The Evidence for Authorship*, undertook to assess the matters of fact at stake in the 'authorship controversy' that had preoccupied a generation of *Piers* scholarship – and effectively closed the books on the question, at least in the form in which it had been posed; the other, *The Autobiographical Fallacy in Chaucer and Langland Studies*, examined some of the literary effects of a tantalisingly 'real' and rounded authorial presence in first-person fictions of the later Middle Ages.[1] Yet these two fertile studies, which appeared in the same year, are even more fruitful when viewed as companion pieces, and the present essay began in just such a consideration. That its end is a renewed appreciation of where and how literary evidence intersects that of other kinds of historical documents is also a tribute to what a generation of Middle English scholars has learned from George Kane.

If the 'autobiographical fallacy' is a critical error, it is not exclusively a modern one. The first of Langland's readers committed to the 'autobiographical fallacy' was, I believe, also the first of his critics to leave us his name: the poet's contemporary John But, who 'made an end' to the A version some time before 1399, and in doing so held out to us the hope of discovering, through his addendum to the text, factual truths concerning a poet whose life is otherwise virtually undocumented in surviving records. Yet whatever may be the value of John But's ending as 'external' documentary evidence about the historical William Langland, it also, and first, offers us priceless internal testimony about what, to a contemporary view, made authorial identity

[1] George Kane, *Piers Plowman: The Evidence for Authorship* (London, 1965), and *The Autobiographical Fallacy in Chaucer and Langland Studies* (London, 1965).

interesting in the construction and development of the poem. We can learn most from what John But has to tell us about William Langland's life if we are also attuned to what, for the 'maker' of 'þis ende', goes without saying about his art – and about why his death required textual commemoration.

The brief Passus 12 of the A text is represented in only three manuscripts, and appears in full in only one of them.[2] The final nineteen lines of the passus – those which refer to 'Will' in the third person rather than as the 'I' of the allegorical action – are usually ascribed to John But (named in line 106), and read as 'external' testimony about the name of the author, his authorship of all three extant versions (the 'other works' of line 101 are generally taken to mean one or the other of the two long versions), and possibly, if we could only identify John But, a *terminus ad quem* for their composition.[3] In scrupulously

---

[2] The manuscripts are described in Kane, to which all citations of the passus and the A Text refer. Their scribal dialects are discussed by M. L. Samuels, 'Langland's Dialect', *MÆ*, 54 (1985), 232–47. The manuscripts are: (1) **U** University College Oxford MS 45 (1400–25; hand II, in which the fragment of A. 12 is written 'belongs to the second quarter of the fifteenth century'), S. Cambridgeshire; has lines 1–19 of Passus 12, after which the MS breaks off damaged. (2) **J** Pierpont Morgan Library MS M818 [*olim* Ingilby] (*c.* 1450); has lines 1–88 of Passus 12, ending with two lines at the top of a leaf, implying that its exemplar had no more of the passus than this. 'Its language . . . and the fragment of a will in the medieval wrapper, suggests SE Lincolnshire as the area of making', according to A. I. Doyle, 'The Manuscripts', *Middle English Alliterative Poetry and Its Literary Background*, ed. David Lawton (Cambridge, 1982), 96. (3) **R** Bodleian MS Rawlinson Poetry 137 [Bodl. MS 14631] (*c.* 1450), SW Sussex; has all of Passus 12 (lines 1–117).

[3] Edith Rickert, 'John But, Messenger and Maker', *MP*, 11 (1913), 107–16, presents evidence to suggest that John But was the king's messenger of that name who was dead by 17 April 1387, when a successor in the office of messenger is named to replace the 'deceased' John But (Cal. Patent Rolls, 1385–9, 290). If Rickert is correct and But speaks knowledgeably of the author, this date thus provides a terminus for all versions of the poem. The identification of But is by no means certain; Rickert presents (107, n. 2) records postdating 1387 of persons of that name, including two (her nos. 1 and 2) that place a John But in the south-west of England in 1400 and 1402. Oscar Cargill, 'The Langland Myth', *PMLA*, 50 (1935), 36–56, favours an identification of John But with a Norfolk mercantile family, members of which are named in several late fourteenth-century records in association with persons of the surname Rokele – the surname, that is, of the poet Langland's father, according to the Latin note of about 1400 in the C manuscript Trinity College Dublin 212. Cargill's analysis of his evidence is sketchy, and his argument very uneven – and in places tendentious – but the records he cites are extremely useful. On the TCD 212 note and other external evidence about authorship, see Kane, *Authorship*, 26–46. Malcolm Parkes has recently stated that the copy of C in TCD 212 'must have been made in the first half of the 1380s'; see George Kane, 'The "Z Version" of *Piers Plowman*', *Speculum*, 60 (1985), 912. This dating would make TCD 212 the earliest extant copy of any version of the poem. For the view that the 'other works' mentioned by But (line 101) are the long version(s) of *Piers Plowman*, see R. W. Chambers, 'The Original Form of the A Text of *Piers Plowman*', *MLR*, 6 (1911), 302–23; this article remains the most thorough treatment of the content of Passus A. 12, and of the arguments concerning But's hand in it.

telling us his name, John But differs from Langland's many other early imitators (apart from this example, their only name is legion); moreover, his concluding prayer for the well-being of Richard II shows that he was Langland's contemporary, and that therefore this report of the poet's sudden death could have been based on direct factual knowledge. But was it? Much that we should like to know about *Piers Plowman* and its author seems to ride on this offered information, and the writer's care to name himself and effectively to date his testimony seems to invite our trust in his good faith and solicitude about the matters on which he reports. Yet But's conclusion also withholds what it seems so provocatively and precisely to offer, since we cannot be sure where in the passus 'this end' begins; moreover, this indeterminacy seems essential to But's design. A firm determination of how much of the passus is John But's work in Chambers's view 'does not admit of proof' in any direction, yet what is and is not 'external' to Langland's work in this passus is crucially important if we are to understand what kind of 'document' it is, and the motives that underwrite its making.[4] Evaluation of its testimony about matters of fact – of its value as 'external evidence' – seems thus inextricably linked to a critical assessment of its literary character and mode. About literary designs, his own and Langland's, John But seems to have had firm, if largely implicit, views that can help us to understand his purpose in 'making a good end' to the poem.

Unlike the anonymous scribe who added seven closing lines to the A text in the Westminster manuscript, But does not consider it necessary to invent a little reprise-in-reverse of the opening lines of the poem in order to bring it to a satisfactory close.[5] The Westminster commentator has Will wake from his

---

[4] See Chambers, 'The Original Form of the A Text', 320–3. Manly believed that But's work began at line 55; Chambers here favours the view that it started at line 89, while admitting the possibility that the whole passus might be But's work. While assenting to Chambers's caveat that there can be no proof of the matter, I shall argue here that But's work begins no later than line 34, and consider it quite possible that the entire passus is his.

[5] See George Kane, 'The Text', *A Companion to Piers Plowman*, ed. John A. Alford (Berkeley, 1988), 1–28; the addition reads:

> And when I was wytterly awakyd I wrote all thys dreame
> And theys mervellys þat I met on mawlverne hyllys
> In a seysoun of sommer as I softe nappyd
> For þe people after ther power wold persen after dowell
> That þe tresure moost tryed and tryacle at neede
> now god gravnt vs grace to make a good ende
> And bryng vs to þe blysse as he bowghte vs on þe Roode
> Amen
>
> R   H

This scribe's seemingly metonymic association of the act of ending the poem with a pious wish that we readers shall have the 'grace to make a good ende', is striking, in the light of But's similar equation, even though the prayer itself is broadly commonplace as

dream to report that he has written it, then turn to us in his own person as writer to laud the 'tresure and tryacle' of dowel that was its substance, and to invoke for his readers the 'grace to make a good ende'. John But, however, seems to regard the content of Will's visions as no fictive 'avanture', no literary dream at all, but authentic spiritual experience, figuratively expressed. What concerns him in the first instance is a 'good ende' to the writer's life, and only secondarily a narratively satisfying closure to the dreamer's 'avanture'. In John But's view Langland as writer has not merely depicted but enacted an exemplary enterprise in the 'making' of this poem. The acts of what Leo Spitzer differentiated as the 'poetic and empirical "I"' are here wholly fused, much as they are by the authors of the Provençal *vidas*, but in this instance the broadly autobiographical *assimilatio* of Langland's 'menyng' has profound implications about poetic form and mode, both John But's and Langland's.[6] Paradoxically, it is because this grateful reader so thoroughly identifies the 'profitable werkes' that enable Will to end well the 'lyf . . . ordeyned for the' (line 90) with the lifelong ambitions and literary project of the poet whose work he respects that the line between his own work and Langland's in this passus is similarly, and artfully, blurred.

The question of where 'þis ende' begins is posed by the literary form John But claims for it: it is not a scribal *explicit* but a tribute in kind, a 'makyng' about a making, an act of both literary criticism and literary imitation.

---

a scribal gesture of conclusion. On the openness of long allegorical narrative to continuations of this sort that both close the narrative action and implicitly make a determination of its broader generic 'intente', see David F. Hult, *Self-Fulfilling Prophecies: Readership and Authority in the First Roman de la Rose* (Cambridge, 1986), 10–64. The Westminster scribe in effect continues the poem in Will's own voice, assuming the persona of dreamer-author to enact the 'avanture' to its conventional narrative closure of waking and retrospective interpretation. John But scrupulously separates his own voice from that of 'Will' the dreamer, yet as I shall suggest, his work extends back into the first-person narration of Will's adventures; But's rationalisation of his own act of closure is thus performed in two voices, that of the dreamer constructed so as to authorise that of his interpreter.

[6] Leo Spitzer, 'Notes on the Poetic and Empirical "I" in Medieval Authors', *Traditio*, 4 (1946), 414–22; Kane, 'Autobiographical Fallacy', 14–15, expresses reservations about the adequacy of this formulation to encompass the strategies of self-presentation by late-medieval authors. On the *vidas* and other forms of biographical and auto-biographical narration of the later middle ages in effect a 'back-formation' from the lyric presentation of the first person, see Paul Zumthor, 'Autobiography in the Middle Ages?' *Genre*, 6 (1973), 29–48; see also Michel Zink, 'Time and Representation of the Self in Thirteenth-Century French Poetry', *PoT*, 5 (1984), 611–27, and Nancy Freeman Regalado, *Poetic Patterns in Rutebeuf* (New Haven, 1970), esp. 190–313. On *assimilatio*, see Judson Boyce Allen, *The Ethical Poetic of the Later Middle Ages* (Toronto, 1982), 248–87, and my essay, 'William Langland's "Kynde Name": Authorial Signature and Social Identity in Late Fourteenth-Century England' (forthcoming).

Fastidious in declaring his own name, John But is equally careful to raise the status of his participation in Langland's enterprise, and his solicitude about its closure, above the merely scribal or documentary. In representing his rôle, and his motives for intervention, as those of a grateful and discriminating reader and amateur versifier, he borrows Langland's own phrase – though stripped of Langland's rueful irony – to tell us so: 'for he [i.e., John But] medleþ of makyng he made þis ende' (109). But the very phrase he quotes from *Piers Plowman* (B. 12. 16) to ally his own pious purpose with the morally edifying designs he sees in Langland's endeavour is taken from perhaps the most devastating systematic indictment of 'making' anywhere in Middle English literature, one which contains a fundamental and self-aware disclosure of Langland's literary designs. John But's small act of 'translation' thus reveals what, as I shall show, we can also confirm by other means – namely that he not only knew of, but knew well, at least one of the long versions of Langland's work, and was here also drawing some important critical inferences about it. Moreover, it opens to us the differences of value and meaning each writer assigns to poetic closure. John But is determined to turn Langland's 'every drem to goode'; Langland himself never loses sight of the possibility, latent in the psychology of penance, that they may bring him to a bad end.

To say, as Ymaginatif does in Langland's B text, that Will's 'meddling with makings' is a waste of time means, within the values assigned to time as the medium of salvation, something far more serious than that it is a fairly witless amateur pastime, to be indulged if not greatly admired, which is the worst indictment of his authorial enterprise that Chaucer has to hear from his fictionalised critics the Man of Law and Queen Alceste.[7] To be sure, Will has certainly been suspected before this point in the poem of trivial and nugatory intentions – of wishing to 'finden up fantasyes' about serious spiritual matters only to serve a turn in table talk. This was Dame Study's dismissive initial view of Will's quest for Dowel, expressed in the passus immediately preceding this one (A. 11. 5–92; cf. B. 10. 5–139). But Ymaginatif's charge in the B continuation (B. 12. 10–19) is far more fundamental and devastating than that of Dame Study. In his view Will's 'makynges', even if understood as earnest didacticism, would at best duplicate 'bokes ynowe' already extant 'to telle men what dowel is', and preachers' use of these 'to preuen what it is'. Yet it is not what Will's 'makings' do or fail to do in the world, but the activity they *replace* that condemns them as otiose and worse.

---

[7] *Canterbury Tales* B[1], 46–89; *Legend of Good Women*, F. 362–72, 412–30, cf. G. 340–52, 398–420. These and other citations of Chaucer are taken from *The Works of Geoffrey Chaucer*, ed. F. N. Robinson, 2nd ed. (Boston, 1957). Ymaginatif's charge appears in Passus 12 of the B text, lines 10–19; this and all citations of B are taken from Kane–Donaldson.

What appears to be most deeply at issue for Ymaginatif here – as it will be for the inquisitors Reason and Conscience, whose interview with Will early in the C text (C. 5. 1–104) largely supplants in argumentative force this part of his encounter with Ymaginatif in B – is not Will's authority to edify, the redundancy of his efforts, or the effect of his writings on others, but their effect on Will himself.[8] In the internal economy of salvation, Ymaginatif suggests, 'makyng' is the mental equivalent of material 'wasting' on the half-acre: it consumes in fruitless dilation precisely those finite temporal gifts of mind that are given to man to sustain spiritual life and health on earth. These commodities – time and memory, and the power to constitute them in mental image and utterance – are loaned to humankind for use, and the manner in which the individual deploys them constitutes an implicit account of his earthly stewardship; they are the counters with which he can of his own will offer a temporal wager for his own salvation. Defining man as a historical being, these faculties are productive in rendering human life as a formal unit, an act of spiritual composition oriented towards 'making a good end'. Will acknowledges as much to Reason and Conscience, when he compares his contrite self–recognition to the merchant's hazard of all he has in one ultimate 'bargayn' by which he will be 'þe bet euere' (C. 5. 96). When time, memory, and imagination are applied instead to the farming of a verse, however, 'makyng' becomes in Ymaginatif's view the very antithesis of penitential discipline – indeed, as it were its demonic double.

Narration, particularly that which 'speaks the self', is thus rendered double-edged. Its ideal use is in the service of confessional 'truth-telling', the contrite return through memory to one's past, enabling the subject to transform the present into a new starting-point from which to make a good end. Yet first-person narration, even if nominally confessional, also carries within it a second kind of hazard. In the psychology of sin implicit in the medieval handbooks, in which the subject's capacity to see and tell the truth about himself is circumscribed by the empty recursiveness formed by his own *habitus*, such utterance is in practice equally capable of deflecting and deferring penitential contrition, enacting a fruitless and endless auto-exegesis which keeps the narrative subject *in medias res*, able only to 'heavily from woe to woe tell o'er', his story a pattern of repetition rather than revelation.[9] Many readers have noted this vivid pattern of habitual return to the 'old man' in Langland's treatment of the Confession of the Deadly Sins: Envy, when urged to penitential sorrow, replies that he is 'seldom other' than sorry, and seems therefore incapable of finding this a restorative state of mind; Glutton falls

---

[8] Citations of the C Text are from Pearsall.

[9] See Lee W. Patterson, 'Chaucerian Confession: Penitential Literature and the Pardoner', *M&H*, ns 7 (1976): 153–73, esp. 156–62; J. A. Burrow, *Ricardian Poetry* (New Haven, 1971), 106–9.

once more into the sins of the tavern while on his way to confession. Not only for these speakers, but often for Will himself, declaration of one's own designs quickly becomes indistinguishable from self-justification, reasons blur into excuses, and confession repeatedly decomposes into *apologia*.

From the first to the last version of Langland's poem the confessional imperative that underwrites both allegorical self-representation and penance – and hence the impulse to narrate – never loses this deep subjective danger and duplicity. Indeed, it would be hard to find an 'idea' in the poem more basic to the workings of Langland's moral and literary imagination, and more fundamental to the form of its realisation, than this notion that 'makyng' is a kind of endless lecture upon the shadow that nevertheless is powerless to deliver us from the 'body of this death' that it can so compellingly envision. As I hope this exercise will suggest, it is the deeper exploration of precisely this idea – and its development in the representation of Will himself, as well as in the early visions through other allegorical figures – that enables and generates the B–C continuation. Sloth, for example, is conceived not simply as social inactivity, but as a habitual complex of a short memory for favours received, an almost obsessive nostalgia about his own carnal powers and pleasures, a delight in revisiting and re-creating the scene of the crime, as well as in amorous delay – all of which are reinforced by idle songs and tales. In what may be Langland's last addition to his poem, the so-called 'autobio-graphical' waking interval between the first and second dreams in the C text, it is Will himself, idle at harvest-time, who is caught 'romynge in remem-braunce' and forced by Reason and Conscience to replay still more fully his humiliating B text confession to Ymaginatif, that beneath his fraudulent pretence to clerical *otium* his far more grievous fault has been that he has 'tyme myspened'.[10] His self-defences and delays finally demolished, he is released by his interlocutors at last 'to bigynne the lyif þat is louable and leele to thy soule' (103). He proceeds to church, to make up for lost time with the requisite penitential countermeasures, and promptly falls asleep, to dream the rest of the poem. Penance, the undertaking of one's own 'good end', is once more deferred by its dilatory double, 'making', in the course of the very imaginative labours which initiate it; what had been a thematic concern is here fully realised as a principle of form.

I have suggested elsewhere that the narrative pattern and generative form of

---

[10] The resemblance of Will's attributes and habits to those of the slothful man have been noticed before; the most thorough and complex treatment of this matter is John M. Bowers, *The Crisis of Will in Piers Plowman* (Washington, D.C., 1986), esp. 128–89. On the disposition of one's earthly time as a topic of examination in the late-medieval confessional, see Jacques LeGoff, 'Merchant's Time and Church's Time in the Middle Ages', and 'Labor Time in the "Crisis" of the Fourteenth Century', in *Time, Work, and Culture in the Middle Ages*, trans. Arthur Goldhammer (Chicago, 1980), 29–42, 43–52.

Langland's poem in all its versions is essentially recursive, an episodic re-enactment in various scenes of a fundamental struggle over the power to determine what counts as edification, and in particular to authorise memorial reconstructions of the past.[11] The conflict takes several forms: a dispute over the interpretation of historical example (such as what conclusions one may draw from Trajan's puzzling salvation), the productive rendering of Christ's life as a model, or of one's own experience of one's life and times; how shall 'al tymes of my tyme' be turned at last to profit, and what kind of profit, and by whom? It is in his prominent representations of penitential motives that Langland reveals the subjective terrors latent in these boldly anti-authoritarian questions – and the almost unbridgeable gap they open between narrative dilation and closure. In such scenes as these Langland explores the deep and abiding instability of 'romyng in remembrance': when at any point penitential reflection may be swamped once more by wasteful nostalgia, narration knows neither progress nor recovery.

'When you hear a man confessing, you know that he is not yet free', declared St Augustine. It was, I suggest, John But's endeavour – deliberate, if not wholly conscious – to free the poet from these profound and disturbing consequences of his own narrative principles that prompted him to 'make this end'. As I have tried to suggest, he was right in perceiving that the poem was imagined most deeply as a memorial abstract of the subject's life, and the subject himself as always on the verge of penitential self-reformation. In 'makyng this end', however, John But must resolve the ambiguities of this project, and to do so he must take the repeatedly proclaimed restitutive intent as final, and take the author at his word. He stabilises Langland's hazardous narrative dynamic in two ways. He 'takes personally' – which is also in part correctly – Langland's representation of a man who is 'thinking of his end', as part of a genuine, if incomplete, confessional self-disclosure of the author, a *confessio ficti* which is potentially salvific (and retroactively effective) for the maker, and not simply an imitation of such an action for the affective edification of the audience.[12] John But regards Will's 'makyng' not as a deferral of penitential reflection but its heroically prolonged enactment, an undertaking of 'profitable werkes' by the author in 'real time' – a time, however, foreclosed by death 'ere Wille myȝte aspie'. He must therefore with his prayers help this unfinished project of reconciliation through a work of sustained self-reflection towards its 'promised end'.

---

[11] On the conflict over the determination of the discursive order of the poem as it is reinscribed in its depicted events, see my essay 'Narration and the Invention of Experience: Episodic Form in *Piers Plowman*', *The Wisdom of Poetry: Essays in Honor of Morton W. Bloomfield*, ed. Larry D. Benson and Siegfried Wenzel (Kalamazoo, Michigan, 1982), 91–122.

[12] On the efficacy of a *confessio ficti*, see Thomas N. Tentler, *Sin and Confession on the Eve of the Reformation* (Princeton, 1977), 273–80.

A second translation is implicit in the first. Diverging from Langland's understanding of what kind of act begins the making of a good end, he must also assign real rather than contingent and gestural value to the *specie* in which 'Will' offers to purchase paradise. Works – in this case that which 'here is wryten and oþer werkes boþe' – become in John But's account equivalent coin to that contrite recollection which, in Langland's own view, they repeatedly drive out of the spiritual economy. For him, 'profitable werkes' are in effect the just price that God exacts for the salvation that is his to give in return. In Langland's view, which is both more theologically complex and less reassuring to those in search of moral art in his poem, they are but the sign of an empowering grace obtained by an initiatory wager of faith, a transaction in which man is at most a willing beholder and partaker, not a 'maker'. Langland's Will does not, and cannot, on his own behalf 'make a good end', but must endure his going hence even as his coming hither, giving over the narration of his story to the master historical pattern in whose image it has been made.

We are now in a position to engage in a retrospection of our own, moving backward through the passus in search of where 'this end' begins. It seems appropriate to take this analytic regression in three main steps, corresponding to three distinct narrative motions in the passus: (1) lines 99–105, which speak of Will in the third person as having

> . . . wrouȝthe þat here is wryten and oþer werkes boþe
> Of peres þe plowman and mechel puple also.
> And whan þis werk was wrouȝt, ere wille myȝte aspie,
> Deþ delt him a dent and drof him to þe erþe
> And is closed vnder clom, crist haue his soule.
>
> (A. 12. 101–5);

(2) lines 55–98, in which Will, in the first person, falls in with Hunger and Fever and seeks to die; and (3) lines 1–54, which continue from the preceding passus Will's quest for Dowel, as he is sent on from the house of Clergy and Scripture to Kynde Wit for further instruction.

While in principle anything before line 106 *could* have been written by Langland, lines 99–105 have generally, since Skeat, been seen as fully continuous with what follows, and assigned to John But – correctly, as I believe can now be demonstrated. Though Skeat's case has rested, largely for lack of interest since the lights went out on the 'authorship controversy', John Norton-Smith has recently reopened it, assigning these lines to Langland as instancing a well-known 'concluding topos' of the end of an author's writing life.[13] Norton-Smith cites in evidence Chaucer and Gower – by which he apparently means the *Retractions* and the end of the *Confessio Amantis*. At

---

[13] John Norton-Smith, *William Langland* (Leiden, 1983), 11–12.

first glance, Gower's work might seem to offer a particularly close parallel: he divides his fictitious *persona* Amans from his own authorial identity in a way broadly analogous to the division between the dreaming and writing self that Norton-Smith here attributes to Langland. Lines 99–105 deviate significantly, however, from the analogues Norton-Smith cites – and from other late-medieval examples of this 'concluding topos' – as well as from Langland's own literary *usus* elsewhere in the poem in ways that decisively rule out his composition of any part of this passage.

The topos, as Norton-Smith sees it operating here, consists of two gestures: the poet claims his own work (lines 99–102) and reports his own death (103–5).[14] Neither Chaucer nor Gower, however, nor any other late-medieval poet portraying himself and his designs from the perspective of the borders of death, represents himself as actually dying and, in effect, pulling the tomb lid down over himself – much less in an untimely and unprepared-for fashion, as Norton-Smith would have Langland do in lines 103–5.[15] Rather, poets who use this device in poetic closure present the authorial self in the act of final rectification through testament, penance, and prayer – the performative rituals necessary to disposing one's earthly effects and spiritual intentions, enabling one to 'make a good end'. Even when travestied, as they are by Villon, these final preparatory deeds, not death itself, form the focal point of this 'topos' wherever it is used, the *raison d'être* of the literary representation – and they are entirely absent from the lines Norton-Smith would assign to Langland. We must therefore, I believe, consider lines 103–5, reporting the poet's death, literarily 'ungrammatical' as issuing from the author of *Piers Plowman*, and assign them to John But's 'making'. If they are fiction, the fiction is not Langland's.

The first half of this 'topos' is equally unlikely to have been from Langland's hand, for reasons that we have already examined. Here (lines 99–102) the 'profitable werkes' enjoined upon Will for his final spiritual

---

[14] The shift from the first to the third person at this point would not in itself necessarily rule out Norton-Smith's claim: earlier in A Langland has named Will in the third person – the first time, in fact, as penitent, the first to weep at Repentance's sermon.

[15] Another famous dreamer and pilgrim named William – Guillaume deGuilleville, at the end of his *Pelerinage de la Vie Humaine*, in the early fourteenth century – closes his long allegorical quest-narrative by staging allegorically his own approaching death. He is old, and feels himself growing weak and faint, but as Death swings his scythe at Guillaume, he wakes from his dream. Even the more elaborately self-dramatising Villon does not quite place himself in his grave in his *Testament*. He does set down wonderfully precise instructions for his funeral, specifying the prayers his mourners should say, and the clothes they should wear, and he composes his own epitaph. The final stanzas of the poem, his own eulogy, record his last moments in the third person. While Villon saw to it that the reports of his death would always be greatly exaggerated, even they offer no more satisfactory analogue to what Norton-Smith claims for lines 103–5 than Chaucer and Gower do.

rectification are said to consist in the 'making' of 'þat here is wryten and oþer werkes boþe'. Such activities are the salvific 'werkes' enjoined upon Will as a substitute for the immediate 'deþ' he seeks by following 'Feuere' (line 88). The latter, Death's 'masager' (who has a 'confessoures face'), persuades Will instead to remain on earth until his allotted years are finished, meanwhile to 'lyue as þis lyf is ordeyned for the', engaged in 'preyeres and profitable werkes' (89–98). This turn of events closely resembles that of the final passus of B and C, when, after a buffeting by Elde and various infirmities, Will's despairing plea to Kynde to be taken 'out of care' is met instead by Kynde's command that he enter into Unity 'and hold þee þere euere til I sende for þee'. The difference, however, between these two similar moments is telling. Where in the final passus (as also in Will's two earlier confrontations about how he should spend his remaining earthly time) the time between now and judgement is to be spent in penitential labours that *supplant* and 'turn to profit' Will's former waste of time in 'making' and other spiritually empty pursuits, the lines in question here assign saving power to the farming of a verse. Perceiving 'soþe' in Feuere's counsel, Will responds, not by turning towards prayer (as he does in the face of Reason and Conscience's rebuke, and as Piers does in renouncing his occupation) but by turning his hand *to* rather than *from* his 'makings' (99–100): his reprieve from death merely buys him more time to write his great work.

This is a plausible construction of his pious continuator John But, who then puts paid to these salvific if uncompleted labours by adding his own prayers for the poet's soul. It is, however, completely opposed to Langland's own treatment of the relations between 'making' and penance everywhere else in the poem, and must rule out his authorship, not only of the lines depicting his death (103–5) but those in which, according to Norton-Smith, he claims his works. If Norton-Smith's analogues fail to support as Langland's the second gesture of this 'topos' – Will's representation of his own death – massive internal evidence undermines the attribution to Langland of this account of the ethical and representational value of Will's 'makings', and their relation to 'making a good end'. Again, Skeat's judgement as textual critic is vindicated by the *ratio* of the literary scholar: Langland's work can extend no further in this passus than line 98.

Indeed, the internal evidence against Langland's authorship of these lines goes still deeper than their treatment of 'making' as salvific labour, and extends backward in the passus to call into question 'Feuere's' counsel as well; John But's construction of Will's final spiritual rectification appears to begin no later than line 89.[16] At no point in the poem does Langland himself

---

[16] Chambers's view was that But's work began here, with Feuere's reply to Will. He cites in support the Pierpont Morgan manuscript, which stops the passus with line 88, leaving most of the leaf blank below it, thus strongly suggesting that this scribe's exemplar went no further.

concede to those who live under the New Law the capacity to win their salvation simply by applying energetically and with earnest conviction some temporal 'one talent it is death to hide'. Much as Langland is willing to 'allow' to the 'treuthe' of the virtuous pagans – and as we know from his handling of the legend of Trajan it is a great deal – for Will and his contemporaries the principle of *facere quod in se est*, 'do what is in you', is a great deal more intractable and less optimistic than that.[17] Will's enduring resistance to its implications is evident in his staunch nostalgia for primal precedent, and his stubborn conviction, under the sign of satire in the early stretches of Dowel, that at least he has a firm ethical grip on historical example – a conviction seriously shaken as he watches Piers unmake his own entirely virtuous occupation in the Pardon scene. The problem for all of those living in the commune Langland depicts, including himself in Will, is that they cannot by either study or introspection *know* 'what is in them', and therefore they cannot render it as continuous narration; they can only find out 'as in a mirror', by revealing it in prayer and penance to God. The individual's story cannot be told wholly in the first person; as Augustine acknowledged, 'I have become a puzzle to myself'.

The belief that one may win heaven by works alone is everywhere for Langland the original and final delusion of mankind, yet it is so very tenacious, and so very reasonable – especially to those who care as deeply as Langland does about civil virtue – that it always in this poem requires a violent shock to dislodge. Every major reversal in the poem witnesses to the power of this delusion: Piers's dismantling of his occupation in the Pardon scene, Will's vertiginous fall into himself in the Lond of Longyng when Scripture 'scorns' his pursuit of knowledge, and the ultimate failure of the poem's seemingly most secure principle of virtuous action and considered choice, Conscience, in the final passus, immediately following an exposure as devastating as Augustine's own of the insufficiency of the four classical virtues to secure peace on earth, and health to the human spirit.[18] For nearly six hundred years, all that most deeply dismays those determined to regard

---

[17] On the righteous heathen, and the principle of *facere quod in se est* – matters beyond the scope of the present essay – see G. H. Russell, 'The Salvation of the Heathen: The Exploration of a Theme in *Piers Plowman*', *JWCI*, 29 (1966), 101–16; Janet Coleman, *Piers Plowman and the Moderni* (Rome, 1981), 108–46; Pamela Gradon, '*Trajanus Redivivus*: Another Look at Trajan in *Piers Plowman*', *Middle English Studies Presented to Norman Davis*, ed. Douglas Gray and E. G. Stanley (Oxford, 1983), 93–114; Gordon Whatley, '*Piers Plowman* B. 12, 277–94: Notes on Language, Text, Theology', *MP*, 82 (1984), 1–12; idem, 'The Uses of Hagiography: The Legends of Pope Gregory and the Emperor Trajan in the Middle Ages', *Viator*, 15 (1984), 25–63.

[18] Augustine, *Civ. Dei*, 19. 4, cited from *The City of God*, trans. Henry Bettenson (New York, 1972). Much of the developing logic of the allegorical narrative in the long versions of *Piers Plowman* from civil satire to cosmic history seems to track the course of the argument of Book 19.

Piers Plowman as morally improving reading emanates from the thousand-volt mortal shocks administered by such moments as this. John But, I suggest, was such a reader, and it was through such reasoning that he became the admiring continuator who undertook – not only with his prayers but with a retrospective rereading of the value of the 'profitable werkes' to which he wrote a pious closure – to deliver the poet Langland from the dreadful logic of his represented pursuit and untimely ambush by the forces of mortality; the seamless grammar that links John But's prayers to the terms of his rescue tends to confirm that they are the work of this second 'maker'.[19]

The narrative logic that produces this resolution extends, however, yet further back into the antecedent events of this passus, which as we have seen closely follow a similar sequence in the final passus of the B–C continuation. In the course of lines 55–98 – and nowhere else in the A text – Will's fundamental effort to Dowel, here realised in his proximate quest for Kynde Wit, abruptly yields to increasingly mortal guidance. Almost immediately upon setting forth, he is diverted, first by hunger and then by surfeit, and ultimately by despair of attaining 'mesure' between them; this vicious circle of moral causality echoes that played out earlier among the folk on the field in the Hunger episode. It is in this demoralised condition, despairing at the grim prospects of attaining by his own efforts any restoration of moral equilibrium, that he meets Feuere, and quickly volunteers to follow him on his mission from 'Deþ þat is oure duk' to kill Lyf. Only in the final passus of B and C, under the disciplinary ravages of Conscience's assistants Kynde and Elde, do we again find Will as despairing and eager for death as he is in these lines. There, in a world threatened by the forces of Antichrist, the sheer self-preserving vitality of Life resists Conscience's first round of warnings, in the form of diseases sent by Kynde, which are intended to summon the endangered folk within the stronghold of Unity. Life continues vigorously wasting the commune through his demonic progeny: with his 'lemman' Fortune he engenders Sleuthe, who spreads 'drede of dispair a doȝeyne myle aboute', causing Conscience to send in his second-strike force, Elde, to combat this

---

[19] Langland's first printer, Robert Crowley, was another; see 'William Langland's "Kynde Name"'. I do not, of course, claim that in constructing his ending John But consciously undertook the chain of reasoning applied here to Langland's poem, merely that his general view of it as edifying narrative, chiefly promoting good works, tended in effect to gloss over the moral and theological difficulties that Langland's own treatment renders visible – and in particular to submerge those aspects of their dynamic representation that become especially problematic at the end of A. What John But seems to have perceived was not the exact nature of the philosophical and practical difficulty, but a general dissonance that he seeks to resolve with a coda in a major key. My argument is that this dissonance was not local or accidental, generated in the hiatus between the first version and the continuations, but pervasive and programmatic – and demanded from But in the execution surprisingly programmatic and sweeping narrative measures to resolve.

spreading wanhope. It is on his way to attack Life that Elde runs over Will's head, making him bald; when Will refuses to take this insult lightly, he adds for good measure deafness, toothlessness, gout, and, worst of all, impotence. As in Passus A. 12, the assaults of despair lower the resistance of both Will and the commune generally to the forces of Antichrist, and only true contrition and satisfaction will restore health to the sick.

This entire apocalyptic sequence at the end of the B and C texts replays as a universal historical process and prophetic revelation what these versions had staged earlier, roughly at the midpoint of the two long texts, as Will's personal recognition of the meaning of his craft, and a rededicatory turning point in his life. 'Scorned' by Scripture only a few lines into the B–C continuation for wishing to know everything but himself, Will falls into Fortune's realm of 'middelerd', where he eagerly accepts as 'lemman' all of Fortune's handmaids (who are the three temptations), only to recognise the mortality of their charms when Elde approaches and they abandon him to his decrepitude and the prospect of a death unprepared for.[20] It is to interpret this encounter as a warning that it is time to 'mynne on þyn ende' that Ymaginatif next intervenes, urging Will to reconceive the seductions and terrors of the days he has seen under the sign of penance rather than 'makyng' – to begin to take his visionary 'avantures' personally rather than as mere 'wonders'. Yet it is precisely the expanded penitential and prophetic dimension of Will's pursuit of death in the final passus of B and C that 'this end' elides. In Passus A. 12 Will remains simply an individual soul both in search and in terror of death, much as he was in Fortune's Lond of Longyng, before his enterprise was 'translated'.

Like Kynde in the final episode, Feuere rejects Will's despairing plea to die. But while the Will of the B and C text 'comsed to rome thoruȝ Contrition and Confession til I cam to vnitee', empowered by the 'craft' of love, Will in this passus earns John But's prayers for his soul simply by remaining in this harsh world a while longer to exercise the 'maker's' craft, continuing a morally edifying story of his individual deliverance from despair through 'profitable werkes'. If faith without feat cannot go, in the end all 'werkes' walk blind, and in Langland's enterprise it is ultimately only the underwriting of 'werkes' by a penitent will that can heal the wounded world.

Lines 55–98 of this passus therefore appear to be not Langland's sketch for later work, but John But's partial 'back-formation' from the B–C ending, its events stripped of the universal apocalyptic overtones they acquire by following the long intervening narrative of the redemption as historical process, and rendered instead as a continued figurative narration of Will's personal quest to know and Dowel – the matter immediately in the foreground at the end of the A text. John But's view, explicit from line 99 on, of the edifying power of

---

[20] See my essay 'William Langland's "Kynde Name"'.

Langland's 'werkes' – and his concomitant sense of their unity of theme and purpose – authorises such a construction. The passus from at least line 55 appears to be a critical act in the form of an imitation, undertaken in the attempt both to understand the further development of the poem, and to apply this understanding to clarifying and interpreting the form of the text at hand, and the narrative occasion it offered for an intellectually and morally satisfying conclusion.[21]

If the last half of Passus A. 12 offers a 'fast-forward' version of the major developments in the first and last moments of the B–C continuation, lines 1–54 likewise repeat, and still more mechanically, antecedent plot developments in A.[22] The first half of this passus closely parallels the *histoire* of the immediately preceding episode, recapitulating it point-for-point with different actors. It disposes within fifty lines Will's encounter with Clergy and Scripture, the second husband-and-wife team who have attempted to teach him, in exactly the same terms as his earlier meeting with Wit and his scolding wife Dame Study, who had sent him here – and with precisely the same narrative outcome. Like Study (A. 11. 1–92) – though unlike Scripture in her earlier appearance in A (11. 225–57) – Scripture in A. 12 is something of

---

[21] George Kane has recently made a similar argument about the longest continuous run of distinctive verses in the so-called Z text; see 'The "Z Version" of *Piers Plowman*', *Speculum*, 60 (1985), 910–30, a review of *Piers Plowman: The Z Version*, ed. A. G. Rigg and Charlotte Brewer (Toronto, 1983). The lines in the Z manuscript called by the editors 'Meed's denunciation of Conscience for avarice' do not appear in any other version at this point in Meed's speech; Kane argues that this passage 'records the Z writer's attempt to understand the role of Conscience in the B version of the poem' (922–3), and that the substance of Meed's charges, incongruous and incorrect at this point in the narrative, is a conflation of Conscience's several actions in the final passus of the long versions – an interpolated 'back-formation' prompted by, and based on, these final dismaying events, inviting the kind of ideational intervention from the scribe that I here attribute to John But in his making of 'þis ende'.

[22] A similar instance of the 'fast-forward' approach to concluding a long and complex allegorical narrative may be seen in the spurious ending to Guillaume de Lorris's text of the *Roman de la Rose*. In 78 lines, this anonymous continuator has Bone Amor open the gate to allow Biauté – accompanied by Pitié, Bel Acueil, Loiauté, Douz Regart, and Simplece – to bring to Amis the bud he desires, and to exact his continued service as the price of his keeping it from repossession. For the text of these lines see *Le Roman de la Rose*, ed. Ernest Langlois (Paris, 1920), 2. 330–3. The crucial requirement of closure, to this continuator, seems to have been swift attainment of the ultimate narrative objective, the lover's obtaining of the rose, with little regard to the delicately balanced proprieties and powers of each of Guillaume's personifications in developing the symbolic structure of desire; the relentless continuity of *histoire* drowns out the claims of *discours*. In a similar fashion, both Feuere's and Kynde Wit's rôles in Passus A. 12 seem both inexact in their suitability to the actions they are here assigned, and at odds with their proprieties elsewhere in the poem; here they are broadly personified agencies capable of filling a slot in the all-important resolution of the action. On the decorum of other scribal-editorial interventions in the textual traditions of the *Rose*, see Hult, 34–55.

a scold (12–33). Like Study's tirade, her storm of 'skorn' (a term otherwise associated with Scripture only in the opening lines of the B–C continuation) drives her more temperate spouse from further discourse (A. 11. 93–9; cf. A. 12. 34–7); Clergy's abashed creeping into a 'caban' at this point also closely echoes a much earlier shamefaced retreat – the one Lady Meed accuses Conscience of effecting in the king's troops in Normandy (A. 3. 178). Like Study earlier (A. 11. 109), Scripture is finally mollified by Will's gestures of formal obeisance (A. 12. 38–46), and – again like her predecessor – to his great joy gives him detailed road-directions to his next instructor, who is in each case her 'cosyn' (A. 11. 110–24; cf. A. 12. 47–54).

These resemblances to the anterior text are more detailed than broadly reduplicated events: throughout this dialogue, and the ensuing narration that sends Will out on the road again, there are also insistent verbal echoes of the Prologue and the Meed episode: sustained similarities of vocabulary, and even direct quotation of whole lines (A. 12. 58; cf. A. Pro. 62). Moreover, the resemblances are not only to the A version of these episodes. To accompany Will on his journey to Kynde Wit her 'cosyn', Scripture summons a companion, *omnia probate*, who is to remain with him as far as 'þe burgh *quod bonum est tenete*' – or as far as Will wishes (A. 12. 49–52). The same Latin text (I Thess. 5: 21) is reified (and similarly as a pair of separated phrases, distanced from each other by the turn of a 'leef'), in Conscience's reply to Meed's charges – but that passage is introduced into Conscience's speech only with the B revision (B. 3. 337–43). The verse that introduces *omnia probate* as 'a pore þing withalle' (A. 12. 50) follows the pattern of the one that introduces the 'lunatik' as a 'leene þyng wiþalle' in the coronation scene added to the B text prologue (B. Pro. 121).

The differences, however, between these features of Langland's poem and their use in A. 12 are far more telling than the similarities: neither the *discours* nor the *histoire* of the passage is as coherent as – or consonant with – what precedes or follows it in Langland's poem. 'Trying all things' does not by any means produce or lead to 'that which is good'; this is precisely Conscience's point in turning the division of the Biblical verse against Lady Meed. How such a course of action might lead Will to Kynde Wit is equally puzzling, as are Scripture's specific qualifications for recommending it. Even if 'Kynde Wit' implies here the power of knowing one's own good, a natural and enlightened self-interest (the sense of the term in Holichurche's speech: A. 1. 53–4), it is far from obvious how the logic of progression in Langland's series of instructors in the third dream, extending from Thought to Wit to Study to Clergy to Scripture, could produce this figure as the next in the set – and the narrative logic of sudden *regression*, provided by Will's precipitous fall at Scripture's 'scorn' in the long versions, is here precluded by Scripture's retraction of her initial insult. The preparatory rôle here forecast for Kynde Wit is fulfilled in the long versions by Ymaginatif, who helps Will to integrate what text and experience, Clergie and Kynde, present to the inner sight, but it is narratively required only by the radical break in Will's progress that passus A. 12 elides.[23]

Moreover it is unlikely that Langland would thus conflate the essentially prudential self-preservative powers of Kynde Wit, who lodges 'wiþ lyf þat lord is of erþe', with the projective and even prophetic capacities of the imaginative faculty. Ymaginatif defines Kynde Wit as springing from *quod vidimus*, 'of siȝte of diuerse peple' (B. 12. 67); along with 'catel' it 'acombreth ful manye' (B. 12. 55). At its most informative and enlightened it is wisdom of this world, and has no knowledge of the wellsprings of grace (B. 12. 69). While it may indeed, as a prudential faculty, conduce to the exercise of virtue, the identification of virtuous practices is no longer the chief question before Will at the end of A. 11; it is rather their salvific efficacy in the face of the inscrutable operations of grace. With her last words in that passus, Scripture insists on the simultaneous necessity of good works and on their insufficiency *per se* as the means for a Christian's salvation. It is in the dismaying apparent gulf her words open between virtuous practice and salvation that Will remains, 'in wandring mazes lost', at the end of A. What is wanted from this point is an understanding of specifically that kind of well-doing that finds favour in God's sight. Its two complementary forms, prayer and penitential self-knowledge, bracket the gap between the end of A – as the *paternoster* that pierces the 'paleis of heuene' in its final sentence – and the first episode of the B continuation, which reorients Will's reflective capacities towards thoughts of his 'ende' in response to the shock of Scripture's catalytic 'scorn'.

Scripture's commendation of Will to Kynde Wit in A. 12 is thus radically at odds with both Langland's definition of this faculty's powers early in A and in the B continuation, and with the allegorical logic of the immediately preceding episode. This high valuation of Kynde Wit as an instructor in the nature of virtuous deeds is, however, entirely of a piece with the restitutive and exemplary value placed on good works later in this passus. It is hard to avoid the conclusion that everything from line 34 on is the work of the same maker – and that, on the grounds of a vocabulary of philosophical distinction elsewhere powerfully attested in the poem, that their maker was not Langland.

A similar suspicion attaches to the substantial narrative developments in the first thirty-three lines as well. Scripture's insistence (A. 12. 14–15) that before Will can receive further instruction from Clergy or herself, he must be shown (or shriven by) 'þe kynde cardinal wit' and 'christned in a font' is open

---

[23] On the meaning and rôle of Ymaginatif, see Alastair J. Minnis, 'Langland's Ymaginatif and Late-Medieval Theories of Imagination', *Comparative Criticism: A Yearbook*, 3 (1981), 71–103; Ernest N. Kaulbach, 'The "Vis Imaginativa" and the Reasoning Powers of Ymaginatif in the B-Text of *Piers Plowman*', *JEGP*, 84 (1985), 16–29.

to the same charges of elementary conflict with the literal sense of the antecedent text.[24] It is the fact that Will is already a baptised Christian that denies him the scrap of comfort about the possibility of his own salvation that he seeks to infer from the tales of deathbed conversion and baptism he desperately seizes and hurls against Scripture in the preceding passus (A. 11. 232–45). If prior guidance by Kynde Wit as a condition for further tutelage by Scripture means no more than the orthodox dictum that one must attain the age of reason before being instructed in the articles of faith, it is irreproachable advice, but inapplicable to Will's condition at this point in the narrative. The lines seem to suggest, however inexactly, that a sacramental intervention of some kind is a prerequisite of Will's further adventures, and will somehow empower his understanding of Dowel. If Kynde Wit's rôle in such a transformation is unclear from this text, this development at least registers, if it does not solve, the impasse to which Passus A. 11 had brought Will.

All that one can discern of an authentically Langlandian development, germane to this specific point in the allegorical narrative, lies in Scripture's subsequent argument: that in the face of wilful and recalcitrant sinfulness one may, and ought, rightfully to remain silent rather than utter sacred truths as correction, where the condition of the audience precludes their efficacy (17–33). The impression of authenticity in this passage is in part stylistic. Of the entire passus, it is this speech alone, cogently adducing three Latin texts in nineteen lines, that shows the Langlandian manner of using scriptural quotation; in comparison, the deployment of *omnia probate* – the only other Latin scriptural verse in the passus – is lame and unconvincing.[25] It is not merely Scripture's manner here, however, but the matter of her speech that shows some specific appropriateness to the immediate narrative and argumentative impasse in Langland's poem. She articulates a question first voiced by Study, but raised repeatedly, with increasing fullness and self-assurance, in the development of the B and C texts: the value, appropriate manner, and social effectiveness of the public orator's or writer's enterprise of moral correction, and the blocking effect of the hearer's unregenerate discourses upon those of his appointed scourge and minister, the truthteller. Scripture's speech in A. 12 resembles both that of Lewte, early in the B continuation, and

---

[24] 'Schriven' is the emendation proposed by Kane for what is clearly a defective line.
[25] On this 'Langlandian manner', based on the practice John Alford has called the 'method of concordance', see John A. Alford, 'The Role of the Quotations in *Piers Plowman*', *Speculum*, 52 (1977), 80–99, and Judson Allen, 'Langland's Reading and Writing: *Detractor* and the Pardon Passus', *Speculum*, 59 (1984), 342–59. The nature of Langland's specific cleverness at deploying this technique of the preacher's and glossator's expository *inventio* is beyond the scope of this essay, though several detailed local readings of passages in recent years have given exemplary accounts of how this can be demonstrated.

that of Study in A. 11, in exposing the prospect of certain defeat for any literary enterprise conceived chiefly as a 'Retorik to arate dedly synne'.

Like Study in A. 11, Scripture in A. 12 finally charges Will with seeking knowledge only to retail it for praise:

> For he cam not by cause to lerne to dowel
> But as *ho* seyþ, such I am, when he with me carpeþ.
>
> A. 12. 32–3[26]

But her approach to this condemnation more closely parallels the concerns of Lewte in B. 11. 84–106 about the problematic 'publishing' of corrective discourse. Early in the B continuation, when Will, after vehemently denouncing the avarice of the friars, wonders aloud whether he dares 'amonges men þis metels auowe' (B. 11. 86), Lewte draws him to articulate the limits of the socially licit for the speaker who undertakes to '[legge] þe soþe' by telling tales – even true ones – to expose 'falsnesse [and] faiterie' in the interest of public moral edification (B. 11. 84–106). In A. 12, however, Scripture provides, with apposite scriptural precedents, the considerations that might authorise the just man to remain silent in the face of extreme provocation to reasonable and truthful corrective utterance. The speech goes beyond Study's condemnation of the unworthy hearer and prideful retailer of truth, in that it registers the dynamic according to which the recalcitrance of the sinful world is at once the stimulant, topic, and defeat of the moral reformer's project. As a forcer of intolerable paradoxes, the Scripture of A. 12 is thus conceptual kin to both the Scripture of A. 11, who insists on both the necessity and the insufficiency of works, and the Scripture of B. 11, who follows Lewte's speech by 'skipping on high' to preach on the very theme that had left Will in a 'weer' at the end of A: 'wheiþer I were chosen or noȝt chosen'. If there is anything of Langland's in this concluding passus of the A text, it seems likeliest to be the argument that rationalises the didactic poet's principled retreat into silence.[27]

---

[26] I have here chosen the reading of the Pierpont Morgan MS 'ho' over the Kane–Donaldson text's 'he', which is that of the Rawlinson MS.

[27] This view of Scripture's speech sorts ill with the suspicion that what initiates it (14–15) is intellectually incoherent and inconsistent with Langland's usage. But these opening lines of Scripture's speech are also textually corrupt, to a degree difficult to determine from the paucity of attestation of this passus. One could make both for and against Langland's authorship of lines 1–33 arguments of some precision – in particular, from the evidence of versification, of which until quite recently no detailed study adequate to the state of the texts has been made or even attempted. Hoyt Duggan's analysis of the 'normal' Middle English alliterative line, and of Langland's characteristic (and apparently unique) divergences from it, could be turned to good account upon this passus as well as the 'Z text'. See Duggan, 'The Shape of the B-Verse in Middle English Alliterative Poetry', *Speculum*, 61 (1986), 564–92, esp. 577; 'Alliterative Patterning as a Basis for Emendation in Middle English Alliterative Poetry', *SAC*, 8 (1986), 73–105; and 'The Authenticity of the Z Text of *Piers Plowman*: Further Notes on Metrical Evidence', forthcoming in *MÆ*.

It is in this part of the passus that one can see how 'þis ende' might have begun: in the attempt to join the sacramental implications of Scripture's final strictures in A. 11 to the sudden gulf of despair and anxiety at the prospect of imminent death that her 'scorn' opens before Will in the first moments of the B continuation – and that gapes still wider in Will's, and the world's, sickness unto death in the final passus. As the last half of this passus shows an attempt to assimilate and interpret in terms of personal morality the prospect of death and dissolution which constitute Langland's own severe ending to all his 'werkes', its first half attempts to give a constructive context to Will's final despair and produce the reconciliation that could lead him, through the 'sawes' he made, to win a 'good end'. John But's 'making' thus becomes a way to stabilise and unify the moral truth of the text that he knew circulated in the world in more than one form. It was his effort to make that truth canonical and final that underlay his construction and benediction of the poet's good end.

Was his report of Langland's death then false? or a fiction? Like George Kane, I doubt that But, whose profound respect for the poet is evident in this performance, would have knowingly promulgated a false or erroneous report, or even hazarded a mistaken guess, about this matter, if he had the means of ascertaining its truth, and the impetus to do so from the material in hand. Moreover, as the further records here adduced show, there may even be slightly better reasons, though quite different arguments, than Rickert knew for thinking that the king's messenger might have been in a position to hear of the writer's demise. Nevertheless, within John But's understanding of the kind of wisdom offered by the poem that he knew in at least two versions – each of which failed in his terms to end satisfactorily – the story told here was true, indeed the only one possible. The poet's death, looming unreconciled in all forms of the poem known to him, was probably the only circumstance But could conceive as adequate to explain the state of the texts. Far from an irresponsible inference, it was the sound, natural, and inevitable one from John But's literary premises about the poem and the available material. It was a truth that needed telling outright, an account that needed closing, if one maker were adequately, and without impious presumption, to render tribute to another in kind. Literary truth and historical truth were one and the same, and the poet's end was implicit in 'all times of my time', at every point in his historical life, the end of which alone could have severed him from his work.

John But's pastiche of Langland's work has, however, its own kind of integrity, for it is a serious, if not profound, effort to work through and integrate morally the most intellectually vertiginous moments of the poem. In replacing the austere and imageless speculation of high-scholastic hypothesis with the sensory riot of 'middelerd', the B continuation also lays bare the subjective treacheries that lie at the heart of the initial authorial enterprise, in the depiction of Will's individual course – and his public discourse – of improvement through knowledge, and a didacticism that proceeds by adventurous spectatorship, through the display of readable 'ferlies'. In assimilating Will's story to the exemplification and promotion of pious practices he saw as the pervading intent of Langland's 'works', John But must remain committed to the narrative enterprise of spiritual romance that Langland himself begins to dismantle and reassemble in the two long versions. He dimly understood that what supported the remainder of Langland's literary 'werkes' beyond the text he had in hand – and Will's moral 'werkes', to which he assimilated them – was a self-representation of the 'I' staring face-to-face at the mortality of its own projects, and he chose to build his own ending on that premise. But for him it was simply another exemplary figure, not a sign of a reconceived literary mode or constructive principle. Will-as-maker has earned through his 'werkes' the good end that John But prays for him, much as Trajan's 'treuthe' warrants St Gregory's prayers; but John But is not inquisitive about the questions raised by the terms of either salvation.

Yet what John But does understand of Langland's poem similarly deserves our respect, and like Trajan's 'treuthe' a debt of gratitude for the example of his intent. His reading shows us how a contemporary registered the integrity of purpose in Langland's lifelong project, and what it meant to take the persona of Will 'personally': to assimilate it not chiefly as a term in an allegorical fiction but as a 'profitable' and earnest struggle of a contemporary to understand through 'making' the elements of his own faith as he understood these in Langland's work. And it is hard to resist the appeal of a 'maker' who, in the face of Langland's powerful contrary arguments, persists in believing that a writer can come to a good end.

APPENDIX

Much work remains to be done in unpublished records on the author and his family and possible circle of acquaintance; one published subsequent to Rickert's article, however, may somewhat strengthen her identification, and (along with recent work on the regions of production and dialect distribution of manuscripts of the poem, particularly the C text) weakens Cargill's suggestions that link the John But of this passus with East Anglia.

If the king's messenger is indeed the writer of part of this passus, the following record suggests that he must have been well advanced in years by the time he 'made þis ende':

> Cal. Close Rolls, 1378–81, 343;
> 3 Richard II. Nov. 5, 1379, Westminster:
> John But, one of the king's messengers, is sent to the prior and convent of St Michael's Mount in Cornwall, to have for life such maintenance as Roger Couper deceased had at the late king's command.
> By p.s.

The nature of this position is further clarified by the lengthier record of the grant of it to But's 'deceased' predecessor Roger Couper (Cal. Close Rolls 1369–74, 279; 45 Edw. III, Feb. 22, 1371, Westminster). That document demands to know why the prior and convent have failed to act on an earlier directive 'to admit Roger le Copper the king's yeoman to their house' with all the requested privileges enjoyed by the previous grantee, now outlawed, and the arrears due this predecessor. It orders them at once to 'make fitting provision' for Couper's maintenance, and 'to minister to him as aforesaid', and to make him letters patent under the common seal of the house specifying 'what he shall take', i.e., the terms of support due him.

These details tend to confirm one's initial impression of the grant to John But that it is a retirement position, such as a corrody. (For assistance in interpreting these records, I am indebted to my colleague in history and law, Professor Thomas Barnes.) As an alien priory, St Michael's Mount was in the king's gift. Couper also held a similar grant of maintenance at the nearby convent of Torre: he is described as 'deceased' in a record six years later. (Cal. Close Rolls 1374–7, 528; 51 Edw. III, April 5, 1377, Sheen), which replaces him in this position with one Peter Fraunk, 'one of the king's henchman' (henxtmannorum), much as the deceased But is replaced by a man newly promoted from courier to messenger in the record of 1387 cited by Rickert. The remainder of that record mentions that this grant of wages for the new messenger was cancelled when a life grant of ten pounds a year from

Lincolnshire issues was found for him; possibly the award of lands and tenements in Barton-on-Humber to But in 1378 was a similar substitution.

The pattern of such grants also suggests that they constitute routine forms of patronage placement for a large and miscellaneous cadre of royal functionaries, rather than forms of payment for specific services rendered, or extraordinary honours for exceptional merit. The appellation 'messenger' seems to have designated a status or rank within an increasingly articulated royal officialdom, at least as much as a specific set of duties, and it could cover a multitude of missions, some best left unspecified; see J. R. Alban and C. T. Allmand, 'Spies and Spying in the Fourteenth Century', in *War, Literature and Politics in the Late Middle Ages*, ed. C. T. Allmand (Liverpool, 1976), 73–101. And it does not by any means imply that someone so designated held 'a position at Court where he came into daily contact with the King' (Rickert, p.115).

We may assume from this record that by 1379 the messenger John But is in effect a pensioner, no longer actively employed on the king's business, and living in the west country. If he was the writer who reported the poet's death, his information was likelier derived from sources in this region than in London or East Anglia. It may also cast in a different light another record cited without further comment by Rickert (107; it is no. 5 in her note 2):

> Cal. Patent Rolls, 1381–5, 369;
> 7 Richard II, April 30, 1384:
> Henry Amys, for not appearing to render account to John But, Thomas Mille, Thomas Warde and John Crofte, executors of the will of Alice late the wife of John But, for the time he was her bailiff in Toriton.
> Devon

While nothing indicates that this is the king's messenger, the context, involving a private inheritance rather than a matter devolving from his status as royal servant, would not in any case require or elicit such a notation. If this man is the retired messenger, then this record would tend further to confirm his continued residence in the west country from late 1379 until 1384. And if he is also the writer of 'þis ende' who reports William's death, it would justify a much closer look at Cargill's Record No. 21, cited (50) from the Fine Rolls for 6 Richard II (1383–4), which mentions one 'William Rokle' as a collector in Devon. (Cargill, who only summarises this unpublished text, uses the phrase 'collector of the tax', leaving it unclear to what actual office it refers.)

One other record cited by Rickert associates John But 'messager' with the south-western quadrant of England in this period. A 'vyneter' of London, one Philip Derneford, has returned to him (Cal. Patent Rolls 1377–81, 615; 4 Richard II, March 30, 1381, Westminster) 'all his goods and chattels' formerly 'forfeited on account of his outlawry'; the occasion of the initial forfeit was a 'trespass in the county of Gloucester' prosecuted by John But. It should be noted that although the record is dated March 1381, it refers to a sequence of prior events which is likely to have spanned several months; the initial offence in Gloucester might have occurred in 1379 or even earlier.

Moreover, the act which the 'messager' is said to have prosecuted may as well have been the subject of a private suit as a matter of the king's business; we need not infer from this designation (as Rickert repeatedly does) that in this instance But was involved in his capacity as a royal officer (Rickert, 110). Notice of But's employment here may only mean that he himself had initially invoked it in making a charge to give additional weight or credibility to his case. Several scenarios are of course possible behind this sketchy report, among them a trespass on property in which But had some interest. However it started, But's prosecution was unsuccessful: the accused vintner was found innocent.

If it was John But the messenger who 'made þis ende' and recorded for posterity the death of William Langland, the record missed by Rickert offers one clear indication of where he spent the 1380s, and taken together with those already known, it places him close to the west-south-west Midlands area from which the C text appears to have been disseminated. It slightly strengthens the case for his knowledgeable report of the poet's death, while it also shifts the likely base of it from general literary reputation to local information. John But's pious record thus looks from this perspective similar in kind to the TCD 212 inscription: a preservation of regional knowledge about a writer whose local habitation was as important as his name in purchasing him a literary epitaph.

University of California, Berkeley

Piers Plowman *and the Chancery Tradition*

JOHN H. FISHER

For some years I have been examining the relationship between the English of the fifteenth-century Chancery documents and that of non-bureaucratic prose and verse. In this essay, I should like to turn to the relationship between Chancery practice and the *Piers Plowman* manuscripts.[1]

I shall not here be dealing with the question of Langland's own orthography and morphology. George Kane has in hand a fourth volume of the Athlone edition of *Piers Plowman*, in which he will provide an analytic glossary and a study of the language. In the Introduction to the edition of the B version, he and E. T. Donaldson have already discussed the poet's own verse system[2] and concluded that 'much of his language accords with London English of his time' (215n.). We will learn more about the poet's individual practice when Kane's Volume 4 appears.

My interest is in the way in which the *Piers Plowman* manuscripts increasingly reflect Chancery practice, and the light they may throw on the method of manuscript production. A definitive study would call for a detailed examination of the hands and spellings of all fifty-two manuscripts – a task beyond the reward that might be expected. I have based my study on the superb manuscript descriptions and textual analyses in Kane and Kane–Donaldson and on photocopies of the first five pages of each of the B-version manuscripts, which Professor Kane has kindly made available to me. These materials reveal the growing normalisation of the manuscripts and something of the process by which they may have come into existence.

Evidently, as with the Chaucer manuscripts – and unlike the Gower manuscripts – none of the *Piers Plowman* manuscripts dates from the

---

[1] This essay should be taken in the context of 'Chancery and the Emergence of Standard Written English in the Fifteenth Century', *Speculum*, 52 (1977), 870–99; 'Chancery Standard and Modern Written English', *Journal of the Society of Archivists*, 6 (1979), 136–44; *An Anthology of Chancery English* (Knoxville, 1984); and 'Caxton and Chancery English', *Fifteenth Century Studies*, ed. Robert F. Yeager (Hamden, Conn., 1984).

[2] Kane–Donaldson, 132ff. All citations of the B version are from this edition.

author's lifetime.[3] Only four are dated from the fourteenth century (Table A). Thirty-eight manuscripts date from the first half of the fifteenth century; seven from the second half of the fifteenth century; and three (and the Crowley imprint) from the sixteenth century. The sixteen manuscripts of the B version (counting R^1 and R^2 as one, and omitting the Crowley)[4] give us an adequate spread over the century in which Chancery English was being regularised: four date from the turn of the century (Bm, Bo, C, W); three from the early fifteenth century (Hm, L, R); six from the first half of the century (C^2 Cot, F, M, O, Y); one from the second half of the century (H^3); and two from the sixteenth century (G, S). We will note the increasing appearance of Chancery forms in the manuscripts and consider whether this reflects the effect of Chancery Standard on the accidentals in the text.

The first influence of Chancery is on the script. Laying the photocopies of the opening pages of the B manuscripts side by side, one can observe the changes which support the dating. The seven before *c*. 1410 (Bm, Bo, C, W, Hm, L, R) are all in book hands designated by Kane and Donaldson 'anglicana formata'. Those that date after *c*. 1410 are in more cursive hands designated 'anglicana'. The two manuscripts from the sixteenth century, in even more cursive hands, are designated 'secretary'. These designations follow M. B. Parkes,[5] whose analysis does not seem to me to make sufficient allowance for the hands used in the Signet and Chancery offices, which I have called Chancery hand.[6] Parkes renames as 'anglicana' the traditional business script previously called 'court hand' after the guild of 'scriptores litere curiales' first mentioned in London in 1357.[7] In the second half of the fourteenth century, this court or anglicana hand was modified by certain

---

[3] The discussion of the chronology of The Canterbury Tales manuscripts in J. M. Manly and Edith Rickert, *The Text of the Canterbury Tales*, 8 vols. (Chicago, 1940), 2. 48 *et passim*, has now been superseded by N. F. Blake, *The Textual Tradition of the Canterbury Tales* (London, 1985); and that of the chronology of the *Troilus* manuscripts in R. K. Root, ed., *The Book of Troilus* (Princeton, 1926) by B. A. Windeatt, ed., *Geoffrey Chaucer, Troilus & Criseyde* (London, 1984). That of the chronology of the Gower manuscripts in G. C. Macauley, ed., *The Works of John Gower*, 4 vols. (Oxford, 1899–1902), 2, cxxxviii ff. *et passim*, and in John H. Fisher, *John Gower: Moral Philosopher and Friend of Chaucer* (New York, 1964), 99ff. *et passim*, will no doubt soon be superseded by the Catalogue of the Manuscripts of the Works of John Gower now in preparation by Jeremy Griffiths, Kate Harris, and Derek Pearsall.
[4] For manuscript identifications see Table A.
[5] M. B. Parkes, *English Cursive Book Hands 1250–1500* (1969; London, 1979).
[6] See the plates and discussion in *An Anthology of Chancery English*, 1–5; but see the strictures in the review by Lister Matheson, *Speculum*, 61 (1986), 646–50.
[7] The traditional discussions of court hand are Hilary Jenkinson, *English Court Hand AD 1066–1500*, 2 vols. (Oxford, 1915), and L. C. Hector, *The Handwriting of English Documents* (London, 1958).

TABLE A

Manuscript dates and and abbreviations compiled from the descriptions by Kane and Donaldson. Italic, A version; large caps, B version; small caps, C version. I have converted N. R. Ker's system, used by Kane–Donaldson, for dating manuscripts.

1. *c.* 1350–90 (XIV^2) G (Camb. U. Dd.3.13)

2. *c.* 1390 (XIV.ex) *E* (Bodley Laud misc. 656); K (BL Digby 171); V (Dublin, Trinity Coll. 212)

3. *c.* 1400 (XIV/XV) *T* (Camb., Trinity Coll. R.3.14); *V* (Bodley, Vernon MS); Bm (BL Add. 10574); Bo (Bodley 814); C (Camb. U. Dd.1.17); W (Camb., Trinity Coll. B.15.17); N (John Holloway); M (BL Cotton Vespasian B.XVI); U (BL Add. 35157); X (Huntington HM 143); Z (Bodley 851)

4. *c.* 1400–10 (XV.in) *L* (Lincoln's Inn 150); *M* (Soc. of Antiquaries 687); *N^1* (Natl. Library of Wales 733B); *U* (Oxford, Univ. Coll. 45); *Ch* (Liverpool U., Chaderton F.4.8); Hm (Huntington HM 128); L (Bodley Laud Misc. 581); R^1 (BL Landsdowne 398); R^2 (Rawlinson 38); J (London U. S.L.V. 88); P (Huntington HM 137); P^2 (BL Add. 34779); Q (Camb. U. Add. 4325)

5. *c.* 1410–50 (XV^1) *H^2* (BL Harley 6041); *K* (Bodley, Digby 145); C^2 (Camb. U. Ll.4.14); Cot (BL Cotton Caligula A.XI); F (Oxford, Corpus Christi Coll. 201); M (BL Add. 35287); O (Oxford, Oriel Coll.); Y (Camb., Newnham Coll. Yates-Thompson); A (London U. S.L.V. 17); Ca (Camb., Gonville and Caius Coll. 669/646); D (Bodley, Douce 1041); F (Camb. U. Ff.5.35); S (Camb., Corpus Christi Coll. 293); Y (Bodley, Digby 102); N^2 (BL Harley 2376)

6. *c.* 1450 (XV) *J* (Morgan M818); *R* (Bodley, Rawlinson 137)

7. 1450–90 (XV^2) *A* (Bodley, Ashmole 1468); *D* (Bodley, Douce 323); *E* (Dublin, Trinity Coll. D.4.12); *H* (BL Harley 875); *W* (Duke of Westminster); H^3 (BL Harley 3954)

8. After 1500 (XVI) G (Camb. U. Gg.4.31); Cr (Crowley imprints); S (Sion Coll. Arc. L. 40 2/E); R (BL Royal 18B)

shapes adopted from the *chancellerie royale* in Paris, notably the single compartment a (vs. anglicana double compartment a), single compartment g (vs. anglicana double compartment g), short r (vs. anglicana long r), and modern s (vs. anglicana s with its large, closed lower compartment extending below the line).[8] It has been suggested that these characters were imported by

---

[8] The fourteenth-century developments are discussed by Parkes, xix–xxi; Hector, 52–4; and Pierre Chaplais, *English Royal Documents 1199–1461* (Oxford, 1972), 52.

the scribes of the Privy Seal office of the Black Prince.[9] They are first found in the episcopal chancellaries of York, London, and Canterbury, and in the royal Chancery.[10] All of the signet letters of Henry V, written by some thirteen different scribes, use these forms, which were gradually adopted by other government clerks and then by clerks of the guilds and private households and by independent scriveners until, by the end of the century, they became the normal forms in Tudor secretary.[11]

The principal difference between anglicana and Tudor secretary, however, was the more fluent duct and greater legation of letters in the latter. Until the advent of printing, formal documents were published in the trained, set hands designated respectively as anglicana, court, chancery, and bastard. But as printing assumed the burden of formal publication, handwriting came to be reduced to a medium for private memoranda and communication, and scripts became increasingly free and personal.[12] Intervening between the set anglicana of the fourteenth century and the cursive secretary of the sixteenth was a set hand much like anglicana, although with increasingly freer duct and with the continental letter shapes enumerated above which lent themselves to a more cursive script: single compartment a, single compartment g, short r, and modern s. This intermediary hand is what in the *Anthology of Chancery English* I designate Chancery hand.[13]

It is interesting to observe how the B-version manuscripts illustrate the fifteenth-century developments towards Chancery. In the first place, they illustrate its inconsistency. Changes in language can be perceived over long periods of time, but at any given moment, all we can see is variety. Table B

[9] Chaplais, 52.

[10] Parkes, xx.

[11] On the movement outward from Chancery, Hilary Jenkinson writes ('Elizabethan Handwriting', *Library*, 3 [1922–3], 3–4): 'Fashions in these hands were largely set by the Royal Courts and other departments of public administration, and in developments which occurred in public administration from the 13th century downwards we find a very close connexion with those of writing, methods of authentication of executive documents, the conventional forms of these documents, the departments or functionaries which controlled and issued them, and even the language in which they were written – all these went through a series of changes closely parallel to each other and to those of handwriting.' M. T. Clanchey, *From Memory to Written Record* (London, 1979), 50–7, discusses the way in which the practice of producing authenticated documents spread from the royal Chancery and Exchequer to episcopal sees and civic guilds and corporations. The earliest bishops to inaugurate registers had both been Chancery officials.

[12] The plates in Anthony G. Petti, *English Literary Hands from Chaucer to Dryden* (Cambridge, 1977) nicely illustrates the movement of hands from public to personal (and see my review in *Speculum*, 54 [1979], 183–4).

[13] That this script was recognised is evidenced when John Clopton ends a 1454 letter to John Paston: 'wretyn with my chauncery hand, in ryth gret haste': *The Paston Letters*, ed. James Gairdner, 6 vols. (London, 1904), 2. 315.

illustrates the adoption of the new letter forms by the scribes of the B manu-scripts. The leftmost column of the table presents the B manuscripts, listed according to the Kane–Donaldson sigles and arranged by date of writing. As indicated in the table, the development of the single compartment a form in manuscripts does not show the expected drift. By the time we reach the sixteenth century, both manuscripts have this a, but until that time all but C^2 have anglicana a. Single compartment g is more regular. Until 1410 all manuscripts have anglicana g; after 1410, five of nine manuscripts have single compartment g; after 1450 all three manuscripts have it. The move-ment towards short r is even more regular – nearly always long r until 1410, nearly always short after that. The forms of s are as inconclusive as those of a. The two earliest manuscripts have the anglicana form regularly, but only the relatively early Hm shows the modern s form regularly. In the latest two, the anglicana form has disappeared, but the only short s is final and a very cursive stroke. Through most of the manuscripts the anglicana s is initial and the modern form final; often initially, and nearly always medially, the modern s form is long.

The introduction of the Chancery forms into the scripts raises questions about the method of manuscript production. After Laura Hibbard's influential article on the Auchinleck manuscript, it was customary to associate the production of large literary codices with the emergence of commercial book-shops,[14] where a master scrivener supervised the work of a number of clerks on a regular basis. Recently, however, Ian Doyle and Malcolm Parkes have called into question the existence of such shops on the grounds that they implied too great a capital investment and that no evidence has been found for the existence of such a commercial scriptorium. They adopt instead the suggestion of Graham Pollard, that books and documents were always pro-duced to order. A public scrivener, the 'stationarius', might accept the order for a large project and do some of the copying himself, but he would subcontract sections of the book to independent scribes who would carry them off to their own quarters for simultaneous copying.[15] The existence of manuscripts in multiple hands offers a clue to the nature of such book

---

[14] Laura Hibbard Loomis, 'The Auchinleck Manuscript and a Possible London Bookshop of 1330–40', *PMLA*, 57 (1942), 595–627.

[15] A. I. Doyle and M. B. Parkes, 'The production of copies of the *Canterbury Tales* and the *Confessio Amantis* in the early fifteenth century,' *Medieval Scribes, Manuscripts, and Libraries: Essays Presented to N. R. Ker*, ed. M. B. Parkes and A. G. Watson (London, 1978), 163–210. The preceding article in the same volume, Graham Pollard, 'The *pecia* system in the medieval universities,' 143–61, discusses the production of texts in the universities by simultaneous copying, which might have paved the way for the commercial production of texts as described by Doyle and Parkes. Graham Pollard's article suggesting the 'bespoke' nature of book production is 'The Company of Stationers before 1557', *Library*, 4th Ser. 18 (1937), 1–37.

TABLE B

R regular
r *forms*: or short r after o
s *forms*: i initial (usually long); f final; x only long s initially, very cursive stroke finally

FORMS	anglicana	single compartment	anglicana	single compartment	long	short	anglicana	modern
	a	a	g	g	r	r	s	s
MSS								
c. 1400								
Bm	R		R		R	or¹	R	R
Bo	R		R		R	or	R	
C	R		R		R	or	i	f
W	R		R		R	or	i	f
1400–10								
Hm	R		R			R		R
L	R		R		R	or	i	f
R	R		R		R	or	i	f
1410–50								
C²		R	R		R	or	R	
Cot	R			R		R	i	f
F	R		R			R	R	
M	R		R		[mixed]		i	
O	R			[mixed]	R	or	i	f
Y	R		R		R	or	i	f
1450–90								
H³	R			R		R		f
after 1500								
G		R	R	R		R		x
S		R	R	R		R		x

¹ Also short r after e, Passus 1.1.

production. Doyle and Parkes base their argument on the identification of five different hands in Trinity College, Cambridge, MS R.3.2 of Gower's *Confessio Amantis*, and other manuscripts copied in the same hands. One (Scribe B) copied both the Hengwrt and Ellesmere manuscripts of *The Canterbury Tales*. Another (Scribe D) copied six manuscripts of the *Confessio Amantis*, two of *The Canterbury Tales*, one of Trevisa, and the *Piers Plowman* section of MS J (see Table A). Scribe E (Thomas Hoccleve) copied collections of his own works as well as documents in the Privy Seal. Timothy Shonk has recently produced a convincing description of the way the Auchinleck manuscript itself could have been put together by a principal scribe who did some of the copying and put together and numbered sections copied by five other scribes. His analysis provides a better explanation for the awkward transitions in the manuscript than any other that has been put forward.[16]

As described by Kane and his associates, eight of the *Piers Plowman* manuscripts show multiple hands. Three (H, Bo, Z) have different hands in different quires in a manner that would have permitted simultaneous copying. Three others (J, Yates-Thompson, Digby 102) show enough variation to be perhaps by different hands. Manuscripts C^2 and U show different hands, but the *Piers* portion of each is in a single hand. The other forty-four *Piers* texts are in single hands. Several of these hands must have belonged to scribes working in Westminster and Chancery Lane during the fifteenth century. The Inns of Chancery provided the training for most of these clerks.[17] Chancery hands have been identified in the teams described by both Shonk (Scribe III) and Doyle and Parkes (Scribes C and E – Hoccleve). At least five of the sixteen B manuscripts are in Chancery hands: Hm, Cot, and Yates-Thompson, described by Kane–Donaldson as 'anglicana with secretary forms', C^2 described as 'small anglicana tending to currency', and F which is quite plainly Chancery.

There seems no possibility that Langland himself was one of this scribal cohort. In the most thorough examination of the possibility, E. T. Donaldson points out that Langland himself never mentions such occupation, that all of his autobiographical references support the notion of 'a married clerk, of an order certainly no higher than an acolyte, who made his living in an irregular fashion by saying prayers for the dead and for the living who supported him'.[18] So it would appear that the Chancery characteristics in the manuscripts are all due to later copyists rather than to the author himself.

English orthography and morphology were gradually being regularised in

---

[16] Timothy Shonk, 'A Study of the Auchinleck Manuscript: Bookmen and Bookmaking in the Early Fourteenth Century,' *Speculum*, 60 (1985), 71–91.

[17] Fisher, 'Chancery and the Emergence of Standard English', 891–2.

[18] E. Talbot Donaldson, *Piers Plowman: The C-Text and Its Poet* (New Haven, 1949), 208, 219.

the fifteenth century by the same cohort of Chancery and Chancery-trained scribes. M. L. Samuels has discerned three stages in the emergence of the written standard.[19] The first stage was the Wycliffite/Lollard manuscripts produced towards the end of the fourteenth century in the north midlands. This writing he finds much more standard than the London English of the same period. Not until government began to be carried on in English after 1417 by the secretariat of Henry V was there any significant movement towards the standardisation of London English; but by 1430 the drift towards Chancery Standard both within and outside the government was well under way.[20]

The movement of the orthography of the B-version manuscripts towards Chancery Standard is revealed by Table C. As in Table B, the leftmost column of this table presents the B manuscripts, listed according to the Kane–Donaldson sigles and arranged by date of writing. The other columns present the results of comparing selected orthographic features with the analytical glossary in the *Anthology of Chancery English*. I have chosen twelve items for comparison. Two provide multiple instances in the pages examined (the first five for each manuscript): the first person pronoun 'I', and the unstressed vowel before s in plural and past tense inflections. The remaining ten items are individual words; if, in any given MS, the target word does not occur (due to textual variation or loss), I have substituted another word with the same phonetic characteristics, indicating the line from which it comes. Arabic numbers following words in the table are line references to Kane–Donaldson, and are to the Prologue unless otherwise indicated.

The first person pronoun was quickly restricted to I in Chancery Standard; y appears only five times in early documents as against I 154 times. Y is regular in the opening lines of the pre-1410 *Piers* manuscripts, and one later, although even in these it is interesting to see I in line 2. However, as columns 1–2 in Table C indicate, the drift was clearly towards I.

Spelling of the unstressed vowel in plural and past tense inflections developed steadily towards e in Chancery Standard,[21] and so it is in the B manuscripts. As indicated in columns 3–4 in Table C, only the early Bm has i/y regularly. The later F and H[3] frequently use i/y with s (hillis, wawys) and e with d (leuede, lokede). But in general the e spellings conform to Chancery.

The preservation of the gh spelling for the gutteral as it died out in pronunciation is one of the most distinctive features of Chancery usage. The

---

[19] M. L. Samuels, 'Some Applications of Middle English Dialectology,' *ES*, 44 (1963), 81–94, introduced the term 'Chancery Standard' to designate fifteenth-century government English. On the influence of Henry V, see Malcolm Richardson, 'Henry V, the English Chancery, and Chancery English,' *Speculum*, 55 (1980), 726–50, and *Anthology of Chancery English*, Introduction.

[20] *Anthology of Chancery English*, 5ff.

[21] See the lists in *Anthology of Chancery English*, 31–3.

TABLE C

FORMS MSS	1	2	3	4	+ Chancery forms		R regular		U usual			TOTAL OF CHANCERY FORMS
	I	Y	i/y	e	þoȝte 6 (5)	heiȝ 13 (6)	seiȝ 14 (7)	plouȝ 20 (8)	noȝt 9 (9)	chosen 31 (10)	swiche 32 (11)	
c. 1400												
Bm	2	R			fouȝten 42	eȝen 74	say	+plough	+not	chesen	+suche	3
Bo	2	R	[even]		fouȝten 42	eiȝen 74	say	+plough	+not	chesen	+suche	3
C	+R			+R	+thoughte	+heighe	seigh	+plowth	+nouȝt	chesen	swillkee	5
W	+R			+R	þoȝte	heiȝ	seiȝ	plouȝ	noȝt	+chosen	swiche	3
1400–10												
Hm	+R	R			thougthe	+hye	+saw	+plough	nouȝt	chesen	+suche	6
L	+R		[even]	+R	thouȝte	hieȝ	seigh	+plow	+nought	+chosen	+suche	6
R★	+R			+R	wrouȝte 1.13	miȝt 156	seiȝ 218	þouȝ 205	nouȝt 152	X	swiche 5.152	2
1410–50												
C²	+R		[even]		thouȝt	+hie	+sauȝt	+plow	+not	schoysn	swyche	5
Cot	+R				thorgh 108[1]	myȝte 38	sey	+plough	+nat	chesen	+such	5
F	2,6	R	i/ys		thowhte	heyȝ	seyȝ	plowh	nowht	+chosen	swiche	1
M	+R		ed	+R	thouȝte	heiȝgh	say	+plow	nowȝt	+chosen	+suche	5
O	+R		[even]	+R	þouȝte	hyȝ	+sawȝ	+plow	+not	+chosen	swiche	5
Y	+R			+R	+thoughte	+heigh	seigh	+plowe	+nought	+chosen	swich	7
1450–90												
H³	+R		i/ys	e/yd	thouthe	hey	+saw	+plow	nout	+chose	sweche	4
after 1500												
G	+R			+R	thougt	+heygh	seyghe	+plogh	+noght	+chose	+such	7
S★	+R		[even]		+caught 107	+highe 128	se 218	+plow 119	+not 152	X	X	5

★ R and S are defective at the beginning; R starts with Prologue 125, S with Prologue 73.
[1] þorgh = through.

gh/h spelling is found in the Midlands and London from early Middle English, but forms with ȝ are favoured in most provincial dialects (see Samuels, Figure 2). We can see the drift towards gh in the B manuscripts in 'thought' (Table C, column 5) and 'high' (column 6). For 'thought' gh appears in the Chancery glossary eight times, 'thowte' once, and ȝ not at all. In the B manuscripts, ȝ appears in five of the seven manuscripts before 1450 and four of the nine manuscripts after 1450. Chancery gh appears in one manuscript before 1450 and three after 1450.

For 'high' the drift is more pronounced. In the Chancery glossary, gh appears forty-seven times, the hie/hye form eighteen times, and ȝ not at all. In the B manuscripts, gh appears once before 1450 and five times after 1450; ȝ appears six times before 1450 and four times afterwards; and i/y appears once before 1540 and twice afterwards.

'Plough/plow' offers another sort of problem. It lost the gutteral in the south of England early enough to develop the w spelling (the earliest *MED* example is 1150/1250), but the gutteral was preserved in the Midlands and the North much later (it is still preserved in Scots). Hence the word has come into Modern Standard English with variant spellings. It appears in the Chancery glossary three times as 'plogh', once as 'plough', and not at all with w or ȝ. The drift in the B manuscripts is towards w: before 1450 ȝ appears four times, gh three, and w twice. After 1450 w appears seven times, gh twice, and ȝ not at all. It would appear that modern usage was taking shape: pronunciation Southern with w; spelling variant, w and gh.

'Not' has two forms in Modern Standard English: the negative particle spelled 'not', and the substantive spelled 'naught'. These distinctions had begun to appear in Chancery usage. The Chancery glossary has only gh forms for the substantive, and non-gh forms for most negative particles (189 times nat/not; thirty-two with gh/h, fifteen with ȝ). The form in Table C, column 9, is the particle ('Coueiten noȝt in contree to [cairen] aboute', l. 29). It appears twice without gh before 1450 and five times after 1450, six times with ȝ before 1450, and once afterwards; and once with gh before 1450 and three times afterwards.

The preterite of 'see' (Table C, column 7) appears three times as 'sawe' in the Chancery glossary, once as 'sye', and never with gh/h/ȝ. The B-version manuscripts show no clear drift. 'Saw' appears only once before 1450 and once afterwards. Vocalised forms with something approaching the vowel of the present appear twice before 1450 and three times afterwards. But forms with gh and ȝ appear in both periods, five of eight before 1450, five of nine after 1450.

The infinitive and present subjunctive of 'choose' in the Chancery glossary is always 'chese', but the past participle is always 'chose/chosen'. The drift in the B manuscripts (Table C, column 10) is normal: o forms twice in the pre-1450 manuscripts and e forms four times; o forms six times in the post-1450 manuscripts and the e forms once.

The 'such' forms show devolution. The u was the preferred Chancery form (185 times to 17 with wi/wy), but u appears four out of eight in the pre-1450 B manuscripts, and only three out of eight in the post-1450 (Table C, column 11).

This sort of comparison could go on ad infinitum, but enough has been presented to indicate the drift of both the hand and the spelling of the B version manuscripts of *Piers Plowman* in the direction of Chancery usage. In Table C Chancery forms have been marked with a plus (+), and the numbers in the final column indicate the number of Chancery forms among those noted in each manuscript. Although there is variation, the totals in the post-1450 manuscripts are generally greater than in the pre-1450 manuscripts.

Table C indicates also that in choosing W as their base manuscript for the edition of the B version, Kane and Donaldson chose the most archaic of the three that might have served (see Kane–Donaldson, 214–15). In Table C it shows only three Chancery forms, compared with six for L and seven for Y. In L ʒ alternates with gh, while in Y ʒ has disappeared completely. Use of the ʒ gives the Kane–Donaldson text a more archaic flavour than that of modern editions of Chaucer and Gower. Samuels cites MS W and the Ellesmere manuscript of *The Canterbury Tales* as especially representative of London English at the beginning of the fifteenth century.[22] But it is noteworthy that both the Hengwrt and Ellesmere use gh/h, as does the Fairfax (Macaulay's copy text for the *Confessio Amantis*). Thus, the choice of *Piers Plowman* W over L (see Kane–Donaldson, 214), which nearly always uses gh, sets the edition less in the mainstream of linguistic development. The prevalence of ʒ forms in the early manuscripts of the B version may indeed suggest that this was Langland's own usage. But W creates an impression of Langland's language different from what Ellesmere and Hengwrt create for Chaucer's language. Samuels suggests that the 'thorw' form of the *Equatorie* may be Chaucer's own spelling,[23] but we read him with the 'thurgh' of the Ellesmere and Hengwrt.

The literary manuscripts of the fifteenth century all show more or less Chancery colouring in both hand and language. It is the responsibility of the editor to sort through the variations and arrive as nearly as possible at the author's ideolect and ideograph. But inconsistency in this process conveys to the modern reader greater differences than may actually have existed in the authorial forms. And to the historian of the language, there is an intrinsic interest in observing the process by which the ideolect is absorbed into the

---

[22] Samuels, 'Some Applications', 411.
[23] Samuels, 'Chaucer's Spelling', *Middle English Studies Presented to Norman Davis*, ed. D. Gray and E. G. Stanley (Oxford, 1983), 17–37.

language. The B-version manuscripts of *Piers Plowman* provide a tangible example of this evolution in process, just as the editorial methods of Kane and Donaldson provide a methodology for recovering the ideolect.

University of Tennessee

Some Creative Misreadings in Le Bone Florence of Rome: An Experiment in Textual Criticism

NICOLAS JACOBS

One of the most distinctive of the types of scribal variant defined by George Kane in the influential Introduction to his edition of the A text of *Piers Plowman* is that for which he proposes the designation *homoeograph*. Such variants are characterised as 'readings which preserve something of the shape of the supplanted, original words and phrases, but little or nothing of their meaning or relation to the context'.[1] Kane goes on to explain these as a scribe's response to a reading in his exemplar of which he could make nothing, and lists a number of ways in which scribes might respond in practice to such a situation: 'They might consciously write in its place a word of similar shape; they might mistakenly identify it with a word of similar shape but distinct, sometimes quite inappropriate meaning with which they were acquainted and write that; they might set down in distraction a meaning-less group of letters of shape similar to the supplanted word.' Homoeographs are thus conceived as essentially the product of a conscious response; but the second of the three responses postulated by Kane already allows for an element of misreading in their production, and he concedes at the outset that 'a few may be visual errors'.

I have referred elsewhere[2] to the difficulty of applying a hard-and-fast categorisation to scribal variants: not only does it frequently happen that a reading may be explained in terms of more than one observable tendency of scribal interference, but there is a considerable likelihood that two or more mental processes may have influenced the scribe at the same time. In view of the similarity of result between Kane's homoeographic alterations and the type of error which he describes earlier[3] in terms of a scribe's forming a wrong visual impression of his copy, it is questionable whether they may usefully be distinguished. The difficulty of differentiating between these visual errors

---

[1] Kane, 132–3.
[2] 'The Processes of Scribal Substitution and Redaction: a Study of the Cambridge Fragment of *Sir Degarre*', *MÆ*, 53 (1984), 26–48; see especially 29.
[3] Kane, 118–19.

and 'deliberate substitution of a seemingly apt word of similar shape' is conceded in the discussion; and the latter in turn would appear to differ from homoeographs only in their greater plausibility, which is arguably a matter of degree rather than of mutually exclusive categories. I would conclude that it is unsafe to attempt too rigid a distinction between these types of variant, and would suggest rather that the ambiguities of interpretation characteristic of homoeographs in the wider sense thus implied are the result of their occupying an area of uncertain demarcation between mechanical error and deliberate alteration. Some might indeed be characterised as creative misreadings, in which either a particular idea on which a scribe's mind is running[4] or simply an otherwise frustrated creative impulse lead him to see in his copy or to make of it something which is not there. The degree to which he is conscious of what he is doing will affect their place in Kane's classification, but they are perhaps better seen as a continuum than as two distinct types; the distinction is particularly difficult to draw when the homoeograph extends over two or more words.

The demonstrable occurrence of homoeographs where the evidence of more than one manuscript is available suggests that they may also be postulated to explain corruption in texts which survive only in a single manuscript. Where more than one manuscript survives, the general tendency of scribal alteration to simplify expression[5] justifies the common principle of preferring the *lectio difficilior*. Yet there are limits to the principle, for some readings are so eccentric in syntax or expression as to make no sense, or, if any sense can be wrung from them, to show no sign of being intended for any deliberate effect which might justify their strangeness. It is in the nature of homoeography to generate such aberrations, and where independent witnesses are available the variants can often be confidently attributed to it. Thus similar eccentricities in a unique manuscript ought to be examined for possible homoeographic copying of a straightforward text. In the case of comparatively simple variants some homoeographic error is probably to be expected in any text of reasonable length. The more elaborate and ingenious instances, as exemplified by the line from *Sir Degarre* cited earlier, are likely to be of rarer occurrence, while their detection is likely to depend on sheer luck combined with a talent for solving crossword puzzles and can seldom, if ever, be a matter of certainty.

[4] For example *Degarre* 352 *and venym eke* in the Cambridge MS for *and vnimete* in a description of a dragon; compare *Florence* 2117, below.

[5] Kane, 133–6. A generalised conclusion of this kind is, in part, based on a circular argument, in that the direction of variation was initially inferred on the assumption that the variant with majority support was probably original (p. 127), and this assumption is invalid where a majority of witnesses descend from a single hyparchetype and reproduce its altered readings. Kane is presumably influenced here by the multiplicity of conflicting variant groupings in the *Piers* manuscripts and the probability of their cancelling one another out; his conclusion in any case corresponds in practice to the impression gained by most scholars who have attempted to edit a text.

But one or two persuasive instances in a text will, to the extent that they are accepted, tend to corroborate some of the more marginal cases, since their effect is to suggest that the text has passed through the hands of a scribe with a propensity towards this type of alteration.

The text of *Le Bone Florence of Rome* recommends itself for an investigation of this kind for two reasons. Its unique surviving manuscript offers a number of readings in which the text is remarkably difficult either to construe or to interpret[6] and demands some kind of editorial attention, and it occurs in Cambridge University Library MS Ff 2. 38 close to the version of *Sir Degarre* in which two certain and a number of probable instances betray the activity of a scribe with a talent for creative misreadings.[7] The danger of a circular argument here must be borne in mind, for if the occurrence of these variants in *Degarre* is used to corroborate supposed instances in *Florence*, the latter, though it may be possible to restore some corrupt passages in it, cannot be used as evidence for the common transmission of the two texts. It is permissible, however, as a working hypothesis, to consider independently the possibility of variants of the appropriate type in *Florence*, and then if, and only if, the evidence proves sufficient to stand on its own it may be possible to work towards conclusions regarding the compilation of the manuscript as a whole.

Florence 2060 *And to the wode Y went for wrathe* is a clear example of the simpler type of homoeograph: *wrathe* gives an inappropriate sense and *wathe* 'danger' (ON *váði*) is as certain an emendation as any emendation can be. But the homoeographic element is not beyond doubt, for *wrathe* would be an obvious word for a scribe to substitute deliberately not only if he did not understand *wathe* but also if he took it for a predecessor's error.[8]

Some other emendations based on the supposition of a similar process should probably be made. 312 *Avysyd myght he be* (sc. to make the circuit of the walls of Rome in a summer's day) can mean only 'he could take advice (whether to do so)' and this gives an exceptionally feeble sense. Reading some form of *bisied* or, better, *abisied* 'occupied' we may translate 'he would be fully occupied', 'he would have his work cut out', and this restores the sense, beside giving point to the reference to the *summer's* day, the duration of which provides a measure for the circumference of the city. Though *b* and *v* are not

---

[6] Despite the silence of the most recent editor: see Carol F. Heffernan, ed., *Le Bone Florence of Rome* (Manchester, 1976).

[7] Jacobs, 'Cambridge Fragment', 39, and Textual Commentary *ad loc.*

[8] Users of Dr Heffernan's edition will have noted two other apparent cases of homoeography: *fame* written for *sawe* at 252, and *gode* for ʒode or *yode* at 393. But Heffernan's readings are ghost-words: the MS clearly has *sawe*, as sense and rhyme demand, and while the initial ʒ of ʒode is not perfectly clear it certainly bears no resemblance to *g*, whereas in form it is an acceptable variant of the scribe's normal ʒ. Both previous editors read the MS correctly, though Ritson, in accordance with his usual practice, prints *y* for ʒ; Heffernan's readings, together with her attempts to justify them, are the merest perversity.

at all alike in this manuscript, they are easily confused in some hands,[9] and in any case close similarity of all letter-forms is not necessary for homoeographs as defined by Kane, though the wider definition I have proposed allows for it. 537 *Syr Emere hym behelde* again gives only the feeblest sense: *behelde* cannot sustain the sense 'looked at with contempt'. *Betelde* 'spoke against' is a likely correction; for the form compare *selde* in rhyme at 562. The rarity of *betelle* associates this alteration with that at 2060. 654 *Among þem can they store* (*:feyre, heyre, pere* 'pear') is plainly wrong; neither 'steer' nor 'stir' will give a suitable rhyme or good sense, and we should read *steyre* (ON **steyra* 'thrust, pierce?', cf. *staurr* 'stake' and Norw. *støyra* 'prick'; see *OED* s.v. *stair* v.[2]), though the absolute use is not elsewhere recorded and the change of subject from 653 to 654 suggests further corruption. MS *store* is probably a scribal slip for *stere*, which would be an understandable, if semantically inept, substitution for a very rare word. 659 *And arayed his batels in þat bere* is impugned by the rhyme on *ire*, with which *bere* 'uproar', 'clamour' cannot possibly rhyme. *Bire* 'onslaught' (ON *byrr*) is an obvious correction. 852 *Loke now that taste* is doubtful. *Taste* 'attempt' is only once recorded in *OED* and gives but indifferent sense. Original *caste* 'purpose' is possible; see *MED* s.v., 3d, for many examples. *c* and *t* could be fairly easily confused in the type of hand represented by the manuscript, though there is no doubt of this reading. It is, however, better regarded as a simple misreading rather than as a homoeograph.

The instances considered so far have been simple and do not point to any particular ingenuity on the part of the scribe or scribes responsible. A possible instance of a more elaborate homoeograph occurs at 1474 *Chorle, God yf þe schames dedd*. *Yf* must conceal the present subjunctive of 'give', and it is so glossed by Heffernan, though the comma after *God* in her text obscures the sense. What is not certain is that 'give' has been understood at all stages of the transmission: it is possible that a scribe has at some stage formed a mistaken impression of the whole line, perhaps taking *schames* as the 3 sing. pres. ind. of an impersonal verb, and that a homoeographic alteration such as *yff* for *gyffe* is associated with the misconstruction. Subjunctive forms of this verb without termination do, however, exist in ME (though most of these are before a vowel; see *OED* s.v. *give* v.A.4): the instance is on the whole doubtful and of no evidential value. The evidence of 1450–1 is likewise unreliable; the reading is plainly wrong, but cannot be unequivocally attributed to homoeography. *Tyll eyder odur mekyll care | The lady hungurd wondur sare* makes no sense with the lines taken together, since the ravisher Mylys is hardly likely to be concerned with the comfort of Florence, and, even if he were, *eyder odur* implies a reciprocal rather than a shared feeling and *eyder tyll*

---

[9] For an instance involving the same word, see my note 'Two Corrections to the Auchinleck *Sir Degarre*', *N&Q*, 214 (1969), 205–6. Professor A. J. Bliss observes that the *Florence* scribe may have taken *avysyd* as 'well advised'; but this again gives no acceptable sense and cannot be what the poet intended.

odur would in any case be expected. 1450 thus needs a main verb and at least a semicolon at the end of the line. Can *mekyll* conceal a verb in *-yth*? Historic presents are not characteristic of this text, but there is other evidence that a scribe may have smoothed some of them out. At 1894 we read *Of Seynt Hyllary the churche ys*, where the context makes it clear that *churche* is for original *feste*: the scribe could not have altered *ys* to *was* here without disrupting the rhymes, and so alters to something which makes sense *ad hoc* with a present verb at the cost of making none in the context as a whole. If this parallel be considered valid, *mekyll* may be a homoeograph for *ekyth* or *wakyth* (not *makyth*, which would, inappropriately, suggest complaint).

There remain three cases where there is a more substantial possibility of larger-scale homoeography. In 844–5 *Syr Garcy went crowlande for fayne/ As rampande eyen do in the rayne* the second line is sufficiently bizarre for corruption to be suspected. Heffernan translates *rampande* as 'rearing' and *eyen* as 'young hawks'. The comparison is not inconceivable: any bird that had its feathers soaked might be expected to shiver. But Heffernan's attribution to the comparison of a proverbial quality is unsupported by any existing proverb. *Eyen* 'young hawks' is not elsewhere attested, the etymological connection with *eyas* being unexplained, and the sense is only tentatively suggested by *MED* (s.v. *eie* n. 3b), whereas *OED* (s.v. *eye* sb.[3]) comments, more judiciously, 'of doubtful meaning: perh. some error'. *Rampande* appears to be used elsewhere only of four-footed beasts, implying as it does a specific movement of the forefeet. Even were the sense of *eyen* acceptable and *rampande* an appropriate epithet, the detail would be curiously distracting in the context of the comparison. It is conceivable that *rampande eyen* may be a homoeographic alteration of *papangeyen* or some such form, the initial *p* being taken as long *r*. This would give a more appropriate comparison for two reasons. In the first place parrots were traditionally supposed to have a particular aversion to rain. Thus we read in Alexander Neckam, *de naturis rerum*, I. xxxvi: *Ferunt etiam multum psittacorum cohortem in montibus Gelboe nidificationi indulgere, eo quod super ipsos nec ros nec pluvia descendit. . . . Cito enim quod psittacus in fata cedit, cute ipsius multum aquis madefacta.* The same passage is cited by Vincent of Beauvais, *Speculum maius*, XVI, cxxxv, who adds the comment *Psitacus aquas alias quocunque modo patitur, sed pluvia moritur.* Secondly, parrots appear in English as emblems of lechery: compare Chaucer, *Shipman's Tale* B 1559 *Hoom he gooth murye as a papyniay* and, more apposite still since the reference is to the senile lust of Januarie, *Merchant's Tale* E 2322 *Syngeth ful murier than the papeiay.* Syr Garcy is portrayed in 94–117 in terms of extreme decrepitude and degenerate sexuality; the emendation would restore an appropriate and memorable image for a seemingly pointless one. 1464 *Ye schall haue dere damysell Y say* is far too long for the tail-line. I suggest that *dar y say* has been misread as *damysell* and *y say* added as a correction instead of beginning again. *Dere* has all the appearance of a subsequent heightening. The reading is rather more than a mere homoeograph, but the presumed initial stage fits the definition. 2117 *He seyde Y fynde yow iiii in fere* gives a trivial sense (influenced perhaps by 2014ff.) and we should perhaps read *þe fende yow fonge in fere*; *fecche* would be more idiomatic, but *fonge* gives a more likely homoeograph.

None of these three homoeographic alterations, unlike some of the one-word instances discussed earlier, can be confidently assumed to have occurred, but each explains and corrects an otherwise unsatisfactory text, and their similarity to those known to have occurred in *Sir Degarre* affords some reason for associating *Florence* with *Degarre*. But if the same scribe is indeed responsible for homoeographs in both, the apparent absence of such variants from *Roberd of Cisyle*, the intervening text in the manuscript, suggests that the scribe of Ff 2. 38 was not responsible.[10] It would then follow that *Florence* and *Degarre* were copied together at an earlier stage of the tradition. It may be hoped that examination of the other texts in Ff 2. 38 will further clarify the processes by which that manuscript was compiled.

Jesus College, Oxford

---

[10] Other explanations are possible: *Roberd of Cisyle* is a short text and the absence of ingenious homoeographs may be a matter of chance, or its exemplar may have been more easily legible than that of *Florence* and *Degarre*. The second hypothesis depends on associating homoeography with the physical appearance of the exemplar rather than the psychology of scribes; if accepted it would point back to the transmission of *Florence* and *Degarre* possibly together and certainly separately from *Roberd*.

Trevisa's Original Prefaces on Translation: a Critical Edition

RONALD WALDRON

The two original English prefaces on translation into English which Trevisa prefixed to his translation of Higden's *Polychronicon*, the *Dialogus Inter Dominum et Clericum* and the dedicatory *Epistola* to his patron Lord Thomas of Berkeley, have long been recognised as important documents in the history of the English language and English literature, and (because of their subject matter) as important social and religious documents as well. The first of these pieces was sometimes confused by cataloguers with the dialogue on relations between Church and state which was translated from Latin by Trevisa independently of the *Polychronicon* – the similarly titled *Dialogus Inter Militem et Clericum*,[1] which is sometimes also copied in manuscripts of the *Poly-chronicon*. Though it is not possible to date Trevisa's translation of this Latin dialogue in relation to his translation of the *Polychronicon* (which he finished in 1387), it seems likely it was done earlier and that its form suggested to him the form of his own dialogue.

In view of their importance and perennial interest to scholars, it is surprising that no edition of the *Dialogus* and *Epistola* from the manuscripts has been published in modern times.[2]

The two pieces were printed (as preliminaries to editions of the *Poly-chronicon*) by Caxton in 1482, by Wynkyn de Worde in 1495, and by Peter Treveris in 1527; the latter two editions are very dependent on Caxton and it seems unlikely that either printer had independent recourse to a manuscript.

The early seventeeth-century antiquary John Smyth, who wrote *The Lives of the Berkeleys* in 1620 or thereabouts (it was first printed in an edition by Sir

---

[1] *Trevisa's Dialogus Inter Militem et Clericum*, ed. A. J. Perry, EETS, 167 (London, 1924).

[2] An edition of the two texts, made from the Huntington MS with collation of Cotton and Harley, comprises part of the (unpublished) 1974 University of Washington Ph.D. dissertation 'The English *Polychronicon*: a text of John Trevisa's Translation of Higden's *Polychronicon*, based on Huntington MS 28561' by Richard Arthur Seeger (*DAI*, 36 (1975), 3663A). I am grateful to Dr Seeger for making a copy of his dissertation available to me and for his interest in the present project.

John Maclean in 1883–5), says a little about Trevisa's connection with the family and reproduces a version of the *Epistola*. Though Smyth assures us that it is set down in 'Trevisa's own words', it is in fact (at least in the version printed by Maclean) from Caxton or one of his successors in slightly modernised form.[3]

Part of the *Dialogus* was printed by the Rev. James Townley in 1821 in a work called *Illustrations of Biblical Literature*. Townley cites as his source 'Polychronicon, lib.i.Dyalogue Fo ii', and makes mention of MS Harley 1900. Townley's description of the contents of this manuscript suggests that he had indeed seen it, but the transcription of part of the dialogue is again almost certainly from Caxton or one of his successors. The spelling is not by any means a faithful reproduction of Caxton's, however, but seems to have been made slightly more antique by impressionistic 'old' spelling.[4]

The Rolls Series edition of the *Polychronicon* was begun by Churchill Babington in 1865 on the basis of only two Trevisa manuscripts and Caxton's printed version.[5] Babington chose two de luxe manuscripts, St John's College Cambridge H1 – his base manuscript – and British Library Additional 24194, but quickly came to realise that these had been unfortunate choices as far as the text was concerned. By Vol. II, published in 1869, use is being made in the footnotes of readings from both Harley and Cotton. In the printed Cotton catalogue of 1800, the latter manuscript is referred to as wanting, but by the 1860s it has been found and restored to use by Madden; Babington came to know of it through Morris's *Specimens of Early English*,[6] which contains some extracts from it. Babington also noticed that Cotton contains

---

[3] *The Berkeley Manuscripts by John Smyth*, ed. J. Maclean, 3 vols, Bristol and Gloucestershire Archaeological Society (Gloucester, 1883–5), 1. 343. In spite of Perry's statement (cxxvii) that the Dialogue is also printed at 1. 141 of this edition of Smyth's *Lives*, I have not been able to find it at this reference or elsewhere in the work.

[4] Rev. James Townley, *Illustrations of Biblical Literature*, 3 vols. (London, 1821), 2. 50. Dependence on Caxton rather than Harley is clearly evidenced by, e.g.:
Harley (fo. 42ᵛ): for þei beþ neuer þe wiser for þe latyn but it be tolde
Caxton (fo. 2ʳ): for they be neuer the wyser/ For the latyn but it be told
Townley: for they be neuer the wiser. For the latyn but it be tolde
　　(l. 113f. of the present edition)
Harley (fo. 43ʳ): translate seynt gregories bokes dialoges: out of latyn into saxon
Caxton (fo. 2ʳ): to translate seynt gregoryes bookes. the dialogues out of latyn in to Saxons
Townley: to translate saynt Gregoryes bokes the Dyalogues out of latyn into Saxons
　　(l. 139f. of the present edition)

[5] *Polychronicon Ranulphi Higden Monachi Cestrensis; together with the English translation of John Trevisa and of an unknown writer of the fifteenth century*, ed. Churchill Babington (Vols. I and II) and Joseph R. Lumby (Vols. III–IX), 9 vols. (London: Rolls Series 41, 1865–86).

[6] Richard Morris, ed., *Specimens of Early English, Selected from the Chief English Authors, AD 1250–AD 1400* (Oxford, 1867), pp. 333–44.

the *Dialogus* and *Epistola*. He had cited some extracts from the Caxton version in footnotes to the Introduction to Vol. I,[7] but the two pieces happened not to be present in either of the two manuscript witnesses chosen for the Rolls Series edition at the outset and the opportunity of incorporating them in full was lost by the time other manuscripts were collated.

Thus it came about that the only complete modern printed text of these two pieces has been that in A. W. Pollard's *Fifteenth Century Prose and Verse*,[8] where, though composed in the fourteenth century, they find a place by virtue of the fact that Pollard prints them from Caxton. He follows Caxton's text closely, only modernising spelling and punctuation and apparently emending once or twice. Modern critics have been obliged to quote Trevisa from this version or from Caxton; a new critical edition from the known manuscripts is therefore an obvious desideratum.

Of the fourteen manuscripts of the English *Polychronicon* known to be extant,[9] six contain copies in whole or in part of the two pieces here edited:[10]

	Dialogus	*Epistola*
London, British Library		
MS Cotton Tiberius D VII (C)	present	present
MS Stowe 65 (S)	present	present
MS Harley 1900 (H)	present	present
Glasgow, University Library		
MS Hunter 367 (G)	present	
San Marino, Huntington Library		
MS HM 28561 (B)	present	present
Princeton, University Library		
Taylor MS (T)		present
Also cited:		
Caxton's 1482 print (K)	present	present

[7] Babington, lx.

[8] A. W. Pollard, *Fifteenth Century Prose and Verse* (London, 1903), 203–10. The anthology is a revision of an earlier collection edited by Edward Arber under the title *An English Garner*, 8 vols. (1877–96).

[9] A full list is given by Anthony S. G. Edwards in 'The Influence and Audience of the *Polychronicon*: Some Observations', *PLPLS-LHS*, 17 (1980), 113–19. See also his chapter 'John Trevisa' in *Middle English Prose: A Critical Guide to Major Authors and Genres*, ed. A. S. G. Edwards (New Brunswick, N.J., 1984), 133–46.

[10] I am grateful to the authorities of the libraries named, and also to Mr Robert H. Taylor, for their generous help and specifically for their permission to use and quote from the manuscripts in their possession. My sincere thanks are due also to the following for replies to my inquiries about the manuscripts and other matters: Dr Jean F. Preston and Mrs Nancy Coffin, Princeton University Library, Miss A. C. Snape, Chetham's Library, Manchester, Mr N. Canwick, Liverpool City Libraries, Dr R. Page, Corpus Christi College, Cambridge, Dr Mary L. Robertson, Huntington Library, Dr Tony Edwards, Dr D. C. Fowler, Dr Henry Hargreaves, Mr Richard A. Linenthal, Dr Jeremy Smith, Dr G. A. Lester, Mr Jeremy Griffiths, and Dr M. C. Seymour.

A feature which may turn out to be of some interest for manuscript relations is that there is a short and a long version of each piece: S and G end their copies of the *Dialogus* in exactly the same place, before the brief doctrinal coda which is found in C, H, and B. Similarly, S and T omit a (briefer) doctrinal coda which is found in the other copies (again C, H, and B) of the *Epistola*. S has the two texts at the end of the main work, along with other short pieces which usually precede it in *Polychronicon* manuscripts.

The choice of Cotton as copytext is dictated by the fact that its language has a more Western character even than Stowe and is probably closest of the set to the dialect of the area of origin of the text, which is Gloucestershire.[11] It is also a better text. Babington says of it, somewhat wistfully, 'It differs much from the standard Manuscript [St John's College Cambridge H.1] and from [BL Additional 24194] in the form of the pronouns, and preserves in some cases the true text, where they have corrupted it.'[12] (It was cited sporadically in the notes to that edition from Bk II, Ch. ii [Babington and Lumby, 2. 211] as both editors came to recognise its value.) Cawley also notes in his study of the manuscripts of the *Polychronicon*: 'Cotton has unique archaic words which are replaced in all the other MSS by later and more familiar words. The examples . . . seem to show that Cotton preserves the oldest tradition of all the MSS.'[13]

This view of Cotton is borne out by the edition of the preliminary pieces here presented. The first folio is somewhat damaged, it should be said, but defective words can be confidently supplied from the other manuscripts. An additional difficulty has been that the first three folios have been subjected to the attentions of a corrector who has replaced some of the original forms, especially of pronouns and verbs: e.g., *þei* for *hy* or *a* (lines 10, 44), *hauythe* for *habbeþ* (line 8), etc. He has not been very systematic or persistent, however, and it is not difficult as a rule to recover the scribe's regular forms from later, uncorrected parts of the manuscript, even if the original reading is not still legible under the correction, as it sometimes is.

This is not the place for a full analysis of the derivation and context of Trevisa's views on translation;[14] attention may here be drawn, however, to three places where the present edition from the manuscripts gives a significantly better reading than the Caxton version we have been accustomed to

[11] The Middle English Dialect Survey provisionally locates the Cotton MS to the immediate neighbourhood of Berkeley, Gloucestershire, and finds its language very similar to that of MS Chetham 11379. I am indebted to Professor M. L. Samuels and Dr Jeremy Smith for providing this information in advance of publication of *A Linguistic Atlas of Late Medieval English*, ed. A. McIntosh, M. L. Samuels and M. Benskin (Aberdeen, 1986).

[12] 2. xxxviii; cf. Lumby's Introduction in 3. xxv.

[13] A. C. Cawley, 'The Relationships of the Trevisa Manuscripts and Caxton's *Polycronicon*', *London Medieval Studies*, 1 (1939/1948), 463–82.

[14] For a judicious discussion of Trevisa's practice as a translator see Traugott Lawlor, 'On the Properties of John Trevisa's Major Translations', *Viator*, 14 (1983), 267–88.

hitherto. The less familiar word *ser* 'various' (line 7), which is unique to Cotton, is more to the point than *fer* 'distant' in the context of *Dominus*'s argument, and is undoubtedly original. In line 6, *alwey deef ys alwey dombe* 'one who has always been deaf is always dumb' makes a reasonable assertion; Caxton has the patently absurd *alway he that is deef is alway dombe* 'always one who is deaf is always dumb'. (The addition *he that is* looks like a Caxton correction, in that it is not supported by either H or B – the manuscripts closest to Caxton – or indeed any of the manuscripts, except C, where it is written above the line in another hand.) Finally, a number of pieces of text have been lost from the HBK group, of which the most important is in lines 132f.: *Also holy wryt was translated out of Hebrew ynto Gru and out of Gru into Latyn.* If this were the only reference to the translation of the Bible in the dialogue one would be inclined to put down this omission in HBK to censorship, rather than to simple eyeskip (*Latyn – Latyn*). Nevertheless, the restoration of the omitted passage does make the relevance of the dialogue to the Bible controversy more conspicuous.

In editing the text I have expanded all contractions silently and (without citing variants) have placed angle brackets, <>, around defective readings reconstructed from the other manuscripts. Square brackets, [ ], are reserved for emendations, whether conjectural or supported by the other manuscripts. In places where the original reading is legible under a correction I have recorded the original as the text, relegating the correction to the notes along with other variants. Some readings have been made with the aid of ultra-violet light or photography.

MS Cotton Tib. D VII, fo. 1

[*Dialogus*[1] *inter dominum et clericum*][1]   1
[*Dominus:*][2] Seþthe[3] þat baby<1>[4] was ybuld men <spe>keþ[5]
dyuers tonges, so[6] þat dy<uer>s men bu<þ> strau<nge t>o
oþer and knoweþ[7] noȝt of here[7] speche. Speche ys noȝt
ykno<we> bote ȝif hyt be lurned. <Com>myn lurnyng of   5
speche ys by huy<r>yng. And so alwey[8] deef ys alwey dombe,
vor he may noȝt hure speche vor to lurne. So men of ser[9]
contrayes and londes þat ha[bbeþ][10] dyuers speches ȝef noþer[11]
of ham haþ lurned oþeres speche,[12] neyþer[13] of ham wot what
oþer meneþ [þey[14] hy][15] meete[16] and haue greet neode of[17]   10
informacion and of loore, of talkyng and of speche. Be þeo
<neode neue>r so gret, neyþer[18] of ham vnderstondeþ oþeres[19]
speche no moore þan gaglyng[20] of gee<s>. For iangle þe[on][21]
neuere so vaste þe oþer[22] ys neuere þe wyser[23] [þey[24] a][25] schrewe
hym in stude of good morowe. Þis ys a gret meschef þat volweþ   15
now mankuynde; bote God of hys mercy and grace haþ
o<rd>eynd doubel remedy. On[26] ys þat som man lurneþ and

knoweþ meny²⁷ dyuers speches. And so, bytwene²⁸ strange men
of þe whoche noþer²⁹ vnderstondeþ oþeres³⁰ speche, such a man
may be mene and telle eyþ<er> what þoþer³¹ wol³² mene. Þe³³   20
oþer remedy ys þat on langage ys ylurned,³⁴ yvsed and yknowe
in meny nacyons and londes. And so Latyn ys³⁵ ylurned,
yknowe and yvsed specialych a þys half Grees in al þe nacions
and londes of Europa. Þarfore clerkes of here godnes and cortesy
makeþ and wryteþ here bokes in Latyn vor here wrytyng and   25
bokes scholde be vnderstonde in dyue<rs> nacyons and londes.
And so Ranulph,³⁶ monk of Chester, wrot yn Latyn hys
book[es]³⁷ of cro<n>y<kes>³⁸ þat discreueþ þe world aboute yn
lengthe and yn brede and makeþ mencyon³⁹ and [mu]ynde³⁹,⁴⁰
of doyngs and of⁴¹ dedes <o>f meruayls and of wondres and   30
rekneþ þe⁴² ʒeres to hys laste dayes fram⁴³ þe vurste makyng of
heuene and of erþe. And so⁴⁴ þarynne ys noble⁴⁵ and gret⁴⁵
informacion and lore to h<e>m þat can þarynne rede and
vnderstonde. [Þarvor]e⁴⁶ [Ic]h⁴⁷ wolde haue þeus⁴⁸ bokes of
cronyks⁴⁹ translated out of Latyn ynto Englysch, for þe mo men   35
scholde hem vnderstonde and haue þereof konnyng,⁵⁰ infor-
mac<ion> and lore.

*Clericus:*⁵¹ Þeus bokes of cronyks⁵² buþ ywryte yn Latyn and
Latyn y<s> yvsed and vnderstonde a þys half Grees yn al þe
<naci>ons and londes of Europa, and comynl<ych⁵³ Eng>lysch   40
ys noʒt so wyde vnderstonde, yvsed and⁵⁴ yk<no>w<e>; and
þe Engly<sch t>ra<n>slacion <sc>hold<e no man>⁵⁵ vnderstonde bote Englyschmen <alone. Þanne> how <s>cho<lde
þe⁵⁶ mo men> vndersto<nde þe cro>nyks⁵⁷ þey [a]⁵⁸ were
translated <out of Latyn þat ys so> wyde yv<s>ed <and   45
yknowe in>to⁵⁹ En<glysch⁶⁰ þat> ys noʒt yvsed and⁶¹ yknowe
bote of <En>gly<s>chmen alone?

*Dominus:*⁶² Þes <question and doute ys> esy to assoyle,⁶³ vor
ʒef þeu<s⁶⁴ cro>nyk<s>⁶⁵ w<ere trans>lated <out> of
Latyn <into> E<ng>ly<sch, þanne by⁶⁶ so> meny⁶⁷ þe mo   50
men scholde vnderston<de⁶⁸ ham as⁶⁹ vnderstondeþ Englysch
and> no L<a>ty<n>.

*Clericus:*⁷⁰ [ʒe cunneþ]⁷¹ speke and⁷² re<de> and vnderstonde
Latyn. Þann<e hyt> nedeþ noʒt to haue such <a>n <Englysch
tran>slacion.   55

*Dominus:*⁷³ Y denye þys argument, fo<r þey> [Ich]⁷⁴ <cu>nne⁷⁵
speke <and>⁷⁶ rede and vnderst<onde Latyn þer> ys moche
Laty<n> in þeus bokes of cron<yks⁷⁷ þat Y can> noʒt vnderstonde, noþer⁷⁸ þou wi<þoute studyinge and ⁷⁹ au>ysement
and lokyng of oþer bokes. <Also þey> hyt wer<e> noʒt   60

neodful vor me <hyt is neodfol vor oþere m>en þat vnderstondeþ no La<tyn>.

Clericus:[80] M<en> þat vnderstondeþ[81] no <Latyn may lerne
and vnderstonde>.

Dominus:[82] <N>oȝt <a>lle. For som may noȝt vor o<þ>er   65
maner bysynes, som <vor elde, som vor> (fo. 1ᵛ) defaute o<f>
wyt, som vor defaute of katel oþer of frendes to vynd<e> ham
to scole <and> som <vor oþere> dyuers defautes and lettes.

Clericus:[83] Hyt neodeþ noȝt þat al soche knowe þe cronykes.[84]

D<ominus>:[85] Spek noȝt to streytlych of þyng þat neodeþ, for   70
<str>eytlych to speke of þyng þat neodeþ on<lych>[86] þyng þat
ys and may[87] noȝt fayle nedeþ to be, and so hyt neodeþ þat God
be for <God ys and may> noȝt faile; and so vor to speke no man
nedeþ to[88] knowe þe[89] cronykes[90] vor hyt myȝte and may <be>
þat no man [ham][91] knoweþ. Oþerwyse to speke of þyng þat   75
neodeþ, somwhat neodeþ vor to[92] susteyne[93] oþer <to> haue
oþer þinges þarby, and so mete and dryngke nedeþ vor kepyng
and sustenaunce of lyf, <and> so vor to speke no man neodeþ
to[94] knowe[89] þe cronyks.[95] Bote in þe þridde manere to speke of
þing þat neodeþ, al þat ys profytable nedeþ, and so vor to speke   80
al men neodeþ[96] to knawe þe cronykes.[97]

Clericus:[98] Þanne [hy][99] þat vnderstondeþ no Latyn mowe axe
and be informed and ytauȝt of [ham][100] þat vnderstondeþ Latyn.

Dominus:[101] Þou spekst wonderlych, vor þe lewed man wot noȝt
what [a][102] scholde axe, and namelych of lore of dedes þat come   85
neuere in hys [mu]ynde,[103] noþer[104] wot comynlych[105] of whom[105]
[a][106] scholde[107] axe. Also noȝt[108] al men þat vnderstondeþ Latyn
ha[bbeþ][109] such bokes[110] to informe lewed[111] men. Also som
konneþ noȝt and[112] [som] wol noȝt[112] and som mowe noȝt a
whyle;[113] and so[114] hyt nedeþ to haue an Englysch translacion.   90

Clericus:[115] Þe Latyn ys boþe good and fayr. Þarvore hyt neodeþ
noȝt to h[an][116] an Englysch translacion.

Dominus:[117] Þis reson ys wor<þy> to be plonged yn a plod and
leyd in pouþer of lewednes and of schame. Hyt myȝte wel be þat
þou makest þys reson[118] onlych in murthe and in game.[119]   95

Clericus:[120] Þe reson mot[121] stonde bot hyt be assoyled.

Dominus:[122] A blere-yȝed man, bote he were al blynd of wyt,
myȝte yseo þe solucion of þis reson; and [þey a][123] were blynd
[a][124] myȝte grope þe solucion, bote ȝef[125] hys[126] velyng hym
faylede. Vor ȝef þis reson were oȝt worþ, by such manere[127]   100
argement[128] [me][129] m]yȝt[130] preoue þat þe þre score and ten,[131]
and Aquila, Symachus, Theodocion, and[132] he þat made þe
vyfte[133] translacion,[132] and Origenes were lewedlych ocupyed

whanne [hy]¹³⁴ translated holy wryt out of Hebrew¹³⁵ into Grw;
and also þat Seint Ierom was lewedlych ocupyed whanne he   105
translatede holy wryt out of Hebreu ynto Latyn, vor þe Hebreu
ys boþe good and feyre and ywryte by¹³⁶ inspiracion of þe Holy
Gost; and al þeuse vor here translacions¹³⁷ buþ hyȝlych ypreysed
of al holy cherche. Þann<e þe v>orseyde lewed reson ys¹³⁸
worþy to be pouþred,¹³⁹ yleyd a water and ysouced. Also holy   110
wryt in Laty<n ys boþe> good and fayr, and <ȝet> for to
make a sermon of holy wryt al yn Latyn to men þat konneþ
Eng<lysch> and no Latyn hyt were a lewed dede, vor [hy]¹⁴⁰
buþ n<euere þ>e wyser vor þe Latyn bote¹⁴¹ hyt be told
h<e>m¹⁴² [a]n¹⁴³ Englysch what hyt ys to mene, and hyt may   115
<noȝt> be told an Englysch what þe Latyn ys to mene withoute
translacion out of La<tyn> in[to]¹⁴⁴ E<nglysch. Þ>an<ne>
hyt nedeþ to haue an Engly<sch> translacion. And for¹⁴⁵ to
kepe hyt in [mu]y<n>de¹⁴⁶ þat hyt be noȝt vorȝu<t hyt> ys
be<tre> þat such a translacion be ymad and ywryte þan¹⁴⁷   120
yseyd and noȝt ywryte. And so þis <v>orseyde lewed reson
scholde meeue no man þat haþ eny wyt to leue þe ma<k>yng of
Englysch translacion.
<C>lericus:¹⁴⁸ A gret¹⁴⁹ del of þeuse bokes stondeþ moche by
holy wryt, by holy doctors and by philosofy. Þanne þeus<e¹⁵⁰   125
boke>s scholde noȝt be translated ynto Englysch.
Dominus:¹⁵¹ Hyt ys wonder þat þou makest so feble argementys
and <hast> ygo so long to scole. Aristoteles¹⁵² bokes and oþere
bokes also of logyk and of philosofy were translated out of Gru
into Latyn. <Also, atte> prayng of K<yng> Charles, Iohn   130
Scot translatede Seint¹⁵³ Denys hys¹⁵⁴ bokes out of Gru ynto
Latyn. <Al>so¹⁵⁵ holy wryt was <tran>sla(fo. 2)ted out of
Hebre<w> ynto Gru and out of Gru into Latyn¹⁵⁵ and <þanne>
out of¹⁵⁶ Latyn y<n>to Frensch. Þanne what haþ Engly<sch>
trespased þat hyt myȝt noȝt be translated into Englysch? Also   135
Kyng Alured, þat foundede þe vnyuersite of Oxenford, translatede þe beste lawes into Englysch tonge and a gret del of þe
Sauter out of <Latyn> into Englysch, and made¹⁵⁷ Wyrefryth,¹⁵⁸
byschop of Wyrcetre,¹⁵⁹ translate¹⁶⁰ Seint¹⁶¹ Gregore hys¹⁶² bokes
Dialoges¹⁶³ out of Latyn ynto Saxon.¹⁶⁴ Also Cedmon of¹⁶⁵   140
Whyteby was inspired of þe Holy Gost and made wonder¹⁶⁶
poesyes an¹⁶⁷ Englysch nyȝ of¹⁶⁸ al þe storyes of holy wryt. Also
þe holy man Beda translatede Seint Iohn hys¹⁶⁹ gospel out of
Latyn ynto Englysch. Also þou wost where þe Apocalips ys
ywryte in þe walles and roof of a chapel boþe in Latyn and yn   145
Freynsch. Also þe gospel and¹⁷⁰ prophecy and þe ryȝt [fey]¹⁷¹ of

holy churche mot[172] be tauȝt[173] and ypreched to Englyschmen þat conneþ[174] no Latyn. Þanne þe gospel and[175] prophecy and þe ryȝt fey[176] of holy cherche mot[177] be told[178] ham an[179] Englysch, and þat ys noȝt ydo bote by[180] Englysch translacion.[181] Vor[182] such Englysch prechyng ys verrey Englysch[183] translacion,[182] and such Englysch prechyng[184] ys good and neodful;[185] þanne Englysch translacion ys good and neodfol.[186]

Clericus:[187] Ȝef a[188] translacion were ymad þat myȝte be amended yn eny poynt, som men hyt wolde blame.

Dominus:[189] Ȝef men blameþ þat ys noȝt worþy to be blamed, þanne [hy][190] buþ to blame. Clerkes knoweþ[191] wel ynow[192] þat no synfol man doþ so wel þat he[193] ne myȝte[194] do betre, noþer makeþ[195] so good a[196] translacyon þat he ne myȝte make a[197] betre. Parvore Orygenes made twey translacions and Ierom translatede þryes þe Sauter. Y[198] desire no[199] translacion of þeus bokes,[200] þe[201] beste þat myȝte be, for þat were an ydel desyre vor eny man þat ys now[202] here[203] alyue, bote [Ich][204] wolde haue a skylfol translacion þat myȝt be knowe and vnderstonde.

Clericus:[205] Wheþer ys ȝow leuere haue a translacion of þeuse cronyks[206] in ryme oþer yn prose?

Dominus:[207] Yn prose, vor comynlych prose ys more cleer þan ryme, more esy and more pleyn to knowe and vnderstonde.

Clericus:[208] Þanne God graunte[209] grace [greiþlyche][210] to[211] gynne,[212] <w>yt and wysdom wysly to wyrche, myȝt and [mu]ynde[213] of ryȝt menyng to make translacion[214] trysty[215] <and> truwe, plesyng to þe Trynyte, þre[216] persones and o god in maieste, þat euer was and euere schal be, and made heuene and erþe and lyȝt vor to schyne, and departede lyȝt [and][217] derknes and clepede[218] lyȝt 'day' and derknesse 'nyȝt'; and so was maad euetyde[219] and morowe tyde [on[220] day þat had no morow tyde].[220] Þe secunde day he made þe firmament betwene[221] watres and departede þe[222] watres þat were vnder þe firmament vram[223] watres þat were aboue þe firmament and clepede[224] þe firmament 'heuone'.[225] Þe þridde day he gadrede þe[226] watres þat buþ vnder heuene[227] ynto on place and made þe erþe vnheled and clepede þe gadryngs[228] of watres 'sees' and drye erþe[229] 'lo<n>d', and made tren and gras. Þe verþe day he made sonne and moone and sterres and sette hem yn þe fermament of heuene, þar vor[230] to schyne and to be toknes and sygnes to departe tymes and ȝeres and[231] nyȝt and day. Þe vyfte day he made voules and bryddes yn aer[232] and fysches yn þe water. Þe sixte day he made bestes of þe lond and man of erþe[233] and put hym[234] yn[235] paradys for he scholde worche and wone[236] þarynne.

Bote man brak God hys heste: he[237] vyl ynto synne and was pot   190
out of paradys ynto wo and sorowe worþy to be dampned to þe
peyne of helle wiþoute eny ende. Bote þe Holy Trynyte hadde
mer<s>y of man and þe Vad<er[238] sende þ>e Sone, and þe
Holy Gost alyȝte on a mayde, and þe Sone tok vlesch and blod of
þat blysfol mayde, and <de>yde[239] on þe Rode to saue   195
<m>ankynde, and aros þe þridde day, gloryous and blysfol,
and tauȝte hys disciples, and styȝ[240] into heuene <whanne hit>
(fo. 2ᵛ) was tyme, and scha<l> come att<e> day <of do>me
and deme quyk and ded. Þanne al m<en>[241] þat buþ ywryte yn
þe bok of lyf schal wende <wiþ> hym ynto þe blysse of heuene   200
and be <þere in b>ody and in[242] soul, and se and knowe hys
godhede and manhede [in[243] ioye wiþout eny ende].[243]
Explicit Dialogus.[216, 244]

Incipit Epistola.[245]
Welthe and worschip to my worþy and worschypfol lord Sire   205
<Th>omas,[246] lord of Berkeleye, Y Iohn Treuysa ȝoure preost
and ȝoure[247] bedman, obedyent[248] and boxum to worche ȝoure
wylle, holde in herte and[249] þenke in þoȝt and meue[250] in
[mu]ynde[251] ȝoure meedfol[252] menyng and speche þat ȝe speke
and seyde þat ȝe wolde haue Englysch translacion of Ranulf[253]   210
of Chestre hys[254] bokes of[255] cronikes.[256] Þarvore Y wol[257]
[vonde][258] to take þat trauayl and make Englysch translacion of
þe same bokes as God graunteþ[259] me grace. For blame of
bakbyters wol Y noȝt blynne,[260] for enuye of enemys, for euel
spyȝtyng and speche of euel spekers wol Y noȝt leue to do þis   215
dede. For trauayl wol Y noȝt spare. Comforte [Ich][261] haue in
medfol makyng and plesyng to God, [and[262] in wytynge][262] þat Y
wot þat[263] hyt ys ȝoure wylle. For to make þis translacion cleer
and pleyn to be knowe and vnderstonde, in som place Y schal
sette word vor[264] word and actyue[265] vor[264] actyue[266] and passiue   220
vor[267] passyue arewe ryȝt[268] as a[269] stondeþ withoute changyng
of þe ordre of wordes. But yn som place Y mot[270] change[271] þe[272]
rewe and[272] þe ordre of wordes and sette þe[273] actyue[274] vor[275]
þe[276] passiue[277] and aȝenward.[278] And yn som place Y mot[279]
sette a reson vor[280] a word to[281] telle[282] what hyt meneþ. Bote   225
vor[283] al such chaungyng, þe menyng schal stonde and noȝt be
ychanged. Bot som wordes and[284] names: of contrayes, of londes,
of cites, of wat[er]s[285] <of> ryuers, of mounteyns and hulles, of
persones and of places, mot[286] be yset and stonde vor[287] hem sylf
in here oune kuynde,[288] as: Asia, Europa, Affrica and Siria,   230
Mont Athlas, Syna and Oreb, Marach, Iordan and Arnon,

Bethleem, Nazareth, Ierusalem and Damascus, Hanybal, Rasyn,[289] Assuerus and[290] Cirus, and meny suche wordes and names. Ʒef[291] eny man makeþ[292] of þeus[293] bokes of cronyks[294] a betre[295] Englysch translacion and more profitable, God do 235 hys[296] mede. And for[297] ʒe make me do <þys> medfol dede, He þat quyteþ al good dedes quyte ʒoure mede yn þe blys of heuene, in[298] welthe and lykyng wiþ alle þe holy seyntes of mankunde and þe nyʒen[299] ordres of angles: angels,[300] arch-angels, pryncipates, potestates, virtutes, dominaciones, thrones, 240 cherubyn, and seraphyn, to se God on[301] Hys blysfol face yn ioye wiþoute eny ende.[298] Amen.
Explicit Epistola.[302]

King's College, London

295

¹ *Dialogus . . clericum*] S; *om* CHGBK. ² *Dominus*] S; om CHGBK. ³ Seþthe]
Syth the tyme K. ⁴ babyl] babel SHB; C *defective*; Babilon G; the grete and
high tour of babilone K. ⁵ spekeþ] SHGB; C *defective*; haue spoken with K.
⁶ so] in such wise K. ⁷ knoweþ . . . here] understonde not others K. ⁸ alwey]
a. he þat is CK (*above line, another hand*, C). ⁹ ser] fer SHGBK. ¹⁰ habbeþ] S;
hauyþe CHGBK (uyþe *over erasure, another hand*, C). ¹¹ noþer] neiþer HBK.
¹² speche] langage HBK. ¹³ neyþer] noþer SG. ¹⁴ þey] þeiȝ S; þough CHGK
(*over erasure, another hand*, C). ¹⁵ hy] hey S; þei CHGK (*above line, another
hand*, C). ¹⁶ meete] miȝte S. ¹⁷ of] *blotted* G. ¹⁸ neyþer] noþer SG. ¹⁹ oþeres]
other G. ²⁰ gaglyng] SHGBK; ganglyng C. ²¹ þe on] S; þat oon HGBK; þey (y
over erasure, another hand, C. ²² þe oþer] HB; þe oon S; þet oþer CGK (t *above
line, ?another hand*, C). ²³ wyser] in stede of go *cancelled after it* S. ²⁴ þey] S;
þogh CHGBK (*over erasure, another hand*, C). ²⁵ a] S; he HGBK; he be *above
line, another hand*, C. ²⁶ On] that one G. ²⁷ meny] mony (o *altered from e?*) G;
manye SHBK. ²⁸ bytwene] bitwixe HB. ²⁹ noþer] neiþer HBK. ³⁰ oþeres]
other G. ³¹ þoþer] oþer SHGBK. ³² wol] wold G. ³³ Þe] Þat HGBK.
³⁴ ylurned] y. & HB. ³⁵ ys] *om* G. ³⁶ Ranulph] Ranulphus K. ³⁷ bookes]
SHBK; book CG. ³⁸ cronykes] SHK; cronykles GB; C *defective*. ³⁹ mencyon
and muynde] mynde and mencioun G. ⁴⁰ muynde] mynde CSHGBK (*erasure
of two minims before it* C). ⁴¹ of] *om* K. ⁴² þe] his S. ⁴³ fram] fro SK. ⁴⁴ so] *om*
B. ⁴⁵ noble and gret] gret and noble GK. ⁴⁶ Þarvore] Therfore CSHGBK
(Therfor *over erasure, another hand*, e (2) *original*, C). ⁴⁷ Ich] SH; y CG (*over
larger erasure, original* h *legible*, C); I BK. ⁴⁸ þeus] þe þees B. ⁴⁹ cronyks]
cronykles GB. ⁵⁰ konnyng] comyn G. ⁵¹ *Clericus*] The Clerke K. ⁵² cronyks]
cronikles GB. ⁵³ comynlych] m *altered from* nl? C. ⁵⁴ and] ne K. ⁵⁵ no man]
SK; no men HB; non men G; C *defective*. ⁵⁶ þe] SHK; *om* GB; C *defective*.
⁵⁷ cronyks] cronykles GB. ⁵⁸ þey a] þei a S; though þey CHGBK (though
above line, another hand; þey *original, erasure after it*, C). ⁵⁹ into] o *partly erased*
H. ⁶⁰ Englysch] enghissh B. ⁶¹ and] nor G. ⁶² *Dominus*] inserted H; The lorde
K. ⁶³ assoyle] assaylle K. ⁶⁴ þeus] þis B. ⁶⁵ cronyks] cronykles GB. ⁶⁶ by]
SHGB; by that K; C *defective*. ⁶⁷ meny] monyn? G. ⁶⁸ vnderstonde] v *blotted*
H. ⁶⁹ as] SHGK; as al þoe þat B; C *defective*. ⁷⁰ *Clericus*] The clerk K. ⁷¹ ȝe
cunneþ] SHGBK; to them þat can *over erasure, ?another hand*, C. ⁷² and] *om*
K. ⁷³ *Dominus*] The lord K. ⁷⁴ Ich] S; y G; I CHBK (*?correction* C). ⁷⁵ cunne]
can HGBK. ⁷⁶ and] SHB; *om* GK; C *defective*. ⁷⁷ cronyks] cronykles GB.

[78] noþer] neþer HBK. [79] and] SHBG; *om* K; C *defective*. [80] *Clericus*] The clerke K. [81] vnderstondeþ] vnderdeþ B. [82] *Dominus*] The lord K. [83] *Clericus*] The Clerke K. [84] cronykes] cronykles GB. [85] *Dominus*] The lord K. [86] onlych] english G. [87] may] be *cancelled after it* S. [88] to] for to K. [89] þe . . . knowe] *copied twice* S (þe] *om* S (1)). [90] cronykes] cronykles GB. [91] ham] SHGBK; *om* C. [92] to] *above line* C. [93] susteyne] svnsteyne B. [94] to] for to K. [95] cronyks] cronikles GB. [96] neodeþ] knowiþ *cancelled before it* H. [97] cronykes] cronykles GB. [98] *Clericus*] *in margin* H; The clerke K. [99] hy] hey S; þei HGBK; þo *over erasure, another hand*, C. [100] ham] hem CSHGK (he *over erasure, another hand*, C); theym G. [101] *Dominus*] The lord K. [102] a] S; he CHGBK (*another hand, over erasure of one letter*, C). [103] muynde] mynde CSHGBK (*erasure, probably of two minims, before it* C). [104] noþer] neþer HB; ner K. [105] comynlych of whom] of whom comynly K. [106] a] S; he CKGBK (*another hand, over erasure of one letter*, C). [107] scholde] e *over erasure* S. [108] noȝt] *om* G. [109] habbeþ] S; hauithe CHB (uithe *over erasure, another hand*, C); haue K; haue not G. [110] bokes] o *lost in fold* G. [111] lewed] men *cancelled before it* H. [112] and . . . noȝt] SG; and wol noȝt C; *om* HBK. [113] a whyle] *om* G. [114] so] *om* B. [115] *Clericus*] The clerke K. [116] han] haue SHGBK; hem (e *over erasure*, m *altered from* n, *another hand*) C. [117] *Dominus*] The lord K. [118] þys reson] *om* K. [119] game] *erasure after it* H. [120] *Clericus*] The Clerke K. [121] mot] most GK. [122] *Dominus*] The lord K. [123] þey a] S; þough he CHGBK (*another hand*, þough *over erasure*, he *above line*, C). [124] a] S; he CHGBK (*another hand* C). [125] ȝef] *om* S. [126] hys] h *altered from* b S. [127] manere] maner of G. [128] argement] arguyng SHGBK. [129] me] men *over erasure, another hand*, C. [130] myȝt] *first minim corrected* C. [131] ten] t. jnterpretours K. [132] and . . . translacion] *om* HBK. [133] vyfte] fyrst G. [134] hy] hey S; þei CHGBK (*another hand*, þ *over erasure*, ei *above line*, C). [135] Hebrew] h *altered from* b S. [136] by] by the G. [137] translacions] c *rubbed* G. [138] ys] is most S. [139] pouþred] p. and CGB (& *above line, another hand*, C). [140] hy] hey S; þei CHGBK (*another hand*, þ *over erasure*, ei *above line*, C). [141] bote] but if G. [142] hem] *above cancelled* alatyn S. [143] an] SHB; in CGK (i *over erasure, another hand*, C). [144] into] SHGBK; in C. [145] for] *om* G. [146] muynde] mynde CSHGBK (*erasure, probably of two minims, before it*, C). [147] þan] then to be G. [148] *Clericus*] The Clerke K. [149] gret] greeet K. [150] þeuse] the G. [151] *Dominus*] The lord K. [152] Aristoteles] Aristotel G. [153] Seint] *om* HBK. [154] Denys hys] denys is S; Denys HGBK. [155] Also . . . Latyn] *om* HBK. [156] of] *om* B. [157] made] caused K. [158] Wyrefryth] Wynefrith S. [159] Wyrcetre] wircestre SH. [160] translate] to t. K. [161] Seint] t *over erasure?* S. [162] Gregore hys] gregori is S; gregories HBK; Gregori G. [163] Dialoges] Dialogus (*unabbr*.) G; the dialogues K. [164] Saxon] Saxons K. [165] of] *above line* C. [166] made wonder] mader B. [167] an] in GBK. [168] of] *om* S. [169] Iohn hys] Iohn is SG; Iones HK; Ione B. [170] and] a. þe B. [171] fey] SHB; feiþe CGK (*over erasure, another hand*, C). [172] mot] most GK. [173] tauȝt] tolde tauȝt G. [174] conneþ] *above cancelled* cowþe S; n (2) *corrected (from beginnings of* e?) H. [175] and] a. the G. [176] fey] SHB;

feyth CGK (th *above line, another hand*, C). [177] mot] most GK. [178] told] tauȝt
& ypreched *cancelled before it* H. [179] an] in HGBK. [180] bote by] without G.
[181] translacion] tranlacion K. [182] Vor . . . translacion] *om* S. [183] Englysch] *in
margin, ?same hand*, H; *om* GK. [184] prechyng] *om* G. [185] neodful, [186] neodfol]
nedeful (nede *over erasure, both*) H. [187] *Clericus*] The clerke K. [188] a] *om* S.
[189] *Dominus*] The lord K. [190] hy] hey S; þei CHGBK (*over erasure* C).
[191] Clerkes knoweþ] *Clericus* Know hit G. [192] ynow] *om* G. [193] he] it K.
[194] myȝte] *beginnings of* k *cancelled after it* S. [195] noþer makeþ] neþer m. HB;
ne make K. [196] a] *om* G. [197] make a] make G; be K. [198] Y] *Dominus* I G. [199] no]
not HBK. [200] bokes] *om* K. [201] þe] on the G. [202] ys now] now is SHGB.
[203] here] *om* K. [204] Ich] SH; y CGBK (*over erasure, ?another hand*,
C). [205] *Clericus*] The Clerk K. [206] cronyks] cronykles GB; Cronykrs K.
[207] *Dominus*] The lord K. [208] *Clericus*] The Clerke K. [209] graunte] SG; g. vs
CHBK (vs *above line, ?another hand*, C). [210] greiþlyche] SHGBK; truly to *over
erasure, another hand*, C. [211] to] *attempt at alteration* (to be?) C. [212] gynne]
begynne G. [213] muynde] mynde CSHGBK (*erasure, probably of two minims,
before it* C). [214] translacion] SHGBK; þis t. (þis *above line, another hand*) C.
[215] trysty] SHGBK; trystyly (ly *added, another hand*) C. [216] þre . . . *Dialogus*]
Amen S; *om* G. [217] and] HBK; fro *over erasure* (*of* &?), *another hand*, C.
[218] clepede] callid K. [219] euetyde] HBK; euentyde (*macron added, another ink*)
C. [220] on . . . tyde] HBK; *om* C. [221] betwene] bytwene (e (1) *altered from*
o) H. [222] þe] *om* HBK. [223] vram] from þe HBK. [224] clepede] called K.
[225] heuone] o *altered to* e C. [226] þe] *om* HBK. [227] heuene] the firmament K.
[228] gadryngs] gadryng K. [229] erþe] *om* B. [230] vor] *attempt at alteration, with
erasure, to* ffro C. [231] and] *om* K. [232] aer] þe eyr HBK. [233] erþe] þe e. HBK.
[234] hym] hem K. [235] yn] into B. [236] wone] *attempt at alteration to* dwelle C.
[237] he] and HBK. [238] Vader] ff *over* v C. [239] deyde] d (1) *over erasure* H.
[240] styȝ] ascended K. [241] men] *om* HB; tho K. [242] in] *om* HBK. [243] in . . .
ende] HBK; *om* C. [244] *Explicit Dialogus*] Thus endeth the dyalogue K; *om* B.
[245] *Incipit Epistola*] The Epystle of sir Iohan Treuisa chapelayn vnto lord
Thomas of Barkley vpon the translacion of Polycronycon in to our Englysshe
tongue K; *om* HBT. [246] Thomas] Thomras (ra *abbr. for* a) H. [247] ȝoure] *om* K.
[248] obedyent] obedien S. [249] and] *om* K. [250] meue] meen K. [251] muynde]
mynde CSHBTK (*erasure, probably of two minims, before it* C). [252] meedfol]
nedefful K. [253] Ranulf] Ranulphus K. [254] Chestre hys] Chestere is S; Chestres
HBK; Chestre T. [255] of] and B. [256] cronikes] cronycles B. [257] wol] wolde B.
[258] vonde] SHBTK; besy me *over erasure, another hand*, (me *above line*) C.
[259] graunteþ] ra *abbr. misplaced* C. [260] blynne] blynue K. [261] Ich] SH; I CTK
(*over erasure* C); y B. [262] and in wytynge] SHBTK (wytynge] knowyng K); &
to your plesing *over erasure, another hand*, C. [263] þat] *om* T. [264] vor (*both*)] ff
over v C. [265] actyue] ff *over* u C. [266] actyue] ff *over* u C; passif T. [267] vor] ff *over*
v C. [268] ryȝt] *om* T. [269] a] it TK; þei HB. [270] mot] CSHBT (*altered to* woll C);
muste K. [271] change] chaung B. [272] þe rewe and] *om* K. [273] þe] *om* K.

²⁷⁴ actyue] ff *over* u C. ²⁷⁵ vor] ff *over* v C. ²⁷⁶ þe] *om* K. ²⁷⁷ passiue] ff *over* v C.
²⁷⁸ aȝenward] *altered from* aȝenword C. ²⁷⁹ mot] CSHTB (*altered to* woll C);
muste K. ²⁸⁰ vor] ff *over* v C. ²⁸¹ to] and HBK. ²⁸² telle] e (1) *rubbed* H. ²⁸³ vor]
ff *over* C. ²⁸⁴ and] of ST. ²⁸⁵ waters] er *abbr. missing* C. ²⁸⁶ mot] CSHBT
(*altered to* most C); muste K. ²⁸⁷ vor] ff *over* v C. ²⁸⁸ kuynde] kyndr K.
²⁸⁹ Rasyn] Risyn B. ²⁹⁰ and] *om* T. ²⁹¹ ȝef] If (I *blotted*) T. ²⁹² makeþ] make K.
²⁹³ þeus] þis T. ²⁹⁴ cronyks] cronicles B. ²⁹⁵ betre] bett B. ²⁹⁶ hys] hym K.
²⁹⁷ for] by cause K. ²⁹⁸ in . . . ende] *om* ST. ²⁹⁹ nyȝen] nynȝen C. ³⁰⁰ angels]
As angels K. ³⁰¹ on] in K. ³⁰² *Explicit epistola*] Thus endeth he his Epistle K;
om ST.

Concerning Three Names in Le Morte Darthur – 'Roone', 'The Welshe Kyng', and 'Chastelayne' – and Malory's Possible Revision of His Book

R. M. LUMIANSKY

Three minor aspects of Sir Thomas Malory's account of Arthur's war against the Roman Emperor Lucius, as it appears in the Winchester manuscript, have not in my view been convincingly explained by earlier commentators. The problems centre about the three names listed in the title for this paper, and in their small way bear upon the larger question of the relationship of the Winchester manuscript to Malory's book as it appears in Caxton's edition.

I. Roone[*]

After King Arthur has disposed of the giant on Mont St Michael, the marshal of France speaks to the king. The marshal

> seyde to the kynge how the Emperour was com into Fraunce and hath destroyed much of oure marchis and is com into Burgayne and many borowys hath destroyed and hath made grete slaughtir of your noble people and where that he rydyth all he destroyes And now he is comyn into dowse Fraunce and ther he brennys all clene Now all the dowse leperys[1] bothe deukys and other and the perys of Parys towne ar fledde downe into the lowe contrey towarde Roone.[2]

Arthur immediately sends a body of knights led by Bors, Lionel, Bedivere, and Gawain to command Lucius either to leave the king's lands or to join battle. The Emperor's defiant reply includes the statement that he 'woll ryde

---

[*]After submitting this paper for publication, I learned of P. J. C. Field's 'Malory's Place-Names: Roone and the Low Country', N&Q, 230 (1985), 452–3, in which Roone is identified as Rouen. I have retained the discussion of Roone here because of its pertinence for the larger matter discussed in the final section of this paper, which Field did not treat.

[1] leperys: obviously a scribal error for perys.
[2] The Winchester Malory: A Facsimile, introd. N. R. Ker, EETS SS, 4 (London, 1976), fos. 78ᵛ–79ʳ.

downe by Sayne and wynne all that therto longes and aftir ryde unto Roone and wynne hit up clene'.[3]

The account of the Roman War as it appears in Caxton's edition of the *Morte* does not include these two appearances of 'Roone';[4] and the alliterative *Morte Arthure*, upon which Malory's account is based, does not seem to provide any help in glossing the two occurrences of 'Roone' in the Winchester manuscript.[5] Eugène Vinaver, in his edition of the Winchester manuscript, glossed 'Roone' in both occurrences as 'Rhine'.[6] R. W. Ackerman's gloss is 'River Rhine?'.[7] Most recently we have the gloss 'Rhine' for 'Roone' by Bert Dillon.[8] Vinaver considered the first occurrence of 'Roone' deserving of a note:

> In view of the fact that the peers of Paris would not normally have fled to Rome through the Netherlands it is not altogether unlikely that M[alory]'s remark is based on some hopelessly corrupt reading. . . . The alternative would be to regard 'Roone' as a misreading of 'Rhine'.[9]

In my view, Vinaver's gloss and note for 'Roone', which we found reflected by Ackerman and Dillon, do not make sense. First, there is no reason to believe that 'towarde Roone' could mean that the French noblemen would be fleeing from Paris towards Rome right into the hands of the enemy. That they would flee eastward towards the Rhine also into the hands of an enemy advancing westward seems equally incomprehensible. Second, Vinaver assumes that 'the lowe contrey' means the Netherlands and in his editions presents it capitalised as 'the Lowe Contrey'. But in the Winchester manuscript, where specific place names are usually presented capitalised in distinctive ink, that is not the case with 'lowe contrey'. Thus Malory does not seem to be saying that the French noblemen fled from Lucius through the Netherlands towards Rome or towards the Rhine.[10]

---

[3] *Winchester Malory*, fo. 79ᵛ.

[4] *Sir Thomas Malory, Le Morte D'Arthur*, printed by William Caxton 1485, Scolar Press facsimile (London, 1976); see liber quintus, capitulum v and capitulum sextum.

[5] Edmund Brock, ed., *Morte Arthure*, EETS, 8 (1865; new edn, 1871; rptd London, 1961), ll. 1231–1340.

[6] *The Works of Sir Thomas Malory* (Oxford, three volumes, 1947), 3. 1689. The same gloss appears in Vinaver's second three-volume edition (1967) and in his second three-volume edition reprinted with corrections and additions (1973).

[7] *An Index of the Arthurian Names in Middle English* (Stanford, 1952), 207.

[8] 'A Dictionary of Names and Places', *Caxton's Malory*, ed. J. W. Spisak (Berkeley, 1983), 842.

[9] *Works* (1947), 1374. The same comment appears in Vinaver's later editions.

[10] Ackerman (149) does not include 'Lowe Contrey' as a place name. Dillon (834) includes 'Lowe Countrey' and defines it as the Low Countries; he strangely interprets Malory's statement to indicate that 'all the people flee before Arthur from Paris down into the Low Countries toward the Rhine (?)'. But the French people are fleeing from Paris because of Lucius' approach, not Arthur's.

A much likelier explanation, in my view, is that for Malory 'Roone' in both occurrences in the Winchester manuscript means the city Rouen, and the 'lowe contrey' means the region from Paris towards the shore. That the French noblemen would flee westward because of the Emperor Lucius' advance seems obvious; and that they would flee from Paris towards Rouen, the capital city of Normandy, seems easily understandable. Further, Lucius' threat (fo. 79^v) that he will ride down the Seine and conquer all that lies along its banks, and afterwards ride 'unto Roone' and conquer it, fits the location of Rouen: situated on the north bank of the Seine river about ninety miles north-west of Paris. I would gloss Malory's 'Roone' as 'Rouen'.[11]

II. The Welshe Kyng

When Emperor Lucius enters the Vale of Sessoyne with his army, he finds that Arthur has already disposed his troops in battle array. The Emperor then vigorously urges his men to 'do doughtly this day' so that 'the felde is ourys'. This exhortation has the following immediate result:

> Than anon the Welshe kyng was so nygh that he herde sir Lucyus Than he dressed hym to the vycounte his avow for to holde His armys were full clene and therein was a dolefull dragon and into the vawarde he prykys hym with styff spere in honde and there he mette wyth the valyaunte Vyllers hymself that was vycounte of Rome and there he smote hym thorow the short rybbys with a spere that the bloode braste oute on every syde and so fylle to the erthe and never spake mo wordys aftir.[12]

In this fight we have 'the Welshe kyng' – whoever he is – attacking 'the vycounte' after hearing Lucius' exhortation to his troops in order to carry out 'his avow'; but then we find lack of clarity as to who rushes into the 'vawarde' in 'full clene armys' and with spear in hand, and as to just how the resulting death involves 'the valyaunt Vyllers' and the 'vycounte of Rome'. The passage is omitted from the account of the Roman War in Caxton's edition, and the alliterative *Morte* provides little help with the passage.

McCarthy suggested that 'the Welsh King' is a title for Arthur, but Field rightly identified him as one of Arthur's vassals.[13] Wilson read 'hymself' as the 'vycounte' and the following 'he' as Vyllers; but Vinaver took the 'he' who

---

[11] Keith Baines's rendering of 'Roone' as the Rhone river, which turns south from Lyons and empties into the Mediterranean near Marseilles, seems as unacceptable geographically as the Rhine. See *Malory's 'Le Morte D'Arthur'* (New York, 1962), 103. Baines's choice of 'Rhone' for Malory's 'Roone' does, however, indicate his awareness of the improbability of Vinaver's 'Rhine'.

[12] *The Winchester Malory*, fo. 85^r.

[13] T. McCarthy, 'Malory's King of Wales', *N&Q*, 216 (1971), 327–9; P. J. C. Field, 'Malory's *Morte Arthure* and the King of Wales', *N&Q*, 217 (1972), 285–6.

rushes into the 'vawarde' and 'hymself' as the Welsh kyng, and 'the vycounte', 'the valyaunte Vyllers', and 'the vycounte of Rome' as one individual.[14] Perhaps a clearer understanding of this passage can be reached by starting with the Welsh King's 'avow'.

Early in the account of the Roman War in the Winchester manuscript the following passage occurs:

> Than spake a myghty deuke that was lorde of Weste Walys 'Sir I make myne avowe to God to be revenged on the Romaynes and to have the vawarde and there to vynquysshe with vyctory the vyscounte of Roome For onys as I paste on pylgrymage all by the Poynte Tremble than the vyscounte was in Tuskayne and toke up my knyghtys and raunsomed them unresonable And than I complayned me to the Potestate the Pope hymself but I had nothynge ellys but plesaunte wordys other reson at Roome myght I none have and so I yode my way sore rebuked And therefore to be avenged I woll arere of my wyghteste Walshemen and of myne owne fre wagis brynge you thirty thousand.' (fo. 72ʳ⁻ᵛ; not in Caxton's edition)

Then, when Arthur later moves his army into Sessoyne, we find this passage in the Winchester manuscript:

> And there sir Vyllers the valyaunte made his avow evyn byfore the kynge [Arthur] to take other to sle the vycounte of Rome or ellys to dye therefore. (fo. 84ᵛ; not in Caxton's edition)

From these two passages it would seem that in Malory's mind Sir Vyllers the Valiant is the 'myghty deuke that was lorde of Weste Walys' who makes his 'avow' to Arthur 'to have the vawarde' and to slay the Viscount of Rome. Therefore the likelihood is that for Malory 'the Welshe kyng' who heard Lucius' exhortation to his troops and 'dressed hym to the vycounte his avow for to holde' is also Sir Vyllers the Valiant, and that it is he who, with 'armys full clene' portraying the fearsome dragon, and with a strong 'spere' in his hand, rushes 'into the vawarde' as he had earlier promised. If such is the case, the 'he' who met with the valiant Vyllers is 'hymself that was vycounte of Rome', as Wilson suggested; and then 'he', Sir Vyllers the Valiant, smites 'hym', the Viscount of Rome, through the short ribs unto death, thus successfully carrying out the 'avow' which he earlier twice made.

III. Chastelayne

Somewhat farther along in Malory's account of the Roman War in the Winchester manuscript, Arthur sends out a group of knights to forage for

---

[14] R. H. Wilson, 'Some Minor Characters in the *Morte Arthure*', *MLN*, 71 (1956), 480; Vinaver, *Works* (1967), 3. 1390, n. 220. 4–6.

cattle. In the course of this group's subsequent fighting against Arthur's enemies, we are told that

> Chastelayne a chylde of kyng Arthurs chambir he was a warde of Sir Gawaynes of the weste marchis He chasis to Sir Cheldrake that was a chyfteyne noble and with his spere he smote thorow Cheldrake and so that chek that chylde cheved by chaunce of armys. (fos. 92ʳ–93ᵛ)

A few lines later we learn that 'that chylde' is pursued and killed (fo. 93ʳ), and his death is later reported to Arthur (fo. 93ᵛ).

The three mentions of Chastelayne in the Winchester manuscript follow closely the lines in the alliterative *Morte Arthure* (Brock, 2952–3028). But in Caxton's edition the information is reduced to 'in that stoure was syr Chestelayne a chyld and ward of syre Gawayne slayne wherfore was mooche sorou made and his dethe was soone avengyd' (liber quintus, capitulo xi).

Vinaver transcribes 'weste marchis' of the first passage in Winchester as 'Weste marchis',[15] and he follows Brock's lack of any punctuation for the statement in the alliterative *Morte*: 'Was warde to Sir Wawayne of the weste marches' (l. 2953). Then, in his Index of Proper Names, Vinaver enters 'Weste Marchis, Gawain's fief'. Ackerman (p. 243) includes 'West Marches. Region associated with Gawain', and Dillon (p. 847) has 'West Marchis, Gawain's fief'.

The points I wish to make are (1) that here associating Gawain, elsewhere regularly associated with Orkney, with the 'weste marchis' – presumably the borders of Wales – is difficult to accept; and (2) that editorial commas setting off 'of the weste marchis' in Winchester would make clear what I believe that Malory meant: that Chastelayne, a young knight, a 'chylde' of Arthur's court and a ward of Sir Gawain, was a native of 'the weste marchis', the borders of Wales – not that those 'weste marchis' belonged to Gawain of Orkney.

The fact that the first two of the three aspects of the Winchester manuscript discussed above are omitted entirely from the much shorter version of Arthur's Roman War as it appears in Caxton's edition, and that the third aspect is shortened and clarified in that edition, is deserving of some comment. Not long before his death, William Matthews prepared a paper entitled 'Who Revised the Roman War Episode in Malory's *Morte Darthur*?' That paper was presented by Professor Roy F. Leslie on 14 August 1975, at the Eleventh International Arthurian Congress; unfortunately, the paper has not yet been published. Whereas Vinaver had maintained that Caxton rewrote this section of Malory's book 'from beginning to end', Matthews argued that the version in Caxton's edition represented revision by Malory himself.[16]

---

[15] *Works* (1947), 1. 239. The same transcription is present in the later editions.
[16] For Vinaver's view see *Works*, volume one, Introduction, p. xxx. I have a copy of the typescript for Matthews's paper; see James W. Spisak, ed., *Caxton's Malory* (Berkeley, 1983), 618.

Among other circumstances in support of his argument,[17] Matthews pointed out that the same technique of omitting or clarifying passages not essential to the narrative which Malory used in reducing the alliterative *Morte Arthure* for the account of the Roman War in the Winchester manuscript is evident when the shorter account of that War in Caxton's edition is compared with the longer matching section of the manuscript. That the three minor aspects of the account discussed above are illustrative of that technique perhaps furnishes additional support for Matthews's argument for Malory as reviser.

Then in 1981 Charles Moorman presented a paper at the Sixteenth International Congress on Medieval Studies, entitled 'Caxton's *Morte Darthur*: Malory's Second Edition', in which he further developed Matthews's argument by maintaining that many of the minor readings in Caxton's edition which are clearly preferable to readings in the Winchester manuscript resulted from Malory's own revision. He examined those readings from 'Gareth of Orkney' as it appears in Caxton's edition which Vinaver starred in his three-volume edition as preferable to comparable readings in the Winchester manuscript, and he found a pattern that in his view points to their resulting from Malory's revising.[18]

Accepting or rejecting Matthews's and Moorman's contentions – that the shorter account of the Roman War in Caxton's edition represents revision by Malory of the longer account as it appears in the Winchester manuscript, and that many minor differences elsewhere in Caxton's edition resulted similarly – depends in large part upon one's view of the exemplar from which Caxton printed the book. So far as we know, that exemplar does not now exist. Although the Winchester manuscript was in Caxton's printshop, it includes no markings for compositors and could not have been Caxton's exemplar.[19] Vinaver believed (a) that the 'copye unto me delyverd', which Caxton mentions in his Preface, was – except for the missing pages in the Winchester manuscript – exactly like that manuscript; and (b) that from this 'copye'

---

[17] Three additional circumstances which Matthews notes seem particularly persuasive: (1) that the shorter version is much more distant from the source and fits much better with the rest of Malory's book; (2) that Caxton, who in his other publications regularly informs the reader of changes he has made in the exemplar from which he printed, states in the case of the *Morte* that he divided it into books and Chapters but gives no indication that he revised the account of the Roman War; and (3) that the shorter account of the Roman War in Caxton's edition includes material not present in the longer account from the alliterative *Morte* and Hardyng's *Chronicle*, English sources which Malory used but which Caxton is not likely to have known: in his Preface and Colophon Caxton specifies only 'Frensshe' sources for Malory's book.

[18] Unfortunately Moorman's paper, like Matthews's, has not been published; I have a typescript of the paper.

[19] See Lotte Hellinga, 'The Malory Manuscript and Caxton', *Aspects of Malory*, ed. T. Takamiya and D. S. Brewer (Cambridge, 1981), 127–41; see also R. L. Kindrick, 'Which Malory? *Morte* or *Works*', *Ralph*, 6. 2 (1979), 3.

Caxton prepared the exemplar for his compositors, dividing it into Books and Chapters, deleting most of the explicits, revising the account of the Roman War, altering the language in numerous instances throughout, adding the Preface, Table of Contents, and Colophon, and deliberately giving it the misleading title *Le Morte Darthur*.[20]

In my view, however, it is far more likely that the now lost 'copye unto me delyverd' was a revision by Malory of the book as we know it from the Winchester manuscript, which included the shorter version of the Roman War and many of the minor improvements present elsewhere in Caxton's edition, and in the margins of which Caxton indicated for the compositors his divisions into Books and Chapters, and to which he added his Preface, Table of Contents, and Colophon.

Concerning Caxton's alleged deletion of some of the explicits which appear in the Winchester manuscript and his supposed creation of the title for the book, considerable scepticism also seems to me appropriate. Since the Winchester manuscript lacks pages at the beginning and at the ending, we cannot be sure – as everyone seems to assume – that Malory did not there give the book a title, or that his final explicit there exactly matched that explicit in Caxton's edition. Three of Malory's important sources provide precedent for the title *Le Morte Darthur*: the Middle English alliterative *Morte Arthure* and stanzaic *Morte Arthur* and the Old French *Mort Artu*, all three of which include much more than just an account of Arthur's death. It could be that Malory, not Caxton, is responsible for the title; Caxton's statement about the title in his Colophon – 'notwythstondyng it treateth of . . .' – sounds to me as if he is saying 'I realise that this title is not comprehensively adequate for the contents of the whole book, but I must reproduce the title Malory gave it'. Also, in Malory's final explicit, which we know only from Caxton's edition, the information about the author duplicates that which is given in the earlier explicits in the Winchester manuscript allegedly deleted by Caxton for his edition. That Malory in revising his book decided that a single final presentation of that information was sufficient and himself deleted the earlier explicits seems to me not beyond the realm of possibility.

We have moved a long way from the three minor names in the Winchester manuscript discussed earlier. But, as I see it, they can contribute their small part to our realising the fundamentally important possibility that the exemplar from which Caxton printed his edition of *Le Morte Darthur* – the 'copye unto me delyverd' – may have represented Malory's own revision of his book as it appears in the Winchester manuscript, and that Caxton may be totally innocent of the charges of tampering beyond his stated division of the work into Books and Chapters which have been levelled against him since the

---

[20] See Chapter II, 'The Story of the Book', in the Introduction to *Works*. See also N. F. Blake, *Caxton and His World* (London, 1969), 108–13.

discovery of the Winchester manuscript. Further, if such is the case, the Winchester manuscript is not the 'more authentic' version of Malory's book which Vinaver took it to be; it is a very interesting step along the way to the exemplar, the revised 'copye unto me delyverd', which Caxton used in preparing his edition.[21]

New York University

---

[21] For a further discussion of this matter, see my article 'Sir Thomas Malory's *Le Morte Darthur*, 1947–1987: Author, Title, Text', *Speculum* 62 (1987), 878–97.

History and Literature in the Vernacular in the Middle Ages?

MORTON W. BLOOMFIELD

Because we are accustomed to think of history and literature as separate disciplines, we can discuss without qualms the differences and similarities between them. But both, in fact, go back to the same Greek word and during much of their existence have lived together amicably. Herodotus was both a historian and a story teller. There is literature in history and history in literature. In fact, it is difficult to distinguish the two in European vernaculars before the late fourteenth century.

Since the eighteenth century, however, historians have been at odds with story tellers and critics. Many historians, together with some philosophers, do not see literary studies as serious and learned activities. Historians, they say, deal with facts and wrestle with real problems; story tellers just make up stories. These critics even harbour the suspicion that writers are in some sense dishonest or insincere. Of course historians and philosophers enjoy literature like anyone else, but that is not the same as recognising the truth in literature and the value of teaching it.

Pre-literate cultures did not share this suspicion of literature. There was no distinguishing between truth and fiction. Audiences believed the tales were true. The tellers of tales stood before them; they talked of heroes and battles they had known or heard of. The tellers authenticated what they had to say by their very presence and would often make the point explicit.

It was not only pre-literate audiences that felt stories should be true; many contemporary readers share their feeling. Either the tale must be true, or claim to be true, or if it is not true, it must be recognised as a special violation of the truth. Many regard pure fiction, except under very controlled circumstances, to be unworthy of serious attention. Nancy Hale tells of the shock a clergyman's wife displayed at a dinner party when told that one of Hale's stories was not true.[1] Few people today would share the wife's distress; but deep down many still feel a story should be true and if the author does not make such a claim or disclaims it, there is at the least some discomfort.

[1] *The Realities of Fiction: A Book about Writing* (Boston, 1961), 8.

Exceptions to this general rule include fables, which teach morals, animal stories, humorous tales, lyrics, and drama. It is chiefly narrative which historians and philosophers target, possibly because narrative is heavily sequential and like the nature of existence. There were exceptions in pre-literate cultures, too. Among the Ashanti, for example, when the teller wants to talk about subjects ordinarily taboo or obviously not true, he will say, 'We don't really mean to say so; we don't really mean to say so!' With this disclaimer, he can talk openly; laugh at taboo subjects and ridicule them.[2]

Some two hundred years ago David Hume wrote, 'Poets . . . though liars by profession, always endeavor to give an air of truth to their fictions, and where that is totally neglected, their performances however ingenious, will never be able to afford much pleasure'. He speaks for many philosophers; the issue itself was raised by Plato. Today, however, the philosophers who are interested in the question wrestle with the problem of what ontic status fictional characters and their actions have. This is a fascinating question because art seems to violate the dualistic principle that things or people either exist or do not exist. Fiction seems to be somewhat in between.

Writers and literary critics wrestle with a different aspect of the issue. Henry James, for example, criticises Trollope in 'The Art of Fiction'[3] for admitting in his novels that 'the events he narrates have not really happened'. Cervantes writes in his *Viaje del Parnaso*, 'Falsehood satisfies when it looks like truth and is written in a delightful way'.[4] James and Cervantes are not bothered by the ontic problem; they are concerned to protect the claim that stories are true on some level.

Historians have a different approach to and definition of their subject-matter. Their goals are accuracy and past truths. They avoid dreams and stories about imaginary people, and steel themselves against imagining what happened. This fear of imagination makes literature an enemy. As Suzanne Gearheart recently put it, 'History is undermined by its other (fiction), which, in the form of the irrational, the ideal, the unexperienced or unconscious, is already within us'.[5]

Historians today wish to raise their subject-matter out of time; they try to find principles and unique events which require separate study. Hayden White has summed up their problem this way: 'It is precisely because the narrative mode of representation is so natural to human consciousness, so much an aspect of everyday speech and ordinary discourse, that its use in any field of study aspiring to the status of a science must be suspect.'[6]

[2] R. S. Rattray, *Akan-Ashanti Folktales* (Oxford, 1930), x–xii.
[3] Ed. Morris Roberts (New York, 1948), 5–6 and 59–60.
[4] Quoted in E. C. Riley, *Cervantes's Theory of the Novel* (London, 1964), 19.
[5] *The Open Boundaries of History and Fiction* (Princeton, 1984), 288.
[6] 'The Question of Narrative in Contemporary Historical Theory', *History and Theory*, 23 (1984), 1.

What about works of fiction? What are their truthful elements or even their claim to truth? It is obvious that part of fiction must normally be true, just as true as history. History itself is partially untrue; it is not easy to find out the truth of the past, but that is a separate and complex subject. The point I want to make here is the historians' *principle* to uncover the truth.

Students of literature, on the other hand, do not use the truth criterion in the same way. In their attempt to answer the attacks of Hume, and others who accuse poets and writers of being liars, they deny that their literary works are products of the imagination only. They claim that truth can be presented through the imagination just as lies can be presented through what seems to be true. Literature is partially really true and history is partially imaginary. Literature makes use of reality and history makes use of the imagination.

Some ten years ago there appeared in English a short book by M. I. Steblin-Kamenskij, *The Saga Mind*,[7] which argued that the modern distinction between history and literature is not an ancient distinction but a recent development. Steblin-Kamenskij's focus was on the sagas. The Russian scholar neglects, however, the rôle of Latin. Men trained in Latin, although a small percentage of the medieval population, were fully aware of the distinction between history and literature.

After this rather long prolegomenon, let us turn to the Middle Ages. In the early Middle Ages there were two traditions: the Latin and the vernacular. When universities first appeared in Western Europe in the twelfth century, Latin was the language of learning and Latinists were well aware of the differences between history and literature. Still, these disciplines were not studied as major subjects. Classical writings and mathematics were the two major subjects taught in the schools. Later, studies in classical writings were divided into three subjects, grammar, rhetoric, and logic. These were the famous trivium. After mastering the trivium, the applicant for a bachelor's degree passed on to the quadrivium of geometry, music (its theory from celestial down to earthly music theory), arithmetic (mathematics), and astronomy. It was as part of grammar that some literature and history were taught, because the two were clearly separated in Latin studies.

With a few exceptions, history as a separate discipline in the vernaculars began in the twelfth and thirteenth centuries, although a firm distinction between history and literature is always hard to make until the fourteenth century. It was first made in French writings. At this time the vernaculars were beginning to come into their own all over Europe and historical writings, together with works of religious instruction, were the most common forms of writing. Literature of course had flourished in the European vernaculars with the help of history for a long time, much of it in the form of oral rather than

---

[7] It appeared in Russian in 1971 and English in 1973 (trans. Kenneth H. Ober [Odense, 1973]).

written communication, and in oral communication history and imagination were mingled. Myth was kept alive in translations from Ovid. All these changes were largely due to the increase in the number of educated men and women and the decline of Latin.

During the early, formative period, perceptions varied. To many the Arthurian tradition was history. But William of Malmsbury, an historian of note who wrote in Latin, was deeply suspicious of the truth of these legends. Modern scholars think there may be some truth in Geoffrey of Monmouth and the historians of the Britons (or perhaps we should call them Welshmen), but they are cautious. There were, of course, some chronicles written in the vernacular which were justly accepted as history, particularly those accounts kept by the monastic scribes. I think that we may safely say of vernacular literature in the Middle Ages that most literary works in narrative form were considered historical. Imaginative works like some poems, utopias, and dream visions were considered to be future-oriented and not history.

The more popular the literary work the more likely the distinction between literary and historical was minimised if at all recognised, and the greater was the emphasis on history. The more educated the audience, the more likely the distinction was recognised. If one remembers that both literature and history were admitted to the halls of academe only in the nineteenth century it is hardly surprising that the distinction was blurred in earlier times.[8]

History was thought to be the more important because of its truth claim. Even chronicles, however, would occasionally report miracles of weather and sky, events which hardly qualify as history. The information was thought to portend the future or explain punishments for past misdeeds and hence was directly linked to God. As John Leyerle has pointed out, 'The deeds of Arthur's knights were regarded as history. . . . The modern distinction between romance and history hardly has relevance in the medieval outlook.'[9]

Although Arthurian material is the main Western medley of history and literature from the twelfth century on there were many other examples. Non-Arthurian romances were also considered true by the populace. Religious miracles were multiplied and extensively admired. They were both literature and history to the populace. They entertained but even more important they stimulated faith inasmuch as they were regarded as true. Even the expressed doubts of learned priests and churchmen had little effect on the masses. Men and women wanted to believe and did.

[8] See also Maurice Keen's 'Chivalry, Heralds, and History', *The Writing of History in the Middle Ages, Essays Presented to Richard William Southern*, ed. R. H. C. Davis and J. M. Wallace-Hadrill (Oxford, 1981), 393–414, especially 394ff. He writes *inter alia*, 'Those who listened to *chansons* and histories do not seem to have worried very much about the distinction between them' (395).
[9] 'Conclusion: the Major Themes of Chivalric Literature', *Chivalric Literature*, ed. Larry D. Benson and John Leyerle (Kalamazoo, 1980), 132.

Turning to the variety of verbal narrative, we may say that most narratives fall into one of three divisions – myth, history, or fiction (in the broad sense of the word). Myth is the oldest of the three and at one time probably included history and fiction. Myth includes fairy tales, animal tales, tales of the gods, and other narratives dealing with strange or unusual phenomena. The heart of the mythic tale is the myth dealing with the acts of the gods in their relations to each other, their actions against their enemies (other supernatural beings), and their relations with this world. Their principal function was to explain conditions and events which puzzled early man.

Literary and historical stories have tended to overwhelm myth in the West in the last few centuries, but they have not succeeded in burying it. Myth lives in the plots of mystery stories and science fiction, and today, just as in the past, some myths become a kind of history and some historical events become myths.[10]

Returning to the early Middle Ages, we find a mixture of narrative forms: history, myth, and fiction. Both *Beowulf* and the *Chanson de Roland* have a historical core which is overladen with both. In his most important work, R. W. Chambers has discussed the historical aspect of *Beowulf*. Chambers shows that the *Beowulf* author wove early Germanic history into his imaginary story.[11] We know a number of names that are rooted in actuality – names of warriors and queens and some of their sons and daughters. A small number of the episodes are historical and others may be historical. While it is sometimes difficult to separate the history from the fiction, it is clear that history is embedded in some of the stories.

As far as the *Chanson de Roland* is concerned, we face a similar mix although it is perhaps harder to separate the history from the fiction and myth. We know there was a Roland and a minor invasion by the Franks into northern Spain but the written sources for Carolingian history are not as related to the epic as are the written sources for English history in the case of *Beowulf*. As far as I know no one has done for the *Chanson* what Chambers did for *Beowulf*. The whole range of French epics or chansons, which run from the eleventh to the thirteenth centuries, contains imaginary *and* real people and events. In some cases we cannot tell one from the other and on the whole we probably have more imagination than truth.

What is happening, of course, is that stories of major historical figures are moving from epic to romance with the latter about to replace the former. Thus, the late *chansons* show a mixture of epic and romance and the later romances contain only a small history component. A few 'proto-romances'

[10] See Mary R. Lefkowitz, 'Women in Greek Myth', *The American Scholar*, 54 (1984–5), 209.
[11] See his *Beowulf, an Introduction to the Study of the Poem with a Discussion of the Stories of Offa and Finn*, with a supplement by C. L. Wrenn, 3rd ed. (Cambridge, England, 1967).

also appear earlier in Germany, usually written in Latin. As far as the audiences of these works were concerned, I feel quite certain they did not think of them as literature, myth, or history, but simply as good entertainment.

In medieval Latin, the genres of classical and late classical Latin were breaking down, possibly because of the growing strength of the vernaculars. Yet on the whole, history is not confused with fiction in medieval Latin narrative. In the vernacular, these genres criss-crossed in narrative.

Another factor to consider is that medieval historians, even those who wrote in the vernaculars, almost certainly did not have a large audience. The chronicles in the later Middle Ages were probably not widely read. Scriptoria in monasteries usually found their audiences there; whereas, if we can judge by the number of MSS, romances and stories were popular. It is true that short *exempla* (introductory stories used by preachers) did have some popularity as guides to preachers who wished to enliven their sermons. Some *exempla* were true and hence historical, some were partially true, and some were imaginative.

History or assumed history was certainly used by religious and political groups to further certain aims. Those who joined the Peasants' Revolt in England in Chaucer's time used parts of the Bible as well as other texts for the justification of their aims. The Wycliffites also used their concept of history to justify their position. To many people then (and I might add now), history, regardless of its truth content, was usable in order to attain certain goals. Fiction as fiction was not used as such, but inasmuch as the difference was not clearly understood, we find there was as much appeal to literature as to imaginary history. I'm thinking, of course, of the Arthurian tradition. As late as the seventeenth century, Milton was planning to follow Spenser's example and write his major work about Arthur. Only later did he shift to the Creation story which was full of apocryphal material.

In the Middle Ages, then, history and fiction were often distinguished in Latin writing, but rarely in vernacular literature, and the notion that history and fiction were in conflict with one another, if it existed at all, was quite peripheral until the end of the period. Literature taught and gave pleasure but was not a model for anything else. History was a bag of material assumed to be true (and for the most part accurate). It was intermingled with fiction and occasionally with myth and used as needed.

History was a major intellectual industry in the nineteenth century, the century that elevated history into an integration of science, philosophy, literature, and history proper. In the Middle Ages, there was nothing of the sort. History was largely the presentation of events, real or imaginary, and a report of the weather, assassinations, wars, and coronation of kings (and occasional queens). The aim was accuracy and the true consequences.

By the fourteenth century English had become the dominant language in the British Isles. This elevation of English with accompanying growth in vocabulary and its popularity with all classes helped England to see the difference between history and literature which enabled a clearer distinction between the two subjects to be made.

The real battle between history and literature only surfaced in the late seventeenth and early eighteenth centuries, leading to the acceptance of English literature and history in the university curriculum in the mid-nineteenth century. Truth became the historians' strongest weapon.

For the Middle Ages, there was a distinction between history and literature for scholars but for other social groups the boundaries were blurred; the truth element was assumed. Unlike Pilate, the Middle Ages did not ask 'what is truth?' They took it for granted. With Hayden White tearing down many of the distinctions today between literature and history, we may be moving back to medieval attitudes. I'm inclined to believe, however, that the distinction is not going to break down. Historians will still condemn literature as Hume and Carlyle did in the preceding centuries and literary scholars will continue to defend their discipline and its claims to eternal truths.

Harvard

The Other, the Self: Speculations Concerning an Aspect of Western Culture and Medieval Literature

DEREK BREWER

Our very first utterance as we are separated from our mothers is a cry which suggests that this first enabling separation is pain. It also suggests that you recognise reality outside yourself primarily because it hurts.

The new born child, a tiny cluster of tremendous desires to live and experience, cannot distinguish the universe of his cradle, his mother's breast, the house, the city, the stars in the sky, from his own self. Everything in the world for the new born child, as far as we can deduce, though by definition we cannot know, seems to be its own self. Consequently it has no knowledge of itself. The self engulfs the world; the world is the self, and the self is an undifferentiated totality ignorant of itself.

Soon some elementary distinctions, some primal separations are made. The mother's breast is not available, and because not there, is not-self. The foot is distinguished from the end of the cot. In each case the lack or the distinction is greeted with pain. We discover that the universe will not always do what we want it to do, and that is how we know that we are in it, and separate from it and that there is such a thing as 'the other', something that is 'not-self'. The huge ego of the baby that includes the whole universe has to contract little by little as what is other invades and limits it. It is reasonable to believe that as new born children we conceive life essentially as pleasure; feeding and excreting with a glorious satisfaction that we shall never achieve in our conscious lives. No doubt we feel, though we cannot know, that that life, which is ourselves, is good, and even real, and that this is how life ought to be. It seems equally reasonable to suppose that our first experience of life other than as an extension of the unreflective self comes from recognising what is separate and being separate, outside, not-self, that it is less than ourselves, less than identical with our own interests, less than friendly. Our first experience of the other must be that it, or he or she or they, is something hostile. Our first sense of the other is of deficiency imposed on us, or of our own failure to achieve.

But the self has immense powers which when the lack or deficiency manifests itself immediately become potent desires. We desire the not-self, in a way we love it though we resent it when we become conscious of the other; we wish to dominate it, absorb it, unify it with ourselves, turn it from being not-self into self. We almost immediately therefore have a profound ambivalence in our relation to the other. In its separateness it is an offence to us. Yet that very offence makes us wish usually to desire it, either to possess it, or be unified with it, or to annihilate it.

As we develop in our capacity to separate ourselves materially from the world, so we begin also to classify the other into various categories, primarily the good and the bad. The good for example is the food that we so ardently desire which we suck up and turn into ourselves. The bad is either purely negative, the absence of that food, or what will not lend itself to our desire to dominate, possess, and become united with.

The situation therefore rapidly becomes very much more complicated because we find that the existence of the other is necessary to ourselves. We cannot do without food. As we learn to walk so we learn that we cannot do without the hard resistant material universe on which to move, even though that hurts us when we fall upon it. If it hurts you know it's real; and later in life one is sometimes inclined to say, if it's real, it hurts. That is why our greatest twentieth-century poet in English said that humankind cannot bear very much reality.

So far I have taken the notion of 'the other' in its broadest sense as simply what is not the self, and in purely physical terms. But going along with the discovery of the material 'other' is something very much more complex; the discovery of the personal other, the realisation that there are other human beings in the world. At an elementary level we recognise them in those two mighty divinities the Mother and the Father. Later subsidiary divinities will appear who take part in the divinity of the father and mother images. The father and mother divinities themselves divide first into their good aspects and their bad, and those aspects then split off into separate incarnations of the good and the bad. Here we come to a difficulty. The process that I am discussing is largely subconscious. Our recognition of the existence of other people is superficially conscious, but our responses to them are creative and largely subconscious. Those aspects of the Mother or the Father which we hate, we find hard consciously to reconcile with aspects in the same person which are good. One way to distinguish them is in stories in which the psychological projections which we make within our minds, based on the main persons we know, are represented as separate characters which we may call 'splits'. The bad or the apparently hostile aspects of the Mother, for example, are represented in the stepmother of the fairy-tale. The threatening aspect of the Father in the fairy-tale is represented by the giant. It may console all young men that all giants in fairy-tales are stupid, and without exception are easily deceived and killed, just as Oedipus found it perfectly easy to kill his own father. For young men killing the Father is rarely a problem. The problem, as Oedipus found, and as fairy-tale heroes find, is getting away from the Mother.

But to what extent are these personal figures, these projections and splits of parents whom we recognise in our own individual psychological pantheons, who act so vigorously in so many stories, actual representations of 'the other'? They must, to some extent, be based upon our experience of genuinely other people, our parents and those associated with them, even our siblings, because we know them as other, because we cannot survive without their care and protection, nor usually without their reproof and correction. We depend upon them, yet they will not always do what we want them to do, and at least to that extent we recognise their separateness, their distinctness from our own selves, their objective existence. But it is a commonplace of ordinary psychological knowledge that those images of Father and Mother figures which we half perceive and half create as we grow up, images which divide into numerous splits, characters good, bad, and indifferent, are quite as much the subjective creations of our own minds as they are genuinely objective real persons. It is also a commonplace in the history of culture that archaic societies make very little distinction between objective and subjective perceptions, or between the material and the personal universe. That is to say, mountains, rivers, the sea, trees, rocks, all kind of natural objects, have attributed to them in an archaic society a real personality. This personality is of the same kind as that attributed to actual persons, Mother figures, Father figures. Gods, goddesses, heroes, and other divine and semi-divine figures are products of the same cultural mixture of objective and subjective. Although the individual in an archaic society must have some sense of his or her separation from the universe, this sense of separation is far less distinct than what we have been accustomed to in Western Europe and North America since the seventeenth century. To modern ways of thought what happens in an archaic society is that the individual projects upon the whole range of his experience of the universe, both personal and material, his own feelings, thoughts, and ideas. When the gods threaten it may well be because the individual is frightened of thunder, but it is also because he is projecting upon the gods his own sense of ill-doing or his own sense of obligation that there is something he must do, or his own image of the Father. In other words, from this point of view the inner drives of the individual are projected upon his external experience both of people and things in such a way as to reduce their otherness. Something other than the individual must exist to act as a basis for the projection he makes, but the basis is very often totally covered by the projection. The basis is no more than a foundation upon which an amazingly elaborate subjectively created building can be erected. As often in the Middle Ages the building moreover may be far too elaborate for the foundations, and when the shocks of cultural change come those splendid buildings decay and fall, though the foundations remain in the earth of the individual in relation to the universe. Although I speak of archaic societies, we ought to remember that many apparently modern societies retain large archaic elements, as we ourselves do personally, though the young are paradoxically usually more archaic than the mature.

Our notion of the other, then, must derive in the first place from every individual's experience of birth and growing up. The notion of the other includes both people and things, but from now on I shall leave out the relationship to things and concentrate on the sense of personal relationships.

The sense of the other must begin at a very early age in the individual's development, but it becomes overlaid by the projections, thoughts, and ideas of the individual in complex relationship with the actual other persons who are, we may believe, somewhere 'out there'. This relationship is also modified by very complex historically conditioned forces so that these figures representing our recognition of the personal other differ from period to period. Different cultures also create different relationships between the individual and the other.

We should further note that what an archaic culture or person believes to be 'the other' may be so only in a very limited way; in such a culture the 'other' is really less the 'other' than a projection of the self.

If what I have sketched is a correct representation in general terms, then there must be along with notions of the other in so far as they are genuinely other and not merely projections of the self, some corresponding development of consciousness of the self as a separate self-contained unit, the central interest of our lives, but nevertheless self-conscious and different from the other, or others, even if only one among many. It seems probable, at any rate in Western culture, that the development of the individual self has been one of the main drives of the cultural developments of our period from the Dark Ages onwards. It is the sense of the self, that is, of self-awareness or self-consciousness, which corresponds with 'other-awareness', that is, with consciousness of others.

Such consciousness of self and others, within our period, must fluctuate. It is very deeply rooted. It can be found even in the Old Testament, just as it can be found in the writings of Classical Antiquity. It is first in Leviticus that we find the instruction to love God and also to love our neighbour, that is, the other, as we love ourselves. This perception of the otherness of God and of the otherness of other people is something very profound. We all know how very difficult it is. No wonder our sense of the other varies and sometimes disappears altogether.

There is a good argument put forward by W. J. Ong[1] that the sense of otherness belongs much more to the Father image than to the Mother image. We find it extraordinarily difficult, perhaps impossible, to dissociate ourselves from the Mother for obvious biological reasons. Fathers never have the same biological and psychological umbilical cords with the child that the

---

[1] W. J. Ong, *Fighting for Life*, Ithaca, N.Y., and London, 1981, pp. 174–7.

mother has. It is for this reason, Ong argues, that we have to attribute something analogous to masculinity to God because it is only from the Father that we can become truly separate, as we obviously do from God. It may well be that we can only develop a true sense of the 'other' as entirely separate, entirely alienated therefore, in a highly masculine paternalistic society, like that of the ancient Hebrews, or indeed of the European Middle Ages. It may be that if we achieve separateness, the extent to which we achieve unity with God, or our neighbour, therefore depends on the counterbalancing sense of the feminine, or even the maternal, which represents unity rather than separateness. It is clear that nowadays we live in a progressively more feminised age, and also that in general our culture is developing a greater and greater dislike of individual separateness. That is why loneliness is nowadays felt to be one of the worst psychological afflictions. We are moving from a masculinised society to a feminised society: masculinisation has created separate individualism and difference which feminisation with its longing for unity, for the collective, for the eradication of difference, finds very painful.

The old jest, 'Vive la différence' is very masculine. I am sure no woman ever made it.

I am using the terms 'masculine' and 'feminine' as a wide-ranging metaphor, based on sexual difference but including much else. The metaphor is not a value judgement, nor an estimate of strength. A society in which the collective sense is strong and the sense of individual separateness is weak may well be much more powerful than a society in which individualistic separatism flourishes. Complex societies will have different areas of masculinisation and femininisation, while all persons of whichever sex are a mixture of masculine and feminine elements.

Within the cultural development of Europe we can see the sense of individuality and collectivity varying in different proportions. In the high civilisation of Classical Antiquity it seems clear that there was a high degree of individualism and a corresponding weakness in the sense of the collective. That civilisation was destroyed by collective barbarian hordes, which if feminine in one sense were also extremely fierce. From the sixth century onwards Europe had to make a painful recovery of civilisation of a special kind.

There were many cultural developments in the West which contributed to the development of the concept of the self and therefore of the other. Consider the logical adversarial habit of mind most clearly demonstrated at a marked stage of its development by Abelard's *Sic et Non*. This adversarial analytical logical concept has its roots to some extent of course in human nature. Physical reality continually says 'yes' and 'no' to us, usually 'no'. Logical analysis derives from the turn that Greek thought took in the fourth century BC in Plato's dialogues where the Socratic method of question and answer, which is essentially adversarial, developed. I believe there is nothing like this in the early history of the other major world cultures. Clearly the adversarial method of investigation involves a distinction of the self from the other, be it a point of view or an opponent arguing in a debate. Adversarial thought processes leading to analysis are what distinguish Western European civilisation from the other great cultures of the world.

There are also other developments which lead to the concept of 'the other'. One of these which has marked European civilisation particularly is the concept of erotic love. Although love is common to all cultures, since it is a part of physical human make-up, it has occupied very different parts in them.

I shall take a very simplified form of love-story as it is known at all levels of culture, to illustrate how I think it has contributed to our sense of 'the other'. The form is that kind of folk-tale known as fairy-tale, or wonder-tale. It underlies the more sophisticated literature of many centuries as I have shown in my book *Symbolic Stories*. The form in which we know fairy-tales derives, including the name, from the French author Perrault writing in the late seventeenth century, but fairy-tales, or wonder-tales, can be traced back over many centuries through many cultures. The story of Cinderella, for example, seems to begin in the ninth century in China and there are said to be 900 variants of it. It is better to call them wonder-tales because their original audience was not limited to children and there are hardly any fairies in them.

The essence of the wonder-tale is the growing-up of the hero or the heroine. Cinderella is the archetype. The story is of the emergence of the individual person and from our point of view it is useful to emphasise that the beginning of the fairy-tale sees essentially the heroine at the very centre with two other major characters, the Father and the Mother, each of whom may equally well be regarded as a projection of the mind of the heroine. The mind of the heroine is the content of the story as a whole. The Mother's and Father's attitudes in these wonder-tales may vary to some extent but they conform to simple stereotypes which are of immense importance in the history of Western culture. The stereotypes tell us for example that if the protagonist of the story is a girl, then the Mother is either dominant or absent. If she is dominant she is hostile and the aim of the heroine is to get out of her clutches. The Mother figure may even attempt to murder the heroine, as happens for example in the story of 'Snow White and the Seven Dwarfs'. The Father figure, on the other hand, is almost always present. If he is dominant, he is hostile, or, worse than hostile, over-loving and wishing to marry his daughter. Only if he is weak is he good. The essence of the wonder-tale is the protagonist's attempts to separate himself or herself from the parent figures. If the protagonist is male, he normally runs away or escapes or has to take a journey away from home in order to achieve some special objective. If the protagonist is female then the drama normally continues at home, and is centred on the kitchen. This is the case even in one of the major variants of Cinderella called in English 'Catskin', where the daughter, fleeing from the unwelcome attentions of her widowed father, who wishes to marry her, goes to the household of a neighbouring king and lives as his kitchen maid. She still settles as it were at home. The nature of these adventures of course reflects the normal social conditions of men and women in earlier society when it was so much easier for men to get away and women were largely though not entirely restricted to the home. This basic structure of protagonist confronting parent figures is to be found in many of the romances of the Middle Ages and continues in the underlying structure of many novels of the nineteenth and twentieth century. The point that concerns us here is the crisis which enables the protagonist, who is now in mid-adolescence, to escape from what used to be comforting but is now the stifling crushing unduly demanding family circle. The crisis comes when the protagonist needs to find his or her as they nowadays say 'significant other'. The crisis may be precipitated by the father wishing to marry the daughter, which is probably best understood as the undue domination of the father rather than any literal widespread anxiety about incest. It is natural for a young woman to wish to find somebody of her own age as a sexual companion and the same is true for young men. The essence of the wonder-tale is to tell how the protagonist disengages from the parents. The only way this can be done is by finding the significant other who cracks the mould of the family and draws to himself or herself the emotional bonds which have in the life of the protagonist up to now been made with the parents. In other words the young hero needs to deflect the love that he felt for his mother as a baby to the princess whom he will discover and rescue. In deflecting this love it is changed into more obviously sexual love. Very few men want to marry their mothers. As I have earlier suggested, many of the feelings which the protagonist attributes to the parents may well be reflections or projections of the protagonist's own feelings towards the parents. It is natural in one part of yourself to hate your parents, but you experience it as if the parents or a parent hates you. Furthermore, if the heroine feels that her father loves her too much it may be because she herself in one part of herself loves her father too much, while the other vigorous growing new part of herself passionately needs a more suitable other person on whom to lavish such affection. This is a common psychological phenomenon not limited to families though in families the biological basis is clear enough: but Western European literature of a secular and imaginative kind seems to have given this phenomenon peculiar force and vitality in the Middle Ages. In the wonder-tale the central point of view, the experiencing consciousness, is always that of the protagonist. In some of the wonder-tales the protagonist regards the other when first met with hostility, as it were in the third person, as an intruder, clearly seen in such a story as 'Beauty and the Beast'. Here the ugly Beast carries off the heroine from her father against her will because of the father's foolishness in making a promise to the Beast. It is a more optimistic version of the ancient biblical folk-tale of Jephtha's daughter. 'The other' in this case is at first an unwelcome intruder, which is why by grammatical analogy I describe him (or it could be her if the protagonist is male) as in the third person. In 'Beauty and the Beast' the situation of the emerging adult forces the heroine to look differently at the other and on acquaintance she finds that what was ugly can be loved. The story says that love is in the eye of the beholder. As soon as the heroine is prepared to love the other, she can regard him directly in the second person as it were, to call him thou, so the other is transformed into a handsome prince and the constricting parental mould has been successfully broken.

Love poetry, whether religious or secular, seems to express the I/thou relationship at a more complex level. The other has been discovered, and the protagonist of the poem now moves to make the other his own, in fact to break down the otherness, for otherness, as I have said, is often painful. Shelley said our sweetest songs are born of saddest thought, and all his songs are love-lyrics. We speak of the 'lyric I' since we need to have the concept of the self in order to have the concept of the other, but as soon as the self realises itself the natural verb to follow the first person singular is 'want' and the natural pronoun to follow that is 'you', or to be more pedantically grammatical, 'thee'. One might almost say that this is the history of the European love-lyric, 'I want thee'. When the lover has attained his aim he usually gives up writing songs of longing. He does not need them and he has better things to do.

I have started with wonder-tale and gone on to the lyric, but perhaps the most important literary expression of the sense of the other is a kind of combination of these two, found in the medieval romance. The basis of medieval romance is almost always the wonder-tale, or the constituent elements of the wonder-tale, sweetened by the expressiveness of lyric, and then made immensely complex by many other cultural elements, by social education and pressures, Latin learning, rhetoric, the genius of the author.

The Middle Ages were inevitably, like all cultures with a weak technology, a highly masculinised society. One of the advantages of the progressive discovery of 'the other' was that, for historical reasons, 'the other' was normally seen as a woman. There are obvious biological and evolutionary advantages in this, but it need not have been so. In the Biblical story of David, for example, the 'other' was Jonathan. I do not suggest that David was a homosexual – the slightest acquaintance with his story would show how unlikely that was. But the 'significant other' was one of his own sex. This often happens in military societies, and is the basis in war of much loyalty and self-sacrifice without any suggestion of perversion. I saw it myself during the Second World War and in medieval literature one need think only of Roland and Oliver.

In European literature, however, the trend was to take the other as being of the other sex. Since the initiative lay with men this involved the elaboration of the idea of woman as a separate exalted entity, and, as a consequence, an almost insurmountable barrier between a young man and woman as equals in the same class. This situation lasted till I was a young man, and it would be interesting to know to what extent, now that the barriers are down between the sexes, or whether at all the notion of the other can persist, at least in the same way, as an element in a sexual relationship. A companion, a mate, or a sex-object, is each in its own way an extension of the self, rather than a separate otherness with its intrinsic strangeness.

The medieval distance of the knight or lover from his lady, the consequent magic and poetic sense of feminine otherness, strangeness and mystery in masculine minds, reinforced certain masculine characteristics. On the whole it seems to have had a softening and ennobling effect, though clear historical, as opposed to literary, evidence is hard to find. If Froissart's story of Queen Philippa begging for the lives of the burghers of Calais is true, it is an example of the civilising influence of women. But Queen Anne is said to have gone on her knees to the Lords Apellant to save Sir Simon Burley's life without effect. In literature, if we take Malory and Arthurian legend as an example, there is no doubt that the Pentecostal oath to protect helpless women, or the nobility of Lancelot, are results of men's response to women as other, with consequent improvement of men's moral quality.

It may be that this, too, is now changing. There are some feminists, I suspect, who would fiercely deny that women are gentler, kinder, better than men, and it may be that it was only cultural pressures, not genetic drives, that made them so. Whether the products of nurture or nature, however, gentleness and kindness, pity, love, are civilising characteristics, and to some extent they were fostered by the medieval discovery of the lady as the other.

Despite the felt moral superiority of women expressed in the medieval secular love-ethic, that very superiority, seen as pity as well as love, in turn paradoxically promoted, when related to a hierarchical social culture that attributed other kinds of superiority to men, a degree either of equality or of alternating superiority in a maturing relationship between a knight and a lady. Equality in human relationships was difficult to achieve in the Middle Ages, but Chaucer solves the problem neatly by proposing different kinds of superiority at the beginning of *The Franklin's Tale*. Another solution is found in *Pearl*, where equality and hierarchy in heaven are subsumed in God's power to love.

The characteristic of wonder-tales and romances dealing with 'the other' is that they have happy endings. This seems to me to indicate the key quality and mark of true romance. After all, most of us grow up and make some sort of show of relating successfully to other people whether through love or not: tragedy, failure to relate, is not so wide-spread at this elementary level as we sometimes think. The happy ending signalises the discovery of the other and relationships between the self and the other which is a sign of maturity and ability to live, however imperfectly or intermittently.

But not all stories have happy endings and I would pick out two kinds. First that in which the other is found but not won. This is, or used to be, regarded as one of the most painful human situations. Chaucer's *Troilus* deals with it. The best one can say is with Tennyson, ''Tis better to have loved and lost, than never to have loved at all.' Life is full of irremediable pain and some things must simply be endured.

The other kind, however, is the great tragic love-stories of Lancelot and Guinivere, and Tristan and Isolde. As stories they differ from each other and ought to have separate treatment, but the element which they share in most versions of each is that for each knight there is a depth of abasement which deprives the lady of equality. She is psychologically irremediably superior to such an extent that no lasting fulfilled mature relationship with her can be achieved. We might say that in the structure of imaginative bonds there is a disastrously filial element in their love. Guinivere must in any version of the story be older than Lancelot. Isolde need not be older than Tristan, but she is the wife of his uncle. Uncles are recognisably splits of Father-figures, as Hamlet makes plain, and the wife of a Father figure is a Mother-figure. Both Lancelot and Tristan are in love with women who are to some extent Mother-figures. As I argued earlier, the Mother can never become fully other. We can no more achieve total independence of Mothers than we can of nature. If parents dominate children the children at least metaphorically die. That was Oedipus's problem: his disastrous fate lay not in killing his father but in loving and marrying his mother, that is, in being unable to escape the ultimately deadly bond which started by being our life-line. An enormous amount of literature is devoted to the struggle to get away from Mother, to become oneself, which is often simultaneously the attempt to find the other, who may begin by being the superior but will ultimately become the equal, while still remaining other. (*The Times*, on Tuesday, 2 December 1986, commented in an article that modern literary artists seem obsessed with this problem. It seems likely that in the current femininisation of our culture, with the emphasis on togetherness, homogeneity, equality, collectivism, the problems of achieving the self and therefore of recognising the genuinely other may increase.)

The concept of love lasted in Europe from the twelfth century until almost the other day. It has evoked both the concept of the self and the self's necessary relationship with the other, to whom it is bound in ties of affection and loyalty. While not coterminous with marriage the concept was always concerned with marriage and humanised marriage. Marriage is the natural end in both senses of erotic love of this kind, its aim, and its conclusion. Marriage itself initiates further, and different, and much more variable stages of love and unities of association. The association of the individual self with another self then leads ultimately to the existence of other selves, who have to find themselves and their own significant others.

The ultimate aim must be to relate not only to the other, but to others; both to concentrate on the individual and to see the individual as one of a human social group, without relapsing into mindless collectivism.

Emmanuel College, Cambridge